SACRED READING

"*Sacred Reading* offers a superb introduction to Ignatian prayer that anyone can use. Too often Ignatian prayer is seen as something reserved only for Jesuits, for people trained in the Spiritual Exercises, or for those who have time for a directed retreat. But this book, created by experts in the traditions of Ignatian prayer, helps the reader to encounter Jesus through short scripture passages, inviting questions and accessible reflections. It's an innovative way to be invited, with gentle wisdom, into meeting Jesus in your prayer."

Rev. James Martin, S.J.
Author of *Jesus: A Pilgrimage*

"*Sacred Reading: The 2016 Guide to Daily Prayer* is an indispensable resource in deepening your prayer and devotional life. Lectio divina will change how you see your relationships—with the Lord, with others, and with yourself. Highly recommended!"

Most Rev. David L. Ricken
Bishop of Green Bay

"Communion with God increases dramatically as we grow in knowledge of God's Word. For most people the problem is simply getting started: determining where to begin. A most ancient and venerable practice is *lectio divina*, scripture reading that is meditation and contemplation but also application. *Sacred Reading* is an uncommonly useful tool in really getting into scripture in just this way."

Rev. Michael White and Tom Corcoran
Authors of *Rebuilt*

"In just six simple steps, *Sacred Reading* opens our minds and hearts to scripture in refreshing and profound ways. The daily meditations are clear and concise and yet filled with wisdom and promise. Reading scripture daily is good; reading scripture daily with *Sacred Reading* as guide is awesome."

Marge Fenelon
Author of *Imitating Mary*

"This guide through the gospel texts of the daily lectionary offers a fully-embodied experience that includes the mind, heart, imagination, desire, and behavior. This way of prayerfully reading the gospels as the Spirit-empowered word of God shows us how to open our lives to be continually formed in Christ."

Stephen J. Binz
Speaker and author of *Conversing with God in Scripture*

"In his apostolic exhortation *The Joy of the Gospel*, Pope Francis invites us to be people of prayer. *Sacred Reading* is an excellent aid in responding to that invitation. This book offers a clear, helpful, and inspirational guide to deepen our love for scripture as we ponder God's Word and live it out in our daily lives."

Most Rev. Robert F. Morneau
Auxiliary Bishop Emeritus of Green Bay

"I am thankful for the ministry of the Apostleship of Prayer and their many ways of drawing people to active lives of encounter with a living God. I encourage anyone looking to deepen their prayer life to spend time learning this ancient practice of lectio divina, and coming to know a God who dances freely in our imaginations if we will but go there with him."

Tim Muldoon
Author of *Six Sacred Rules for Families*

"*Sacred Reading* is the perfect companion for the lectio journey."

Sonja Corbitt
Author of *Unleashed*

SACRED READING

The 2016 Guide to Daily Prayer

Apostleship of Prayer

Douglas Leonard, Executive Director

Ave Maria Press AVE Notre Dame, Indiana

Unless otherwise noted, all scripture quotations are from the *New Revised Standard Version* of the Bible, © 1989 by the Division of Christian Education of the National Council of the Churches of Christ in the United States of America. Used by permission. All rights reserved.

Founded in 1865, Ave Maria Press is a ministry of the United States Province of Holy Cross.

www.avemariapress.com

Paperback: ISBN-13 978-1-59471-607-2

E-book: ISBN-13 978-1-59471-608-9

Cover image © Thinkstock.

Cover and text design by David Scholtes.

Printed and bound in the United States of America.

CONTENTS

INTRODUCTION

Christians throughout the world are rediscovering a powerful, ancient form of prayer known as sacred reading (lectio divina). What better way to deepen one's friendship with Jesus Christ, the Word of God, than by prayerfully encountering him in the daily Gospel reading? This book will set you on a personal prayer journey with Jesus from the start of Advent in November 2015 through the end of Ordinary Time in November 2016: the entire Church year.

Sacred reading takes up this ancient practice of lectio divina in order to help you engage the words of the daily Gospel reading, guided by the Holy Spirit. As you read and pray this way, you may find—as many others have—that the Lord speaks to you in intimate and surprising ways. The reason for this is simple: as we open our hearts to Jesus, he opens his heart to us.

St. Paul prays beautifully for his readers:

> For this reason I bow my knees before the Father, from whom every family in heaven and on earth takes its name. I pray that, according to the riches of his glory, he may grant that you may be strengthened in your inner being with power through his Spirit, and that Christ may dwell in your hearts through faith, as you are being rooted and grounded in love. I pray that you may have the power to comprehend, with all the saints, what is the breadth and length and height and depth, and to know the love of Christ that surpasses knowledge, so that you may be filled with all the fullness of God. (Eph 3:14–19)

This book moves you through each day's Gospel by prompting you at each step, getting you started with reading, observing, praying, listening, and resolving to act. But most important is your own response to the Word and the Spirit, for that is how you will grow in your relationship with Jesus. If you are sincerely seeking God, the Holy Spirit will lead you in this process.

How to Use This Book

The *Sacred Reading* prayer book is intended to guide your prayerful reading during the entire Church year. (Small booklets, suitable for use in parish groups, are also available for Advent and Lent.) Each weekday reflection begins with the date as well as a reference to any feast days for which there is a special lectionary gospel reading. Sunday reflections include both the date and its place in the liturgical calendar. For the sake of simplicity, most other memorials to saints are not cited except when there is a Gospel reading proper to that saint: that is, unless the Gospel has been chosen with specific relevance to the saint.

In prayerful reading of the daily Gospels, you join your prayers with those of believers all over the world. Following the readings for each season of the liturgical calendar (including solemnities and holy days of obligation), you will be invited each day to reflect on the Gospel text for the day in six simple but profound steps:

1. Know that God is present with you and ready to converse.

At all times God is everywhere, including where you are in this very moment. The human mind is incapable of fully grasping the mystery of God, but we do know some things about God from scripture. God is the transcendent ground of all being, invisible, eternal, and infinite in power. God is Love, with infinite love for you and me. God is one with and revealed through the Word, Jesus Christ, who became flesh. Through him all things were made, and by him and for him all things subsist. Jesus is the Way, the Truth, and the Life. He says that those who know him also know his Father. Through the passion, death, and resurrection of Jesus, we are reconciled with God. If we believe in Jesus Christ, we become the sons and daughters of Almighty God.

God gives us the Holy Spirit to lead us to truth and understanding. The Holy Spirit also gives us power to live obedient to the teachings of Jesus. The Holy Spirit draws us to prayer and works in us as we pray. No wonder we come into God's presence with gladness. All God's ways are good and beautiful. We can get to know God better by encountering God in the Word, which is Jesus himself.

The prompt prayer at the beginning of each day's reading is just that: a prompt, something to get you started. In fact, all the elements in the process of sacred reading are meant to prompt you to your own conversations with God. After reading the prompt, feel free to continue to pray in your own words: respond in your own way, pray in your own way, and hear God speaking to you personally. Your goal is to make sacred reading your own prayer time each day.

2. Read the Gospel.

The entire Bible is the Word of God, but the gospels (Matthew, Mark, Luke, and John) specifically tell the Good News about Jesus Christ. Throughout the Church year, the daily Gospel readings during Mass will come from all four gospels. To help you focus on each day's readings, we have referenced only solemnities and holy days of obligation on the liturgical calendar when the Gospel relates to the feast. For the sake of simplicity, no other feast days have been included.

The Sacred Reading series (the prayer books as well as the seasonal booklets for Advent / Christmas and Lent / Easter) concentrates on praying with the daily Gospels. These readings contain the story of Jesus' life, his teachings, his works, his passion and death on the cross, his resurrection on the third day, and his ascension into heaven.

The gospels interpret Jesus' ministry for us. Much more, by the Holy Spirit, we can find in the Gospels the very person of Jesus Christ. Prayerful reading of the daily Gospel is an opportunity to draw close to the Lord: Father, Son, and Holy Spirit. As we pray with the gospels, we can be transformed by the grace of God—enlightened, strengthened, and moved. Seek to read the Gospel with a complete openness to what God is saying to you. Many who pray with the Gospel recommend rereading it several times.

3. Notice what you think and feel as you read the Gospel.

Sacred reading can involve every faculty—mind, heart, emotions, soul, spirit, sensations, imagination, and much more—though usually not all at once. Different passages touch different keys in us. Sometimes we may laugh. Sometimes we may need to stop and worship before we continue. Sometimes we will be puzzled, amazed, stung, abashed, reminded of something lovely, or reminded of something we had wanted to forget.

Seek to feel all of your emotions as you read. Apply your intellect, too. You will confront problems of context and exegesis on a daily basis. That's okay. Sometimes you may experience very little. That's okay, too. God is at work anyway. Give yourself to the Gospel and take from it what is there for you each day.

Most important, notice what in particular jumps out at you, whatever it may be. It may be a word, a phrase, a character, an image, a pattern, an emotion, a sensation—some arrow to your heart. Whatever it is, pay attention to it, because the Holy Spirit is using it to accomplish something in you.

Sometimes a particular Gospel repeats during the liturgical year of the Church. To pray through the same Gospel even on successive days presents no problem whatsoever to your sacred reading. Saint Ignatius of Loyola, founder of the Jesuits and author of *The Spiritual Exercises*, actually recommends repeated meditation on passages of scripture. Read in the Spirit, gospel passages have unlimited potential to reveal to us the truths we are ready to receive. For the receptive soul, the Word of God has boundless power to illuminate and transform the prayerful believer.

4. Pray as you are led for yourself and others.

Praying is just talking with God. Believe God hears you. Believe God will answer you. Believe God knows what you need even before you ask. Jesus says so in the Gospel. So your conversation with God can go far beyond asking for things. You may thank, praise, worship, rejoice, mourn, explain, question, reveal your fears, seek understanding, or ask forgiveness. Your conversation with God has no limits. God is the ideal conversationalist. God wants to spend much time with you.

Being human, we can't help being self-absorbed, but praying is not just about our own needs. We are often moved by the Gospel to pray for others. We will regularly remember our loved ones in prayer. Sometimes we will be led to pray for someone who has hurt us. At other times we will be moved to pray for a class of people in need, wherever they are in the world, such as persecuted Christians, refugees, the mentally ill, teachers, the unborn, or the lonely.

We may also pray with the universal Church by praying for the pope's prayer intentions. Those intentions are entrusted to the Apostleship of Prayer and are available through its website and its annual and monthly leaflets. You may get your own copy of this year's papal prayer intentions by contacting the Apostleship of Prayer. The Apostleship is the pope's prayer group, with more than fifty million members worldwide. Jesus asked us to unite in prayer, promising that the Father would grant us whatever we ask for in his name.

5. Listen to Jesus.

Jesus the Good Shepherd speaks to his own sheep, who hear his voice (see Jn 10:27). This listening is a most wonderful time in your prayer experience. The italicized words in this passage are the words I felt impressed upon my heart as I prayed with these readings. I included them in order to help you to listen more actively for whatever it is the Lord might be saying to you.

Jesus speaks to all in the gospels, but in *Sacred Reading* he can now speak exclusively to you. If you can, write down what he says to you and reread his words during the day. Put all of Jesus' words to you in a folder or keep a spiritual notebook. Believers through the ages have recorded the words of Jesus to them, holy mystics and ordinary believers alike.

It takes faith to hear the voice of Jesus. This faith will grow as you practice listening. Ideally, we will learn to hear what Jesus is saying to us all day long, such as when we face difficult situations. Listening to the voice of Jesus is practicing the presence of God. As Saint Paul said, "In him we live and move and have our being" (Acts 17:28).

Saint Ignatius of Loyola called this conversation with Jesus *colloquy*. That word simply means that two or more people are talking. Saint Ignatius even urges us to include the saints in our prayer conversations. We believe in the communion of saints. If you have a patron saint, don't be afraid to talk to him or her. In her autobiography, Saint Thérèse of Lisieux, who was a member of the Apostleship of Prayer, describes how she spoke often with Mary and Joseph, as well as with Jesus.

6. *Ask God to show you how to live today.*

Pope Benedict XVI commented that sacred reading is not complete without a call to action: something in our praying leads us to do something in our day. Perhaps we find an opportunity to serve, to love, to give, to lead, or to do something good for someone else. Perhaps we find occasion to repent, to forgive, to ask forgiveness, to make amends. Open your heart to anything God might want you to do. Try to keep the conversation with God going all day long.

Asking God to show you how to live is the last step of the *Sacred Reading* prayer time, but that doesn't mean you need to end it here. Keep it going. You may drift off in the presence of God, lose attention, or even fall asleep, but you can come back. God is always present, seeking to love you and to be loved. God is always seeking to lead us to the green pastures. God is our strength, our rock, our ever-present help in time of trouble. God is full of mercy, ready to forgive us again and again. God sees us through very difficult times. God heals us. God gives his life to us constantly. God is our Maker, Father, Mother, Lover, Servant, Savior, and Friend. We know that from the Gospel. He is an inexhaustible spring of blessing and holiness in our innermost selves. The sanctification of our souls is God's work, not our own.

As you read, ask the Holy Spirit to lead you in this process. With genuine faith, open yourself to respond to the Word and the Spirit, and your relationship with Jesus will continue to deepen and to grow just as the infant Jesus grew within the womb of the Blessed Mother. This in turn will lead you to share the love of Christ with all those you encounter—just as the Blessed Mother draws all those who encounter her directly to her Son.

Other Resources to Help You

These Sacred Reading resources, including both the seasonal books and this annual prayer book, are enriched by the spirituality of the Apostleship of Prayer. Since 1844 our mission has been to encourage Catholics to pray each day for the good of the world, the Church, and the prayer intentions of the Holy Father. In particular, we encourage Christians to respond to the loving gift of Jesus Christ by making a daily offering of themselves each day. As we give the Lord our hearts, we ask him to make them like his own heart, full of love, mercy, and peace.

These prayer books are intended to guide you to a prayer experience that you will find personally helpful and spiritually enriching. In addition to the daily prayers in the book, you can also adapt your prayer time in ways that are best suited to your particular needs. For example, some choose to continue to reflect upon each day's reading in writing, either in the book or in a separate journal or notebook, to create a record of their spiritual journey for the entire year. Others supplement their daily reading from the book with the daily videos and other online resources available through the Apostleship of Prayer website (apostleshipofprayer.org).

For more information about the Apostleship of Prayer ("the pope's prayer group") and about the other resources we have developed to help men and women cultivate habits of daily prayer, visit our website at www.apostleshipofprayer.org.

I pray that this experience may help you walk closely with God every day.

Douglas Leonard, PhD
Executive Director
Apostleship of Prayer

We Need Your Feedback!
Ave Maria Press and the Apostleship of Prayer would like to hear from you. After you've finished reading, please go to avemariapress.com/feedback to take a brief survey about your experience with *Sacred Reading: The 2016 Guide to Daily Prayer*. We'll use your input to make next year's book even better.

The Advent and Christmas Seasons

INTRODUCTION

Advent is all about waiting for Jesus Christ. The Gospel readings of Advent make us mindful of three ways we await Jesus—past, present, and future. First, we remember and accompany Mary, Joseph, and the newborn Jesus. Second, we prepare for the celebration of his birth this Christmas so that the day doesn't pass us by with just meaningless words and worthless presents. Third, we anticipate the second coming of Jesus Christ, who will come in power and glory for everyone to see and establish his kingdom of peace and justice upon the earth.

Christ is born, and we follow him in exile and in those joyful early years with the Holy Family. We are blessed, but we are challenged, too, to understand the ways of God and how we personally may understand and respond to them now.

Sunday, November 29, 2015
First Sunday of Advent

Know that God is present with you and ready to converse.

We begin by taking a moment to quiet our hearts, offering back to God any distractions or cares that might cause us to miss what he wants to say.

When you are ready, invite God to speak to you with words such as these: "I seek you in your Word, my God. Jesus, you are the Word of God. You are present with me now."

Read the Gospel: Luke 21:25–28, 34–36.

Jesus said: "There will be signs in the sun, the moon, and the stars, and on the earth distress among nations confused by the roaring of the sea and the waves. People will faint from fear and foreboding of what is coming upon the world, for the powers of the heavens will be shaken. Then they will see 'the Son of Man coming in a cloud' with power and great glory. Now when these things begin to take place, stand up and raise your heads, because your redemption is drawing near. . . .

"Be on guard so that your hearts are not weighed down with dissipation and drunkenness and the worries of this life, and that day does not catch you unexpectedly, like a trap. For it will come upon all who live on the face of the whole earth. Be alert at all times, praying that you may have the strength to escape all these things that will take place and to stand before the Son of Man."

Notice what you think and feel as you read the Gospel.

This Advent begins with a reminder of Jesus' second coming, making us think about the areas of our lives that need to be put in order.

Take a moment to consider what this Gospel passage suggests to you about how you can best prepare to celebrate the Lord's coming in the Incarnation, and to anticipate his return.

Pray as you are led for yourself and others.

"I am often anxious at this time of year, Lord. How does the Gospel help me prepare myself for your coming? How can I share your Incarnation with others?" (Continue in your own words.)

Listen to Jesus.

My child, I am preparing you every day. I am your strength. Put yourself in my care. Follow me into my eternal kingdom. What else is Jesus saying to you?

Ask God to show you how to live today.

As we conclude our time of prayer, we invite God to remain with us. While it is true that God is always with us, this prayer helps us to offer our day to God and to be more mindful of his presence in our daily lives.

"When I find myself anxious today, Lord, let me offer it to you and find your peace. Amen."

Linger in God's presence a few more moments.

Monday, November 30, 2015
Saint Andrew, Apostle

Know that God is present with you and ready to converse.

Take a moment to quiet your heart before you begin. "Lord, I come with my heart open to you. I need you here with me. We are together."

Read the Gospel: Matthew 4:18–22.

As Jesus walked by the Sea of Galilee, he saw two brothers, Simon, who is called Peter, and Andrew his brother, casting a net into the lake—for they were fishermen. And he said to them, "Follow me, and I will make you fish for people." Immediately they left their nets and followed him. As he went from there, he saw two other brothers, James son of Zebedee and his brother John, in the boat with their father Zebedee, mending their nets, and he called them. Immediately they left the boat and their father, and followed him.

Notice what you think and feel as you read the Gospel.

Jesus knew those he called to be his apostles. He did not interview them. They did not question him either, for the call of the Son of God was compelling. These men left jobs and family to be with him. What were they expecting?

Pray as you are led for yourself and others.

"Jesus, let me be willing to abandon all to follow you. I am in this place, doing this work. Do you want me in another place, or to do something else? How may I please you, Lord?" (Continue in your own words.)

Listen to Jesus.

Thank you for giving me time to speak with you when you pray. As I see your love for me growing in your heart, I am happy. Give yourself to me, so I can give more of myself to you. What else is Jesus saying to you?

Ask God to show you how to live today.
"Holy Spirit, show me ways to please God and to show love to others today. Amen."

Linger in God's presence a few more moments.

Tuesday, December 1, 2015

Know that God is present with you and ready to converse.
"You are here with me, Jesus. Help me as I read your Word."

Read the Gospel: Luke 10:21–24.
At that same hour Jesus rejoiced in the Holy Spirit and said, "I thank you, Father, Lord of heaven and earth, because you have hidden these things from the wise and the intelligent and have revealed them to infants; yes, Father, for such was your gracious will. All things have been handed over to me by my Father; and no one knows who the Son is except the Father, or who the Father is except the Son and anyone to whom the Son chooses to reveal him."

Then turning to the disciples, Jesus said to them privately, "Blessed are the eyes that see what you see! For I tell you that many prophets and kings desired to see what you see, but did not see it, and to hear what you hear, but did not hear it."

Notice what you think and feel as you read the Gospel.
The disciples were blessed to see Jesus, to hear and touch him. They recognized him instantly. Do we? Or are we often too self-absorbed and skeptical to see the Lord at work in our lives?

As you read this Gospel, what impression does it leave with you?

Pray as you are led for yourself and others.
"Make me like a child, Lord, so that I may recognize you in the events and people of my life. I want . . ." (Continue in your own words.)

Listen to Jesus.
If you know me, you know my Father and the Spirit. We are one. This is a mystery of love. You can find us in all the people of your life. What else is Jesus saying to you?

Ask God to show you how to live today.

"Lord, thank you for speaking to me privately, as you spoke to your disciples. Keep speaking to me, Lord. I hear you saying . . ." (Continue in conversation with Jesus awhile.)

Wednesday, December 2, 2015

Know that God is present with you and ready to converse.

"Let me be here with you now, Jesus. Let me hear what I need to hear from you today."

Read the Gospel: Matthew 15:29–37.

After Jesus had left that place, he passed along the Sea of Galilee, and he went up the mountain, where he sat down. Great crowds came to him, bringing with them the lame, the maimed, the blind, the mute, and many others. They put them at his feet, and he cured them, so that the crowd was amazed when they saw the mute speaking, the maimed whole, the lame walking, and the blind seeing. And they praised the God of Israel.

Then Jesus called his disciples to him and said, "I have compassion for the crowd, because they have been with me now for three days and have nothing to eat; and I do not want to send them away hungry, for they might faint on the way." The disciples said to him, "Where are we to get enough bread in the desert to feed so great a crowd?" Jesus asked them, "How many loaves have you?" They said, "Seven, and a few small fish." Then ordering the crowd to sit down on the ground, he took the seven loaves and the fish; and after giving thanks he broke them and gave them to the disciples, and the disciples gave them to the crowds. And all of them ate and were filled; and they took up the broken pieces left over, seven baskets full.

Notice what you think and feel as you read the Gospel.

See how Jesus' heart goes out to the crowd. Many of them are desperate; he heals them and then feeds them. What else do you notice?

Pray as you are led for yourself and others.

"Lord, I need healing and feeding and other necessities of life. There are people I love who also need these things. Please give us . . ." (Continue in your own words.)

Listen to Jesus.

When you pray my prayer from the heart, "Give us this day our daily bread," I hear you. I give you what you need. When you pray, "Thy will be done," you are expressing your trust in me . . . What else is Jesus saying to you?

Ask God to show you how to live today.

"I give myself to you, body and soul, Lord. I am ready to receive from you what you want to give me to serve you. Make me mindful of your gifts today. Amen."

Thursday, December 3, 2015
Saint Francis Xavier, priest

Know that God is present with you and ready to converse.

"I come into your presence with hope, Lord. Prepare me to hear you."

Read the Gospel: Matthew 7:21, 24–27.

Jesus said, "Not everyone who says to me, 'Lord, Lord,' will enter the kingdom of heaven, but only one who does the will of my Father in heaven.

"Everyone then who hears these words of mine and acts on them will be like a wise man who built his house on rock. The rain fell, the floods came, and the winds blew and beat on that house, but it did not fall, because it had been founded on rock. And everyone who hears these words of mine and does not act on them will be like a foolish man who built his house on sand. The rain fell, and the floods came, and the winds blew and beat against that house, and it fell—and great was its fall!"

Notice what you think and feel as you read the Gospel.

Feel the buffeting of rain and wind on your face. On what rock are you building your house?

Pray as you are led for yourself and others.

"How do I do the will of your Father, Jesus? Teach me . . ." (Continue in your own words.)

Listen to Jesus.

To seek me is to find me, my child. When you give yourself to God, you are building upon the rock. Trust me to keep you safe. What else is Jesus saying to you?

Ask God to show you how to live today.

"I offer myself today, Lord, for the good of all those you have given me. Show me how to serve. Amen."

Friday, December 4, 2015

Know that God is present with you and ready to converse.

"We are here together, Lord. I praise you."

Read the Gospel: Matthew 9:27–31.

As Jesus went on from there, two blind men followed him, crying loudly, "Have mercy on us, Son of David!" When he entered the house, the blind men came to him; and Jesus said to them, "Do you believe that I am able to do this?" They said to him, "Yes, Lord." Then he touched their eyes and said, "According to your faith let it be done to you." And their eyes were opened. Then Jesus sternly ordered them, "See that no one knows of this." But they went away and spread the news about him throughout that district.

Notice what you think and feel as you read the Gospel.

Jesus heard the cry of those in need and touched them. And they could not contain their joy.

Pray as you are led for yourself and others.

"Touch me, Lord. I want to see . . ." (Continue in your own words).

Listen to Jesus.

I have given you the gift of faith in me. See your circumstances with eyes of faith, dear disciple. What else is Jesus saying to you?

Ask God to show you how to live today.

"I offer myself today, Lord, for the good of all those I encounter. Help me to play a part in opening their eyes to your love and care. Amen."

Saturday, December 5, 2015

Know that God is present with you and ready to converse.
"Thank you for being here with me now, Lord."

Read the Gospel: Matthew 9:35–10:1, 5a, 7–8.
Then Jesus went about all the cities and villages, teaching in their synagogues, and proclaiming the good news of the kingdom, and curing every disease and every sickness. When he saw the crowds, he had compassion for them, because they were harassed and helpless, like sheep without a shepherd. Then he said to his disciples, "The harvest is plentiful, but the laborers are few; therefore ask the Lord of the harvest to send out laborers into his harvest."

Then Jesus summoned his twelve disciples and gave them authority over unclean spirits, to cast them out, and to cure every disease and every sickness. . . . These twelve Jesus sent out with the following instructions: ". . . As you go, proclaim the good news, 'The kingdom of heaven has come near.' Cure the sick, raise the dead, cleanse the lepers, cast out demons. You received without payment; give without payment."

Notice what you think and feel as you read the Gospel.
Jesus has a heart for the needy; he calls his disciples to serve. Then he gives them power to do what is needed. What does this say to you?

Pray as you are led for yourself and others.
"How are you calling me to serve, Jesus? What power are you giving me to serve? I ask that . . ." (Continue in your own words.)

Listen to Jesus.
I need you where you are, dear one, to do what you can do. Show love to others in every way you can. I give you power to do that. What else is Jesus saying to you?

Ask God to show you how to live today.
"Jesus, you gave yourself to others every day. Help me do the same. Amen."

Sunday, December 6, 2015
Second Sunday of Advent

Know that God is present with you and ready to converse.

We begin by taking a moment to quiet our hearts, offering back to God any distractions or cares that might cause us to miss what he wants to say. When you are ready, invite God to speak to you with words such as these:

"Let me come into your presence with joy, Lord."

Read the Gospel: Luke 3:1–6.

In the fifteenth year of the reign of Emperor Tiberius, when Pontius Pilate was governor of Judea, and Herod was ruler of Galilee . . . the word of God came to John son of Zechariah in the wilderness. He went into all the region around the Jordan, proclaiming a baptism of repentance for the forgiveness of sins, as it is written in the book of the words of the prophet Isaiah,

"The voice of one crying out in the wilderness:
'Prepare the way of the Lord,
make his paths straight.
Every valley shall be filled,
and every mountain and hill shall be made low,
and the crooked shall be made straight,
and the rough ways made smooth;
and all flesh shall see the salvation of God.'"

Notice what you think and feel as you read the Gospel.

John was set in motion by the Word of God, who is Jesus, to preach repentance. Repentance prepares the way of the Lord.

Take a moment to consider: How do these words of Isaiah move you?

Pray as you are led for yourself and others.

"Lord, I repent of my sins so that you can come to me. Show me the ways I resist your love, help me to forsake all habits of sin, and give me grace to . . ." (Continue in your own words.)

Listen to Jesus.

You are mine, enfolded in arms of love and peace. I forgive you and make you whole. I am strengthening you in your spirit. What else is Jesus saying to you?

Ask God to show you how to live today.

As we conclude our time of prayer, we invite God to remain with us. While it is true that God is always with us, this prayer helps us to offer our day to God, and to be more mindful of his presence in our daily lives.

"Thank you for your mercy, Jesus. How shall I become what you want me to be? What shall I do today? Amen."

Linger in God's presence a few more moments.

Monday, December 7, 2015

Know that God is present with you and ready to converse.

"I welcome you into my day, Lord. Let me be with you all day long."

Read the Gospel: Luke 5:17–26.

One day, while Jesus was teaching, Pharisees and teachers of the law were sitting nearby (they had come from every village of Galilee and Judea and from Jerusalem); and the power of the Lord was with him to heal. Just then some men came, carrying a paralyzed man on a bed. They were trying to bring him in and lay him before Jesus; but finding no way to bring him in because of the crowd, they went up on the roof and let him down with his bed through the tiles into the middle of the crowd in front of Jesus. When he saw their faith, he said, "Friend, your sins are forgiven you." Then the scribes and the Pharisees began to question, "Who is this who is speaking blasphemies? Who can forgive sins but God alone?" When Jesus perceived their questionings, he answered them, "Why do you raise such questions in your hearts? Which is easier, to say, 'Your sins are forgiven you,' or to say, 'Stand up and walk?' But so that you may know that the Son of Man has authority on earth to forgive sins"—he said to the one who was paralyzed—"I say to you, stand up and take your bed and go to your home." Immediately he stood up before them, took what he had been lying on, and went to his home, glorifying God. Amazement seized all of them, and they glorified God and were filled with awe, saying, "We have seen strange things today."

Notice what you think and feel as you read the Gospel.

What an incredible scene as the friends of the paralyzed man let him down through the roof on a stretcher! Even as witnesses to his mercy and healing power, some people find fault with Jesus. What else do you see in this passage?

Pray as you are led for yourself and others.

"I, too, can find fault with my circumstances, questioning you in my heart for some trouble or some good thing I feel has been withheld from me. Give me grace to cooperate with your will, to work with you as you bring good out of all things in my life. I glorify you for . . ." (Continue in your own words.)

Listen to Jesus.

My child, I love you and I love spending this time with you. I am always near you. Look for me in your circumstances and especially in others. Do not worry about anything. What else is Jesus saying to you?

Ask God to show you how to live today.

"You deserve honor and glory, Lord. Let me worship you for your goodness. Let me know more about you, my Good Shepherd. Amen."

Tuesday, December 8, 2015
The Immaculate Conception of the Blessed Virgin Mary

Know that God is present with you and ready to converse.

"I come to you today, Lord, seeking you. You are here now. Thank you."

Read the Gospel: Luke 1:26–38.

In the sixth month the angel Gabriel was sent by God to a town in Galilee called Nazareth, to a virgin engaged to a man whose name was Joseph, of the house of David. The virgin's name was Mary. And he came to her and said, "Greetings, favored one! The Lord is with you." But she was much perplexed by his words and pondered what sort of greeting this might be. The angel said to her, "Do not be afraid, Mary, for you have found favor with God. And now, you will conceive in your womb and bear a son, and you will name him Jesus. He will be great, and will be called the Son of the Most High, and the Lord God will give to him the throne of his ancestor David. He will reign over the house of Jacob forever, and of his kingdom there will be no end."

Mary said to the angel, "How can this be, since I am a virgin?" The angel said to her, "The Holy Spirit will come upon you, and the power of the Most High will overshadow you; therefore the child to be born will be holy; he will be called Son of God. And now, your relative Elizabeth in her old age has also conceived a son; and this is the sixth month for her who was said to be barren. For nothing will be impossible with God." Mary said, "Here am I, the servant of the Lord; let it be with me according to your word." Then the angel departed from her.

Notice what you think and feel as you read the Gospel.

Mary cannot comprehend Gabriel's stunning announcement. But she surrenders to God's will and gives her consent. She must have had many feelings about what the angel told her. What do *you* feel as you read this passage?

Pray as you are led for yourself and others.

"Hail Mary, full of grace, thank you for your willingness to give your life to the Holy Spirit so that the holy Son of God could come and redeem us. Lord Jesus, because 'nothing is impossible with God,' I ask you . . ." (Continue in your own words.)

Listen to Jesus.

I hear your prayer, my good friend. I am the One who puts love and faith in your heart. In me and through me, your prayer changes things for good. What else is Jesus saying to you?

Ask God to show you how to live today.

"I want to spend this time with you, Jesus. I have so much to learn about loving and serving you. Amen."

Wednesday, December 9, 2015

Know that God is present with you and ready to converse.

"I feel you within me and all around me, Lord. May I grow closer to you in this time of prayer."

Read the Gospel: Matthew 11:28–30.

Jesus said, "Come to me, all you that are weary and are carrying heavy burdens, and I will give you rest. Take my yoke upon you, and learn from me; for I am gentle and humble in heart, and you will find rest for your souls. For my yoke is easy, and my burden is light."

Notice what you think and feel as you read the Gospel.

Jesus invites those who are already burdened to take up his yoke. That seems surprising, until Jesus beautifully explains. What else do you hear Jesus saying?

Pray as you are led for yourself and others.

"Lord, let me learn from you. Let me take up the yoke to love God and others. Give me your own heart, gentle and lowly, that I might find rest for . . ." (Continue in your own words.)

Listen to Jesus.

Beloved, I want to speak to your heart. I know your labor and your burdens. Lay them on me. What else is Jesus saying to you?

Ask God to show you how to live today.

"How will you change my heart, Lord, to make it like your own? What shall I do today to act upon your Word? Amen."

Thursday, December 10, 2015

Know that God is present with you and ready to converse.

"Give me the joy of your presence here and now, Lord. You are the Word of God."

Read the Gospel: Matthew 11:11–15.

Jesus said: "Truly I tell you, among those born of women no one has arisen greater than John the Baptist; yet the least in the kingdom of heaven is greater than he. From the days of John the Baptist until now the kingdom of heaven has suffered violence, and the violent take it by force. For all the prophets and the law prophesied until John came; and if you are willing to accept it, he is Elijah who is to come. Let anyone with ears listen!"

Notice what you think and feel as you read the Gospel.

Some might find the words of Jesus here a bit puzzling. How can the least in the kingdom be greater than John? We were not there in Jesus' day. How does our faith in the Messiah differ from John's?

Pray as you are led for yourself and others.

"Jesus, give me ears to hear you calling me into the kingdom of heaven. Give me courage to follow fearlessly and with obedience . . ." (Continue in your own words.)

Listen to Jesus.

In time, I will show you the kingdom of heaven, leading you to something beyond human imagining. Know that heaven is a world of love, and you will share my glory. What else is Jesus saying to you?

Ask God to show you how to live today.

"My ears and my heart are open to you, Savior. Teach me. Amen."

Friday, December 11, 2015

Know that God is present with you and ready to converse.

"Speak to me, Lord. Your servant is with you now, listening."

Read the Gospel: Matthew 11:16–19.

Jesus said: "But to what will I compare this generation? It is like children sitting in the marketplaces and calling to one another,

'We played the flute for you, and you did not dance;
we wailed, and you did not mourn.'

"For John came neither eating nor drinking, and they say, 'He has a demon'; the Son of Man came eating and drinking, and they say, 'Look, a glutton and a drunkard, a friend of tax collectors and sinners!' Yet wisdom is vindicated by her deeds."

Notice what you think and feel as you read the Gospel.

Jesus seems to be saying that those of his generation would respond neither to John the Baptist's stern call to repentance nor to Jesus' welcoming call to the kingdom. What about my generation? What about me?

Pray as you are led for yourself and others.

"Lord, I don't want to be a complainer. Let me respond to you with wisdom. Give me what I need to share your love with my generation . . ." (Continue in your own words.)

Listen to Jesus.

My child, my purpose has always been your salvation—and the salvation of every person everywhere, for all of human history. I am glad you love me and want others to love me, too. Start by loving them; then you will know what to say and do. What else is Jesus saying to you?

Ask God to show you how to live today.

"Jesus, make me the person you want me to be. I give myself to you. Amen."

Saturday, December 12, 2015
Our Lady of Guadalupe

Know that God is present with you and ready to converse.

Let me be brave, Lord, and not afraid as I spend this time with you, your Word, and your mother.

Read the Gospel: Luke 1:26–38.

In the sixth month the angel Gabriel was sent by God to a town in Galilee called Nazareth, to a virgin engaged to a man whose name was Joseph, of the house of David. The virgin's name was Mary. And he came to her and said, "Greetings, favored one! The Lord is with you." But she was much perplexed by his words and pondered what sort of greeting this might be. The angel said to her, "Do not be afraid, Mary, for you have found favor with God. And now, you will conceive in your womb and bear a son, and you will name him Jesus. He will be great, and will be called the Son of the Most High, and the Lord God will give to him the throne of his ancestor David. He will reign over the house of Jacob forever, and of his kingdom there will be no end."

Mary said to the angel, "How can this be, since I am a virgin?" The angel said to her, "The Holy Spirit will come upon you, and the power of the Most High will overshadow you; therefore the child to be born will be holy; he will be called Son of God. And now, your relative Elizabeth in her old age has also conceived a son; and this is the sixth month for her who was said to be barren. For nothing will be impossible with God."

Then Mary said, "Here am I, the servant of the Lord; let it be with me according to your word." Then the angel departed from her.

Notice what you think and feel as you read the Gospel.

Mary, the handmaid of the Lord, is also the handmaid of the Church, the Body of her son Jesus. He is the Son of the most high God who will rule over his kingdom forever.

Pray as you are led for yourself and others.

"Jesus, I honor your mother, whom you have also honored in heaven as Queen. You are a loving son to her, and as she loves you, she loves us. Mary, for love of Jesus, pray for us sinners now and at the hour of our death . . ." (Continue in your own words.)

Listen to Jesus.

I do love my mother and will honor her forever. Those who love me love her. And those who love her do the will of God and will be great in the kingdom of heaven. There is love and joy for all. What else is Jesus saying to you?

Ask God to show you how to live today.

"Lord, I delight in your promises. Your goodness overwhelms me. I am part of your family. Show me who needs my prayers today. Amen."

Sunday, December 13, 2015
Third Sunday of Advent

Know that God is present with you and ready to converse.

Begin by taking a moment to quiet your heart, offering back to God any distractions or cares that might cause you to miss what he wants to say. When you are ready, invite God to speak to you with words such as these:

"I am before you, my God. Teach me your ways by your Word and Spirit."

Read the Gospel: Luke 3:10–18.

And the crowds asked John the Baptist, "What then should we do?" In reply he said to them, "Whoever has two coats must share with anyone who has none; and whoever has food must do likewise." Even tax collectors came to be baptized, and they asked him, "Teacher, what should we do?" He said to them, "Collect no more than the amount prescribed for you." Soldiers also asked him, "And we, what should we do?" He said to them, "Do not extort money from anyone by threats or false accusation, and be satisfied with your wages."

As the people were filled with expectation, and all were questioning in their hearts concerning John, whether he might be the Messiah, John answered all of them by saying, "I baptize you with water; but one who is more powerful than I is coming; I am not worthy to untie the thong of his sandals. He will baptize you with the Holy Spirit and fire. His winnowing fork is in his hand, to clear his threshing floor and to gather the wheat into his granary; but the chaff he will burn with unquenchable fire."

So, with many other exhortations, he proclaimed the Good News to the people.

Notice what you think and feel as you read the Gospel.

John is a practical man, preaching generosity, justice, and truthfulness in one's affairs. When people wonder whether he is the Christ, John strongly opposes them. He baptizes with water, he says; the Christ will baptize with the Spirit and fire. Take a moment to consider what all these images—the winnowing fork, threshing floor, wheat, chaff, and fire—say to you.

Pray as you are led for yourself and others.

"There is something great at stake, Lord, for me and for the whole world. Let me respond from my heart to John's message of repentance, for I, too, have been baptized with water. I look to you for my baptism with the Holy Spirit . . ." (Continue in your own words.)

Listen to Jesus.

You may not realize what a great change I have made in your life, dear child. The Spirit of God works in you, drawing you to me, washing and making you holy, giving you power to love others. Tell me what you need. What else is Jesus saying to you?

Ask God to show you how to live today.

Mindful of and thankful for the ways God has already changed us, we invite God to work in the moments of the day ahead. "Lord, show me today how I can serve you and others. Bring people before my mind and let me know what I can do for them that will bring glory to you. Amen."

Linger in God's presence a few more moments.

Monday, December 14, 2015

Know that God is present with you and ready to converse.

"I believe you are with me now, Savior. I seek you with my mind, my heart, and my soul."

Read the Gospel: Matthew 21:23–27.

When Jesus entered the Temple, the chief priests and the elders of the people came to him as he was teaching and said, "By what authority are you doing these things, and who gave you this authority?" Jesus said to them, "I will also ask you one question; if you tell me the answer, then I will also tell you by what authority I do these things. Did the baptism of John come from heaven, or was it of human origin?" And they argued with one another, "If we say, 'From heaven,' he will say to us, 'Why then did you not believe him?' But if we say, 'Of human origin,' we are afraid of the crowd; for all regard John as a prophet."

So they answered Jesus, "We do not know." And he said to them, "Neither will I tell you by what authority I am doing these things."

Notice what you think and feel as you read the Gospel.

Authority is an important principle in human affairs, and it is important in godly matters as well. The chief priests and elders are trying to pin Jesus down, perhaps with genuine curiosity, but the way Jesus answers them suggests he knows they are trying to find fault. How does he turn the tables on them?

Pray as you are led for yourself and others.

"Jesus, I believe your authority is from the Father. You know all people's hearts, including mine. Let me open myself to hearing what you have to say to me today, even if it's something I may not want to hear . . ." (Continue in your own words.)

Listen to Jesus.

I love you. You are mine. I wait for you to be ready to hear what I have to say. What have I put in your heart to do for me? For someone else? What else is Jesus saying to you?

Ask God to show you how to live today.

"God, I want you to help me make plans for today and even beyond. I am your servant; show me how to serve. Amen."

Tuesday, December 15, 2015

Know that God is present with you and ready to converse.

"Jesus, you spoke even to those who opposed you when you walked the earth. You tried to instruct them. Thank you for being here now to instruct me."

Read the Gospel: Matthew 21:28–32.

Jesus said: "What do you think? A man had two sons; he went to the first and said, 'Son, go and work in the vineyard today.' He answered, 'I will not'; but later he changed his mind and went. The father went to the second and said the same; and he answered, 'I go, sir'; but he did not go. Which of the two did the will of his father?" They said, "The first." Jesus said to them, "Truly I tell you, the tax collectors and the prostitutes are going into the kingdom of God ahead of you. For John came to you in the way of righteousness and you did not believe him, but the tax collectors and the prostitutes believed him; and even after you saw it, you did not change your minds and believe him."

Notice what you think and feel as you read the Gospel.

God is far above human values and expectations. The first son is defiant, but he repents and does his father's will. The second son assents but is both disobedient and a liar.

Pray as you are led for yourself and others.

"Lord, where am I in this story? Am I more like the repentant son or the one who failed to follow through? Show me the areas of my life where I am prone to self-righteousness and hypocrisy . . ." (Continue in your own words.)

Listen to Jesus.

This is the way the human heart works—even yours, beloved friend. And yet, if you come to me, I will give you a new heart, a heart full of grace and truth, so that you can give yourself for others who need you. What else is Jesus saying to you?

Ask God to show you how to live today.

"What do I need to know and do, Lord? I want to receive your truth. Amen."

Wednesday, December 16, 2015

Know that God is present with you and ready to converse.

"You meet me here in Word and in Spirit, Lord. I love you."

Read the Gospel: Luke 7:18b–23.

So John summoned two of his disciples and sent them to the Lord to ask, "Are you the one who is to come, or are we to wait for another?" When the men had come to him, they said, "John the Baptist has sent us to you to ask, 'Are you the one who is to come, or are we to wait for another?'"

Jesus had just then cured many people of diseases, plagues, and evil spirits, and had given sight to many who were blind. And he answered them, "Go and tell John what you have seen and heard: the blind receive their sight, the lame walk, the lepers are cleansed, the deaf hear, the dead are raised, the poor have good news brought to them. And blessed is anyone who takes no offense at me."

Notice what you think and feel as you read the Gospel.

Jesus was a great wonder-worker, not for himself, but for others, especially the sick and the poor. He does not seek his own glory but lets the works speak for themselves.

Pray as you are led for yourself and others.

"Jesus, let my works also speak for themselves, that I am your friend and servant. I stumble sometimes, I sin, but I keep coming back to you for forgiveness and grace to do better. Help me to do your will . . ." (Continue in your own words.)

Listen to Jesus.

You have my grace today, my friend. Stop often to enjoy my presence with you. This is the secret of all prayer. Think about the opportunities you will have to do that today. What else is Jesus saying to you?

Ask God to show you how to live today.

"Lord, I give you all my joys and sorrows and worries. I give you all the people that you have given to me. How may I serve you in serving them? Amen."

Thursday, December 17, 2015

Know that God is present with you and ready to converse.

"This is our time together, Lord. Let my meditation be pleasing to you, and let me attend to your voice."

Read the Gospel: Matthew 1:1–7a, 11–13, 16–17.

An account of the genealogy of Jesus the Messiah, the son of David, the son of Abraham. Abraham was the father of Isaac, and Isaac the father of Jacob, and Jacob the father of Judah and his brothers, and Judah the father of Perez and Zerah by Tamar, and Perez the father of Hezron, and . . . Salmon the father of Boaz by Rahab, and Boaz the father of Obed by Ruth, and Obed the father of Jesse, and Jesse the father of King David.

And David was the father of Solomon by the wife of Uriah, and Solomon the father of Rehoboam, and Rehoboam the father of Abijah, and . . . Josiah [was] the father of Jechoniah and his brothers, at the time of the deportation to Babylon.

And after the deportation to Babylon: Jechoniah was the father of Salathiel, and Salathiel the father of Zerubbabel, and . . . Jacob the father of Joseph the husband of Mary, of whom Jesus was born, who is called the Messiah.

So all the generations from Abraham to David are fourteen generations; and from David to the deportation to Babylon, fourteen generations; and from the deportation to Babylon to the Messiah, fourteen generations.

Notice what you think and feel as you read the Gospel.

While it may be tempting to gloss over these strange names of those in the line of Jesus, even in this abridged version of the text, a closer look at their lives reveals that Jesus Christ was the descendent of people who were both good and bad. For example, the great King Solomon was the fruit of the adulterous union of King David and the wife of Uriah the Hittite (see 2 Sm 11:5–27). In the birth of Christ, God turned even wicked actions to a good result. I contemplate God's mysterious ways.

Pray as you are led for yourself and others.

"Lord, let me trust you in all my circumstances, whether they seem good or bad. I know that you use them all for my good and the good of others. Help me to abandon myself completely to you . . ." (Continue in your own words.)

Listen to Jesus.

I came to redeem humanity. I came to save you, dear one. Love is the sole motive behind God's mysterious ways. Trust in the mercy of God even in hard circumstances, such as you face now. What else is Jesus saying to you?

Ask God to show you how to live today.

"You know about my difficulties, Lord. Bring to my mind your blessings in my life. Amen."

Friday, December 18, 2015

Know that God is present with you and ready to converse.

"God, you are always with me. You are 'Emmanuel,' the God who is with us (Is 7:14) to the very end of the world (Mt 28:20)."

Read the Gospel: Matthew 1:18–25.

Now the birth of Jesus the Messiah took place in this way. When his mother Mary had been engaged to Joseph, but before they lived together, she was found to be with child from the Holy Spirit. Her husband, Joseph, being a righteous man and unwilling to expose her to public disgrace, planned to dismiss her quietly. But just when he had resolved to do this, an angel of the Lord appeared to him in a dream and said, "Joseph, son of David, do not be afraid to take Mary as your wife, for the child conceived in her is from the Holy Spirit. She will bear a son, and you are to name him Jesus, for he will save his people from their sins." All this took place to fulfill what had been spoken by the Lord through the prophet:

> "Look, the virgin shall conceive and bear a son,
> and they shall name him 'Emmanuel,'
> which means, 'God is with us.'"

When Joseph awoke from sleep, he did as the angel of the Lord commanded him; he took her as his wife, but had no marital relations with her until she had borne a son; and he named him Jesus.

Notice what you think and feel as you read the Gospel.

Joseph was a reasonable man who sought to do right by Mary. But he must have been baffled by the situation. Through the angel in the dream, the Lord turned Joseph completely around. He obeyed, but he still had to wonder. What do you think Joseph was wondering?

Pray as you are led for yourself and others.

"I wonder, too, Lord, about the circumstances in my own life. Please help me to know what you want me to do and give me the strength to obey even if I cannot fully understand . . ." (Continue in your own words.)

Listen to Jesus.

My child, I do understand your circumstances. I know you thoroughly. And I love you. You are right to give to me all your concerns. When you do that, you will see me work in your life. What else is Jesus saying to you?

Ask God to show you how to live today.

"Lord, I long to see your face. How may I see you today? Amen."

Saturday, December 19, 2015

Know that God is present with you and ready to converse.

"Let me be in your presence now without fear, Lord, for you are the Good Shepherd who is always gentle with me."

Read the Gospel: Luke 1:5–15a; 18–25.

In the days of King Herod of Judea, there was a priest named Zechariah, who belonged to the priestly order of Abijah. His wife was a descendant of Aaron, and her name was Elizabeth. Both of them were righteous before God, living blamelessly according to all the commandments and regulations of the Lord. But they had no children, because Elizabeth was barren, and both were getting on in years.

Once when he was serving as priest before God and his section was on duty, he was chosen by lot, according to the custom of the priesthood, to enter the sanctuary of the Lord and offer incense. Now at the time of the incense-offering, the whole assembly of the people was praying outside. Then there appeared to him an angel of the Lord, standing at the right side of the altar of incense. When Zechariah saw him, he was terrified; and fear overwhelmed him. But the angel said to him, "Do not be afraid, Zechariah, for your prayer has been heard. Your wife Elizabeth will bear you a son, and you will name him John. You will have joy and gladness, and many will rejoice at his birth, for he will be great in the sight of the Lord. . . ."

Zechariah said to the angel, "How will I know that this is so? For I am an old man, and my wife is getting on in years." The angel replied, "I am Gabriel. I stand in the presence of God, and I have been sent to speak to you and to bring you this good news. But now, because you did not believe my words, which will be fulfilled in their time, you will become mute, unable to speak, until the day these things occur."

Meanwhile, the people were waiting for Zechariah, and wondered at his delay in the sanctuary. When he did come out, he could not speak to them, and they realized that he had seen a vision in the sanctuary. He kept motioning to them and remained unable to speak. When his time of service was ended, he went to his home.

After those days his wife Elizabeth conceived, and for five months she remained in seclusion. She said, "This is what the Lord has done for me when he looked favorably on me and took away the disgrace I have endured among my people."

Notice what you think and feel as you read the Gospel.

What might have gone through Elizabeth's mind when Zechariah returned to her, unable to speak? What does this passage suggest to you about how God answers prayer?

Pray as you are led for yourself and others.

"Almighty Lord of Hosts, heaven and earth are full of your glory. Give me eyes to see, a heart of love and trust, and strength to do what you want me to do . . ." (Continue in your own words.)

Listen to Jesus.

I have made you for myself, my beloved. Your prayers are like the sweetest incense to me. What else is Jesus saying to you?

Ask God to show you how to live today.

"How may I give myself quietly to you today, Lord? Amen."

Sunday, December 20, 2015
Fourth Sunday of Advent

Know that God is present with you and ready to converse.

Begin by taking a moment to quiet your heart, offering back to God anything that might cause you to miss what he wants to say. When you are ready, invite God to speak to you with words such as these:

"Holy Spirit, you are here with me. Let me receive you fully into my soul while I listen to the Word of God."

Read the Gospel: Luke 1:39–45.

In those days Mary set out and went with haste to a Judean town in the hill country, where she entered the house of Zechariah and greeted Elizabeth. When Elizabeth heard Mary's greeting, the child leapt in her womb. And Elizabeth was filled with the Holy Spirit and exclaimed with a loud cry, "Blessed are you among women, and blessed is the fruit of your womb. And why has this happened to me, that the Mother of my Lord comes to me? For as soon as I heard the sound of your greeting, the child in my womb leapt for joy. And blessed is she who believed that there would be a fulfillment of what was spoken to her by the Lord."

Notice what you think and feel as you read the Gospel.

Notice how the Holy Spirit reveals himself both through Mary, with Jesus in her womb, and through Elizabeth, with the infant John in her womb. How does the Holy Spirit reveal his presence in your life?

Pray as you are led for yourself and others.

"Pray through me, Holy Spirit. Let me pronounce blessings upon the people in my life, particularly those in some difficulty, including . . ." (Continue in your own words.)

Listen to Jesus.

My Spirit enfolds you; you are mine. Walk in grace today and all the days of your life. Receive my peace; receive my joy. What else is Jesus saying to you?

Ask God to show you how to live today.

As our time of prayer concludes, invite God to remain with you. Although God is always with us, this prayer helps us to offer our day to God and to be more mindful of his presence.

"Who needs me today, Lord? Is there something special I can do? Amen."

Linger in God's presence a few more moments.

Monday, December 21, 2015

Know that God is present with you and ready to converse.

"You are present in your Word, Lord, and present in my heart. I am listening."

Read the Gospel: Luke 1:39–45.

In those days Mary set out and went with haste to a Judean town in the hill country, where she entered the house of Zechariah and greeted Elizabeth. When Elizabeth heard Mary's greeting, the child leapt in her womb. And Elizabeth was filled with the Holy Spirit and exclaimed with a loud cry, "Blessed are you among women, and blessed is the fruit of your womb. And why has this happened to me, that the Mother of my Lord comes to me? For as soon as I heard the sound of your greeting, the child in my womb leapt for joy. And blessed is she who believed that there would be a fulfillment of what was spoken to her by the Lord."

Notice what you think and feel as you read the Gospel.

After Mary had received the startling announcement from the angel, she acted immediately. First her heart was willing to believe God, then her words consented, and then she hurried to visit her elderly cousin.

Pray as you are led for yourself and others.

"Lord, give me openness to your word like Mary's. Let me believe, say yes to you, and act in the loving ways you wish for me to act . . ." (Continue in your own words.)

Listen to Jesus.

I give you what you ask, my love. Today I give you opportunities to show your faith and to show your willingness to do God's will. Little acts of love are great acts. What else is Jesus saying to you?

Ask God to show you how to live today.

"Give me wisdom, Lord, so that I can show your love to others. Amen."

Tuesday, December 22, 2015

Know that God is present with you and ready to converse.

"You are the Almighty One, the Lord, my God, yet you are pleased to be with me now."

Read the Gospel: Luke 1:46–56.

And Mary said,
"My soul magnifies the Lord,
and my spirit rejoices in God my Savior,
for he has looked with favor on the lowliness of his servant.
Surely, from now on all generations will call me blessed;
for the Mighty One has done great things for me,
and holy is his name.
His mercy is for those who fear him
from generation to generation.
He has shown strength with his arm;
he has scattered the proud in the thoughts of their hearts.
He has brought down the powerful from their thrones,
and lifted up the lowly;
he has filled the hungry with good things,

and sent the rich away empty.
He has helped his servant Israel,
in remembrance of his mercy,
according to the promise he made to our ancestors,
to Abraham and to his descendants forever."

And Mary remained with her for about three months and then returned to her home.

Notice what you think and feel as you read the Gospel.

God opposes the proud, the mighty, and the rich. God extends blessings to those who fear God, the lowly, and the hungry. In what ways can you identify with these groups?

Pray as you are led for yourself and others.

"Lord, you know how I can be proud and self-sufficient. I do not want to be that way. Give me the blessed humility of Mary. Give me hunger for you and have mercy on me . . ." (Continue in your own words.)

Listen to Jesus.

I forgive you, child. I love to bestow mercy. Walk in it today. Who needs mercy from you? What else is Jesus saying to you?

Ask God to show you how to live today.

"My Jesus, how may I become lowly like your Blessed Mother? Amen."

Wednesday, December 23, 2015

Know that God is present with you and ready to converse.

"You promised to be with me always, Lord. You are here with me now. Mold me to your Word."

Read the Gospel: Luke 1:57–66.

Now the time came for Elizabeth to give birth, and she bore a son. Her neighbors and relatives heard that the Lord had shown his great mercy to her, and they rejoiced with her.

On the eighth day they came to circumcise the child, and they were going to name him Zechariah after his father. But his mother said, "No; he is to be called John." They said to her, "None of your relatives has this name." Then they began motioning to his father to find out what name he wanted to give him. He asked for a writing tablet and wrote, "His name is John." And all of them were amazed. Immediately his mouth was opened and his tongue freed, and he began to speak, praising God. Fear came over all their neighbors, and all these things were talked about throughout the entire hill country of Judea. All who heard them pondered them and said, "What then will this child become?" For, indeed, the hand of the Lord was with him.

Notice what you think and feel as you read the Gospel.

The neighbors and relatives do not approve of the name Elizabeth and Zechariah had chosen for their son. Yet when they obey by calling him John, the Lord confirms their choice publicly by removing Zechariah's impediment so he can speak again. Through obedience to God, we experience the greatest freedom.

Pray as you are led for yourself and others.

"Lord, the approval of neighbors and relatives is not the proper motive of my actions. I wish only to obey you. Help me to know your will and give me the strength to do it even in the face of disapproval . . ." (Continue in your own words.)

Listen to Jesus.

My beloved, I will bless you for your sincere efforts to put God first in your life. Love God and others in your thoughts, words, and actions. That is the whole will of God. What else is Jesus saying to you?

Ask God to show you how to live today.

"How shall I put you first today, Lord? Amen."

Thursday, December 24, 2015

Know that God is present with you and ready to converse.

"In the name of the Father, the Son, and the Holy Spirit, I sit with the living Word of God."

Read the Gospel: Luke 1:67–79.

Then his father Zechariah was filled with the Holy Spirit and spoke this prophecy:

> "Blessed be the Lord God of Israel,
> for he has looked favorably on his people and redeemed them.
> He has raised up a mighty savior for us
> in the house of his servant David,

as he spoke through the mouth of his holy prophets from of old,
that we would be saved from our enemies and from the hand of all who hate us.
Thus he has shown the mercy promised to our ancestors,
and has remembered his holy covenant,
the oath that he swore to our ancestor Abraham,
to grant us that we, being rescued from the hands of our enemies,
might serve him without fear, in holiness and righteousness
before him all our days.
And you, child, will be called the prophet of the Most High;
for you will go before the Lord to prepare his ways,
to give knowledge of salvation to his people
by the forgiveness of their sins.
By the tender mercy of our God,
the dawn from on high will break upon us,
to give light to those who sit in darkness and in the shadow of death,
to guide our feet into the way of peace."

Notice what you think and feel as you read the Gospel.

". . . the dawn from on high will break upon us, to give light to those who sit in darkness and in the shadow of death." These beautiful words express a glorious promise. The Savior, the Christ, is coming soon.

Pray as you are led for yourself and others.

"Lord, you are great. You keep your promises. Blessed are you. Blessed are all those who trust in you. Let me be one of those . . ." (Continue in your own words.)

Listen to Jesus.

I bless you today, dear friend. Wait for me in every moment and we will walk together. What else is Jesus saying to you?

Ask God to show you how to live today.

"Lord, show me the events and people of this day as you see them. Give me your heart as I give mine to you. Amen."

Friday, December 25, 2015
The Nativity of the Lord (Christmas)

Know that God is present with you and ready to converse.

"You have made your dwelling among us, Lord. You have taken human flesh and blood to fulfill the purposes of God."

Read the Gospel: John 1:1–18.

In the beginning was the Word, and the Word was with God, and the Word was God. He was in the beginning with God. All things came into being through him, and without him not one thing came into being. What has come into being in him was life, and the life was the light of all people. The light shines in the darkness, and the darkness did not overcome it.

There was a man sent from God, whose name was John. He came as a witness to testify to the light, so that all might believe through him. He himself was not the light, but he came to testify to the light. The true light, which enlightens everyone, was coming into the world.

He was in the world, and the world came into being through him; yet the world did not know him. He came to what was his own, and his own people did not accept him. But to all who received him, who believed in his name, he gave power to become children of God, who were born, not of blood or of the will of the flesh or of the will of man, but of God.

And the Word became flesh and lived among us, and we have seen his glory, the glory as of a father's only son, full of grace and truth. (John testified to him and cried out, "This was he of whom I said, 'He who comes after me ranks ahead of me because he was before me.'") From his fullness we have all received grace upon grace. The law indeed was given through Moses; grace and truth came through Jesus Christ. No one has ever seen God. It is God the only Son, who is close to the Father's heart, who has made him known.

Notice what you think and feel as you read the Gospel.

The infant and the man Jesus is true God. He reveals God's glory from everlasting to everlasting, and, accepting him, we receive the power to become children of God.

Pray as you are led for yourself and others.

"Word of God, full of grace and truth, let me bathe in your light. Let me know you and love you with every atom of myself, for I was made for you. Take me and my . . ." (Continue in your own words.)

Listen to Jesus.

My child, you know I love you, teach you, and guide you on your journey. Thank you for placing yourself in my care. You may trust me. I give you my peace. What else is Jesus saying to you?

Ask God to show you how to live today.

"I am still listening, Lord. How may I please you? Amen."

Saturday, December 26, 2015
Saint Stephen, first martyr

Know that God is present with you and ready to converse.

"You were present at the death of Saint Stephen, Lord, and you are present with me now."

Read the Gospel: Matthew 10:17–22.

Jesus said: "Beware of them, for they will hand you over to councils and flog you in their synagogues; and you will be dragged before governors and kings because of me, as a testimony to them and the Gentiles. When they hand you over, do not worry about how you are to speak or what you are to say; for what you are to say will be given to you at that time; for it is not you who speak, but the Spirit of your Father speaking through you. Brother will betray brother to death, and a father his child, and children will rise against parents and have them put to death; and you will be hated by all because of my name. But the one who endures to the end will be saved."

Notice what you think and feel as you read the Gospel.

"Beware of them," Jesus says, and he goes on to describe the atrocities people will inflict, and still do inflict, upon his followers. How have you experienced these things?

Pray as you are led for yourself and others.

"Lord, Lamb of God, Prince of Peace, strengthen and comfort all who are persecuted for your sake. Give them your Spirit to speak your words and to endure to the end. I pray for peace and love in my family . . ." (Continue in your own words.)

Listen to Jesus.

Be at peace, dear friend, for I am bringing good out of each act of hatred and violence. Trust me. Give my peace to each person you encounter, especially anyone who hates you. What else is Jesus saying to you?

Ask God to show you how to live today.

"Holy Spirit, give me the words to say when I am persecuted, abused, scorned, or neglected. Amen."

Sunday, December 27, 2015
The Holy Family of Jesus, Mary, and Joseph

Know that God is present with you and ready to converse.

Begin the week by placing yourself deliberately in God's presence. Take a moment to offer to him any distractions or cares that might cause you to miss what he wants to tell you. Acknowledge the gift of his presence.

"I know you are present, around me and within me now. I depend on that, my God."

Read the Gospel: Luke 2:41–52.

Now every year Jesus' parents went to Jerusalem for the festival of the Passover. And when he was twelve years old, they went up as usual for the festival. When the festival was ended and they started to return, the boy Jesus stayed behind in Jerusalem, but his parents did not know it. Assuming that he was in the group of travelers, they went a day's journey. Then they started to look for him among their relatives and friends. When they did not find him, they returned to Jerusalem to search for him.

After three days they found him in the Temple, sitting among the teachers, listening to them and asking them questions. And all who heard him were amazed at his understanding and his answers. When his parents saw him they were astonished; and his mother said to him, "Child, why have you treated us like this? Look, your father and I have been searching for you in great anxiety." He said to them, "Why were you searching for me? Did you not know that I must be in my Father's house?" But they did not understand what he said to them. Then he went down with them and came to Nazareth, and was obedient to them. His mother treasured all these things in her heart.

And Jesus increased in wisdom and in years, and in divine and human favor.

Notice what you think and feel as you read the Gospel.

Imagine how anxiously Mary and Joseph must have looked for their boy, Jesus. Jesus' behavior is a reminder that he was a boy like other boys, just as he was to become a man like other men. Yet he was always uniquely aware of his relationship to his Father.

Pray as you are led for yourself and others.

"Jesus, through you I also have a relationship with the heavenly Father. Let me love God more truly, more deeply, more completely than I ever have. I want to pray for these children today . . ." (Continue in your own words.)

Listen to Jesus.

You and I are truly children of my Father, Creator of heaven and earth, all things and all people. Rejoice in that. Know that you can trust God to care for you as long as you live. What else is Jesus saying to you?

Ask God to show you how to live today.

As you conclude this time of prayer, invite God to remain with you and to make you more mindful of his presence throughout the day.

"What will heaven be, Lord? How may I prepare for my service to you? Amen."

Linger in his presence a few moments longer.

Monday, December 28, 2015
The Holy Innocents, martyrs

Know that God is present with you and ready to converse.

"You are with me here every day in joy or in sorrow. Thank you for that."

Read the Gospel: Matthew 2:13–18.

Now after they had left, an angel of the Lord appeared to Joseph in a dream and said, "Get up, take the child and his mother, and flee to Egypt, and remain there until I tell you; for Herod is about to search for the child, to destroy him." Then Joseph got up, took the child and his mother by night, and went to Egypt, and remained there until the death of Herod. This was to fulfill what had been spoken by the Lord through the prophet, "Out of Egypt I have called my son."

When Herod saw that he had been tricked by the wise men, he was infuriated, and he sent and killed all the children in and around Bethlehem who were two years old or under, according to the time that he had learned from the wise men. Then was fulfilled what had been spoken through the prophet Jeremiah:

"A voice was heard in Ramah,
wailing and loud lamentation,
Rachel weeping for her children;
she refused to be consoled, because they are no more."

Notice what you think and feel as you read the Gospel.

The mysterious juxtaposition of God's power and man's free will is seen clearly in this passage. Wicked Herod massacres all those babies and toddlers, as Jeremiah prophesied; yet God protects the Holy Family.

Pray as you are led for yourself and others.

"I am at a loss to understand you in this Gospel, God. Many terrible things happen in this world. Help me to know what I should do. Help me to trust you in all things . . ." (Continue in your own words.)

Listen to Jesus.

I want you to trust in God in all things. I know this is sometimes difficult. I, too, have felt afraid and forsaken. In hard times, give yourself entirely to God. God will see you through. What else is Jesus saying to you?

Ask God to show you how to live today.

"Lord, show me what my response should be to violent and frightening world events. Amen."

Tuesday, December 29, 2015

Know that God is present with you and ready to converse.

"Open me to your nearness, Lord. Open my heart to your Word."

Read the Gospel: Luke 2:22–35.

When the time came for their purification according to the law of Moses, Mary and Joseph brought Jesus up to Jerusalem to present him to the Lord (as it is written in the law of the Lord, "Every firstborn male shall be designated as holy to the Lord"), and they offered a sacrifice according to what is stated in the law of the Lord, "a pair of turtle doves or two young pigeons."

Now there was a man in Jerusalem whose name was Simeon; this man was righteous and devout, looking forward to the consolation of Israel, and the Holy Spirit rested on him. It had been revealed to him by the Holy Spirit that he would not see death before he had seen the Lord's Messiah. Guided by the Spirit, Simeon came into the Temple; and when the parents brought in the child Jesus, to do for him what was customary under the law, Simeon took him in his arms and praised God, saying,

> "Master, now you are dismissing your servant in peace,
> according to your word;
> for my eyes have seen your salvation,
> which you have prepared in the presence of all peoples,
> a light for revelation to the Gentiles
> and for glory to your people Israel."

And the child's father and mother were amazed at what was being said about him. Then Simeon blessed them and said to his mother, Mary, "This child is destined for the falling and the rising of many in Israel, and to be a sign that will be opposed so that the inner thoughts of many will be revealed—and a sword will pierce your own soul, too."

Notice what you think and feel as you read the Gospel.

Simeon prophesizes that Jesus is destined to be a sign to be contradicted, opposed, and pierced. (Even his mother will be pierced.) What do you think it means that through their suffering "the inner thoughts of many will be revealed"?

Pray as you are led for yourself and others.

"Lord, you suffered and died at the hands of your tormenters. Your side was pierced, and blood and water gushed out for the salvation of the world. Let the hearts of many embrace you, for you are the light for the Gentiles and glory for your people Israel . . ." (Continue in your own words.)

Listen to Jesus.

I died a violent death to bring salvation, life, and peace to all who come to me. You have come to me, my beloved. Be my own. What else is Jesus saying to you?

Ask God to show you how to live today.
"How may I give myself to you today, Lord? Amen."

Wednesday, December 30, 2015

Know that God is present with you and ready to converse.
"Like the prophetess Anna, let me recognize your presence with me now, Lord, and give you thanks."

Read the Gospel: Luke 2:36–40.
There was also a prophet, Anna the daughter of Phanuel, of the tribe of Asher. She was of a great age, having lived with her husband for seven years after her marriage, then as a widow to the age of eighty-four. She never left the Temple but worshiped there with fasting and prayer night and day. At that moment she came and began to praise God and to speak about the child to all who were looking for the redemption of Jerusalem.

When they had finished everything required by the law of the Lord, they returned to Galilee, to their own town of Nazareth. The child grew and became strong, filled with wisdom; and the favor of God was upon him.

Notice what you think and feel as you read the Gospel.
What marvelous things happened in the life of the Holy Family! The hearts of Mary and Joseph must have been filled with joy and amazement. They watched Jesus grow and become strong, full of wisdom and the favor of God.

Pray as you are led for yourself and others.
"Jesus, I am a child, too. I await my own redemption and the redemption of the many I love. I thank you that I am growing in God's wisdom and favor . . ." (Continue in your own words.)

Listen to Jesus.
Grow in God's wisdom, child. It's not complicated. The secret is simply to give yourself to me and to those I give to you. What else is Jesus saying to you?

Ask God to show you how to live today.
"Show me how to walk in your way today, Lord. Amen."

Thursday, December 31, 2015

Know that God is present with you and ready to converse.

"I belong to you, Lord, not to the world. I know you are with me."

Read the Gospel: John 1:1–18.

In the beginning was the Word, and the Word was with God, and the Word was God. He was in the beginning with God. All things came into being through him, and without him not one thing came into being. What has come into being in him was life, and the life was the light of all people. The light shines in the darkness, and the darkness did not overcome it.

There was a man sent from God, whose name was John. He came as a witness to testify to the light, so that all might believe through him. He himself was not the light, but he came to testify to the light. The true light, which enlightens everyone, was coming into the world.

He was in the world, and the world came into being through him; yet the world did not know him. He came to what was his own, and his own people did not accept him. But to all who received him, who believed in his name, he gave power to become children of God, who were born, not of blood or of the will of the flesh or of the will of man, but of God.

And the Word became flesh and lived among us, and we have seen his glory, the glory as of a father's only son, full of grace and truth. (John testified to him and cried out, "This was he of whom I said, 'He who comes after me ranks ahead of me because he was before me.'") From his fullness we have all received grace upon grace. The law indeed was given through Moses; grace and truth came through Jesus Christ. No one has ever seen God. It is God the only Son, who is close to the Father's heart, who has made him known.

Notice what you think and feel as you read the Gospel.

There is no beginning with God. Before the beginning, God already was, with Jesus, the eternal Word of God. Through him, with him, and in him all things were made, and all things exist.

Pray as you are led for yourself and others.

"I give you glory, Word of the Father. Thank you for shedding your true light on me. May darkness never overcome it . . ." (Continue in your own words.)

Listen to Jesus.

I am close to you now. Our words come together in holy conversation. I am listening to you. What else is Jesus saying to you?

Ask God to show you how to live today.

"Plant your words in me, Lord, and let them grow for the good of others. Amen."

Remain with Jesus awhile.

Friday, January 1, 2016
Mary, Mother of God

Know that God is present with you and ready to converse.

"I come into your presence with gladness, Lord."

Read the Gospel: Luke 2:16–21.

So the shepherds went with haste and found Mary and Joseph, and the child lying in the manger. When they saw this, they made known what had been told them about this child; and all who heard it were amazed at what the shepherds told them. But Mary treasured all these words and pondered them in her heart. The shepherds returned, glorifying and praising God for all they had heard and seen, as it had been told them.

After eight days had passed, it was time to circumcise the child; and he was called Jesus, the name given by the angel before he was conceived in the womb.

Notice what you think and feel as you read the Gospel.

Simple shepherds are among those privileged to see the infant Jesus; God must have been pleased by their hearts. Mary keeps these wonderful events in her motherly heart.

Pray as you are led for yourself and others.

"Like the shepherds, I offer you my simple thanks, Lord. I thank you and praise you for coming among us for the salvation of people, myself included. Let me be a sign to others of your great goodness . . ." (Continue in your own words.)

Listen to Jesus.

You are mine. It makes me happy when you approach me with love and thanksgiving. Beloved friend, I give your life meaning; live every day for love. What else is Jesus saying to you?

Ask God to show you how to live today.

"God, let me treasure your blessings in my heart, just as Mary did. Amen."

Saturday, January 2, 2016

Know that God is present with you and ready to converse.

"Stir up my heart and mind, Lord, to hear and obey your Word."

Read the Gospel: John 1:19–28.

This is the testimony given by John when the Jews sent priests and Levites from Jerusalem to ask him, "Who are you?" He confessed and did not deny it, but confessed, "I am not the Messiah."

And they asked him, "What then? Are you Elijah?" He said, "I am not."

"Are you the prophet?" He answered, "No."

Then they said to him, "Who are you? Let us have an answer for those who sent us. What do you say about yourself?"

He said,

> "I am the voice of one crying out in the wilderness,
> 'Make straight the way of the Lord,'
> as the prophet Isaiah said."

Now they had been sent from the Pharisees. They asked him, "Why then are you baptizing if you are neither the Messiah, nor Elijah, nor the prophet?"

John answered them, "I baptize with water. Among you stands One whom you do not know, the One who is coming after me; I am not worthy to untie the thong of his sandal." This took place in Bethany across the Jordan where John was baptizing.

Notice what you think and feel as you read the Gospel.

John freely admits he is not the Messiah. He says he is not worthy to untie the sandal of the One who will come after him. How did they likely respond to this?

Pray as you are led for yourself and others.

"Thank you for my baptism by water, Lord. I repent of all my sins and ask for your grace to resist sin today . . ." (Continue in your own words.)

Listen to Jesus.

I give you my forgiveness and my grace as you have prayed. In this way, you are making our way straight, for I want to be with you and walk with you today in love. What else is Jesus saying to you?

Ask God to show you how to live today.

"Lord, some days I feel unworthy of you, but I'm so grateful for your loving presence and your constant grace. Let's walk together today. Amen."

Sunday, January 3, 2016
Epiphany of the Lord

Know that God is present with you and ready to converse.

On this final day of the Christmas season, pause to put yourself in the presence of the Lord, just like the magi.

"Wise men seek you and find you, Lord, right here, in this moment."

Read the Gospel: Matthew 2:1–12.

In the time of King Herod, after Jesus was born in Bethlehem of Judea, wise men from the East came to Jerusalem, asking, "Where is the child who has been born king of the Jews? For we observed his star at its rising, and have come to pay him homage." When King Herod heard this, he was frightened, and all Jerusalem with him; and calling together all the chief priests and scribes of the people, he inquired of them where the Messiah was to be born. They told him, "In Bethlehem of Judea; for so it has been written by the prophet:

'And you, Bethlehem, in the land of Judah,
are by no means least among the rulers of Judah;
for from you shall come a ruler
who is to shepherd my people Israel.'"

Then Herod secretly called for the wise men and learned from them the exact time when the star had appeared. Then he sent them to Bethlehem, saying, "Go and search diligently for the child; and when you have found him, bring me word so that I may also go and pay him homage." When they had heard the king, they set out; and there, ahead of them, went the star that they had seen at its rising, until it stopped over the place where the child was. When they saw that the star had stopped, they were overwhelmed with joy. On entering the house, they saw the child with Mary his mother; and they knelt down and paid him homage. Then, opening their treasure chests, they offered him gifts of gold, frankincense, and myrrh. And having been warned in a dream not to return to Herod, they left for their own country by another road.

Notice what you think and feel as you read the Gospel.

I marvel that God led these mysterious and exotic wise men, magi from the east, to Bethlehem to honor the newborn king. They are overjoyed. What did they know about what they were seeing?

Pray as you are led for yourself and others.

"Lord, I seek you, too. I give you the gift of myself today. Use me as you will. That will be a joy to me . . ." (Continue in your own words.)

Listen to Jesus.

I am always with you, my dear one. We have found one another, for I also seek you. Look for me in everything, especially in the faces of those in need. What else is Jesus saying to you?

Ask God to show you how to live today.

"Show me yourself all along the way, Lord. Give me eyes for only you. Amen."

Monday, January 4, 2016

Know that God is present with you and ready to converse.

"Light of the world, I seek you. You said that one who seeks, finds. I rely on that. Thank you for being here with me."

Read the Gospel: Matthew 4:12–17, 23–25.

Now when Jesus heard that John had been arrested, he withdrew to Galilee. He left Nazareth and made his home in Capernaum by the sea, in the territory of Zebulun and Naphtali, so that what had been spoken through the prophet Isaiah might be fulfilled:

> "Land of Zebulun, land of Naphtali,
> on the road by the sea, across the Jordan, Galilee of the Gentiles—
> the people who sat in darkness

have seen a great light,
and for those who sat in the region and shadow of death
light has dawned."

From that time Jesus began to proclaim, "Repent, for the kingdom of heaven has come near." . . .

Jesus went throughout Galilee, teaching in their synagogues and proclaiming the good news of the kingdom and curing every disease and every sickness among the people. So his fame spread throughout all Syria, and they brought to him all the sick, those who were afflicted with various diseases and pains, demoniacs, epileptics, and paralytics, and he cured them. And great crowds followed him from Galilee, the Decapolis, Jerusalem, Judea, and from beyond the Jordan.

Notice what you think and feel as you read the Gospel.

Jesus responds to John the Baptist's arrest by moving to Galilee and beginning his ministry there. He preaches repentance, proclaims the Gospel, and heals every disease. The Gentiles sitting in darkness there have truly seen a great light.

Pray as you are led for yourself and others.

"Jesus, I am sitting in darkness, too. Light me. I need healing, too. Heal me. I put my trust in you . . ." (Continue in your own words.)

Listen to Jesus.

My beloved, you are right to cast your whole self upon me, for I am the Good Shepherd. I care about you, every part of your life. What else is Jesus saying to you?

Ask God to show you how to live today.

"Dear Lord, you do so much for me. Show me what I may do for you and for others today. Amen."

Tuesday, January 5, 2016

Know that God is present with you and ready to converse.

"I am amazed, Lord, that you are not only with me but also with millions of others at the same time, all turning to you today."

Read the Gospel: Mark 6:34–44.

As Jesus went ashore, he saw a great crowd; and he had compassion for them, because they were like sheep without a shepherd; and he began to teach them many things. When it grew late, his disciples came to him and said, "This is a deserted place, and the hour is now very late; send them away so that they may go into the surrounding country and villages and buy something for themselves to eat." But he answered them, "You give them something to eat." They said to him, "Are we to go and buy two hundred denarii worth of bread, and give it to them to eat?" And he said to them, "How many loaves have you? Go and see." When they had found out, they said, "Five, and two fish." Then he ordered them to get all the people to sit down in groups on the green grass. So they sat down in groups of hundreds and of fifties. Taking the five loaves and the two fish, he looked up to heaven, and blessed and broke the loaves, and gave them to his disciples to set before the people; and he divided the two fish among them all. And all ate and were filled; and they took up twelve baskets full of broken pieces and of the fish. Those who had eaten the loaves numbered five thousand men.

Notice what you think and feel as you read the Gospel.

Jesus' heart is moved with pity for the vast, hungry crowd of five thousand. He feeds them all with five loaves and two fish, with twelve baskets of fragments remaining. That homely, exact detail of the twelve baskets left over delights me.

Pray as you are led for yourself and others.

"Jesus, you have a heart for me and you know my needs. I am hungry—yes, for my daily bread, but also for you. You are the bread of life. I need you today . . ." (Continue in your own words.)

Listen to Jesus.

Disciple and friend, I need you, too. I ask you to be broken like bread for others. You will be surprised at how I can multiply the bread that is you. What else is Jesus saying to you?

Ask God to show you how to live today.

"I am listening, Lord. Show me how my brokenness can be food for others. Amen."

Wednesday, January 6, 2016

Know that God is present with you and ready to converse.

"I sometimes feel alone as I toss in the storms of my life. But wait—you are here."

Read the Gospel: Mark 6:45–52.

Immediately Jesus made his disciples get into the boat and go on ahead to the other side, to Bethsaida, while he dismissed the crowd. After saying farewell to them, he went up on the mountain to pray.

When evening came, the boat was out on the sea, and he was alone on the land. When he saw that they were straining at the oars against an adverse wind, he came towards them early in the morning, walking on the sea. He intended to pass them by. But when they saw him walking on the sea, they thought it was a ghost and cried out; for they all saw him and were terrified. But immediately he spoke to them and said, "Take heart, it is I; do not be afraid." Then he got into the boat with them and the wind ceased. And they were utterly astounded, for they did not understand about the loaves, but their hearts were hardened.

Notice what you think and feel as you read the Gospel.

Jesus' disciples did not understand the incident of the five loaves with which he fed the five thousand. They are astounded by his walking on the water, entering the boat, and quieting the storm. Jesus says, "It is I; do not be afraid."

Pray as you are led for yourself and others.

"Jesus, I am one of them. I do not understand much. I am sometimes so dull I do not even know to be astounded by your working in my life. I am afraid of the storms, those now and the ones I fear . . ." (Continue in your own words.)

Listen to Jesus.

Do not be afraid, because I am with you always, protecting you. You will have storms, but I will be there with you. What storms do you fear, my beloved? What else is Jesus saying to you?

Ask God to show you how to live today.

"Thank you for hearing me, Lord. Show me how to draw close to you to find peace and safety. Amen."

Thursday, January 7, 2016

Know that God is present with you and ready to converse.

"Jesus, you came to your own, but sometimes they did not know who you really were. Let me know you are here with me now."

Read the Gospel: Luke 4:14–22.

Then Jesus, filled with the power of the Spirit, returned to Galilee, and a report about him spread through all the surrounding country. He began to teach in their synagogues and was praised by everyone.

When he came to Nazareth, where he had been brought up, he went to the synagogue on the Sabbath day, as was his custom. He stood up to read, and the scroll of the prophet Isaiah was given to him. He unrolled the scroll and found the place where it was written:

"The Spirit of the Lord is upon me,
because he has anointed me
to bring good news to the poor.
He has sent me to proclaim release to the captives
and recovery of sight to the blind,
to let the oppressed go free,
to proclaim the year of the Lord's favor."

And he rolled up the scroll, gave it back to the attendant, and sat down. The eyes of all in the synagogue were fixed on him. Then he began to say to them, "Today this scripture has been fulfilled in your hearing." All spoke well of him and were amazed at the gracious words that came from his mouth. They said, "Is not this Joseph's son?"

Notice what you think and feel as you read the Gospel.

After reading a messianic passage from Isaiah from the scrolls in the Nazareth synagogue, Jesus tells the people of his hometown that today the passage is fulfilled in their hearing. He tells them the truth with quiet confidence. They ask, "Isn't this the son of Joseph?"

Pray as you are led for yourself and others.

"Jesus, you are not the son of Joseph. You are the Son of God proclaiming glad tidings to the poor, to captives, to the blind, and to the oppressed. May your glad tidings still be proclaimed by the Church, and by me, too . . ." (Continue in your own words.)

Listen to Jesus.

The peoples of the world still need to hear the glad tidings. I have asked all who love me to proclaim the Gospel. Resist the temptation to let others do it. You, too, are called to preach the Gospel. What else is Jesus saying to you?

Ask God to show you how to live today.

"Show me how, Lord. I feel inadequate to do your blessed work of evangelization. Amen."

Friday, January 8, 2016

Know that God is present with you and ready to converse.

"Do you want to be with me right now, Jesus, as I seek you in your Word? Yes, wonderfully, you do."

Read the Gospel: Luke 5:12–16.

Once, when Jesus was in one of the cities, there was a man covered with leprosy. When he saw Jesus, he bowed with his face to the ground and begged him, "Lord, if you choose, you can make me clean." Then Jesus stretched out his hand, touched him, and said, "I do choose. Be made clean." Immediately the leprosy left him. And he ordered him to tell no one. "Go," he said, "and show yourself to the priest, and, as Moses commanded, make an offering for your cleansing, for a testimony to them." But now more than ever the word about Jesus spread abroad; many crowds would gather to hear him and to be cured of their diseases. But he would withdraw to deserted places and pray.

Notice what you think and feel as you read the Gospel.

The leper says, "If you wish, you can make me clean." Knowing he needs reassurance, Jesus says, "I do will it." And he heals the leper.

Pray as you are led for yourself and others.

"Lord, why do I sometimes doubt that you want what is good for me? You do will my good, as you willed to heal the leper. Help me to see you as the good, loving, and generous Savior you are . . ." (Continue in your own words.)

Listen to Jesus.

My child, part of my work is to show you your own heart, so that you come to rely on me and not yourself. You need to see that you need me, even every hour. When you give me your weakness, I can give you my strength. What else is Jesus saying to you?

Ask God to show you how to live today.

"Show me my faults, my weaknesses, my vulnerabilities, Lord, so that I can give them all to you and receive your strength to do good. Amen."

Saturday, January 9, 2016

Know that God is present with you and ready to converse.

"What a privilege to carry everything to God in prayer. You are always with me, Lord, my rock."

Read the Gospel: John 3:22–30.

Jesus and his disciples went into the Judean countryside, and he spent some time there with them and baptized. John also was baptizing at Aenon near Salim because water was abundant there; and people kept coming and were being baptized—John, of course, had not yet been thrown into prison.

Now a discussion about purification arose between John's disciples and a Jew. They came to John and said to him, "Rabbi, the one who was with you across the Jordan, to whom you testified, here he is baptizing, and all are going to him." John answered, "No one can receive anything except what has been given from heaven. You yourselves are my witnesses that I said, 'I am not the Messiah, but I have been sent ahead of him.' He who has the bride is the bridegroom. The friend of the bridegroom, who stands and hears him, rejoices greatly at the bridegroom's voice. For this reason my joy has been fulfilled. He must increase, but I must decrease."

Notice what you think and feel as you read the Gospel.

John compares himself to the friend of the bridegroom, who is Jesus. The friend is joyful because the bridegroom has the bride. The Church—and each one of us—is the bride of Christ. How happy that makes me.

Pray as you are led for yourself and others.

"Lord, may you increase as I decrease. Take all of me and make of me what you will. Most of all, give me your own heart of love for all . . ." (Continue in your own words.)

Listen to Jesus.

Dear bride, I know your heart and your love for God and others. I am happy to keep filling your heart with love, for God is love. What else is Jesus saying to you?

Ask God to show you how to live today.

"If I sit with you, Jesus, will you stay with me in quiet conversation? Amen."

Sunday, January 10, 2016
The Baptism of the Lord

Know that God is present with you and ready to converse.

"Holy Spirit, descend upon me now. Pray with me."

Read the Gospel: Luke 3:15–16, 21–22.

As the people were filled with expectation, and all were questioning in their hearts concerning John, whether he might be the Messiah, John answered all of them by saying, "I baptize you with water; but one who is more powerful than I is coming; I am not worthy to untie the thong of his sandals. He will baptize you with the Holy Spirit and fire. . . ."

Now when all the people were baptized, and when Jesus also had been baptized and was praying, the heaven was opened, and the Holy Spirit descended upon him in bodily form like a dove. And a voice came from heaven, "You are my Son, the Beloved; with you I am well pleased."

Notice what you think and feel as you read the Gospel.

When Jesus prays after his baptism, the Holy Spirit descends upon him and the voice comes from heaven.

Pray as you are led for yourself and others.

"I need you in my life, Holy Spirit, to love, trust, understand, and pray. You are one with Jesus and the Father, Lord. Be one with me, too . . ." (Continue in your own words.)

Listen to Jesus.

As one who follows me, you are one with the Holy Trinity. The kingdom of heaven is already within you. Look to God for all your needs, your own and others'. What else is Jesus saying to you?

Ask God to show you how to live today.

"Guide me, Lord, by your Spirit, today and tomorrow. Show me how to surrender to the Holy Spirit in all things. Amen."

Ordinary Time

INTRODUCTION

Ordinary Time is the time of the year in which Christ walks among us, calling us, teaching us, transforming us. Advent, Lent, and the Easter season are special periods excluded from Ordinary Time. Ordinary Time begins on the Monday following the first Sunday after the Feast of the Epiphany and runs until Ash Wednesday, then continues on the Monday after Pentecost Sunday and runs until the First Sunday in Advent when the new liturgical year begins.

Ordinary Time is called "ordinary" simply because the weeks are numbered. Like the word *ordinal,* the word *ordinary* comes from a Latin word for numbers. Ordinary Time refers to the ordered life of the Church; the gospels of Ordinary Time treat all aspects of Jesus' ministry and sayings more or less in sequence.

Monday, January 11, 2016

Know that God is present with you and ready to converse.

"Hello, dear God, dear Father. Thank you for calling me into your presence today. Let me hear you in your Word and through your Spirit."

Read the Gospel: Mark 1:14–20.

Now after John was arrested, Jesus came to Galilee, proclaiming the good news of God, and saying, "The time is fulfilled, and the kingdom of God has come near; repent, and believe in the good news."

As Jesus passed along the Sea of Galilee, he saw Simon and his brother Andrew casting a net into the sea for they were fishermen. And Jesus said to them, "Follow me and I will make you fish for people." And immediately they left their nets and followed him. As he went a little farther, he saw James son of Zebedee and his brother John, who were in their boat mending the nets. Immediately he called them; and they left their father Zebedee in the boat with the hired men, and followed him.

Notice what you think and feel as you read the Gospel.

Jesus begins to proclaim the Gospel of God immediately after his baptism. His Gospel did not evolve. The kingdom is at hand; repent and believe it.

Pray as you are led for yourself and others.

"Lord, I sometimes struggle with repentance. I don't want to face my sin. Let the scales of denial and rationalization fall from my eyes, so that I can repent well and be cleansed . . ." (Continue in your own words.)

Listen to Jesus.

I am happy to grant your request because it is my will. My work is to sanctify you, to prepare you for heaven, where you shall be like me. What else is Jesus saying to you?

Ask God to show you how to live today.

"Let me open myself, Lord, to all your truth. Help me repent from the heart and be healed. Amen."

Tuesday, January 12, 2016

Know that God is present with you and ready to converse.

"Thank you, Lord, for calling me back to you again. Speak, and I will listen."

Read the Gospel: Mark 1:21–28.

They went to Capernaum; and when the Sabbath came, Jesus entered the synagogue and taught. They were astounded at his teaching, for he taught them as one having authority, and not as the scribes. Just then there was in their synagogue a man with an unclean spirit, and he cried out, "What have you to do with us, Jesus of Nazareth? Have you come to destroy us? I know who you are, the holy one of God." But Jesus rebuked him, saying, "Be silent, and come out of him!" And the unclean spirit, convulsing him and crying with a loud voice, came out of him. They were all amazed, and they kept on asking one another, "What is this? A new teaching—with authority! He commands even the unclean spirits, and they obey him." At once his fame began to spread throughout the surrounding region of Galilee.

Notice what you think and feel as you read the Gospel.

What a world it was, when unclean spirits speak through a man. They recognize Jesus as the holy one of God, worrying that he has come to destroy them. What else do you notice in this passage?

Pray as you are led for yourself and others.

"Jesus, if there is anything unclean in me, please take it away . . ." (Continue in your own words.)

Listen to Jesus.

I have the authority to make you clean, and I thank you for wanting that because I ask you to be holy, as I am holy. Holiness is happiness. What else is Jesus saying to you?

Ask God to show you how to live today.

"Lord, now is the time to amend my life. How may I do that in my thoughts, words, and deeds? Amen."

Wednesday, January 13, 2016

Know that God is present with you and ready to converse.

"Jesus, you are real in my life. I love being alone with you. I find great joy and strength in you. Thank you."

Read the Gospel: Mark 1:29–39.

As soon as they left the synagogue, they entered the house of Simon and Andrew, with James and John. Now Simon's mother-in-law was in bed with a fever, and they told Jesus about her at once. He came and took her by the hand and lifted her up. Then the fever left her, and she began to serve them.

That evening, at sunset, they brought to him all who were sick or possessed with demons. And the whole city was gathered around the door. And he cured many who were sick with various diseases, and cast out many demons; and he would not permit the demons to speak, because they knew him.

In the morning, while it was still very dark, he got up and went out to a deserted place, and there he prayed. And Simon and his companions hunted for him. When they found him, they said to him, "Everyone is searching for you." Jesus answered, "Let us go on to the neighboring towns, so that I may proclaim the message there also; for that is what I came out to do." And he went throughout Galilee, proclaiming the message in their synagogues and casting out demons.

Notice what you think and feel as you read the Gospel.

Jesus rises early to pray. His disciples follow. Do they think he is unaware of the demands people are putting on him? He is aware, but he wants to pray, to be with God.

Pray as you are led for yourself and others.

"Lord, I, too, want to be with God, for I have many demands upon me. I need God to help me . . ." (Continue in your own words.)

Listen to Jesus.

You are right to recognize that the single most important thing you do in life is to maintain your love affair with God. I am easy to love. So are you, for you are mine. What else is Jesus saying to you?

Ask God to show you how to live today.

"Lord, teach me how to pray. Let me pray in ways that please you well. Amen." Remain in Jesus' presence awhile.

Thursday, January 14, 2016

Know that God is present with you and ready to converse.

"Jesus, I join you now in this place. Open my heart to your Word."

Read the Gospel: Mark 1:40–45.

A leper came to Jesus begging him, and kneeling he said to him, "If you choose, you can make me clean." Moved with pity, Jesus stretched out his hand and touched him, and said to him, "I do choose. Be made clean!" Immediately the leprosy left him, and he was made clean. After sternly warning him he sent him away at once, saying to him, "See that you say nothing to anyone; but go, show yourself to the priest, and offer for your cleansing what Moses commanded, as a testimony to them." But he went out and began to proclaim it freely, and to spread the word, so that Jesus could no longer go into a town openly, but stayed out in the country; and people came to him from every quarter.

Notice what you think and feel as you read the Gospel.

Jesus heals the leper and commands him to say nothing about it. He means it, yet Jesus knows the leper will talk freely about his healing. His talking results in Jesus not being able to go into towns but only preach in the country.

Pray as you are led for yourself and others.

"Lord, I don't know how to feel about this passage, for if I were the healed leper, I would probably speak about your healing me, too. I think it is good for me to tell others about your blessings to me now . . ." (Continue in your own words.)

Listen to Jesus.

Yes, share your joy, my child, for I am in your life every day, not just passing through your town. It is good for me and for you to be in this ministry to the world. What else is Jesus saying to you?

Ask God to show you how to live today.

"Will you call to my mind my many blessings and give me proper gratitude? Let me speak of my blessings to others. Amen."

Friday, January 15, 2016

Know that God is present with you and ready to converse.

"My conversation with you, Lord, despite my failings, is my lifeline. I find you again today, merciful Savior."

Read the Gospel: Mark 2:1–12.

When Jesus returned to Capernaum after some days, it was reported that he was at home. So many gathered around that there was no longer room for them, not even in front of the door; and he was speaking the word to them. Then some people came, bringing to him a paralyzed man, carried by four of them. And when they could not bring him to Jesus because of the crowd, they removed the roof above him; and after having dug through it, they let down the mat on which the paralytic lay. When Jesus saw their faith, he said to the paralytic, "Son, your sins are forgiven." Now some of the scribes were sitting there, questioning in their hearts, "Why does this fellow speak in this way? It is blasphemy! Who can forgive sins but God alone?" At once Jesus perceived in his spirit that they were discussing these questions among themselves; and he said to them, "Why do you raise such questions in your hearts? Which is easier, to say to the paralytic, 'Your sins are forgiven,' or to say, 'Stand up and take your mat and walk'? But so that you may know that the Son of Man has authority on earth to forgive sins"—he said to the paralytic—"I say to you, stand up, take your mat and go to your home." And he stood up, and immediately took the mat and went out before all of them; so that they were all amazed and glorified God, saying, "We have never seen anything like this!"

Notice what you think and feel as you read the Gospel.

Jesus connects for the critical scribes his authority to forgive and to heal. He heals the paralytic, and all are amazed, glorifying God, saying, "We never saw anything like this!"

Pray as you are led for yourself and others.

"Lord, I have need for healing, too—in my body, in my mind, and in my spirit. But I need forgiveness first. Forgive, then heal me . . ." (Continue in your own words.)

Listen to Jesus.

Your words please me, for you are my follower, seeking me and the love in my heart. I am working in you every day for healing. Receive it in faith. What else is Jesus saying to you?

Ask God to show you how to live today.

"Lord, you do amazing things no one has ever seen. Give me the gift of wonder, appreciating your powerful works in my life. Amen."

Saturday, January 16, 2016

Know that God is present with you and ready to converse.

"Jesus, you know I am already here with you. Please be here with me."

Read the Gospel: Mark 2:13–17.

Jesus went out again beside the sea; the whole crowd gathered around him, and he taught them. As he was walking along, he saw Levi son of Alphaeus sitting at the tax booth, and he said to him, "Follow me." And he got up and followed him.

And as he sat at dinner in Levi's house, many tax collectors and sinners were also sitting with Jesus and his disciples—for there were many who followed him. When the scribes of the Pharisees saw that he was eating with sinners and tax collectors, they said to his disciples, "Why does he eat with tax collectors and sinners?" When Jesus heard this, he said to them, "Those who are well have no need of a physician, but those who are sick; I have come to call not the righteous but sinners."

Notice what you think and feel as you read the Gospel.

How often do we think of others as unworthy? Yet the Lord ate with sinners and tax collectors, and obviously believed they could be converted—even as the "righteous" (the self-righteous) missed his call. How does this passage speak to you?

Pray as you are led for yourself and others.

"Lord, I pray for myself and all who consider themselves righteous, for none is righteous but God. Lord, what virtue is harder than humility? Give me your humble heart . . ." (Continue in your own words.)

Listen to Jesus.

You are walking in flesh, my dear child. Do not be surprised by your temptation to think too highly of yourself. I am happy that you are seeing that as a problem in our relationship. What else is Jesus saying to you?

Ask God to show you how to live today.

"Lord, I have so far to go to be ready for your kingdom, where I shall be holy like you. What can I do now to please you, to advance in holiness? Amen."

Sunday, January 17, 2016
Second Sunday in Ordinary Time

Know that God is present with you and ready to converse.

Begin this sacred reading by quieting yourself, immersing yourself by faith in the presence of God. Let go of doubt and distraction.

When you are ready, speak to the Lord with words such as these: "I welcome you, Lord. I am moved by your presence with me in this time of prayer."

Read the Gospel: John 2:1–11.

On the third day there was a wedding in Cana of Galilee, and the mother of Jesus was there. Jesus and his disciples had also been invited to the wedding. When the wine gave out, the mother of Jesus said to him, "They have no wine." And Jesus said to her, "Woman, what concern is that to you and to me? My hour has not yet come." His mother said to the servants, "Do whatever he tells you." Now standing there were six stone water jars for the Jewish rites of purification, each holding twenty or thirty gallons. Jesus said to them, "Fill the jars with water." And they filled them up to the brim. He said to them, "Now draw some out, and take it to the chief steward." So they took it. When the steward tasted the water that had become wine, and did not know where it came from (though the servants who had drawn the water knew), the steward called the bridegroom and said to him, "Everyone serves the good wine first, and then the inferior wine after the guests have become drunk. But you have kept the good wine until now." Jesus did this, the first of his signs, in Cana of Galilee, and revealed his glory; and his disciples believed in him.

Notice what you think and feel as you read the Gospel.

Jesus seems to dismiss his mother when she mentions to him the fact that the wedding banquet has run out of wine. But he turns six very large jars of water into excellent wine, the first of his miracles at Cana in Galilee. His disciples believe in him.

Pray as you are led for yourself and others.

"Jesus, it must have been a joy for your disciples to be with you at that wedding in Cana. Let me have the joy of your presence today. Strengthen my faith. I ask you . . ." (Continue in your own words.)

Listen to Jesus.

Dear disciple, I have joy in you and your faith in me, too. I am always the same, always with you. What else is Jesus saying to you?

Ask God to show you how to live today.

Continue conversing with Jesus in words or silently in your heart. Thank him for his closeness to you and his constant protection. You might ask him, "What can I do today to help someone find you or to draw closer to you? Amen."

Monday, January 18, 2016

Know that God is present with you and ready to converse.

"Lord, the days follow one after another, the weather changes, but you are the same and always with me. Thank you."

Read the Gospel: Mark 2:18–22.

Now John's disciples and the Pharisees were fasting; and people came and said to Jesus, "Why do John's disciples and the disciples of the Pharisees fast, but your disciples do not fast?" Jesus said to them, "The wedding guests cannot fast while the bridegroom is with them, can they? As long as they have the bridegroom with them, they cannot fast. The days will come when the bridegroom is taken away from them, and then they will fast on that day.

"No one sews a piece of unshrunk cloth on an old cloak; otherwise, the patch pulls away from it, the new from the old, and a worse tear is made. And no one puts new wine into old wineskins; otherwise, the wine will burst the skins, and the wine is lost, and so are the skins; but one puts new wine into fresh wineskins."

Notice what you think and feel as you read the Gospel.

People questioned Jesus about why his disciples did not fast as John's did. He pointed out that it was a new era, for he, the Bridegroom, was present.

Pray as you are led for yourself and others.

"Lord, I wish to live in the newness of your life rather than in the oldness of my own. You must lead me and show me . . ." (Continue in your own words.)

Listen to Jesus.

You are right to seek me first. It is good for you and those you care for. What else is Jesus saying to you?

Ask God to show you how to live today.

"I will try to stay close to you throughout the day, Lord. Help me do so. Thank you. Amen."

Tuesday, January 19, 2016

Know that God is present with you and ready to converse.

"I come into your presence with feelings, fears, distractions, wants, and needs. Let me begin by thanking you for being here, Lord."

Read the Gospel: Mark 2:23–28.

One Sabbath Jesus was going through the cornfields; and as they made their way his disciples began to pluck heads of grain. The Pharisees said to him, "Look, why are they doing what is not lawful on the Sabbath?" And he said to them, "Have you never read what David did when he and his companions were hungry and in need of food? He entered the house of God, when Abiathar was high priest, and ate the bread of the Presence, which it is not lawful for any but the priests to eat, and he gave some to his companions." Then he said to them, "The Sabbath was made for humankind, and not humankind for the Sabbath; so the Son of Man is lord even of the Sabbath."

Notice what you think and feel as you read the Gospel.

Here we see Jesus as the "Son of Man," revealing the full significance of that which was foreshadowed in the Old Testament. God has come among us. The rules have changed. There is new freedom and fresh grace.

Pray as you are led for yourself and others.

"Jesus, how do I enjoy the new freedom you brought us? What needless restrictions do I observe? What freedoms do I abuse?" (Continue in your own words.)

Listen to Jesus.

Your only need is to walk close to me, dear child. In me find love for God and for others. In me find truth. What else is Jesus saying to you?

Ask God to show you how to live today.

"Lord, lead me to do something today that is pleasing to you, perhaps something I have never done or even thought of doing. Glory to you, Lord. Amen."

Wednesday, January 20, 2016

Know that God is present with you and ready to converse.

"When I was little, I learned that God is everywhere. Now that I am grown, I celebrate that mystery."

Read the Gospel: Mark 3:1–6.

Again Jesus entered the synagogue, and a man was there who had a withered hand. They watched him to see whether he would cure him on the Sabbath, so that they might accuse him. And he said to the man who had the withered hand, "Come forward." Then he said to them, "Is it lawful to do good or to do harm on the Sabbath, to save life or to kill?" But they were silent. He looked around at them with anger; he was grieved at their hardness of heart and said to the man, "Stretch out your hand." He stretched it out, and his hand was restored. The Pharisees went out and immediately conspired with the Herodians against him, how to destroy him.

Notice what you think and feel as you read the Gospel.

Hardness of heart makes Jesus angry. The Pharisees resent Jesus' healing of the man with the withered hand on the Sabbath. Then they immediately meet with the Herodians to discuss how to destroy Jesus.

Pray as you are led for yourself and others.

"Merciful Lord, forgive my hardness of heart. It is easy for me to put others' needs out of my mind or to make excuses. I open myself to you, asking for a clean heart, a heart of flesh, a heart of love like your own . . ." (Continue in your own words.)

Listen to Jesus.

Dear one, I understand and grant your prayer. I do not ask you to do much, but I would like you to do something today that expresses the love I give you. What else is Jesus saying to you?

Ask God to show you how to live today.

"Let me stay with you and listen as you guide me, Lord. Amen."

Thursday, January 21, 2016

Know that God is present with you and ready to converse.

"God is present in the still, small voice within me."

Read the Gospel: Mark 3:7–12.

Jesus departed with his disciples to the sea, and a great multitude from Galilee followed him; hearing all that he was doing, they came to him in great numbers from Judea, Jerusalem, Idumea, beyond the Jordan, and the region around Tyre and Sidon. He told his disciples to have a boat ready for him because of the crowd, so that they would not crush him; for he had cured many, so that all who had diseases pressed upon him to touch him. Whenever the unclean spirits saw him, they fell down before him and shouted, "You are the Son of God!" But he sternly ordered them not to make him known.

Notice what you think and feel as you read the Gospel.

Jesus, doing good to all, is aware that the crowd might crush him if he doesn't take precautions. Yet he continues to heal and cast out demons. Ironically, the demons know who he is but some of the people do not.

Pray as you are led for yourself and others.

"God, you already know what I need before I ask. May I also ask for the needs of others?" (Continue in your own words.)

Listen to Jesus.

Why do you come to me, friend? Do you seek to escape death and destruction? To receive blessing and favor? Or do you seek me for myself alone? What else is Jesus saying to you?

Ask God to show you how to live today.

Saint Ignatius urged people to seek God in all things. "Show me yourself, Lord, where I normally do not see you. Amen."

Friday, January 22, 2016

Know that God is present with you and ready to converse.

"The Lord knew me before the foundation of the world, before my bones were knit in the womb of my mother. He is with me now."

Read the Gospel: Mark 3:13–19.

Jesus went up the mountain and called to him those whom he wanted, and they came to him. And he appointed twelve, whom he also named apostles, to be with him, and to be sent out to proclaim the message, and to have authority to cast out demons. So he appointed the Twelve: Simon (to whom he gave the name Peter); James son of Zebedee and John the brother of James (to whom he gave the name Boanerges, that is, Sons of Thunder); and Andrew, and Philip, and Bartholomew, and Matthew, and Thomas, and James son of Alphaeus, and Thaddaeus, and Simon the Cananaean, and Judas Iscariot, who betrayed him.

Then he went home.

Notice what you think and feel as you read the Gospel.

Jesus gives authority to the Twelve to preach and to cast out demons. He liked to give his chosen ones nicknames, like Peter (Rock) and Sons of Thunder.

Pray as you are led for yourself and others.

"Jesus, you have unique affection for each one you call to be with you. I believe you have unique affection even for me. Do you have a nickname for me?" (Continue in your own words.)

Listen to Jesus.

I do love you for yourself, dear one, and someday will give you a new name as I promise in Revelation 2:17. What else is Jesus saying to you?

Ask God to show you how to live today.

"How may I show your unique affection for someone today, something that lets a person know that he or she is loved for who he or she really is? Amen."

Saturday, January 23, 2016

Know that God is present with you and ready to converse.

"All-powerful, always-present Lord of the universe, I bow to you as I enter your presence."

Read the Gospel: Mark 3:20–21.

And the crowd came together again, so that Jesus and his disciples could not even eat. When his family heard it, they went out to restrain him, for people were saying, "He has gone out of his mind."

Notice what you think and feel as you read the Gospel.

Jesus was under tremendous pressure and criticism as he healed the people who crowded around him. Even some of his friends and relatives questioned his state of mind.

Pray as you are led for yourself and others.

"Thank you, Jesus, for always acting out of love for poor sinners like me, even when we judge you. I pray for those who dismiss you now, including . . ." (Continue in your own words.)

Listen to Jesus.

I came knowing I would be rejected by the people I came to save, but I did my Father's loving will and still do. It is a great happiness for me that you love me and allow me to love you. What else is Jesus saying to you?

Ask God to show you how to live today.

"You know all the secrets of love and service, Jesus, even when you are opposed. Is there a way I haven't seen to help someone else? Show me, Jesus. Amen."

Sunday, January 24, 2016
Third Sunday in Ordinary Time

Know that God is present with you and ready to converse.

Prepare yourself to hear the Word of God by emptying yourself of all the clutter and clatter. Open yourself to God's quiet voice, and begin with words such as these: "Abba, Father. Jesus invited me to speak to you in the most intimate way, as he did. Thank you for allowing me to be with you."

Read the Gospel: Luke 1:1–4; 4:14–21.

Since many have undertaken to set down an orderly account of the events that have been fulfilled among us, just as they were handed on to us by those who from the beginning were eyewitnesses and servants of the word, I too decided, after investigating everything carefully from the very first, to write an orderly account for you, most excellent Theophilus, so that you may know the truth concerning the things about which you have been instructed. . . .

Then Jesus, filled with the power of the Spirit, returned to Galilee, and a report about him spread through all the surrounding country. He began to teach in their synagogues and was praised by everyone.

When he came to Nazareth, where he had been brought up, he went to the synagogue on the Sabbath day, as was his custom. He stood up to read, and the scroll of the prophet Isaiah was given to him. He unrolled the scroll and found the place where it was written:

"The Spirit of the Lord is upon me,
because he has anointed me
to bring good news to the poor.
He has sent me to proclaim release to the captives
and recovery of sight to the blind,
to let the oppressed go free,
to proclaim the year of the Lord's favor."

And he rolled up the scroll, gave it back to the attendant, and sat down. The eyes of all in the synagogue were fixed on him. Then he began to say to them, "Today this scripture has been fulfilled in your hearing."

Notice what you think and feel as you read the Gospel.

After reading the great messianic passage from Isaiah in the synagogue, Jesus says, "Today this scripture has been fulfilled in your hearing." He is the truth, and he tells the truth always—regardless of how he might be received.

Pray as you are led for yourself and others.

"Jesus, let me walk in truth, as you did. How may I make what I say absolutely honest and real? Life is too short for deceptions, selfish secrets, defensiveness, denials . . ." (Continue in your own words.)

Listen to Jesus.

I encourage you to seek honesty and simplicity in your relationships with others. This is an important way to show respect, and it honors God. What else is Jesus saying to you?

Ask God to show you how to live today.

Allow Jesus to speak to you for as long as he wishes. Mark his words. When you are ready, ask him to remain with you. "Lord, I place myself in your hands. Show me how to walk in your truth today and tomorrow. Amen."

Monday, January 25, 2016
Conversion of Saint Paul

Know that God is present with you and ready to converse.

"Stir my heart, great Holy Spirit, so that I may converse with God."

Read the Gospel: Mark 16:15–18.

And Jesus said to them, "Go into all the world and proclaim the good news to the whole creation. The one who believes and is baptized will be saved; but the one who does not believe will be condemned. And these signs will accompany those who believe: by using my name they will cast out demons; they will speak in new tongues; they will pick up snakes in their hands, and if they drink any deadly thing, it will not hurt them; they will lay their hands on the sick, and they will recover."

Notice what you think and feel as you read the Gospel.

After his resurrection, Jesus sends those he called to follow him out into the world to preach the Gospel to every creature and to continue to do the good works he did.

Pray as you are led for yourself and others.

"Lord, I want to obey you, for you called me, too. Help me to speak of you to others, but even more than that, help me to live the Gospel . . ." (Continue in your own words.)

Listen to Jesus.

Beloved friend: yes, speak of me. Why would you hesitate to mention our friendship? Your words about me have power in the hearts of others. What else is Jesus saying to you?

Ask God to show you how to live today.

"Let me see the opportunities to speak of you and do your work to help others. Thank you. Amen."

Tuesday, January 26, 2016
Saints Timothy and Titus

Know that God is present with you and ready to converse.

"You were present with Saint Timothy and Saint Titus when they preached the Gospel. You are present with me now."

Read the Gospel: Mark 3:31–35.

Then Jesus' mother and his brothers came; and standing outside, they sent to him and called him. A crowd was sitting around him; and they said to him, "Your mother and your brothers and sisters are outside, asking for you." And he replied, "Who are my mother and my brothers?" And looking at those who sat around him, he said, "Here are my mother and my brothers! Whoever does the will of God is my brother and sister and mother."

Notice what you think and feel as you read the Gospel.

Jesus makes the point that spiritual relationships are stronger than family ties. We become his brother or sister by doing the will of God.

Pray as you are led for yourself and others.

"Jesus, I pray for my own family. May we all be members of the Holy Family . . ." (Continue in your own words.)

Listen to Jesus.

You are my child, dear one, and I hear your prayers for those you love. Continue to pray for others, for faith is rewarded in perseverance. What else is Jesus saying to you?

Ask God to show you how to live today.

"Show me how to do your will, Lord, in great ways and small. Amen."

Wednesday, January 27, 2016

Know that God is present with you and ready to converse.

"Like the psalmist, I enter your presence with singing. I praise you for your goodness and glory."

Read the Gospel: Mark 4:1–20.

Again Jesus began to teach beside the sea. Such a very large crowd gathered around him that he got into a boat on the sea and sat there, while the whole crowd was beside the sea on the land. He began to teach them many things in parables, and in his teaching he said to them: "Listen! A sower went out to sow. And as he sowed, some seed fell on the path, and the birds came and ate it up. Other seed fell on rocky ground, where it did not have much soil, and it sprang up quickly, since it had no depth of soil. And when the sun rose, it was scorched; and since it had no root, it withered away. Other seed fell among thorns, and the thorns grew up and choked it, and it yielded no grain. Other seed fell into good soil and brought forth grain, growing up and increasing and yielding thirty and sixty and a hundredfold." And he said, "Let anyone with ears to hear listen!"

When he was alone, those who were around him along with the twelve asked him about the parables. And he said to them, "To you has been given the secret of the kingdom of God, but for those outside, everything comes in parables; in order that

'they may indeed look, but not perceive,
  and may indeed listen, but not understand;
so that they may not turn again and be forgiven.'"

And he said to them, "Do you not understand this parable? Then how will you understand all the parables? The sower sows the word. These are the ones on the path where the word is sown: when they hear, Satan immediately comes and takes away the word that is sown in them. And these are the ones sown on rocky ground: when they hear the word, they immediately receive it with joy. But they have no root, and endure only for a while; then, when trouble or persecution arises on account of the word, immediately they fall away. And others are those sown among the thorns: these are the ones who hear the word, but the cares of the world, and the lure of wealth, and the desire for other things come in and choke the word, and it yields nothing. And these are the ones sown on the good soil: they hear the word and accept it and bear fruit, thirty and sixty and a hundredfold."

Notice what you think and feel as you read the Gospel.

The Word of God is good seed, but the ground it falls upon determines how it will bear fruit. I seek to be one who hears and understands, that the seed will take deep root in me and bear much fruit to the glory of God.

Pray as you are led for yourself and others.

"Jesus, I know I need to receive your Word with seriousness, for I have seen how easy it is for people to wander away from you, to lose heart when difficulties come, or to be lured away by pursuit of wealth . . ." (Continue in your own words.)

Listen to Jesus.

Dear one, you are hearing my Word now, and I have put it into your heart to understand it. You have received me within you. In our love for one another, we will grow. What else is Jesus saying to you?

Ask God to show you how to live today.

"Teacher, what can I do for you today? Amen."

Thursday, January 28, 2016

Know that God is present with you and ready to converse.

"If I ascend to the heights of heaven, you are there. If I descend to the depths of hell, you are there. You are here with me now, Lord. I give you glory."

Read the Gospel: Mark 4:21–25.

Jesus said to them, "Is a lamp brought in to be put under the bushel basket, or under the bed, and not on the lampstand? For there is nothing hidden, except to be disclosed; nor is anything secret, except to come to light. Let anyone with ears to hear listen!" And he said to them, "Pay attention to what you hear; the measure you give will be the measure you get, and still more will be given you. For to those who have, more will be given; and from those who have nothing, even what they have will be taken away."

Notice what you think and feel as you read the Gospel.

Jesus outlines some spiritual realities. Nothing will remain hidden. One receives in the proportion that one gives. The one that has will receive more. What else do you notice?

Pray as you are led for yourself and others.

"Lord, open my understanding to receive these sayings. One thing is clear to me: I want to hear you and give much . . ." (Continue in your own words.)

Listen to Jesus.

And I want you to receive much, dear one. The treasures of the kingdom of God are faith, hope, and love. You cannot give them away without receiving much more. What else is Jesus saying to you?

Ask God to show you how to live today.

"Let me begin by giving you myself. Then show me how to give myself and you to others many times today. Amen."

Friday, January 29, 2016

Know that God is present with you and ready to converse.

"Blessed Savior, you are the Lamb of God who takes away the sins of the world."

Read the Gospel: Mark 4:26–34.

Jesus also said, "The kingdom of God is as if someone would scatter seed on the ground, and would sleep and rise night and day, and the seed would sprout and grow, he does not know how. The earth produces of itself, first the stalk, then the head, then the full grain in the head. But when the grain is ripe, at once he goes in with his sickle, because the harvest has come."

He also said, "With what can we compare the kingdom of God, or what parable will we use for it? It is like a mustard seed, which, when sown upon the ground, is the smallest of all the seeds on earth; yet when it is sown it grows up and becomes the greatest of all shrubs, and puts forth large branches, so that the birds of the air can make nests in its shade."

With many such parables he spoke the word to them, as they were able to hear it; he did not speak to them except in parables, but he explained everything in private to his disciples.

Notice what you think and feel as you read the Gospel.

How the kingdom of God grows! It grows quickly from a very small beginning. Clearly the growth of the kingdom is the work of the Lord.

Pray as you are led for yourself and others.

"Master, the growth of the kingdom of God in me is your work. Let me cooperate with you. Let it grow to maturity . . ." (Continue in your own words.)

Listen to Jesus.

The kingdom is within you, for that's where I dwell. Together we will continue to grow until you achieve the kingdom of heaven, our everlasting home. What else is Jesus saying to you?

Ask God to show you how to live today.

"How may I scatter the tiny seeds of your kingdom today, Lord? Amen."

Saturday, January 30, 2016

Know that God is present with you and ready to converse.

"Sometimes I feel afraid in the storms of my life, Lord, but I am safe in you. You are present even when I fear you are not."

Read the Gospel: Mark 4:35–41.

On that day, when evening had come, Jesus said to them, "Let us go across to the other side." And leaving the crowd behind, they took him with them in the boat, just as he was. Other boats were with him. A great windstorm arose, and the waves beat into the boat, so that the boat was already being swamped. But he was in the stern, asleep on the cushion; and they woke him up and said to him, "Teacher, do you not care that we are perishing?" He woke up and rebuked the wind, and said to the sea, "Peace! Be still!" Then the wind ceased, and there was a dead calm. He said to them, "Why are you afraid? Have you still no faith?" And they were filled with great awe and said to one another, "Who then is this, that even the wind and the sea obey him?"

Notice what you think and feel as you read the Gospel.

Jesus questions his disciples for their fear of the stormy sea while he was sleeping. With such ease he calms the storm.

Pray as you are led for yourself and others.

"I am not the only one afraid of the storms of life. I pray for myself and for all of us who have too little faith. Give us faith through the storms, Jesus, until you quiet them . . ." (Continue in your own words.)

Listen to Jesus.

I love you, dear one. I understand your fears. Storms will try your faith in this life. You may be afraid that I do not care or I cannot save you. I do care. I will save you, as I have saved you in the past. Things will not always work out as you want or expect, but I promise you I am with you and will care for you always. What else is Jesus saying to you?

Ask God to show you how to live today.

"Lord, I do a lot of thinking about myself. Turn my gaze outward to others; fill my heart with compassion for those experiencing storms of their own. Show me how to help. Thank you. Amen."

Sunday, January 31, 2016
Fourth Sunday in Ordinary Time

Know that God is present with you and ready to converse.

Jesus came to his own for love, but he was rejected by many. They did not recognize the Word of God among them or the gifts he brought from God.

When you are ready, invite God to speak to you with words such as these: "I stand upon the rock, Lord. I drink your living water. You, Word of the Father, are with me now."

Read the Gospel: Luke 4:21–30.

Then Jesus began to say to them, "Today this scripture has been fulfilled in your hearing." All spoke well of him and were amazed at the gracious words that came from his mouth. They said, "Is not this Joseph's son?" He said to them, "Doubtless you will quote to me this proverb, 'Doctor, cure yourself!' And you will say, 'Do here also in your hometown the things that we have heard you did at Capernaum.'" And he said, "Truly I tell you, no prophet is accepted in the prophet's hometown. But the truth is, there were many widows in Israel in the time of Elijah, when the heaven was shut up three years and six months, and there was a severe famine over all the land; yet Elijah was sent to none of them except to a widow at Zarephath in Sidon. There were also many lepers in Israel in the time of the prophet Elisha, and none of them was cleansed except Naaman the Syrian." When they heard this, all in the synagogue were filled with rage. They got up, drove him out of the town, and led him to the brow of the hill on which their town was built, so that they might hurl him off the cliff. But he passed through the midst of them and went on his way.

Notice what you think and feel as you read the Gospel.

Jesus, rejected as a prophet in his own country, thwarts the angry crowd intent on throwing him headlong down the hill. Mysteriously he passes through the midst of them and goes away.

Pray as you are led for yourself and others.

"Jesus, sometimes people don't like me either. You experienced rejection by your own people as I never have. You forgave them. You loved them so much you died for them, your enemies. Lord, fill me with that Spirit, that I may be like you . . ." (Continue in your own words.)

Listen to Jesus.

My child, my beloved disciple, you seek to follow me. I bless your desire. I give you my Spirit. You have power to be my follower in your own country. What else is Jesus saying to you?

Ask God to show you how to live today.

Consider how the Lord strengthens his disciples in moments of prayer like these. Yet we cannot but be aware of our weaknesses. We may take this occasion to meditate on our own weaknesses and the power we have in him. "How shall I live in my weakness, Lord? How may I act in the power you give me, Lord? Amen."

Monday, February 1, 2016

Know that God is present with you and ready to converse.

"Jesus, you are closer than a brother to me. You are good to speak with me now."

Read the Gospel: Mark 5:1–20.

Jesus and his disciples came to the other side of the sea, to the country of the Gerasenes. And when Jesus had stepped out of the boat, immediately a man out of the tombs with an unclean spirit met him. He lived among the tombs; and no one could restrain him anymore, even with a chain; for he had often been restrained with shackles and chains, but the chains he wrenched apart, and the shackles he broke in pieces; and no one had the strength to subdue him. Night and day among the tombs and on the mountains he was always howling and bruising himself with stones. When he saw Jesus from a distance, he ran and bowed down before him; and he shouted at the top of his voice, "What have you to do with me, Jesus, Son of the Most High God? I adjure you by God, do not torment me." For he had said to him, "Come out of the man, you unclean spirit!" Then Jesus asked him, "What is your name?" He replied, "My name is Legion; for we are many." He begged him earnestly not to send them out of the country. Now there on the hillside a great herd of swine was feeding; and the unclean spirits begged him, "Send us into the swine; let us enter them." So he gave them permission. And the unclean spirits came out and entered the swine; and the herd, numbering about two thousand, rushed down the steep bank into the sea, and were drowned in the sea.

The swineherds ran off and told it in the city and in the country. Then people came to see what it was that had happened. They came to Jesus and saw the demoniac sitting there, clothed and in his right mind, the very man who had had the legion; and they were afraid. Those who had seen what had happened to the demoniac and to the swine reported it. Then they began to beg Jesus to leave their neighborhood. As he was getting into the boat, the man who had been possessed by demons begged him that he might be with him. But Jesus refused, and said to him, "Go home to your friends, and tell them how much the Lord has done for you, and what mercy he has shown you." And he went away and began to proclaim in the Decapolis how much Jesus had done for him; and everyone was amazed.

Notice what you think and feel as you read the Gospel.

What a scene with the demoniac and the swine! Jesus encountered spiritual enemies and subdued them, restoring peace and sanity to the man who had been so oppressed. All he wanted was for the man to tell his friends how much the Lord had done for him.

Pray as you are led for yourself and others.

"Lord, you have done so much for me. Keep me free of spiritual enemies. I want to go with you, too. What do you want me to do?" (Continue in your own words.)

Listen to Jesus.

I want you to sit with me, knowing the power of my love. When you rise to do the things you must do, know that I am with you. Let people know how much the Lord has done for you. What else is Jesus saying to you?

Ask God to show you how to live today.

"Help me to honor you in my thoughts, words, and actions today, Jesus. Amen."

Tuesday, February 2, 2016
The Presentation of the Lord

Know that God is present with you and ready to converse.

"Holy Spirit, welcome. Enlighten me by the living Word of God."

Read the Gospel: Luke 2:22–40.

When the time came for their purification according to the law of Moses, Mary and Joseph brought Jesus up to Jerusalem to present him to the Lord (as it is written in the law of the Lord, "Every firstborn male shall be designated as holy to the Lord"), and they offered a sacrifice according to what is stated in the law of the Lord, "a pair of turtledoves or two young pigeons."

Now there was a man in Jerusalem whose name was Simeon; this man was righteous and devout, looking forward to the consolation of Israel, and the Holy Spirit rested on him. It had been revealed to him by the Holy Spirit that he would not see death before he had seen the Lord's Messiah. Guided by the Spirit, Simeon came into the Temple; and when the parents brought in the child Jesus, to do for him what was customary under the law, Simeon took him in his arms and praised God, saying,

> "Master, now you are dismissing your servant in peace,
> according to your word;
> for my eyes have seen your salvation,
> which you have prepared in the presence of all peoples,
> a light for revelation to the Gentiles
> and for glory to your people Israel."

And the child's father and mother were amazed at what was being said about him. Then Simeon blessed them and said to his mother, Mary, "This child is destined for the falling and the rising of many in Israel, and to be a sign that will be opposed so that the inner thoughts of many will be revealed—and a sword will pierce your own soul too."

There was also a prophet, Anna the daughter of Phanuel, of the tribe of Asher. She was of a great age, having lived with her husband seven years after her marriage, then as a widow to the age of eighty-four. She never left the Temple but worshiped there with fasting and prayer night and day. At that moment she came, and began to praise God and to speak about the child to all who were looking for the redemption of Jerusalem.

When they had finished everything required by the law of the Lord, they returned to Galilee, to their own town of Nazareth. The child grew and became strong, filled with wisdom; and the favor of God was upon him.

Notice what you think and feel as you read the Gospel.

The elderly saints of the Temple in Jerusalem, Simeon and Anna, rejoice in the Holy Spirit as the infant Jesus is presented according to the Law of Moses.

Pray as you are led for yourself and others.

"Jesus, I rejoice with them. I rejoice that I, too, have seen you, tasted you, and loved you in your Word. I want more of you—not just for me, but for those I love and encounter every day . . ." (Continue in your own words.)

Listen to Jesus.

All things of God work by the Spirit of God, my beloved. As you give yourself to the Holy Spirit, you will have knowledge and power to do God's will. Do not be afraid to give yourself to God. What else is Jesus saying to you?

Ask God to show you how to live today.

"I do give myself, Lord. Let me do so without reservation. Amen."

Wednesday, February 3, 2016

Know that God is present with you and ready to converse.

"Infinite, eternal God of the universe, I bow before you, for I am your creation."

Read the Gospel: Mark 6:1–6.

Jesus left that place and came to his hometown, and his disciples followed him. On the Sabbath he began to teach in the synagogue, and many who heard him were astounded. They said, "Where did this man get all this? What is this wisdom that has been given to him? What deeds of power are being done by his hands! Is not this the carpenter, the son of Mary and brother of James and Joses and Judas and Simon, and are not his sisters here with us?" And they took offense at him. Then Jesus said to them, "Prophets are not without honor, except in their hometown, and among their own kin, and in their own house." And he could do no deed of power there, except that he laid his hands on a few sick people and cured them. And he was amazed at their unbelief.

Then he went about among the villages teaching.

Notice what you think and feel as you read the Gospel.

Jesus marvels at the unbelief of the people who have known him and his family for a long time. They are offended by his wisdom and power to heal.

Pray as you are led for yourself and others.

"Lord, do not let my familiarity with you become commonplace. Keep our friendship fresh and ever growing. I pray for all those whose faith in you has stagnated or lapsed, especially for . . ." (Continue in your own words.)

Listen to Jesus.

I rejoice in your coming to me today, my child. I am your life. As long as you remain in me, our friendship will stay fresh, and others will see it and glorify God. What else is Jesus saying to you?

Ask God to show you how to live today.

"During this day, Lord, make me aware of some particular good thing I can do for someone who needs something, large or small. Then give me the grace to do it well. Amen."

Thursday, February 4, 2016

Know that God is present with you and ready to converse.

"I am here with you now, Jesus. Help me receive your Word into my heart."

Read the Gospel: Mark 6:7–13.

Jesus called the Twelve and began to send them out two by two, and gave them authority over the unclean spirits. He ordered them to take nothing for their journey except a staff; no bread, no bag, no money in their belts; but to wear sandals and not to put on two tunics. He said to them, "Wherever you enter a house, stay there until you leave the place. If any place will not welcome you and they refuse to hear you, as you leave, shake off the dust that is on your feet as a testimony against them." So they went out and proclaimed that all should repent. They cast out many demons, and anointed with oil many who were sick and cured them.

Notice what you think and feel as you read the Gospel.

Jesus gives the Twelve power to do the great works that he does and sends them out. He prepares them for rejection. Shake it off and keep going, he says.

Pray as you are led for yourself and others.

"Jesus, I have felt rejection. I know what it is to be discouraged, in worldly things and spiritual things. Strengthen my hope and clarify my purpose so that I can do what you want me to do, for myself and for others . . ." (Continue in your own words.)

Listen to Jesus.

Hope lies between faith and love, dear one, and all of them flow from God. I am your hope. Hope in the Lord and all your hopes will be realized. What else is Jesus saying to you?

Ask God to show you how to live today.

"Jesus, I would like to encourage someone who needs it today. I would like to affirm someone who feels rejected. Help me to see opportunities and act on them in your Spirit. Amen."

Friday, February 5, 2016

Know that God is present with you and ready to converse.

"Eternal Word, Wisdom, I open my heart to you now."

Read the Gospel: Mark 6:14–29.

King Herod heard that Jesus had sent out the Twelve, for Jesus' name had become known. Some were saying, "John the baptizer has been raised from the dead; and for this reason these powers are at work in him." But others said, "It is Elijah." And others said, "It is a prophet, like one of the prophets of old." But when Herod heard of it, he said, "John, whom I beheaded, has been raised."

For Herod himself had sent men who arrested John, bound him, and put him in prison on account of Herodias, his brother Philip's wife, because Herod had married her. For John had been telling Herod, "It is not lawful for you to have your brother's wife." And Herodias had a grudge against him, and wanted to kill him. But she could not, for

Herod feared John, knowing that he was a righteous and holy man, and he protected him. When he heard him, he was greatly perplexed; and yet he liked to listen to him. But an opportunity came when Herod on his birthday gave a banquet for his courtiers and officers and for the leaders of Galilee. When his daughter Herodias came in and danced, she pleased Herod and his guests; and the king said to the girl, "Ask me for whatever you wish, and I will give it." And he solemnly swore to her, "Whatever you ask me, I will give you, even half of my kingdom." She went out and said to her mother, "What should I ask for?" She replied, "The head of John the baptizer." Immediately she rushed back to the king and requested, "I want you to give me at once the head of John the Baptist on a platter." The king was deeply grieved; yet out of regard for his oaths and for the guests, he did not want to refuse her. Immediately the king sent a soldier of the guard with orders to bring John's head. He went and beheaded him in the prison, brought his head on a platter, and gave it to the girl. Then the girl gave it to her mother. When his disciples heard about it, they came and took his body, and laid it in a tomb.

Notice what you think and feel as you read the Gospel.

King Herod had beheaded John the Baptist for crazy and absurd reasons, and his paranoia about John returns when he hears about Jesus. He fears Jesus is John raised from the dead. What else do you see in this passage?

Pray as you are led for yourself and others.

"Jesus, there is much absurdity, ignorance, and mental illness operating in human affairs. Good people are often victims of deluded people with power. Lord, protect the innocent and thwart the violence of people who are deranged. Grant us peace!" (Continue in your own words.)

Listen to Jesus.

Pray for peace, and peace shall come. But do not be disheartened, dear one, by atrocious acts. I am the defender of the poor, the innocent, and the oppressed, and justice will prevail. Everyone will see the justice of God. What else is Jesus saying to you?

Ask God to show you how to live today.

"How may I be a peacemaker today, Jesus? Amen."

Saturday, February 6, 2016

Know that God is present with you and ready to converse.

"You give me life and love day by day, my Lord. I receive you as a great gift."

Read the Gospel: Mark 6:30–34.

The apostles gathered around Jesus, and told him all that they had done and taught. He said to them, "Come away to a deserted place all by yourselves and rest a while." For many were coming and going, and they had no leisure even to eat. And they went away in the boat to a deserted place by themselves. Now many saw them going and recognized them, and they hurried there on foot from all the towns and arrived ahead of them. As he went ashore, he saw a great crowd; and he had compassion for them, because they were like sheep without a shepherd; and he began to teach them many things.

Notice what you think and feel as you read the Gospel.

Weary and overworked, Jesus and the apostles cannot escape the crowds. But Jesus has compassion because they are like sheep without a shepherd.

Pray as you are led for yourself and others.

"How lovable you are, Jesus. You always put people first. You teach us many things. Let your teaching go deep into my heart, that I may honor you with my actions and my words . . ." (Continue in your own words.)

Listen to Jesus.

I love you, servant and friend. When you are weary and overworked, I will give you grace to love and serve others. Let my peace and strength flow through you, for in your weakness, I am strong. What else is Jesus saying to you?

Ask God to show you how to live today.

"I give myself to you today, Lord. Take whatever I am and use me for the good of others. Amen."

Sunday, February 7, 2016
Fifth Sunday in Ordinary Time

Know that God is present with you and ready to converse.

Mysterious God is everywhere, and we may seek God in all things. We need the eyes and ears of the Holy Spirit to see and hear God, even in God's Word.

Place yourself in God's presence with words such as these: "Almighty God, I bow to you now. Let me receive your Word."

Read the Gospel: Luke 5:1–11.

Once while Jesus was standing beside the lake of Gennesaret, and the crowd was pressing in on him to hear the word of God, he saw two boats there at the shore of the lake; the fishermen had gone out of them and were washing their nets. He got into one of the boats, the one belonging to Simon, and asked him to put out a little way from the shore. Then he sat down and taught the crowds from the boat. When he had finished speaking, he said to Simon, "Put out into the deep water and let down your nets for a catch." Simon answered, "Master, we have worked all night long but have caught nothing. Yet if you say so, I will let down the nets." When they had done this, they caught so many fish that their nets were beginning to break. So they signaled their partners in the other boat to come and help them. And they came and filled both boats, so that they began to sink. But when Simon Peter saw it, he fell down at Jesus' knees, saying, "Go away from me, Lord, for I am a sinful man!" For he and all who were with him were amazed at the catch of fish that they had taken; and so also were James and John, sons of Zebedee, who were partners with Simon. Then Jesus said to Simon, "Do not be afraid; from now on you will be catching people." When they had brought their boats to shore, they left everything and followed him.

Notice what you think and feel as you read the Gospel.

Simon's immediate reaction to the miracle of catching fish is to say, "Go away from me, Lord, for I am a sinful man!" There are many ways to react to Jesus' miracles, but this is one of the most endearing, most human. No wonder Jesus gave Simon (Peter) the keys to the kingdom.

Pray as you are led for yourself and others.

"Jesus, I don't want you to depart from me, but I am a sinner, too. Give me the spirit of Peter to speak to you with perfect honesty. Reassure me and enable me to do what you have destined me to do . . ." (Continue in your own words.)

Listen to Jesus.
Do not be afraid, dear one, for I am in you and you are in me, and the truth marches on. My disciples are filling the boats of heaven with people. It's a process. You are part of it. What else is Jesus saying to you?

Ask God to show you how to live today.
Consider what you wish to take away from this time of prayer and intimacy. How will the Word of God change you and the things you do today? You may conclude: "Lord, dear God, I'm not much. I'm less than Peter. If I am going to be part of this great catching of humankind, I need you to show me what to do and how to do it. I offer myself for your work. I am willing, Lord. Amen."

Monday, February 8, 2016

Know that God is present with you and ready to converse.
"You who struck the stars in the sky and laid the stony depths of the seas, I worship you. I am so grateful that you are here for me now."

Read the Gospel: Mark 6:53–56.
When Jesus and his disciples had crossed over, they came to land at Gennesaret and moored the boat. When they got out of the boat, people at once recognized Jesus, and rushed about that whole region and began to bring the sick on mats to wherever they heard he was. And wherever he went, into villages or cities or farms, they laid the sick in the marketplaces, and begged him that they might touch even the fringe of his cloak; and all who touched it were healed.

Notice what you think and feel as you read the Gospel.
I long just to touch the fringe of his garment. As many as touched it were made well.

Pray as you are led for yourself and others.
"Jesus, I am not worthy to converse with you, but I need you. I reach out for the fringe of your garment. Make me well . . ." (Continue in your own words.)

Listen to Jesus.

I make you worthy, child. You are an adopted child of my Father. You are washed in my blood. I gave myself body and soul as a gift to you, and you are made whole, preparing for eternity in the kingdom of heaven. What else is Jesus saying to you?

Ask God to show you how to live today.

"Jesus, thank you. Let it not be only about me. Inspire me to act in your own loving ways today. Let me look back on the day and see how you worked through me. Amen."

Tuesday, February 9, 2016

Know that God is present with you and ready to converse.

"Word of God, I am ready to hear you now."

Read the Gospel: Mark 7:1–13.

Now when the Pharisees and some of the scribes who had come from Jerusalem gathered around Jesus, they noticed that some of his disciples were eating with defiled hands, that is, without washing them. (For the Pharisees, and all the Jews, do not eat unless they thoroughly wash their hands, thus observing the tradition of the elders; and they do not eat anything from the market unless they wash it; and there are also many other traditions that they observe, the washing of cups, pots, and bronze kettles.) So the Pharisees and the scribes asked him, "Why do your disciples not live according to the tradition of the elders, but eat with defiled hands?" He said to them, "Isaiah prophesied rightly about you hypocrites, as it is written,

> 'This people honors me with their lips,
> but their hearts are far from me;
> in vain do they worship me,
> teaching human precepts as doctrines.'

You abandon the commandment of God and hold to human tradition."

Then he said to them, "You have a fine way of rejecting the commandment of God in order to keep your tradition! For Moses said, 'Honor your father and your mother'; and, 'Whoever speaks evil of father or mother must surely die.' But you say that if anyone tells father or mother, 'Whatever support you might have had from me is Corban' (that is, an offering to God)—then you no longer permit doing anything for a father or mother, thus making void the word of God through your tradition that you have handed on. And you do many things like this."

Notice what you think and feel as you read the Gospel.

Human beings, especially those of us who are religious, are ingenious at thwarting the Spirit of God. We have, Jesus says, a "fine way of rejecting the commandment of God."

Pray as you are led for yourself and others.

"Jesus, free me from every human rule that keeps me from obeying God, from loving God with all my heart, mind, and might, for that is the first commandment. Help me avoid rationalizations that keep me from loving and doing good to my neighbor . . ." (Continue in your own words.)

Listen to Jesus.

I am present to lead you into all truth. Walk in the way of love, and you will not err. What else is Jesus saying to you?

Ask God to show you how to live today.

"Lord, let me not be a victim of the unloving devices of those who seek to manipulate your truth. Show me your way of love. Amen."

The Lenten Season

INTRODUCTION

In the Gospel, Jesus says his disciples will fast when he, the Bridegroom, is taken from them. We know that Jesus is always with us, but during the season of Lent we honor him in a special way by entering a forty-day period of prayer, fasting, and almsgiving in preparation for the celebration of the resurrection of the Lord, Easter Sunday. The number of days of Lent corresponds to the forty days Jesus prayed and fasted in the desert before beginning his earthly ministry. Lent is a time to allow God to help us become holy, to help us look to the needs of others and minister to those needs, and, most of all, to grow in faith, hope, and love, for those virtues are of God, motivating and empowering us to live the Gospel.

The season of Lent begins on Ash Wednesday, dividing the cycle of Ordinary Time in the Church year. Sundays in Lent are not counted as fast days. Fast days continue through Holy Saturday, the day before Easter. Lent officially ends on Holy Thursday, the beginning of the Easter Triduum.

Wednesday, February 10, 2016
Ash Wednesday

Know that God is present with you and ready to converse.

As we begin this holy season of Lent, we offer ourselves to God, aware that we are sinners and dust that will return to the earth after our brief journey here. But the Lord will quicken us by the Spirit, and we shall live in him. How can we begin that new life now? "Father, you see me in secret. You are with me now. Let your Word speak life to me."

Read the Gospel: Matthew 6:1–6, 16–18.

Jesus warned, "Beware of practicing your piety before others in order to be seen by them; for then you have no reward from your Father in heaven.

"So whenever you give alms, do not sound a trumpet before you, as the hypocrites do in the synagogues and in the streets, so that they may be praised by others. Truly I tell you, they have received their reward. But when you give alms, do not let your left hand know what your right hand is doing, so that your alms may be done in secret; and your Father who sees in secret will reward you.

"And whenever you pray, do not be like the hypocrites; for they love to stand and pray in the synagogues and at the street corners, so that they may be seen by others. Truly I tell you, they have received their reward. But whenever you pray, go into your room and shut the door and pray to your Father who is in secret; and your Father who sees in secret will reward you. . . .

"And whenever you fast, do not look dismal, like the hypocrites, for they disfigure their faces so as to show others that they are fasting. Truly I tell you, they have received their reward. But when you fast, put oil on your head and wash your face, so that your fasting may be seen not by others but by your Father who is in secret; and your Father who sees in secret will reward you."

Notice what you think and feel as you read the Gospel.

God is not impressed by grand gestures of piety done to impress others. When we do good, we should not gloat in our righteousness. What does this Gospel say about almsgiving, praying, and fasting?

Pray as you are led for yourself and others.

"Father, you want me to have a secret friendship with you. Help me to love and serve you for your own sake, not for appearance's sake . . ." (Continue in your own words.)

Listen to Jesus.

You are beginning the season of Lent, preparing yourself for the Church's commemoration of my passion, crucifixion, and resurrection. How may I help you make this Lent especially meaningful? What else is Jesus saying to you?

Ask God to show you how to live today.

Linger in the presence of Jesus as he offers himself to you again by his Word and his Spirit. Respond to his love for you. "Jesus, you are generous with me. Show me how to be generous with others today. I offer myself and all I am and have to you. Amen."

Thursday, February 11, 2016
Our Lady of Lourdes

Know that God is present with you and ready to converse.

"I am following you, Jesus, in your passion and in your triumphant resurrection."

Read the Gospel: Luke 9:22–25.

Jesus said, "The Son of Man must undergo great suffering, and be rejected by the elders, chief priests, and scribes, and be killed, and on the third day be raised."

Then he said to them all, "If any want to become my followers, let them deny themselves and take up their cross daily and follow me. For those who want to save their life will lose it, and those who lose their life for my sake will save it. What does it profit them if they gain the whole world, but lose or forfeit themselves?"

Notice what you think and feel as you read the Gospel.

Jesus knew the death he would die and sought to prepare his disciples to carry their own crosses. Those who seek to preserve their lives will lose them. What else do you notice in this Gospel?

Pray as you are led for yourself and others.

"Jesus, I don't want to gain the whole world at the expense of myself. I don't want to gain the whole world and lose you . . ." (Continue in your own words.)

Listen to Jesus.

Take up your cross today and follow me, for a servant is not greater than the master. My cross is my glory. Your cross shall be yours. What else is Jesus saying to you?

Ask God to show you how to live today.

"Jesus, teach me to embrace my crosses, knowing that they are meaningful because of you. I offer my sufferings for the good of those who suffer today. Amen."

Friday, February 12, 2016

Know that God is present with you and ready to converse.

"You are always with me, Jesus, but you are not present to me as you were to your disciples. I seek greater closeness with you."

Read the Gospel: Matthew 9:14–15.

Then the disciples of John came to Jesus, saying, "Why do we and the Pharisees fast often, but your disciples do not fast?" And Jesus said to them, "The wedding guests cannot mourn as long as the bridegroom is with them, can they? The days will come when the bridegroom is taken away from them, and then they will fast."

Notice what you think and feel as you read the Gospel.

When Jesus, the bridegroom, is taken from them, then will his disciples fast.

Pray as you are led for yourself and others.

"Jesus, I wish to fast and pray during this season. I offer my sacrifices for the good of others. How marvelous that fasting and praying accomplish good in this world . . ." (Continue in your own words.)

Listen to Jesus.

When you fast and pray, you imitate me. When you fast and pray, you draw out of yourself and enter into me. I can teach you what you need to know. What else is Jesus saying to you?

Ask God to show you how to live today.
"Help me, Lord. Show me how to do this well. Amen."

Saturday, February 13, 2016

Know that God is present with you and ready to converse.
"You spend time with sinners, Lord. I am one."

Read the Gospel: Luke 5:27–32.
After this Jesus went out and saw a tax collector named Levi, sitting at the tax booth; and he said to him, "Follow me." And he got up, left everything, and followed him.

Then Levi gave a great banquet for him in his house; and there was a large crowd of tax collectors and others sitting at the table with them. The Pharisees and their scribes were complaining to his disciples, saying, "Why do you eat and drink with tax collectors and sinners?" Jesus answered, "Those who are well have no need of a physician, but those who are sick; I have come to call not the righteous but sinners to repentance."

Notice what you think and feel as you read the Gospel.
Under criticism for fraternizing with tax collectors and sinners, Jesus says he has come to call sinners to repentance.

Pray as you are led for yourself and others.
"Lord, you call me. I come to you repenting . . ." (Continue in your own words.)

Listen to Jesus.
Your sins are covered by my mercy, my beloved. I forgive you and give you power to make amends and avoid those offenses in the future. What else is Jesus saying to you?

Ask God to show you how to live today.
"Jesus, how do I make amends? Amen."

Sunday, February 14, 2016
First Sunday of Lent

Know that God is present with you and ready to converse.

During Lent, we are called to repentance by the words of Jesus. More than that, we are called to holiness, without which no one will see God. We must find it in the Word and be transformed by the Spirit of holiness.

You may begin by opening yourself to the Lord with words such as these: "Jesus, you overcame temptation by the Word of God. Be with me in my temptations and help me overcome them."

Read the Gospel: Luke 4:1–13.

Jesus, full of the Holy Spirit, returned from the Jordan and was led by the Spirit in the wilderness, where for forty days he was tempted by the devil. He ate nothing at all during those days, and when they were over, he was famished. The devil said to him, "If you are the Son of God, command this stone to become a loaf of bread." Jesus answered him, "It is written, 'One does not live by bread alone.'"

Then the devil led him up and showed him in an instant all the kingdoms of the world. And the devil said to him, "To you I will give their glory and all this authority; for it has been given over to me, and I give it to anyone I please. If you, then, will worship me, it will all be yours." Jesus answered him, "It is written,

'Worship the Lord your God,
and serve only him.'"

Then the devil took him to Jerusalem, and placed him on the pinnacle of the Temple, saying to him, "If you are the Son of God, throw yourself down from here, for it is written,

'He will command his angels concerning you,
to protect you,'

and

'On their hands they will bear you up,
so that you will not dash your foot against a stone.'"

Jesus answered him, "It is said, 'Do not put the Lord your God to the test.'" When the devil had finished every test, he departed from him until an opportune time.

Notice what you think and feel as you read the Gospel.

The devil offers Jesus the glory of all the kingdoms of the world in a moment of time, saying they had been delivered to him to give to whomever he wished. What else do you notice in this Gospel?

Pray as you are led for yourself and others.

"Jesus, your kingdom is not of this world. You came to save souls, not to establish an earthly power. In infinite love, you value our souls. Give me that same mind . . ." (Continue in your own words.)

Listen to Jesus.

When you are tempted, cast your mind upon the things of God, all things good and true and beautiful. These are the things that will endure forever. What else is Jesus saying to you?

Ask God to show you how to live today.

"Reveal to me the ways that evil crawls into my life. Make me aware of my temptations and give me grace to resist them. Amen."

Monday, February 15, 2016

Know that God is present with you and ready to converse.

"You are present in the hungry, the thirsty, the stranger, the naked, and the imprisoned. You are also here with me. Teach me, Lord."

Read the Gospel: Matthew 25:31–46.

Jesus said, "When the Son of Man comes in his glory, and all the angels with him, then he will sit on the throne of his glory. All the nations will be gathered before him, and he will separate people one from another as a shepherd separates the sheep from the goats, and he will put the sheep at his right hand and the goats at the left. Then the king will say to those at his right hand, 'Come, you that are blessed by my Father, inherit the kingdom prepared for you from the foundation of the world; for I was hungry and you gave me food, I was thirsty and you gave me something to drink, I was a stranger and you welcomed me, I was naked and you gave me clothing, I was sick and you took care of me, I was in prison and you visited me.' Then the righteous will answer him, 'Lord, when was it that we saw you hungry and gave you food, or thirsty and gave you something to drink? And when was it that we saw you a stranger and welcomed you, or naked and gave you clothing? And when was it that we saw you sick or in prison and visited you?'

And the king will answer them, 'Truly I tell you, just as you did it to one of the least of these who are members of my family, you did it to me.' Then he will say to those at his left hand, 'You that are accursed, depart from me into the eternal fire prepared for the devil and his angels; for I was hungry and you gave me no food, I was thirsty and you gave me nothing to drink, I was a stranger and you did not welcome me, naked and you did not give me clothing, sick and in prison and you did not visit me.' Then they also will answer, 'Lord, when was it that we saw you hungry or thirsty or a stranger or naked or sick or in prison, and did not take care of you?' Then he will answer them, 'Truly I tell you, just as you did not do it to one of the least of these, you did not do it to me.' And these will go away into eternal punishment, but the righteous into eternal life."

Notice what you think and feel as you read the Gospel.

You are judging the nations, Jesus, and you are judging us all. You judge humankind on the basis of what we have done for those in need; for what we do for the least of these, we do to you.

Pray as you are led for yourself and others.

"You challenge me, Jesus, for I seem to be more occupied with ignoring the needy than with helping them. I sometimes forget the poor and hurting, or think that somehow they don't involve me. But they do, for you are there in the faces of the poor . . ." (Continue in your own words.)

Listen to Jesus.

I am truly present in the poor, the sick, the suffering, the homeless, and the imprisoned. It is not your place to judge them, for they are victims. For my sake, have compassion on them and do what you can to help them. What else is Jesus saying to you?

Ask God to show you how to live today.

"Jesus, your kingdom in the making is glorious, for you love us all, even me. Help me to act on what I know to your honor and glory. Amen."

Tuesday, February 16, 2016

Know that God is present with you and ready to converse.

"Father in heaven, you are here with me. I open myself to your Word, Jesus."

Read the Gospel: Matthew 6:7–15.

Jesus instructed, "When you are praying, do not heap up empty phrases as the Gentiles do; for they think that they will be heard because of their many words. Do not be like them, for your Father knows what you need before you ask him.

"Pray then in this way:

Our Father in heaven,
hallowed be your name.
Your kingdom come.
Your will be done,
  on earth as it is in heaven.
Give us this day our daily bread.
And forgive us our debts,
  as we also have forgiven our debtors.
And do not bring us to the time of trial,
  but rescue us from the evil one.

"For if you forgive others their trespasses, your heavenly Father will also forgive you; but if you do not forgive others, neither will your Father forgive your trespasses."

Notice what you think and feel as you read the Gospel.

How do we get through to God? He is not impressed by our piling up many words of prayers. Nor do we need to beg God for what we need. Instead, God and forgiveness are found when we forgive others.

Pray as you are led for yourself and others.

"Our Father, who art in heaven . . ." (Continue in your own words.)

Listen to Jesus.

Do you have unforgivingness in your life, in your heart, dear one? Can you forgive? Forgiveness can be difficult. But this is the way to God. What else is Jesus saying to you?

Ask God to show you how to live today.

"Lord, I don't want just to go through the motions of forgiving someone who has trespassed against me. I want to forgive that person completely from my heart. Then I can put that hurt behind me forever. Help me. Amen."

Wednesday, February 17, 2016

Know that God is present with you and ready to converse.

"Something greater than Solomon is here, Lord. You are here now. I will listen to your Word."

Read the Gospel: Luke 11:29–32.

When the crowds were increasing, Jesus began to say, "This generation is an evil generation; it asks for a sign, but no sign will be given to it except the sign of Jonah. For just as Jonah became a sign to the people of Nineveh, so the Son of Man will be to this generation. The queen of the south will rise at the judgment with the people of this generation and condemn them, because she came from the ends of the earth to listen to the wisdom of Solomon, and see, something greater than Solomon is here! The people of Nineveh will rise up at the judgment with this generation and condemn it, because they repented at the proclamation of Jonah, and see, something greater than Jonah is here!"

Notice what you think and feel as you read the Gospel.

Jesus knows the hearts of humans. He knows our self-interest. He knows our desire for signs and proofs that he is the Messiah. He cannot win over the skeptics no matter what he does.

Pray as you are led for yourself and others.

"Jesus, I do not want to be part of an evil generation, challenging you, doubting you. I want . . ." (Continue in your own words.)

Listen to Jesus.

I want what's best for you, my child and friend. People often hold on to habits of sin because they think they cannot live without them. I tell you truly that you will be happier without them. What else is Jesus saying to you?

Ask God to show you how to live today.

"Lord, I bow before you. Heal me. Lift me up to serve you and those you give to me. Amen."

Thursday, February 18, 2016

Know that God is present with you and ready to converse.

"I seek you, Lord, but you are already found. And you find me here now, ready to be with you."

Read the Gospel: Matthew 7:7–12.

Jesus instructed, "Ask, and it will be given you; search, and you will find; knock, and the door will be opened for you. For everyone who asks receives, and everyone who searches finds, and for everyone who knocks, the door will be opened. Is there anyone among you who, if your child asks for bread, will give a stone? Or if the child asks for a fish, will give a snake? If you then, who are evil, know how to give good gifts to your children, how much more will your Father in heaven give good things to those who ask him!

"In everything do to others as you would have them do to you; for this is the law and the prophets."

Notice what you think and feel as you read the Gospel.

Jesus is teaching. How we judge others determines how we are judged. Rather than look at others' faults, we should look at our own. What we desire and seek from God we receive, for God is good. What else do you notice in this Gospel?

Pray as you are led for yourself and others.

"Lord, forgive me for judging others, forgive my hypocrisies, and forgive me for not doing unto others what I would have others do to me . . ." (Continue in your own words.)

Listen to Jesus.

I grant you what you seek, my child. Ask me now for whatever you want from God for yourself and for others. What else is Jesus saying to you?

Ask God to show you how to live today.

"Lord, alert me when you see me begin to judge someone else, and turn me toward you. I give you this day. I need you. Amen."

Friday, February 19, 2016

Know that God is present with you and ready to converse.

"The Word of God is before me. Jesus is present in Word and in Spirit. Open my heart, Lord."

Read the Gospel: Matthew 5:20–26.

Jesus said, "For I tell you, unless your righteousness exceeds that of the scribes and Pharisees, you will never enter the kingdom of heaven.

"You have heard that it was said to those of ancient times, 'You shall not murder'; and 'whoever murders shall be liable to judgment.' But I say to you that if you are angry with a brother or sister, you will be liable to judgment; and if you insult a brother or sister, you will be liable to the council; and if you say, 'You fool,' you will be liable to the hell of fire. So when you are offering your gift at the altar, if you remember that your brother or sister has something against you, leave your gift there before the altar and go; first be reconciled to your brother or sister, and then come and offer your gift. Come to terms quickly with your accuser while you are on the way to court with him, or your accuser may hand you over to the judge, and the judge to the guard, and you will be thrown into prison. Truly I tell you, you will never get out until you have paid the last penny."

Notice what you think and feel as you read the Gospel.

Jesus emphasizes the importance of moral behavior in our dealings with others. Little things are important. Rudeness and anger toward another violate God's commandment. Do not allow someone to hold a grudge against you, Jesus says. Resolving a human dispute is more important than making an offering to God.

Pray as you are led for yourself and others.

"Jesus, you set moral standards higher than the scribes and Pharisees. Who can stand before you? Wash me and lead me in the way of holiness . . ." (Continue in your own words.)

Listen to Jesus.

My child, I am working in you. I desire your holiness. Take a moment now to consider who may need to forgive you. What can you do to reconcile? What else is Jesus saying to you?

Ask God to show you how to live today.

Lord, you ask much. Give me grace, strength, and courage to do what you ask. Amen."

Saturday, February 20, 2016

Know that God is present with you and ready to converse.

"Heavenly Father, rain down your love upon me as I attend to your Word, my Lord and Savior, your Son, Jesus."

Read the Gospel: Matthew 5:43–48.

Jesus taught, "You have heard that it was said, 'You shall love your neighbor and hate your enemy.' But I say to you, love your enemies and pray for those who persecute you, so that you may be children of your Father in heaven; for he makes his sun rise on the evil and on the good, and sends rain on the righteous and on the unrighteous. For if you love those who love you, what reward do you have? Do not even the tax collectors do the same? And if you greet only your brothers and sisters, what more are you doing than others? Do not even the Gentiles do the same? Be perfect, therefore, as your heavenly Father is perfect."

Notice what you think and feel as you read the Gospel.

Jesus asks us to be perfect, and he also says how we can achieve it: by loving our enemies as well as our family and friends.

Pray as you are led for yourself and others.

"Lord, whom do I hate, dislike, criticize, avoid, or fear? Bring these people to my mind. Put your love for them into my heart . . ." (Continue in your own words.)

Listen to Jesus.

Dear friend, do you see that my way of love is the way to peace and joy? It is also the way of healing and wholeness. Love all people and see the world change around you. What else is Jesus saying to you?

Ask God to show you how to live today.

"Lord, you have given me an assignment today, an exercise in holiness, an exercise of the heart. Give me your heart as I seek to love people that I have forgotten to love. Amen."

Sunday, February 21, 2016
Second Sunday of Lent

Know that God is present with you and ready to converse.

Jesus was present with Moses and Elijah on the mountain. He was present with Peter, James, and John. He was present with the multitudes. He is present with you now.

When you are ready, invite God to speak to you with words such as these: "Thank you for loving me, Lord. I long to see your glory."

Read the Gospel: Luke 9:28b–36.

Jesus took with him Peter and John and James, and went up on the mountain to pray. And while he was praying, the appearance of his face changed, and his clothes became dazzling white. Suddenly they saw two men, Moses and Elijah, talking to him. They appeared in glory and were speaking of his departure, which he was about to accomplish at Jerusalem. Now Peter and his companions were weighed down with sleep; but since they had stayed awake, they saw his glory and the two men who stood with him. Just as they were leaving him, Peter said to Jesus, "Master, it is good for us to be here; let us make three dwellings, one for you, one for Moses, and one for Elijah"—not knowing what he said. While he was saying this, a cloud came and overshadowed them; and they were terrified as they entered the cloud. Then from the cloud came a voice that said, "This is my Son, my Chosen; listen to him!" When the voice had spoken, Jesus was found alone. And they kept silent and in those days told no one any of the things they had seen.

Notice what you think and feel as you read the Gospel.

How fortunate for the disciples to see Jesus transfigured while praying on the mountain and talking with Moses and Elijah. They are talking about Jesus' "departure, which he was about to accomplish at Jerusalem." What is Jesus saying to them? What are they saying to Jesus?

Pray as you are led for yourself and others.

"Lord, you came into this world to depart from it in a violent death, imposed upon you by those you loved and came to save. I love you for that. Let the power of your love live in me . . ." (Continue in your own words.)

Listen to Jesus.

You read about Moses, Elijah, and me revealed in glory. My disciples were in awe. The kingdom of heaven is far beyond whatever glory you can imagine now. I look forward to the day when I can reveal its glory to you. What else is Jesus saying to you?

Ask God to show you how to live today.

"Peter wanted to build three booths to honor Jesus and the prophets. How may I honor you today, Jesus? For you are the Son of God. Amen."

Monday, February 22, 2016
Chair of Saint Peter

Know that God is present with you and ready to converse.

"Word of the Father, I joyfully come into your presence to love you, know you, and serve you."

Read the Gospel: Matthew 16:13–19.

Now when Jesus came into the district of Caesarea Philippi, he asked his disciples, "Who do people say that the Son of Man is?" And they said, "Some say John the Baptist, but others Elijah, and still others Jeremiah or one of the prophets." He said to them, "But who do you say that I am?" Simon Peter answered, "You are the Messiah, the Son of the living God." And Jesus answered him, "Blessed are you, Simon son of Jonah! For flesh and blood has not revealed this to you, but my Father in heaven. And I tell you, you are Peter, and on this rock I will build my Church, and the gates of Hades will not prevail against it. I will give you the keys of the kingdom of heaven, and whatever you bind on earth will be bound in heaven, and whatever you loose on earth will be loosed in heaven."

Notice what you think and feel as you read the Gospel.

Jesus affirms that he is the Christ and proclaims to Peter that he is the rock upon which he will build his Church. Peter is to receive the keys of the kingdom of heaven—powers in heaven and on earth.

Pray as you are led for yourself and others.

"Lord, you are true to your word. Against all odds your Church continues to this day, and it will continue until you return. I pray for your Church and all who serve in it, that they may do so with the love, wisdom, and power that come by your Spirit . . ." (Continue in your own words.)

Listen to Jesus.

You, too, belong to my Church, which is my Body. I ask my followers to love one another so the world will know that I am among you. What else is Jesus saying to you?

Ask God to show you how to live today.

"Jesus, how may I help to unify those who follow you? Amen."

Tuesday, February 23, 2016

Know that God is present with you and ready to converse.

"I am here, Lord. Open my heart to your Word."

Read the Gospel: Matthew 23:1–12.

Then Jesus said to the crowds and to his disciples, "The scribes and the Pharisees sit on Moses' seat; therefore, do whatever they teach you and follow it; but do not do as they do, for they do not practice what they teach. They tie up heavy burdens, hard to bear, and lay them on the shoulders of others; but they themselves are unwilling to lift a finger to move them. They do all their deeds to be seen by others; for they make their phylacteries broad and their fringes long. They love to have the place of honor at banquets and the best seats in the synagogues, and to be greeted with respect in the marketplaces, and to have people call them rabbi. But you are not to be called rabbi, for you have one teacher, and you are all students. And call no one your father on earth, for you have one Father—the one in heaven. Nor are you to be called instructors, for you have one instructor, the Messiah. The greatest among you will be your servant. All who exalt themselves will be humbled, and all who humble themselves will be exalted."

Notice what you think and feel as you read the Gospel.

Jesus says that earthly distinctions, appearance, rank, and status are not the way God sees us. If we aspire to greatness, we should be servants.

Pray as you are led for yourself and others.

"Jesus, you came to serve us, the great and small. Your amazing words and your amazing deeds proclaim the truth. I give myself to you today as your humble servant . . ." (Continue in your own words.)

Listen to Jesus.

There is joy in serving others, my beloved. I want you to know joy as I know it. What else is Jesus saying to you?

Ask God to show you how to live today.

"Jesus, let my love for you translate into actions in my day. I need you to walk with me and guide me in all things. Amen."

Wednesday, February 24, 2016

Know that God is present with you and ready to converse.

"Lord, please don't let me hear your Word and be oblivious to what you are saying to me. Elevate my heart and mind to receive you."

Read the Gospel: Matthew 20:17–28.

While Jesus was going up to Jerusalem, he took the twelve disciples aside by themselves, and said to them on the way, "See, we are going up to Jerusalem, and the Son of Man will be handed over to the chief priests and scribes, and they will condemn him to death; then they will hand him over to the Gentiles to be mocked and flogged and crucified; and on the third day he will be raised."

Then the mother of the sons of Zebedee came to Jesus with her sons and, kneeling before him, she asked a favor of him. And he said to her, "What do you want?" She said to him, "Declare that these two sons of mine will sit, one at your right hand and one at your left, in your kingdom." But Jesus answered, "You do not know what you are asking. Are you able to drink the cup that I am about to drink?" They said to him, "We are able." He said to them, "You will indeed drink my cup, but to sit at my right hand and at my left, this is not mine to grant, but it is for those for whom it has been prepared by my Father."

When the ten heard it, they were angry with the two brothers. But Jesus called them to him and said, "You know that the rulers of the Gentiles lord it over them, and their great ones are tyrants over them. It will not be so among you; but whoever wishes to be great among you must be your servant, and whoever wishes to be first among you must be your slave; just as the Son of Man came not to be served but to serve, and to give his life a ransom for many."

Notice what you think and feel as you read the Gospel.

Jesus tells the Twelve exactly what's going to happen to him in Jerusalem: his passion, death, and resurrection on the third day. What did his disciples understand? They are concerned about their status when he comes into his kingdom. What else do you notice?

Pray as you are led for yourself and others.

"Lord, I guess it is human nature that we want honor and power for ourselves. Thank you for reminding me again that greatness is acquired by serving others. Show me how . . ." (Continue in your own words.)

Listen to Jesus.

Whom can you serve, my dear disciple? The one you serve today will be me. What else is Jesus saying to you?

Ask God to show you how to live today.

"Lord, walking in your humble way is challenging. You ask me to be better than I have ever been. I can accomplish none of it without you. Be with me today. Amen."

Thursday, February 25, 2016

Know that God is present with you and ready to converse.

"Give me ears to hear your Word, Lord, for you are with me."

Read the Gospel: Luke 16:19–31.

Jesus said, "There was a rich man who was dressed in purple and fine linen and who feasted sumptuously every day. And at his gate lay a poor man named Lazarus, covered with sores, who longed to satisfy his hunger with what fell from the rich man's table; even the dogs would come and lick his sores. The poor man died and was carried away by the angels to be with Abraham. The rich man also died and was buried. In Hades, where he was being tormented, he looked up and saw Abraham far away with Lazarus by his side. He called out, 'Father Abraham, have mercy on me, and send Lazarus to dip the tip of his finger in water and cool my tongue; for I am in agony in these flames.' But Abraham said, 'Child, remember that during your lifetime you received your good things, and Lazarus in like manner evil things; but now he is comforted here, and you are in agony. Besides all this, between you and us a great chasm has been fixed, so that those who might want to pass from here to you cannot do so, and no one can cross from there to us.' He said, 'Then, father, I beg you to send him to my father's house—for I have five brothers—that he may warn them, so that they will not also come into this place of torment.' Abraham replied, 'They have Moses and the prophets; they should listen to them.' He said, 'No, father Abraham; but if someone goes to them from the dead, they will repent.' He said to him, 'If they do not listen to Moses and the prophets, neither will they be convinced even if someone rises from the dead.'"

Notice what you think and feel as you read the Gospel.

In the parable of the rich man and poor Lazarus, Jesus connects human behavior in life to final destiny after death. The twist is that Jesus says that many people ignore the messages of the prophets, even the prophet who rose from the dead.

Pray as you are led for yourself and others.
"I desire to receive your words today, risen Lord, and to take them to heart. Lead me to upright behavior and compassionate acts . . ." (Continue in your own words.)

Listen to Jesus.
It is very pleasant to spend time with you, beloved. You are mine and I am yours. What would you like from me? What else is Jesus saying to you?

Ask God to show you how to live today.
"Jesus, you are good to me. Is there a Lazarus in my life whom I can help? Amen."

Friday, February 26, 2016

Know that God is present with you and ready to converse.
"Let me not be one of those who resist your Word, Lord. I wish to live by every word that proceeds from the mouth of God."

Read the Gospel: Matthew 21:33–43, 45–46.
Jesus instructed, "Listen to another parable. There was a landowner who planted a vineyard, put a fence around it, dug a wine press in it, and built a watchtower. Then he leased it to tenants and went to another country. When the harvest time had come, he sent his slaves to the tenants to collect his produce. But the tenants seized his slaves and beat one, killed another, and stoned another. Again he sent other slaves, more than the first; and they treated them in the same way. Finally he sent his son to them, saying, 'They will respect my son.' But when the tenants saw the son, they said to themselves, 'This is the heir; come, let us kill him and get his inheritance.' So they seized him, threw him out of the vineyard, and killed him. Now when the owner of the vineyard comes, what will he do to those tenants?" They said to him, "He will put those wretches to a miserable death, and lease the vineyard to other tenants who will give him the produce at the harvest time."

Jesus said to them, "Have you never read in the scriptures:

'The stone that the builders rejected
has become the cornerstone;

this was the Lord's doing,
and it is amazing in our eyes'?

Therefore I tell you, the kingdom of God will be taken away from you and given to a people that produces the fruits of the kingdom. . . ."

When the chief priests and the Pharisees heard his parables, they realized that he was speaking about them. They wanted to arrest him, but they feared the crowds, because they regarded him as a prophet.

Notice what you think and feel as you read the Gospel.

Jesus tells his own story in this parable of the unjust tenants, and he foretells his own end at the hands of those who reject him. They will kill him, yet the very stone that the builders rejected has become the head of the corner.

Pray as you are led for yourself and others.

"Your words and your ways are marvelous, Jesus, and you are my rock, the stone at the corner of my life . . ." (Continue in your own words.)

Listen to Jesus.

I am happy when you speak to me, listen to me, and follow my motives and desires. For I wish no one ill. Let us be close and embrace all others. What else is Jesus saying to you?

Ask God to show you how to live today.

"As friends, Jesus, we go out together into the world, living your good news, sharing it with everyone. Let me not be afraid of rejection. Amen."

Saturday, February 27, 2016

Know that God is present with you and ready to converse.

"Good Shepherd, when I am lost, you find me; when I come back to you seeking forgiveness, you welcome me. You are above all human praise."

Read the Gospel: Luke 15:1–3, 11–32.

Now all the tax collectors and sinners were coming near to listen to Jesus. And the Pharisees and the scribes were grumbling and saying, "This fellow welcomes sinners and eats with them."

So he told them this parable: . . .

Then Jesus said, "There was a man who had two sons. The younger of them said to his father, 'Father, give me the share of the property that will belong to me.' So he divided his property between them. A few days later the younger son gathered all he had and traveled to a distant country, and there he squandered his property in dissolute living. When he had spent everything, a severe famine took place throughout that country, and he began to be in need. So he went and hired himself out to one of the citizens of that country, who sent him to his fields to feed the pigs. He would gladly have filled himself with the pods that the pigs were eating; and no one gave him anything. But when he came to himself he said, 'How many of my father's hired hands have bread enough and to spare, but here I am dying of hunger! I will get up and go to my father, and I will say to him, "Father, I have sinned against heaven and before you; I am no longer worthy to be called your son; treat me like one of your hired hands."' So he set off and went to his father. But while he was still far off, his father saw him and was filled with compassion; he ran and put his arms around him and kissed him. Then the son said to him, 'Father, I have sinned against heaven and before you; I am no longer worthy to be called your son.' But the father said to his slaves, 'Quickly, bring out a robe—the best one—and put it on him; put a ring on his finger and sandals on his feet. And get the fatted calf and kill it, and let us eat and celebrate; for this son of mine was dead and is alive again; he was lost and is found!' And they began to celebrate.

"Now his elder son was in the field; and when he came and approached the house, he heard music and dancing. He called one of the slaves and asked what was going on. He replied, 'Your brother has come, and your father has killed the fatted calf, because he has got him back safe and sound.' Then he became angry and refused to go in. His father came out and began to plead with him. But he answered his father, 'Listen! For all these years I have been working like a slave for you, and I have never disobeyed your command; yet you have never given me even a young goat so that I might celebrate with my friends. But when this son of yours came back, who has devoured your property with prostitutes, you killed the fatted calf for him!' Then the father said to him, 'Son, you are always with me, and all that is mine is yours. But we had to celebrate and rejoice, because this brother of yours was dead and has come to life; he was lost and has been found.'"

Notice what you think and feel as you read the Gospel.

Jesus speaks of God the Father and himself in this great parable of the prodigal son. The younger son has learned a lesson. What does the older son learn?

Pray as you are led for yourself and others.

"Jesus, you know the human heart. You know me inside and out. I am created for you. Help me fulfill my destiny. Lead me in your way of love for others. I pray for . . ." (Continue in your own words.)

Listen to Jesus.

I hear your prayers, dear one. I am like a father or a mother who wants only what is best for you. What else is Jesus saying to you?

Ask God to show you how to live today.

"We have spent time together, Lord. Let me go forth to do unto others as I would have them do unto me. With your help, nothing is impossible. Amen."

Sunday, February 28, 2016
Third Sunday of Lent

Know that God is present with you and ready to converse.

Jesus preached against judging others. We need humility to walk in his way.

When you are ready to hear his voice in the Word, invite him to teach you in words such as these: "Lord, the world can be a frightening place, with violence, accidents, and disasters. Let me trust you when I am afraid. Let me trust you now."

Read the Gospel: Luke 13:1–9.

At that very time there were some present who told Jesus about the Galileans whose blood Pilate had mingled with their sacrifices. He asked them, "Do you think that because these Galileans suffered in this way they were worse sinners than all other Galileans? No, I tell you; but unless you repent, you will all perish as they did. Or those eighteen who were killed when the tower of Siloam fell on them—do you think that they were worse offenders than all the others living in Jerusalem? No, I tell you; but unless you repent, you will all perish just as they did."

Then he told this parable: "A man had a fig tree planted in his vineyard; and he came looking for fruit on it and found none. So he said to the gardener, 'See here! For three years I have come looking for fruit on this fig tree, and still I find none. Cut it down! Why should it be wasting the soil?' He replied, 'Sir, let it alone for one more year, until I dig around it and put manure on it. If it bears fruit next year, well and good; but if not, you can cut it down.'"

Notice what you think and feel as you read the Gospel.

Jesus cautions us against judging victims of violence in any form. We are not here to judge but to get right with God.

Pray as you are led for yourself and others.

"Lord, I pray for all victims. I hear about them in the news of the world, the nation, and my community. No one deserves to be a victim. You were a victim, Lamb of God, and you had a purpose. Accomplish your purposes now. Send me . . ." (Continue in your own words.)

Listen to Jesus.

I want you to be fruitful, my beloved, because the world needs those who care for others, who aid those in need, speak the truth, and work for justice. What else is Jesus saying to you?

Ask God to show you how to live today.

"Today I offer myself as a living sacrifice. This is how I choose to worship you, Lord. Make of me what you will. Amen."

Monday, February 29, 2016

Know that God is present with you and ready to converse.

"You go to people who are not your own. You speak to sinners. You are here with me. Let me hear your Word, Lord."

Read the Gospel: John 4:5–42.

So Jesus came to a Samaritan city called Sychar, near the plot of ground that Jacob had given to his son Joseph. Jacob's well was there, and Jesus, tired out by his journey, was sitting by the well. It was about noon.

A Samaritan woman came to draw water, and Jesus said to her, "Give me a drink." (His disciples had gone to the city to buy food.) The Samaritan woman said to him, "How is it that you, a Jew, ask a drink of me, a woman of Samaria?" (Jews do not share things in common with Samaritans.) Jesus answered her, "If you knew the gift of God, and who it is that is saying to you, 'Give me a drink,' you would have asked him, and he would have given you living water." The woman said to him, "Sir, you have no bucket, and the well is deep. Where do you get that living water? Are you greater than our ancestor Jacob, who gave us the well, and with his sons and his flocks drank from it?" Jesus said to her, "Everyone who drinks of this water will be thirsty again, but those who drink of the water that I will give them will never be thirsty. The water that I will give will become in them a spring of water gushing up to eternal life." The woman said to him, "Sir, give me this water, so that I may never be thirsty or have to keep coming here to draw water."

Jesus said to her, "Go, call your husband, and come back." The woman answered him, "I have no husband." Jesus said to her, "You are right in saying, 'I have no husband'; for you have had five husbands, and the one you have now is not your husband. What you have said is true!" The woman said to him, "Sir, I see that you are a prophet. Our ancestors worshiped on this mountain, but you say that the place where people must worship is in Jerusalem." Jesus said to her, "Woman, believe me, the hour is coming when you will worship the Father neither on this mountain nor in Jerusalem. You worship what you do not know; we worship what we know, for salvation is from the Jews. But the hour is coming, and is now here, when the true worshipers will worship the Father in spirit and truth, for the Father seeks such as these to worship him. God is spirit, and those who worship him must worship in spirit and truth." The woman said to him, "I know that Messiah is coming" (who is called Christ). "When he comes, he will proclaim all things to us." Jesus said to her, "I am he, the one who is speaking to you."

Just then his disciples came. They were astonished that he was speaking with a woman, but no one said, "What do you want?" or, "Why are you speaking with her?" Then the woman left her water jar and went back to the city. She said to the people, "Come and see a man who told me everything I have ever done! He cannot be the Messiah, can he?" They left the city and were on their way to him.

Meanwhile the disciples were urging him, "Rabbi, eat something." But he said to them, "I have food to eat that you do not know about." So the disciples said to one another, "Surely no one has brought him something to eat?" Jesus said to them, "My food is to do the will of him who sent me and to complete his work. Do you not say, 'Four months more, then comes the harvest'? But I tell you, look around you, and see how the fields are ripe for harvesting. The reaper is already receiving wages and is gathering fruit for eternal life, so that sower and reaper may rejoice together. For here the saying holds true, 'One sows and another reaps.' I sent you to reap that for which you did not labor. Others have labored, and you have entered into their labor."

Many Samaritans from that city believed in him because of the woman's testimony, "He told me everything I have ever done." So when the Samaritans came to him, they asked him to stay with them; and he stayed there two days. And many more believed because of his word. They said to the woman, "It is no longer because of what you said that we believe, for we have heard for ourselves, and we know that this is truly the Savior of the world."

Notice what you think and feel as you read the Gospel.

This passage is a short story with setting, characters, and dialogue. The theme is that Jesus is the Christ, the Savior of the world, for those who receive him in spirit and in truth. Do you identify with the woman at the well?

Pray as you are led for yourself and others.

"Lord Jesus, you came for all people, especially those far from God. I cannot thank you enough. The world cannot glorify you enough. I have springs of living water within me. How may I channel them to others?" (Continue in your own words.)

Listen to Jesus.

The secret to bearing fruit, helping others, is to abide in me. Ours is the key relationship. It's like a good marriage. Everything else will follow. What else is Jesus saying to you?

Ask God to show you how to live today.

"Jesus, I have little idea what is good, what is best, what is your will for me. Show me, enable me, and let it glorify you. Amen."

Tuesday, March 1, 2016

Know that God is present with you and ready to converse.

"God, great Lord of hosts, you are waiting for me to open my mind and my heart to your Word, Jesus, your Son and my Savior. Praise him!"

Read the Gospel: Matthew 18:21–35.

Then Peter came and said to Jesus, "Lord, if another member of the church sins against me, how often should I forgive? As many as seven times?" Jesus said to him, "Not seven times, but, I tell you, seventy-seven times.

"For this reason the kingdom of heaven may be compared to a king who wished to settle accounts with his slaves. When he began the reckoning, one who owed him ten thousand talents was brought to him; and, as he could not pay, his lord ordered him to be sold, together with his wife and children and all his possessions, and payment to be made. So the slave fell on his knees before him, saying, 'Have patience with me, and I will pay you everything.' And out of pity for him, the lord of that slave released him and forgave him the debt. But that same slave, as he went out, came upon one of his fellow slaves who owed him a hundred denarii; and seizing him by the throat, he said, 'Pay what you owe.' Then his fellow slave fell down and pleaded with him, 'Have patience with me, and I will pay you.' But he refused; then he went and threw him into prison until he would pay the debt. When his fellow slaves saw what had happened, they were greatly distressed, and they went and reported to their lord all that had taken place. Then his lord summoned him and said to him, 'You wicked slave! I forgave you all that debt because you pleaded with me. Should you not have had mercy on your fellow slave, as I had mercy on you?' And in anger his lord handed him over to be tortured until he would pay his entire debt. So my heavenly Father will also do to every one of you, if you do not forgive your brother or sister from your heart."

Notice what you think and feel as you read the Gospel.

The master forgives his servant's large debt, but the servant will not forgive a much smaller debt of a fellow servant. Angry, the master delivers the unforgiving servant to jail. Jesus says his Father will do the same to us unless we forgive our brothers from our hearts.

Pray as you are led for yourself and others.

"Lord, this parable ends in justice. But that justice is related to mercy. God has mercy on me and forgives me. So I must do the same . . ." (Continue in your own words.)

Listen to Jesus.

It's a law of grace, my child, that you receive mercy as you extend mercy to those who offend you. What else is Jesus saying to you?

Ask God to show you how to live today.

"Lord, what can I do today to make up for grudges I have harbored for hurts and slights I have received from others? I wish to be free of unforgivingness. Amen."

Wednesday, March 2, 2016

Know that God is present with you and ready to converse.

"Lord, let your Word be my law. I am ready to hear you now."

Read the Gospel: Matthew 5:17–19.

Jesus taught, "Do not think that I have come to abolish the law or the prophets; I have come not to abolish but to fulfill. For truly I tell you, until heaven and earth pass away, not one letter, not one stroke of a letter, will pass from the law until all is accomplished. Therefore, whoever breaks one of the least of these commandments, and teaches others to do the same, will be called least in the kingdom of heaven; but whoever does them and teaches them will be called great in the kingdom of heaven."

Notice what you think and feel as you read the Gospel.

Jesus came not to abolish but to fulfill the law and the prophets. We are to take the commandments seriously and teach others to do the same.

Pray as you are led for yourself and others.

"Lord, you know my heart. I want to obey you because I want to please you in all I think, say, and do . . ." (Continue in your own words.)

Listen to Jesus.

Repentance is a spring of renewal, my child. I hear your confession. I absolve you of your sin. What else is Jesus saying to you?

Ask God to show you how to live today.

"Lord, how may I give alms today? I want to show my gratitude to you for your mercy. Amen."

Thursday, March 3, 2016

Know that God is present with you and ready to converse.

"Jesus, I am with you. Keep me close."

Read the Gospel: Luke 11:14–23.

Now Jesus was casting out a demon that was mute; when the demon had gone out, the one who had been mute spoke, and the crowds were amazed. But some of them said, "He casts out demons by Beelzebul, the ruler of the demons." Others, to test him, kept demanding from him a sign from heaven. But he knew what they were thinking and said to them, "Every kingdom divided against itself becomes a desert, and house falls on house. If Satan also is divided against himself, how will his kingdom stand? For you say that I cast out the demons by Beelzebul. Now if I cast out the demons by Beelzebul, by whom do your exorcists cast them out? Therefore they will be your judges. But if it is by the finger of God that I cast out the demons, then the kingdom of God has come to you. When a strong man, fully armed, guards his castle, his property is safe. But when one stronger than he attacks him and overpowers him, he takes away his armor in which he trusted and divides his plunder. Whoever is not with me is against me, and whoever does not gather with me scatters."

Notice what you think and feel as you read the Gospel.

In response to criticism, Jesus affirms that his authority over demons comes from God, not Beelzebul. He says that the one who does not gather with him scatters.

Pray as you are led for yourself and others.

"Dear Jesus, I gather. I have had enough of scattering. I pray for the many I know who have scattered. Draw them back to you . . ." (Continue in your own words.)

Listen to Jesus.

I care for those who are scattered, too, dear friend. I do not cease to seek them. What else is Jesus saying to you?

Ask God to show you how to live today.

"As I give you my whole self, Lord, show me what to do today for your glory. Amen."

Friday, March 4, 2016

Know that God is present with you and ready to converse.

"Breathe on me, Holy Spirit, outside and inside, heart and mind and soul, and through the Word of God."

Read the Gospel: Matthew 12:28–34.

Jesus said, "But if it is by the Spirit of God that I cast out demons, then the kingdom of God has come to you. Or how can one enter a strong man's house and plunder his property, without first tying up the strong man? Then indeed the house can be plundered. Whoever is not with me is against me, and whoever does not gather with me scatters. Therefore I tell you, people will be forgiven for every sin and blasphemy, but blasphemy against the Spirit will not be forgiven. Whoever speaks a word against the Son of Man will be forgiven, but whoever speaks against the Holy Spirit will not be forgiven, either in this age or in the age to come.

"Either make the tree good, and its fruit good; or make the tree bad, and its fruit bad; for the tree is known by its fruit. You brood of vipers! How can you speak good things, when you are evil? For out of the abundance of the heart the mouth speaks."

Notice what you think and feel as you read the Gospel.

Jesus says he has power by the Holy Spirit and warns those who speak against the Spirit. Jesus shows profound understanding of spiritual realities.

Pray as you are led for yourself and others.

"Lord, I am no better than those you sternly warn. I depend on you to make me good so I can bear good fruit . . ." (Continue in your own words.)

Listen to Jesus.

I want you to bear fruit. You can do much for others. Abide in me, child. What else is Jesus saying to you?

Ask God to show you how to live today.

"Make me mindful of opportunities to show kindness and fairness all through the day, Lord. Amen."

Saturday, March 5, 2016

Know that God is present with you and ready to converse.

"I come into your presence humbly, Lord, exalting you."

Read the Gospel: Luke 18:9–14.

Jesus also told this parable to some who trusted in themselves that they were righteous and regarded others with contempt: "Two men went up to the Temple to pray, one a Pharisee and the other a tax collector. The Pharisee, standing by himself, was praying thus, 'God, I thank you that I am not like other people: thieves, rogues, adulterers, or even like this tax collector. I fast twice a week; I give a tenth of all my income.' But the tax collector, standing far off, would not even look up to heaven, but was beating his breast and saying, 'God, be merciful to me, a sinner!' I tell you, this man went down to his home justified rather than the other; for all who exalt themselves will be humbled, but all who humble themselves will be exalted."

Notice what you think and feel as you read the Gospel.

Presumably the Pharisee did practice his religion, while the tax collector did not. Yet the Pharisee falls short in his prayer, while the tax collector is justified. What makes the difference here?

Pray as you are led for yourself and others.

"The righteous are prone to spiritual pride. Lord, help me avoid this grievous fault. Let me not find fault in others but rather have true humility . . ." (Continue in your own words.)

Listen to Jesus.

Learn from me because I am meek and lowly of heart, my child. You will be exalted for your humility. What else is Jesus saying to you?

Ask God to show you how to live today.

"Is there someone I can lift up today by some common act of service? Amen."

Sunday, March 6, 2016
Fourth Sunday of Lent

Know that God is present with you and ready to converse.

As the prodigal son is welcomed by his father, so we are welcomed each time we return to God. We turn our hearts to our loving Father today.

When you are ready, begin: "Father, you are present in this parable; you are always present in the Word. Let me be present, too."

Read the Gospel: Luke 15:1–3, 11–32.

Now all the tax collectors and sinners were coming near to listen to Jesus. And the Pharisees and the scribes were grumbling and saying, "This fellow welcomes sinners and eats with them."

So he told them this parable: . . .

Then Jesus said, "There was a man who had two sons. The younger of them said to his father, 'Father, give me the share of the property that will belong to me.' So he divided his property between them. A few days later the younger son gathered all he had and traveled to a distant country, and there he squandered his property in dissolute living. When he had spent everything, a severe famine took place throughout that country, and he began to be in need. So he went and hired himself out to one of the citizens of that country, who sent him to his fields to feed the pigs. He would gladly have filled himself with the pods that the pigs were eating; and no one gave him anything. But when he came to himself he said, 'How many of my father's hired hands have bread enough and to spare, but here I am dying of hunger! I will get up and go to my father, and I will say to him, "Father, I have sinned against heaven and before you; I am no longer worthy to be called your son; treat me like one of your hired hands."' So he set off and went to his father. But while he was still far off, his father saw him and was filled with compassion; he ran and put his arms around him and kissed him. Then the son said to him, 'Father, I have sinned against heaven and before you; I am no longer worthy to be called your son.' But the father said to his slaves, 'Quickly, bring out a robe—the best one—and put it on him; put a ring on his finger and sandals on his feet. And get the fatted calf and kill it, and let us eat and celebrate; for this son of mine was dead and is alive again; he was lost and is found!' And they began to celebrate.

"Now his elder son was in the field; and when he came and approached the house, he heard music and dancing. He called one of the slaves and asked what was going on. He replied, 'Your brother has come, and your father has killed the fatted calf, because he has got him back safe and sound.' Then he became angry and refused to go in. His father came out and began to plead with him. But he answered his father, 'Listen! For all these years I have been working like a slave for you, and I have never disobeyed your command; yet you have never given me even a young goat so that I might celebrate with my friends. But when this son of yours came back, who has devoured your property with prostitutes, you killed the fatted calf for him!' Then the father said to him, 'Son, you are always with me, and all that is mine is yours. But we had to celebrate and rejoice, because this brother of yours was dead and has come to life; he was lost and has been found.'"

Notice what you think and feel as you read the Gospel.

Jesus tells a story that rings true today with familiar characters: the foolish younger son, the loving and merciful father, and the jealous older son.

Pray as you are led for yourself and others.

"Father, help me come to my senses as the prodigal son did and return home to you as often as I need to. Help others also experience the joy of confessing their sins and receiving forgiveness from God and from those they have injured. I think of . . ." (Continue in your own words.)

Listen to Jesus.

I too want people to reconcile with God. That is the most important thing. Thank you for sharing my desire and praying for others. What else is Jesus saying to you?

Ask God to show you how to live today.

"Have I been waiting for someone who holds something against me to come to me and make peace? Perhaps I can take the initiative in reconciling. Give me wisdom, Jesus. Amen."

Monday, March 7, 2016

Know that God is present with you and ready to converse.

"I invite you to come where you are already, Lord—here with me. Open my eyes to see you in your Word."

Read the Gospel: John 9:1–41.

As he walked along, Jesus saw a man blind from birth. His disciples asked him, "Rabbi, who sinned, this man or his parents, that he was born blind?" Jesus answered, "Neither this man nor his parents sinned; he was born blind so that God's works might be revealed in him. We must work the works of him who sent me while it is day; night is coming when no one can work. As long as I am in the world, I am the light of the world." When he had said this, he spat on the ground and made mud with the saliva and spread the mud on the man's eyes, saying to him, "Go, wash in the pool of Siloam" (which means sent). Then he went and washed and came back able to see. The neighbors and those who had seen him before as a beggar began to ask, "Is this not the man who used to sit and beg?" Some were saying, "It is he." Others were saying, "No, but it is someone like him." He kept saying, "I am the man." But they kept asking him, "Then how were your eyes opened?" He answered, "The man called Jesus made mud, spread it on my eyes, and said to me, 'Go to Siloam and wash.' Then I went and washed and received my sight." They said to him, "Where is he?" He said, "I do not know."

They brought to the Pharisees the man who had formerly been blind. Now it was a Sabbath day when Jesus made the mud and opened his eyes. Then the Pharisees also began to ask him how he had received his sight. He said to them, "He put mud on my eyes. Then I washed, and now I see." Some of the Pharisees said, "This man is not from God, for he does not observe the Sabbath." But others said, "How can a man who is a sinner perform such signs?" And they were divided. So they said again to the blind man, "What do you say about him? It was your eyes he opened." He said, "He is a prophet."

The Jews did not believe that he had been blind and had received his sight until they called the parents of the man who had received his sight and asked them, "Is this your son, who you say was born blind? How then does he now see?" His parents answered, "We know that this is our son, and that he was born blind; but we do not know how it is that now he sees, nor do we know who opened his eyes. Ask him; he is of age. He will speak for himself." His parents said this because they were afraid of the Jews; for the Jews had already agreed that anyone who confessed Jesus to be the Messiah would be put out of the synagogue. Therefore his parents said, "He is of age; ask him."

So for the second time they called the man who had been blind, and they said to him, "Give glory to God! We know that this man is a sinner." He answered, "I do not know whether he is a sinner. One thing I do know, that though I was blind, now I see." They said to him, "What did he do to you? How did he open your eyes?" He answered them, "I have told you already, and you would not listen. Why do you want to hear it again? Do you also want to become his disciples?" Then they reviled him, saying, "You are his disciple, but we are disciples of Moses. We know that God has spoken to Moses, but as for this man, we do not know where he comes from." The man answered, "Here is an astonishing thing! You do not know where he comes from, and yet he opened my eyes. We know that God does not listen to sinners, but he does listen to one who worships him and obeys his will. Never since the world began has it been heard that anyone opened the eyes of a person born blind. If this man were not from God, he could do nothing." They answered him, "You were born entirely in sins, and are you trying to teach us?" And they drove him out.

Jesus heard that they had driven him out, and when he found him, he said, "Do you believe in the Son of Man?" He answered, "And who is he, sir? Tell me, so that I may believe in him." Jesus said to him, "You have seen him, and the one speaking with you is he." He said, "Lord, I believe." And he worshiped him. Jesus said, "I came into this world for judgment so that those who do not see may see, and those who do see may become blind." Some of the Pharisees near him heard this and said to him, "Surely we are not blind, are we?" Jesus said to them, "If you were blind, you would not have sin. But now that you say, 'We see,' your sin remains."

Notice what you think and feel as you read the Gospel.

It's all about judging sinners. Jesus' disciples ask whether a blind man is blind because he is a sinner. Jesus says no. The Pharisees wonder how a sinner (they mean Jesus) can heal someone. Jesus says that they are truly the blind ones.

Pray as you are led for yourself and others.

"You are the light of the world, Lord. Be my light. I want your light to shine upon all who sit in darkness. I pray for . . ." (Continue in your own words.)

Listen to Jesus.

My child, do not find fault in others. In judging them, you err. Only I know the heart. What else is Jesus saying to you?

Ask God to show you how to live today.

"I have and do make judgments about others. Shine your light on me and show me how to undo my judgments. Amen."

Tuesday, March 8, 2016

Know that God is present with you and ready to converse.

"Jesus is aware of my needs. I will wait for him now."

Read the Gospel: John 5:1–16.

After this there was a festival of the Jews, and Jesus went up to Jerusalem.

Now in Jerusalem by the Sheep Gate there is a pool, called in Hebrew Beth-zatha, which has five porticoes. In these lay many invalids—blind, lame, and paralyzed. One man was there who had been ill for thirty-eight years. When Jesus saw him lying there and knew that he had been there a long time, he said to him, "Do you want to be made well?" The sick man answered him, "Sir, I have no one to put me into the pool when the water is stirred up; and while I am making my way, someone else steps down ahead of me." Jesus said to him, "Stand up, take your mat, and walk." At once the man was made well, and he took up his mat, and began to walk.

Now that day was a Sabbath. So the Jews said to the man who had been cured, "It is the Sabbath; it is not lawful for you to carry your mat." But he answered them, "The man who made me well said to me, 'Take up your mat and walk.'" They asked him, "Who is the man who said to you, 'Take it up and walk'?" Now the man who had been healed did not know who it was, for Jesus had disappeared in the crowd that was there. Later Jesus found him in the Temple and said to him, "See, you have been made well! Do not sin anymore, so that nothing worse happens to you." The man went away and told the Jews that it was Jesus who had made him well. Therefore the Jews started persecuting Jesus, because he was doing such things on the Sabbath.

Notice what you think and feel as you read the Gospel.

The Pharisees always seem concerned about Jesus healing on the Sabbath. Jesus heals the man who had been ill for thirty-eight years.

Pray as you are led for yourself and others.

"Lord, I offer myself in your work of helping others. Let me work alongside you. Jesus . . ." (Continue in your own words.)

Listen to Jesus.

We are working together, my beloved disciple. Do not be discouraged by the difficulties of this world, but live and work in my hope. What else is Jesus saying to you?

Ask God to show you how to live today.

"I will rely on you, Lord, to show me how to live today. Amen."

Wednesday, March 9, 2016

Know that God is present with you and ready to converse.

"Father almighty, you are working in me; Jesus, you are working, too. Let me respond to your Word."

Read the Gospel: John 5:17–30.

But Jesus answered them, "My Father is still working, and I also am working." For this reason the Jews were seeking all the more to kill him, because he was not only breaking the Sabbath, but was also calling God his own Father, thereby making himself equal to God.

Jesus said to them, "Very truly, I tell you, the Son can do nothing on his own, but only what he sees the Father doing; for whatever the Father does, the Son does likewise. The Father loves the Son and shows him all that he himself is doing; and he will show him greater works than these, so that you will be astonished. Indeed, just as the Father raises the dead and gives them life, so also the Son gives life to whomever he wishes. The Father judges no one but has given all judgment to the Son, so that all may honor the Son just as they honor the Father. Anyone who does not honor the Son does not honor the Father who sent him. Very truly, I tell you, anyone who hears my word and believes him who sent me has eternal life, and does not come under judgment, but has passed from death to life.

"Very truly, I tell you, the hour is coming, and is now here, when the dead will hear the voice of the Son of God, and those who hear will live. For just as the Father has life in himself, so he has granted the Son also to have life in himself; and he has given him authority to execute judgment, because he is the Son of Man. Do not be astonished at this; for the hour is coming when all who are in their graves will hear his voice and will come out—those who have done good, to the resurrection of life, and those who have done evil, to the resurrection of condemnation.

"I can do nothing on my own. As I hear, I judge; and my judgment is just, because I seek to do not my own will but the will of him who sent me."

Notice what you think and feel as you read the Gospel.

Jesus affirms that his Father works all the time, and so does he, even on the Sabbath. Like his Father, he gives life to whomever he wishes—even eternal life. The one who believes has already passed from death to life.

Pray as you are led for yourself and others.

"Jesus, you promise resurrection. Your Father has given you all judgment, all authority, all power. I believe in you and your wonderful words of life. I worship you . . ." (Continue in your own words.)

Listen to Jesus.

As my Father loves me, I love you, dear friend. Start here, and reach out to others. What else is Jesus saying to you?

Ask God to show you how to live today.

"I am willing, Lord. I want to do your will as you did the will of your Father. Help me to see it and do it. Amen."

Thursday, March 10, 2016

Know that God is present with you and ready to converse.

"In your presence, Lord, grant me quietness of heart, peace, and joy. I will hear you."

Read the Gospel: John 5:31–47.

Jesus said, "If I testify about myself, my testimony is not true. There is another who testifies on my behalf, and I know that his testimony to me is true. You sent messengers to John, and he testified to the truth. Not that I accept such human testimony, but I say these things so that you may be saved. He was a burning and shining lamp, and you were willing to rejoice for a while in his light. But I have a testimony greater than John's. The works that the Father has given me to complete, the very works that I am doing, testify on my behalf that the Father has sent me. And the Father who sent me has himself testified on my behalf. You have never heard his voice or seen his form, and you do not have his word abiding in you, because you do not believe him whom he has sent.

"You search the scriptures because you think that in them you have eternal life; and it is they that testify on my behalf. Yet you refuse to come to me to have life. I do not accept glory from human beings. But I know that you do not have the love of God in you. I have come in my Father's name, and you do not accept me; if another comes in his own name, you will accept him. How can you believe when you accept glory from one another and do not seek the glory that comes from the one who alone is God? Do not think that I will accuse you before the Father; your accuser is Moses, on whom you have set your hope. If you believed Moses, you would believe me, for he wrote about me. But if you do not believe what he wrote, how will you believe what I say?"

Notice what you think and feel as you read the Gospel.

Jesus challenges the Pharisees and me: How can people believe in Jesus as the Christ when they seek to receive glory from one another and do not seek the glory that comes from God?

Pray as you are led for yourself and others.

"I have enjoyed approval from others, Lord, and I have even been resentful when I didn't get credit I thought I deserved. Let me put all that behind me and seek only you, your approval, your glory . . ." (Continue in your own words.)

Listen to Jesus.

Be generous, honest, and just in your approval of others, especially as you are in authority. You can encourage others by this. Know, too, that people need to do things for their own reasons—and for mine. What else is Jesus saying to you?

Ask God to show you how to live today.

"Lord, give me wisdom to do your will in my relationships. Amen."

Friday, March 11, 2016

Know that God is present with you and ready to converse.

"Speak to me, Jesus, for you come from God; you are God's holy Word of truth."

Read the Gospel: John 7:1–2, 10, 25–30.

After this Jesus went about in Galilee. He did not wish to go about in Judea because the Jews were looking for an opportunity to kill him. Now the Jewish festival of Booths was near. . . .

But after his brothers had gone to the festival, then he also went, not publicly but as it were in secret. . . .

Now some of the people of Jerusalem were saying, "Is not this the man whom they are trying to kill? And here he is, speaking openly, but they say nothing to him! Can it be that the authorities really know that this is the Messiah? Yet we know where this man is from; but when the Messiah comes, no one will know where he is from." Then Jesus cried out as he was teaching in the Temple, "You know me, and you know where I am from. I have not come on my own. But the one who sent me is true, and you do not know him. I know him, because I am from him, and he sent me." Then they tried to arrest him, but no one laid hands on him, because his hour had not yet come.

Notice what you think and feel as you read the Gospel.

Jesus is brave. He speaks the truth boldly, knowing the hearts of those in Jerusalem who want to arrest him. He tells them they do not know the One who sent him.

Pray as you are led for yourself and others.

"Jesus, I am not brave. I need to be a brave person, doing what's right every day, speaking your truth with all humility . . ." (Continue in your own words.)

Listen to Jesus.

I send my Spirit to strengthen you, to give you the words of truth, to give you what you need to touch hearts with love. What else is Jesus saying to you?

Ask God to show you how to live today.

"Lord, thank you. Show me how to allow my weakness to be your strength today. Amen."

Saturday, March 12, 2016

Know that God is present with you and ready to converse.

"You are patient with me, Lord, as I listen to your Word. I long to grow closer to you."

Read the Gospel: John 7:40–53.

When they heard Jesus' words, some in the crowd said, "This is really the prophet." Others said, "This is the Messiah." But some asked, "Surely the Messiah does not come from Galilee, does he? Has not the scripture said that the Messiah is descended from David and comes from Bethlehem, the village where David lived?" So there was a division in the crowd because of him. Some of them wanted to arrest him, but no one laid hands on him.

Then the Temple police went back to the chief priests and Pharisees, who asked them, "Why did you not arrest him?" The police answered, "Never has anyone spoken like this!" Then the Pharisees replied, "Surely you have not been deceived too, have you? Has any one of the authorities or of the Pharisees believed in him? But this crowd, which does not know the law—they are accursed." Nicodemus, who had gone to Jesus before, and who was one of them, asked, "Our law does not judge people without first giving them a hearing to find out what they are doing, does it?" They replied, "Surely you are not also from Galilee, are you? Search and you will see that no prophet is to arise from Galilee."

Then each of them went home.

Notice what you think and feel as you read the Gospel.

Nicodemus, who had spoken with Jesus in secret, now bravely speaks out for him to the chief priests and Pharisees. They want to arrest Jesus, but Nicodemus argues for a fair hearing. They reject his advice.

Pray as you are led for yourself and others.

"Lord, let me be brave in speaking out for you. Let me not be daunted by rejection or ridicule . . ." (Continue in your own words.)

Listen to Jesus.

I know you, dear one. I know what you need. I am the one you need. Ours is a journey of lovers. What else is Jesus saying to you?

Ask God to show you how to live today.

"God, I seek you in all things. Let me see you. Let me glorify you and trust in your ways. Amen."

Sunday, March 13, 2016
Fifth Sunday of Lent

Know that God is present with you and ready to converse.

Jesus reveals to us the mercy of God, for he and the Father are one. We rejoice in his mercy—forgiving us, healing us, and helping us to forgive others.

When you are ready to listen to the Lord, invite him with words such as these: "Jesus, you do not condemn me. Teach me now by your Word and draw me into your love."

Read the Gospel: John 8:2–11.

Early in the morning Jesus came again to the Temple. All the people came to him and he sat down and began to teach them. The scribes and the Pharisees brought a woman who had been caught in adultery; and making her stand before all of them, they said to him, "Teacher, this woman was caught in the very act of committing adultery. Now in the law Moses commanded us to stone such women. Now what do you say?" They said this to test him, so that they might have some charge to bring against him. Jesus bent down and wrote with his finger on the ground. When they kept on questioning him, he straightened up and said to them, "Let anyone among you who is without sin be the first to throw a stone at her." And once again he bent down and wrote on the ground. When they heard it, they went away, one by one, beginning with the elders; and Jesus was left alone with the woman standing before him. Jesus straightened up and said to her, "Woman, where are they? Has no one condemned you?" She said, "No one, sir." And Jesus said, "Neither do I condemn you. Go your way, and from now on do not sin again."

Notice what you think and feel as you read the Gospel.

Jesus escapes the entrapment by the Pharisees, and the woman escapes stoning. Jesus' words, "Let anyone among you who is without sin be the first to throw a stone," freezes them in shame. What does Jesus say to the woman now?

Pray as you are led for yourself and others.

"Jesus, there is meaning here for me as a judger and for me as a sinner. Let me take this to heart when I am prone to judge. Let me take this to heart when I am tempted to sin again . . ." (Continue in your own words.)

Listen to Jesus.

I am your constant friend, dear one. I strengthen your spirit and grant you wisdom. What else is Jesus saying to you?

Ask God to show you how to live today.

"Lord, how does this Gospel change me in my dealings with others? In my dealings with you? Amen."

Monday, March 14, 2016

Know that God is present with you and ready to converse.

"Jesus, let your Word raise me up and give me life."

Read the Gospel: John 11:1–45.

Now a certain man was ill, Lazarus of Bethany, the village of Mary and her sister Martha. Mary was the one who anointed the Lord with perfume and wiped his feet with her hair; her brother Lazarus was ill. So the sisters sent a message to Jesus, "Lord, he whom you love is ill." But when Jesus heard it, he said, "This illness does not lead to death; rather it is for God's glory, so that the Son of God may be glorified through it." Accordingly, though Jesus loved Martha and her sister and Lazarus, after having heard that Lazarus was ill, he stayed two days longer in the place where he was.

Then after this he said to the disciples, "Let us go to Judea again." The disciples said to him, "Rabbi, the Jews were just now trying to stone you, and are you going there again?" Jesus answered, "Are there not twelve hours of daylight? Those who walk during the day do not stumble, because they see the light of this world. But those who walk at night stumble, because the light is not in them." After saying this, he told them, "Our friend Lazarus has fallen asleep, but I am going there to awaken him." The disciples said to him, "Lord, if he has fallen asleep, he will be all right." Jesus, however, had been speaking about his death, but they thought that he was referring merely to sleep. Then Jesus told them plainly, "Lazarus is dead. For your sake I am glad I was not there, so that you may believe. But let us go to him." Thomas, who was called the Twin, said to his fellow disciples, "Let us also go, that we may die with him."

When Jesus arrived, he found that Lazarus had already been in the tomb four days. Now Bethany was near Jerusalem, some two miles away, and many of the Jews had come to Martha and Mary to console them about their brother. When Martha heard that Jesus was coming, she went and met him, while Mary stayed at home. Martha said to Jesus, "Lord, if you had been here, my brother would not have died. But even now I know that God will give you whatever you ask of him." Jesus said to her, "Your brother will rise again." Martha said to him, "I know that he will rise again in the resurrection on the last day." Jesus said to her, "I am the resurrection and the life. Those who believe in me, even though they die, will live, and everyone who lives and believes in me will never die. Do you believe this?" She said to him, "Yes, Lord, I believe that you are the Messiah, the Son of God, the one coming into the world."

When she had said this, she went back and called her sister Mary, and told her privately, "The Teacher is here and is calling for you." And when she heard it, she got up quickly and went to him. Now Jesus had not yet come to the village, but was still at the place where Martha had met him. The Jews who were with her in the house, consoling her, saw Mary get up quickly and go out. They followed her because they thought that she was going to the tomb to weep there. When Mary came where Jesus was and saw him, she knelt at his feet and said to him, "Lord, if you had been here, my brother would not have died." When Jesus saw her weeping, and the Jews who came with her also weeping, he was greatly disturbed in spirit and deeply moved. He said, "Where have you laid him?" They said to him, "Lord, come and see." Jesus began to weep. So the Jews said, "See how he loved him!" But some of them said, "Could not he who opened the eyes of the blind man have kept this man from dying?"

Then Jesus, again greatly disturbed, came to the tomb. It was a cave, and a stone was lying against it. Jesus said, "Take away the stone." Martha, the sister of the dead man, said to him, "Lord, already there is a stench because he has been dead four days." Jesus said to her, "Did I not tell you that if you believed, you would see the glory of God?" So they took away the stone. And Jesus looked upward and said, "Father, I thank you for having heard me. I knew that you always hear me, but I have said this for the sake of the crowd standing here, so that they may believe that you sent me." When he had said this, he cried with a loud voice, "Lazarus, come out!" The dead man came out, his hands and feet bound with strips of cloth, and his face wrapped in a cloth. Jesus said to them, "Unbind him, and let him go."

Many of the Jews therefore, who had come with Mary and had seen what Jesus did, believed in him.

Notice what you think and feel as you read the Gospel.

Jesus did nothing by chance. He proclaims himself to be the resurrection and the life, and he proves it by raising Lazarus, already dead four days. Why does this event so move Jesus to tears?

Pray as you are led for yourself and others.

"Jesus, you experienced the loss of family and loved ones. Death may be natural in this life, but it has no place in your kingdom. I praise you, for you give everlasting life to those who believe in you . . ." (Continue in your own words.)

Listen to Jesus.

You see how difficult it is for some to believe. Let me strengthen your faith in me. If you want that, open your heart to me now. What else is Jesus saying to you?

Ask God to show you how to live today.

"Thank you for strengthening me in faith, hope, and love. Make me an instrument of your peace today. Amen."

Tuesday, March 15, 2016

Know that God is present with you and ready to converse.

"Jesus, Son of the Father, I rejoice in your presence. Let me know you in your Word."

Read the Gospel: John 8:21–30.

Again Jesus said to them, "I am going away, and you will search for me, but you will die in your sin. Where I am going, you cannot come." Then the Jews said, "Is he going to kill himself? Is that what he means by saying, 'Where I am going, you cannot come'?" He said to them, "You are from below, I am from above; you are of this world, I am not of this world. I told you that you would die in your sins, for you will die in your sins unless you believe that I am he." They said to him, "Who are you?" Jesus said to them, "Why do I speak to you at all? I have much to say about you and much to condemn; but the one who sent me is true, and I declare to the world what I have heard from him." They did not understand that he was speaking to them about the Father. So Jesus said, "When you have lifted up the Son of Man, then you will realize that I am he, and that I do nothing on my own, but I speak these things as the Father instructed me. And the one who sent me is with me; he has not left me alone, for I always do what is pleasing to him." As he was saying these things, many believed in him.

Notice what you think and feel as you read the Gospel.

Jesus, who always did what was pleasing to his Father, declares that his message has been the same since the beginning of his ministry. He now prophesies to the ones who doubt him that they will know that "I am he" when they have "lifted up the Son of Man."

Pray as you are led for yourself and others.

"Brave Jesus, you speak of the power of the cross. The shame of crucifixion you would transform to glory, salvation, and life. Your own would recognize you there . . ." (Continue in your own words.)

Listen to Jesus.

I came to the world to reconcile humankind to God. I am joyful for each one who believes in me and receives my salvation. I am happy in you, dear disciple. What else is Jesus saying to you?

Ask God to show you how to live today.

"Jesus, I have many choices today. I begin by choosing you. Be with me in all my choices. Amen."

Wednesday, March 16, 2016

Know that God is present with you and ready to converse.

"Your words are truth and life, Lord. I turn to you now."

Read the Gospel: John 8:31–42.

Then Jesus said to the Jews who had believed in him, "If you continue in my word, you are truly my disciples; and you will know the truth, and the truth will make you free." They answered him, "We are descendants of Abraham and have never been slaves to anyone. What do you mean by saying, 'You will be made free'?"

Jesus answered them, "Very truly, I tell you, everyone who commits sin is a slave to sin. The slave does not have a permanent place in the household; the son has a place there forever. So if the Son makes you free, you will be free indeed. I know that you are descendants of Abraham; yet you look for an opportunity to kill me, because there is no place in you for my word. I declare what I have seen in the Father's presence; as for you, you should do what you have heard from the Father."

They answered him, "Abraham is our father." Jesus said to them, "If you were Abraham's children, you would be doing what Abraham did, but now you are trying to kill me, a man who has told you the truth that I heard from God. This is not what Abraham did. You are indeed doing what your father does." They said to him, "We are not illegitimate children; we have one father, God himself." Jesus said to them, "If God were your Father, you would love me, for I came from God and now I am here. I did not come on my own, but he sent me."

Notice what you think and feel as you read the Gospel.

"If you continue in my word," Jesus says, "you are truly my disciples." We will know the truth, and it will make us free. Why do so many not hear him?

Pray as you are led for yourself and others.

"Jesus, I seek to do my part to continue in your word. Teach me the truth, all that you have for me, and make me free to do God's will, as you did . . ." (Continue in your own words.)

Listen to Jesus.

You are right to seek me here in the Gospels and in prayer. I share with you truth that will bless you and bear fruit all your life. What else is Jesus saying to you?

Ask God to show you how to live today.

"Lord, I place my whole self and my whole day into your care. Show me ways I can care for others. Amen."

Thursday, March 17, 2016
Saint Patrick, bishop

Know that God is present with you and ready to converse.

"Eternal Word of the Father, I sit at your feet. I will hear and keep your Word."

Read the Gospel: John 8:51–59.

Jesus said, "Very truly, I tell you, whoever keeps my word will never see death." The Jews said to him, "Now we know that you have a demon. Abraham died, and so did the prophets; yet you say, 'Whoever keeps my word will never taste death.' Are you greater than our father Abraham, who died? The prophets also died. Who do you claim to be?" Jesus answered, "If I glorify myself, my glory is nothing. It is my Father who glorifies me, he of whom you say, 'He is our God,' though you do not know him. But I know him; if I would say that I do not know him, I would be a liar like you. But I do know him and I keep his word. Your ancestor Abraham rejoiced that he would see my day; he saw it and was glad." Then the Jews said to him, "You are not yet fifty years old, and have you seen Abraham?" Jesus said to them, "Very truly, I tell you, before Abraham was, I am." So they picked up stones to throw at him, but Jesus hid himself and went out of the Temple.

Notice what you think and feel as you read the Gospel.

Jesus says that if anyone keeps his word, that one will not taste death. He redefines life. He reveals God. And those who hear him scorn him and want to kill him.

Pray as you are led for yourself and others.

"Jesus, help me to understand, believe, and keep your word, for I want to live forever. I want to be close to God . . ." (Continue in your own words.)

Listen to Jesus.

It is not so difficult, my child. I draw you into my life with love and truth. Where else would you go? What else is Jesus saying to you?

Ask God to show you how to live today.

"I have fears, Jesus, but I have no one but you. Let me walk in your word today, for my good and the good of others. Amen."

Friday, March 18, 2016

Know that God is present with you and ready to converse.

"Lord, you are good to extend your glory to me, even now as I prepare to converse with you."

Read the Gospel: John 10:31–42.

The Jews took up stones again to stone him. Jesus replied, "I have shown you many good works from the Father. For which of these are you going to stone me?" The Jews answered, "It is not for a good work that we are going to stone you, but for blasphemy, because you, though only a human being, are making yourself God." Jesus answered, "Is it not written in your law, 'I said, you are gods'? If those to whom the word of God came were called 'gods'—and the scripture cannot be annulled—can you say that the one whom the Father has sanctified and sent into the world is blaspheming because I said, 'I am God's Son'? If I am not doing the works of my Father, then do not believe me. But if I do them, even though you do not believe me, believe the works, so that you may know and understand that the Father is in me and I am in the Father." Then they tried to arrest him again, but he escaped from their hands.

He went away again across the Jordan to the place where John had been baptizing earlier, and he remained there. Many came to him, and they were saying, "John performed no sign, but everything that John said about this man was true." And many believed in him there.

Notice what you think and feel as you read the Gospel.

Jesus continues to assert that he is one with the Father and does the works of his Father. They want to stone him or arrest him, but somehow he slips through their fingers, as he has done before. His time has not yet come. Many come to him and believe in him.

Pray as you are led for yourself and others.

"Jesus, I believe in you. I thank the Father for sending you. Where would the world be without you?" (Continue in your own words.)

Listen to Jesus.

I am the light of the world, but some choose to remain in darkness. Do not judge them, but love them. I give you the power of my love. What else is Jesus saying to you?

Ask God to show you how to live today.

"Sometimes I am frustrated that I cannot do more, dear Jesus. Show me ways that I can reflect your light and your love today. Amen."

Saturday, March 19, 2016
Saint Joseph, husband of Mary

Know that God is present with you and ready to converse.

"Master of the universe, I glorify you. You are with me now. Guide me in your perfect way."

Read the Gospel: Matthew 1:16, 18–21, 24a.

And Jacob was the father of Joseph the husband of Mary, of whom Jesus was born, who is called the Messiah. . . .

Now the birth of Jesus the Messiah took place in this way. When his mother Mary had been engaged to Joseph, but before they lived together, she was found to be with child from the Holy Spirit. Her husband, Joseph, being a righteous man and unwilling to expose her to public disgrace, planned to dismiss her quietly. But just when he had resolved to do this, an angel of the Lord appeared to him in a dream and said, "Joseph, son of David, do not be afraid to take Mary as your wife, for the child conceived in her is from the Holy Spirit. She will bear a son, and you are to name him Jesus, for he will save his people from their sins." . . .

When Joseph awoke from sleep, he did as the angel of the Lord commanded him.

Notice what you think and feel as you read the Gospel.

Joseph receives the message from the angel and changes his plans. He stays with Mary and waits for the birth of Jesus, the Savior of the world.

Pray as you are led for yourself and others.

"Joseph, you are a just and wise man. You obeyed God. Let me do as you did. Pray for me . . ." (Continue in your own words.)

Listen to Jesus.

We honor Joseph, friend, because he did the will of God. To be like him, surrender yourself to the will of God. I will show you how. What else is Jesus saying to you?

Ask God to show you how to live today.

"Give me wisdom, Lord. Give me power to act simply and decisively in doing the will of God today and every day of my life. Amen."

Sunday, March 20, 2016
Palm Sunday

Know that God is present with you and ready to converse.

When Jesus entered Jerusalem for the last time, he rode on a borrowed colt, and he humbled himself to receive honor from the people. The people welcoming him did not know that he had come to suffer and die there, but Jesus knew.

When you are ready, begin by joining the crowds praising Jesus: "Blessed is the King who comes in the name of the Lord. Glory in the highest."

Read the Gospel: Luke 19:28–40.

After Jesus had said this, he went on ahead, going up to Jerusalem.

When he had come near Bethphage and Bethany, at the place called the Mount of Olives, he sent two of the disciples, saying, "Go into the village ahead of you, and as you enter it you will find tied there a colt that has never been ridden. Untie it and bring it here. If anyone asks you, 'Why are you untying it?' just say this: 'The Lord needs it.'" So those who were sent departed and found it as he had told them. As they were untying the colt, its owners asked them, "Why are you untying the colt?" They said, "The Lord needs it." Then they brought it to Jesus; and after throwing their cloaks on the colt, they set Jesus on it. As he rode along, people kept spreading their cloaks on the road. As he was now approaching the path down from the Mount of Olives, the whole multitude of the disciples began to praise God joyfully with a loud voice for all the deeds of power that they had seen, saying,

"Blessed is the king
    who comes in the name of the Lord!
Peace in heaven,
    and glory in the highest heaven!"

Some of the Pharisees in the crowd said to him, "Teacher, order your disciples to stop." He answered, "I tell you, if these were silent, the stones would shout out."

Notice what you think and feel as you read the Gospel.

Lord, your kingdom and your glory come into the real world in simple ways, as you come into Jerusalem on a borrowed colt. The multitude rejoice and sing your praises, for if they don't the very stones will cry out.

Pray as you are led for yourself and others.

"Let me praise you, too, good Savior, as you head in ironic triumph toward your passion and death in Jerusalem . . ." (Continue in your own words.)

Listen to Jesus.

I did all out of love for the multitudes, and for love of you, child. I did not seek praise or blame in this world, but I sought only to do my Father's will. What else is Jesus saying to you?

Ask God to show you how to live today.

"How may I learn from you today, Lord? How may I follow you? Amen."

Monday, March 21, 2016

Know that God is present with you and ready to converse.

"Spirit of the Lord, you were present with Jesus, and you are present with Jesus now. Thank you for your presence with me as I read God's Word."

Read the Gospel: Luke 4:16–21.

When Jesus came to Nazareth, where he had been brought up, he went to the synagogue on the Sabbath day, as was his custom. He stood up to read, and the scroll of the prophet Isaiah was given to him. He unrolled the scroll and found the place where it was written:

> "The Spirit of the Lord is upon me,
> because he has anointed me
> to bring good news to the poor.
> He has sent me to proclaim release to the captives
> and recovery of sight to the blind,
> to let the oppressed go free,
> to proclaim the year of the Lord's favor."

And he rolled up the scroll, gave it back to the attendant, and sat down. The eyes of all in the synagogue were fixed on him. Then he began to say to them, "Today this scripture has been fulfilled in your hearing."

Notice what you think and feel as you read the Gospel.

Jesus, you announce yourself before the synagogue in your hometown as the being the One who fulfills the messianic prophesies of Isaiah. The people know you and your parents. What do they think?

Pray as you are led for yourself and others.

"Lord, I sometimes lack understanding of your Word and your ways. Let the Spirit enlighten me that I may serve you better . . ." (Continue in your own words.)

Listen to Jesus.

Practice patience, my child. Quiet yourself before me. I have things to tell you that I want you to know. What else is Jesus saying to you?

Ask God to show you how to live today.

"Thank you for your consoling words, Lord. Let me stay with you and learn from you all day. Amen."

Tuesday, March 22, 2016

Know that God is present with you and ready to converse.

"When I seek you, Lord, you are already found. You work in my heart."

Read the Gospel: John 13:21–33, 36–38.

After saying this Jesus was troubled in spirit, and declared, "Very truly, I tell you, one of you will betray me." The disciples looked at one another, uncertain of whom he was speaking. One of his disciples—the one whom Jesus loved—was reclining next to him; Simon Peter therefore motioned to him to ask Jesus of whom he was speaking. So while reclining next to Jesus, he asked him, "Lord, who is it?" Jesus answered, "It is the one to whom I give this piece of bread when I have dipped it in the dish." So when he had dipped the piece of bread, he gave it to Judas son of Simon Iscariot. After he received the piece of bread, Satan entered into him. Jesus said to him, "Do quickly what you are going to do." Now no one at the table knew why he said this to him. Some thought that, because Judas had the common purse, Jesus was telling him, "Buy what we need for the festival"; or that he should give something to the poor. So, after receiving the piece of bread, he immediately went out. And it was night.

When he had gone out, Jesus said, "Now the Son of Man has been glorified, and God has been glorified in him. If God has been glorified in him, God will also glorify him in himself and will glorify him at once. Little children, I am with you only a little longer. You will look for me; and as I said to the Jews so now I say to you, 'Where I am going, you cannot come.'" . . .

Simon Peter said to him, "Lord, where are you going?" Jesus answered, "Where I am going, you cannot follow me now; but you will follow afterward." Peter said to him, "Lord, why can I not follow you now? I will lay down my life for you." Jesus answered, "Will you lay down your life for me? Very truly, I tell you, before the cock crows, you will have denied me three times."

Notice what you think and feel as you read the Gospel.

When John lies close to the heart of Jesus, the Lord speaks to him secretly about his betrayal by Judas. The other disciples misunderstand. Jesus also identifies the one who would soon deny him three times: Simon Peter.

Pray as you are led for yourself and others.

"I want to be your beloved disciple, lie close to your heart, and hear your secret words just for me. Lord, let me follow you even to death and never deny you . . ." (Continue in your own words.)

Listen to Jesus.

You are my beloved disciple, and I speak to you in secret. Do not be afraid of what is coming. Stay here with me. I will tell you what to do. What else is Jesus saying to you?

Ask God to show you how to live today.

"I resolve to stay close to you, gentle Savior. For how else can I keep your commandments to love God and others with all my heart? Amen."

Wednesday, March 23, 2016

Know that God is present with you and ready to converse.

"You spent that last Passover with your friends, even the one who would betray you. Spend time with me now, Jesus, and teach me by your Word."

Read the Gospel: Matthew 26:14–25.

Then one of the Twelve, who was called Judas Iscariot, went to the chief priests and said, "What will you give me if I betray him to you?" They paid him thirty pieces of silver. And from that moment he began to look for an opportunity to betray him.

On the first day of Unleavened Bread the disciples came to Jesus, saying, "Where do you want us to make the preparations for you to eat the Passover?" He said, "Go into the city to a certain man, and say to him, 'The Teacher says, my time is near; I will keep the Passover at your house with my disciples.'" So the disciples did as Jesus had directed them, and they prepared the Passover meal.

When it was evening, he took his place with the Twelve; and while they were eating, he said, "Truly I tell you, one of you will betray me." And they became greatly distressed and began to say to him one after another, "Surely not I, Lord?" He answered, "The one who has dipped his hand into the bowl with me will betray me. The Son of Man goes as it is written of him, but woe to that one by whom the Son of Man is betrayed! It would have been better for that one not to have been born." Judas, who betrayed him, said, "Surely not I, Rabbi?" He replied, "You have said so."

Notice what you think and feel as you read the Gospel.

Was Judas motivated by thirty pieces of silver? Was he pretending to believe in Jesus all along? Was Jesus able to get through to him? Judas acted by his own choice.

Pray as you are led for yourself and others.

"There are mysteries in your Word, Lord. There are mysteries in my life. Evil is a mystery. But I choose good. I choose you . . ." (Continue in your own words.)

Listen to Jesus.

Pray for those who do evil. All things are possible with God, even the salvation of sinners. What else is Jesus saying to you?

Ask God to show you how to live today.

"Dear Lord and Savior, I need you all day long, your love and your wisdom. Thank you. Amen."

Thursday, March 24, 2016
Holy Thursday

Know that God is present with you and ready to converse.

"Teacher and Lord, I am ready to learn from you today."

Read the Gospel: John 13:1–15.

Now before the festival of the Passover, Jesus knew that his hour had come to depart from this world and go to the Father. Having loved his own who were in the world, he loved them to the end. The devil had already put it into the heart of Judas son of Simon Iscariot to betray him. And during supper Jesus, knowing that the Father had given all things into his hands, and that he had come from God and was going to God, got up from the table, took off his outer robe, and tied a towel around himself. Then he poured water into a basin and began to wash the disciples' feet and to wipe them with the towel that was tied around him. He came to Simon Peter, who said to him, "Lord, are you going to wash my feet?" Jesus answered, "You do not know now what I am doing, but later you will understand." Peter said to him, "You will never wash my feet." Jesus answered, "Unless I wash you, you have no share with me." Simon Peter said to him, "Lord, not my feet only but also my hands and my head!" Jesus said to him, "One who has bathed does not need to wash, except for the feet, but is entirely clean. And you are clean, though not all of you." For he knew who was to betray him; for this reason he said, "Not all of you are clean."

After he had washed their feet, had put on his robe, and had returned to the table, he said to them, "Do you know what I have done to you? You call me Teacher and Lord—and you are right, for that is what I am. So if I, your Lord and Teacher, have washed your feet, you also ought to wash one another's feet. For I have set you an example, that you also should do as I have done to you."

Notice what you think and feel as you read the Gospel.

Facing a horrible death, Jesus thinks about his friends and gives them a great life lesson in humble service of others. Jesus' love and goodness overwhelms me.

Pray as you are led for yourself and others.

"Wash me, Lord, so that I may be clean, and let me also serve others—friends and enemies—that I may be like you, my Teacher and Lord . . ." (Continue in your own words.)

Listen to Jesus.

You understand me, dear student. I love to show you myself. I would love you to do the works that I do. What else is Jesus saying to you?

Ask God to show you how to live today.

"Jesus, it would give me great pleasure to do your works and to do them as you would have me do them. Show your simple child what to do to be like you. Amen."

Friday, March 25, 2016
Good Friday

Know that God is present with you and ready to converse.

"Father, as I read this epic account of the Lord's passion and death, open my eyes to the gift of your love."

Read the Gospel: John 18:1–19:42.

After Jesus had spoken these words, he went out with his disciples across the Kidron valley to a place where there was a garden, which he and his disciples entered. Now Judas, who betrayed him, also knew the place, because Jesus often met there with his disciples. So Judas brought a detachment of soldiers together with police from the chief priests and the Pharisees, and they came there with lanterns and torches and weapons. Then Jesus, knowing all that was to happen to him, came forward and asked them, "Whom are you looking for?" They answered, "Jesus of Nazareth." Jesus replied, "I am he." Judas, who betrayed him, was standing with them. When Jesus said to them, "I am he," they stepped back and fell to the ground. Again he asked them, "Whom are you looking for?" And they said, "Jesus of Nazareth." Jesus answered, "I told you that I am he. So if you are looking for me, let these men go." This was to fulfill the word that he had spoken, "I did not lose a single one of those whom you gave me." Then Simon Peter, who had a sword, drew it, struck the high priest's slave, and cut off his right ear. The slave's name was Malchus. Jesus said to Peter, "Put your sword back into its sheath. Am I not to drink the cup that the Father has given me?"

So the soldiers, their officer, and the Jewish police arrested Jesus and bound him. First they took him to Annas, who was the father-in-law of Caiaphas, the high priest that year. Caiaphas was the one who had advised the Jews that it was better to have one person die for the people.

Simon Peter and another disciple followed Jesus. Since that disciple was known to the high priest, he went with Jesus into the courtyard of the high priest, but Peter was standing outside at the gate. So the other disciple, who was known to the high priest, went out, spoke to the woman who guarded the gate, and brought Peter in. The woman said to Peter, "You are not also one of this man's disciples, are you?" He said, "I am not." Now the slaves and the police had made a charcoal fire because it was cold, and they were standing around it and warming themselves. Peter also was standing with them and warming himself.

Then the high priest questioned Jesus about his disciples and about his teaching. Jesus answered, "I have spoken openly to the world; I have always taught in synagogues and in the Temple, where all the Jews come together. I have said nothing in secret. Why do you ask me? Ask those who heard what I said to them; they know what I said." When he had said this, one of the police standing nearby struck Jesus on the face, saying, "Is that how you answer the high priest?" Jesus answered, "If I have spoken wrongly, testify to the wrong. But if I have spoken rightly, why do you strike me?" Then Annas sent him bound to Caiaphas the high priest.

Now Simon Peter was standing and warming himself. They asked him, "You are not also one of his disciples, are you?" He denied it and said, "I am not." One of the slaves of the high priest, a relative of the man whose ear Peter had cut off, asked, "Did I not see you in the garden with him?" Again Peter denied it, and at that moment the cock crowed.

Then they took Jesus from Caiaphas to Pilate's headquarters. It was early in the morning. They themselves did not enter the headquarters, so as to avoid ritual defilement and to be able to eat the Passover. So Pilate went out to them and said, "What accusation do you bring against this man?" They answered, "If this man were not a criminal, we would not have handed him over to you." Pilate said to them, "Take him yourselves and judge him according to your law." The Jews replied, "We are not permitted to put anyone to death." (This was to fulfill what Jesus had said when he indicated the kind of death he was to die.)

Then Pilate entered the headquarters again, summoned Jesus, and asked him, "Are you the King of the Jews?" Jesus answered, "Do you ask this on your own, or did others tell you about me?" Pilate replied, "I am not a Jew, am I? Your own nation and the chief priests have handed you over to me. What have you done?" Jesus answered, "My kingdom is not from this world. If my kingdom were from this world, my followers would be fighting to keep me from being handed over to the Jews. But as it is, my kingdom is not from here." Pilate asked him, "So you are a king?" Jesus answered, "You say that I am a king. For this I was born, and for this I came into the world, to testify to the truth. Everyone who belongs to the truth listens to my voice." Pilate asked him, "What is truth?"

After he had said this, he went out to the Jews again and told them, "I find no case against him. But you have a custom that I release someone for you at the Passover. Do you want me to release for you the King of the Jews?" They shouted in reply, "Not this man, but Barabbas!" Now Barabbas was a bandit.

Then Pilate took Jesus and had him flogged. And the soldiers wove a crown of thorns and put it on his head, and they dressed him in a purple robe. They kept coming up to him, saying, "Hail, King of the Jews!" and striking him on the face. Pilate went out again and said to them, "Look, I am bringing him out to you to let you know that I find no case against him." So Jesus came out, wearing the crown of thorns and the purple robe. Pilate said to them, "Here is the man!" When the chief priests and the police saw him, they shouted, "Crucify him! Crucify him!" Pilate said to them, "Take him yourselves and crucify him; I find no case against him." The Jews answered him, "We have a law, and according to that law he ought to die because he has claimed to be the Son of God."

Now when Pilate heard this, he was more afraid than ever. He entered his headquarters again and asked Jesus, "Where are you from?" But Jesus gave him no answer. Pilate therefore said to him, "Do you refuse to speak to me? Do you not know that I have power to release you, and power to crucify you?" Jesus answered him, "You would have no power over me unless it had been given you from above; therefore the one who handed me over to you is guilty of a greater sin." From then on Pilate tried to release him, but the Jews cried out, "If you release this man, you are no friend of the emperor. Everyone who claims to be a king sets himself against the emperor."

When Pilate heard these words, he brought Jesus outside and sat on the judge's bench at a place called the Stone Pavement, or in Hebrew Gabbatha. Now it was the day of preparation for the Passover; and it was about noon. He said to the Jews, "Here is your king!" They cried out, "Away with him! Away with him! Crucify him!" Pilate asked them, "Shall I crucify your king?" The chief priests answered, "We have no king but the emperor." Then he handed him over to them to be crucified.

So they took Jesus; and carrying the cross by himself, he went out to what is called the Place of the Skull, which in Hebrew is called Golgotha. There they crucified him, and with him two others, one on either side, with Jesus between them. Pilate also had an inscription written and put on the cross. It read, "Jesus of Nazareth, the King of the Jews." Many of the Jews read this inscription, because the place where Jesus was crucified was near the city; and it was written in Hebrew, in Latin, and in Greek. Then the chief priests of the Jews said to Pilate, "Do not write, 'The King of the Jews,' but, 'This man said, I am King of the Jews.'" Pilate answered, "What I have written I have written." When the soldiers had crucified Jesus, they took his clothes and divided them into four parts, one for each soldier. They also took his tunic; now the tunic was seamless, woven in one piece from the top. So they said to one another, "Let us not tear it, but cast lots for it to see who will get it." This was to fulfill what the scripture says,

"They divided my clothes among themselves,
and for my clothing they cast lots."

And that is what the soldiers did.

Meanwhile, standing near the cross of Jesus were his mother, and his mother's sister, Mary the wife of Clopas, and Mary Magdalene. When Jesus saw his mother and the disciple whom he loved standing beside her, he said to his mother, "Woman, here is your son." Then he said to the disciple, "Here is your mother." And from that hour the disciple took her into his own home.

After this, when Jesus knew that all was now finished, he said (in order to fulfill the scripture), "I am thirsty." A jar full of sour wine was standing there. So they put a sponge full of the wine on a branch of hyssop and held it to his mouth. When Jesus had received the wine, he said, "It is finished." Then he bowed his head and gave up his spirit.

Since it was the day of preparation, the Jews did not want the bodies left on the cross during the Sabbath, especially because that Sabbath was a day of great solemnity. So they asked Pilate to have the legs of the crucified men broken and the bodies removed. Then the soldiers came and broke the legs of the first and of the other who had been crucified with him. But when they came to Jesus and saw that he was already dead, they did not break his legs. Instead, one of the soldiers pierced his side with a spear, and at once blood and water came out. (He who saw this has testified so that you also may believe. His testimony is true, and he knows that he tells the truth.) These things occurred so that the scripture might be fulfilled, "None of his bones shall be broken." And again another passage of scripture says, "They will look on the one whom they have pierced."

After these things, Joseph of Arimathea, who was a disciple of Jesus, though a secret one because of his fear of the Jews, asked Pilate to let him take away the body of Jesus. Pilate gave him permission; so he came and removed his body. Nicodemus, who had at first come to Jesus by night, also came, bringing a mixture of myrrh and aloes, weighing about a hundred pounds. They took the body of Jesus and wrapped it with the spices in linen cloths, according to the burial custom of the Jews. Now there was a garden in the place where he was crucified, and in the garden there was a new tomb in which no one had ever been laid. And so, because it was the Jewish day of preparation, and the tomb was nearby, they laid Jesus there.

Notice what you think and feel as you read the Gospel.

This is the narrative of your passion, Jesus. I empathize with every painful detail, and I love you for taking on the sins of the world. You say to Pilate, "Everyone who is of the truth hears my voice."

Pray as you are led for yourself and others.

"I need to hear your voice, Jesus. May your words in this Gospel give me courage and wisdom when I, too, have a cross to carry or suffering to bear. Lamb of God, have mercy on me . . ." (Continue in your own words.)

Listen to Jesus.

You do console me, beloved disciple. Do you know that I would have gone to my death for you alone? Follow me. What else is Jesus saying to you?

Ask God to show you how to live today.

"The great saints follow you, Lord. I am just myself. Please take me by the hand and help me to do your will. Amen."

Saturday, March 26, 2016
Easter Vigil

Know that God is present with you and ready to converse.

"Rise up in victory, strong Son of God. Let me attend to your Word."

Read the Gospel: Luke 24:1–12.

But on the first day of the week, at early dawn, the women came to the tomb, taking the spices that they had prepared. They found the stone rolled away from the tomb, but when they went in, they did not find the body. While they were perplexed about this, suddenly two men in dazzling clothes stood beside them. The women were terrified and bowed their faces to the ground, but the men said to them, "Why do you look for the living among the dead? He is not here, but has risen. Remember how he told you, while he was still in Galilee, that the Son of Man must be handed over to sinners, and be crucified, and on the third day rise again." Then they remembered his words, and returning from the tomb, they told all this to the eleven and to all the rest. Now it was Mary Magdalene, Joanna, Mary the mother of James, and the other women with them who told this to the apostles. But these words seemed to them an idle tale, and they did not believe them. But Peter got up and ran to the tomb; stooping and looking in, he saw the linen cloths by themselves; then he went home, amazed at what had happened.

Notice what you think and feel as you read the Gospel.

The eleven do not believe the report of the three women after they find the tomb empty and hear the explanation of the two angels. Peter runs to the tomb and confirms that it is empty, and he goes home wondering.

Pray as you are led for yourself and others.

"Jesus, I know the rest of the story, which Peter cannot know. He wonders what this could mean. You would reveal the Resurrection to him later. Reveal it also to me, so I can share in your victory . . ." (Continue in your own words.)

Listen to Jesus.

This was my work, my sign, my glory, that I would take on the sins of the whole world, be put to death, and rise again. Now God is near to all. My kingdom is forever. Whoever will, let him or her come to me. What else is Jesus saying to you?

Ask God to show you how to live today.

"I glorify you, Lord, along with the billions of your redeemed throughout the ages. Stay with us, Lord, to the end. I thank you. Give me gratitude in true recognition of your glory. Amen."

Sunday, March 27, 2016
Easter Sunday

Know that God is present with you and ready to converse.

After Jesus' brutal execution and burial, the disciples discover the empty tomb. They are slow to believe. We recognize the weakness of our own faith, but we know, too, that faith comes by hearing the Word of God.

When you are ready, invite Jesus to reveal himself to you by his Word: "Alleluia. You are risen from the dead. Come into my heart, Lord. Come into my life."

Read the Gospel: John 20:1–9.

Early on the first day of the week, while it was still dark, Mary Magdalene came to the tomb and saw that the stone had been removed from the tomb. So she ran and went to Simon Peter and the other disciple, the one whom Jesus loved, and said to them, "They have taken the Lord out of the tomb, and we do not know where they have laid him." Then Peter and the other disciple set out and went toward the tomb. The two were running together, but the other disciple outran Peter and reached the tomb first. He bent down to look in and saw the linen wrappings lying there, but he did not go in. Then Simon Peter came, following him, and went into the tomb. He saw the linen wrappings lying there, and the cloth that had been on Jesus' head, not lying with the linen wrappings but rolled up in a place by itself. Then the other disciple, who reached the tomb first, also went in, and he saw and believed; for as yet they did not understand the scripture, that he must rise from the dead.

Notice what you think and feel as you read the Gospel.

Finally the disciples Peter and John see the empty tomb. What did they believe? How could anyone take in the fact of Jesus being raised from the dead?

Pray as you are led for yourself and others.

"Lord, I, too, can be slow to faith. Your resurrection was the most amazing event of all time. I pray for those who doubt your resurrection. Let them see the truth . . ." (Continue in your own words.)

Listen to Jesus.

I have shown the power of God to all people, though some choose not to believe it. You do. You are my beloved disciple. I welcome you into my kingdom of life, love, peace, and joy forever. What else is Jesus saying to you?

Ask God to show you how to live today.

"Lord, you do so much for me. How may I serve others in the same spirit, today, tomorrow, and for my whole life? Amen."

The Easter Season

INTRODUCTION

Easter is the greatest feast of the Church year because it celebrates the victory of Jesus Christ over sin and death, a victory not just for himself but for all who believe in him. Jesus is the pioneer who leads us into eternal life. "Just as in Adam all die," wrote St. Paul, "so in Christ all will come to life again . . . Christ the first fruits and then, at his coming, all those who belong to him" (1 Cor 15:22–23). In the risen Christ, we are reconciled with God now and forever.

Our hearts and minds may wonder at the great mystery of resurrection. In the Gospels, we read how the disciples received the amazing news that Jesus is not dead but lives. At first many of them are skeptical, but they come to believe as Jesus shows himself to them again and again. For modern readers, their skepticism turning to faith helps us to believe in this greatest of all miracles.

The season ends with Pentecost, the descent of the Holy Spirit to empower the disciples of Jesus to carry on his great work. The Spirit is given to us, too, as is the work. Let us pray the Gospels of this season with joy and thanksgiving.

Monday, March 28, 2016

Know that God is present with you and ready to converse.

"I praise you for meeting me here, resurrected Lord, in your Word."

Read the Gospel: Matthew 28:8–15.

The women left the tomb quickly with fear and great joy, and ran to tell Jesus' disciples the angel's message. Suddenly Jesus met them and said, "Greetings!" And they came to him, took hold of his feet, and worshiped him. Then Jesus said to them, "Do not be afraid; go and tell my brothers to go to Galilee; there they will see me."

While they were going, some of the guard went into the city and told the chief priests everything that had happened. After the priests had assembled with the elders, they devised a plan to give a large sum of money to the soldiers, telling them, "You must say, 'His disciples came by night and stole him away while we were asleep.' If this comes to the governor's ears, we will satisfy him and keep you out of trouble." So they took the money and did as they were directed. And this story is still told among the Jews to this day.

Notice what you think and feel as you read the Gospel.

Jesus says "hail" to the women who have left the empty tomb. They know him, fall at his feet, and worship him with great joy. What else do you see in this passage?

Pray as you are led for yourself and others.

"Jesus, I fall at your feet. I believe you are risen from the dead regardless of what others may say, for you are here with me. What do you want me to do?" (Continue in your own words.)

Listen to Jesus.

I want you to tell others how much we love one another. Do not be afraid of ridicule or rejection. What else is Jesus saying to you?

Ask God to show you how to live today.

"Lord, I ask you to give me opportunities today to speak of you. Let your Holy Spirit speak through me. Amen."

Tuesday, March 29, 2016

Know that God is present with you and ready to converse.

"Lord, you call me by name. Let me recognize you present with me now."

Read the Gospel: John 20:11–18.

But Mary stood weeping outside the tomb. As she wept, she bent over to look into the tomb; and she saw two angels in white, sitting where the body of Jesus had been lying, one at the head and the other at the feet. They said to her, "Woman, why are you weeping?" She said to them, "They have taken away my Lord, and I do not know where they have laid him." When she had said this, she turned around and saw Jesus standing there, but she did not know that it was Jesus. Jesus said to her, "Woman, why are you weeping? Whom are you looking for?" Supposing him to be the gardener, she said to him, "Sir, if you have carried him away, tell me where you have laid him, and I will take him away." Jesus said to her, "Mary!" She turned and said to him in Hebrew, "Rabbouni!" (which means teacher). Jesus said to her, "Do not hold on to me, because I have not yet ascended to the Father. But go to my brothers and say to them, 'I am ascending to my Father and your Father, to my God and your God.'" Mary Magdalene went and announced to the disciples, "I have seen the Lord"; and she told them that he had said these things to her.

Notice what you think and feel as you read the Gospel.

Mary Magdalene experiences many emotions in this short scene. Weeping at the empty tomb, she turns around and sees Jesus without recognizing him. What happens next?

Pray as you are led for yourself and others.

"Jesus, your Father is my Father, your God is my God, and I will go where you are, for you have taken away my sin . . ." (Continue in your own words.)

Listen to Jesus.

Beloved, seek me in tears and seek me in joy. I am with you. We are together forever. What else is Jesus saying to you?

Ask God to show you how to live today.

"Mary obeyed you in carrying your message to the disciples. How may I obey you today? Amen."

Wednesday, March 30, 2016

Know that God is present with you and ready to converse.

"Lord, sometimes my eyes do not recognize you. Then I discover with joy that you are here."

Read the Gospel: Luke 24:13–35.

Now on that same day two of them were going to a village called Emmaus, about seven miles from Jerusalem, and talking with each other about all these things that had happened. While they were talking and discussing, Jesus himself came near and went with them, but their eyes were kept from recognizing him. And he said to them, "What are you discussing with each other while you walk along?" They stood still, looking sad. Then one of them, whose name was Cleopas, answered him, "Are you the only stranger in Jerusalem who does not know the things that have taken place there in these days?" He asked them, "What things?" They replied, "The things about Jesus of Nazareth, who was a prophet mighty in deed and word before God and all the people, and how our chief priests and leaders handed him over to be condemned to death and crucified him. But we had hoped that he was the one to redeem Israel. Yes, and besides all this, it is now the third day since these things took place. Moreover, some women of our group astounded us. They were at the tomb early this morning, and when they did not find his body there, they came back and told us that they had indeed seen a vision of angels who said that he was alive. Some of those who were with us went to the tomb and found it just as the women had said; but they did not see him." Then he said to them, "Oh, how foolish you are, and how slow of heart to believe all that the prophets have declared! Was it not necessary that the Messiah should suffer these things and then enter into his glory?" Then beginning with Moses and all the prophets, he interpreted to them the things about himself in all the scriptures.

As they came near the village to which they were going, he walked ahead as if he were going on. But they urged him strongly, saying, "Stay with us, because it is almost evening and the day is now nearly over." So he went in to stay with them. When he was at the table with them, he took bread, blessed and broke it, and gave it to them. Then their eyes were opened, and they recognized him; and he vanished from their sight. They said to each other, "Were not our hearts burning within us while he was talking to us on the road, while he was opening the scriptures to us?" That same hour they got up and returned to Jerusalem; and they found the eleven and their companions gathered together.

They were saying, "The Lord has risen indeed, and he has appeared to Simon!" Then they told what had happened on the road, and how he had been made known to them in the breaking of the bread.

Notice what you think and feel as you read the Gospel.

The risen Jesus is making himself known to his disciples. He falls in step with two who are leaving Jerusalem sad, for they had hoped Jesus would be the one to redeem Israel. He chastises them for not believing the scriptures, and he shows them how the prophets speak of him. But they have yet to recognize him . . .

Pray as you are led for yourself and others.

"Jesus, continue to reveal yourself to me by your Word. I am slow of heart to believe. I rejoice that, through suffering, you entered into glory . . ." (Continue in your own words.)

Listen to Jesus.

Look around, friend. I am in everything, waiting for you. What else is Jesus saying to you?

Ask God to show you how to live today.

"Let my heart burn within me as I ponder your Word and your presence today. Guide me to do acts of love. Amen."

Thursday, March 31, 2016

Know that God is present with you and ready to converse.

"You are here, Lord, giving me your peace and joy by your Word."

Read the Gospel: Luke 24:35–48.

Then the two disciples told what had happened on the road, and how Jesus had been made known to them in the breaking of the bread.

While they were talking about this, Jesus himself stood among them and said to them, "Peace be with you." They were startled and terrified, and thought that they were seeing a ghost. He said to them, "Why are you frightened, and why do doubts arise in your hearts? Look at my hands and my feet; see that it is I myself. Touch me and see; for a ghost does not have flesh and bones as you see that I have." And when he had said this, he showed them his hands and his feet. While in their joy they were disbelieving and still wondering, he said to them, "Have you anything here to eat?" They gave him a piece of broiled fish, and he took it and ate in their presence.

Then he said to them, "These are my words that I spoke to you while I was still with you—that everything written about me in the law of Moses, the prophets, and the psalms must be fulfilled." Then he opened their minds to understand the scriptures, and he said to them, "Thus it is written, that the Messiah is to suffer and to rise from the dead on the third day, and that repentance and forgiveness of sins is to be proclaimed in his name to all nations, beginning from Jerusalem. You are witnesses of these things."

Notice what you think and feel as you read the Gospel.

First the disciples think Jesus is a ghost. Then they disbelieve him for joy. Meanwhile Jesus eats a piece of fish and explains succinctly the meaning of his life, death, and resurrection. What does he say?

Pray as you are led for yourself and others.

"Sometimes I wonder what your plans are for me for the day ahead and for my whole life. If I seek to stay close to you, will you lead me all the way?" (Continue in your own words.)

Listen to Jesus.

You are mine, beloved disciple. I have given you people to love and care for. Do it with all your heart. What else is Jesus saying to you?

Ask God to show you how to live today.

"Help me do everything with your love and by your grace day by day. Amen."

Friday, April 1, 2016

Know that God is present with you and ready to converse.

"Your Word is food for me, Lord. Let me eat what you have prepared for me."

Read the Gospel: John 21:1–14.

Jesus showed himself again to the disciples by the Sea of Tiberias; and he showed himself in this way. Gathered there together were Simon Peter, Thomas called the Twin, Nathanael of Cana in Galilee, the sons of Zebedee, and two others of his disciples. Simon Peter said to them, "I am going fishing." They said to him, "We will go with you." They went out and got into the boat, but that night they caught nothing.

Just after daybreak, Jesus stood on the beach; but the disciples did not know that it was Jesus. Jesus said to them, "Children, you have no fish, have you?" They answered him, "No." He said to them, "Cast the net to the right side of the boat, and you will find some." So they cast it, and now they were not able to haul it in because there were so many fish. That disciple whom Jesus loved said to Peter, "It is the Lord!" When Simon Peter heard that it was the Lord, he put on some clothes, for he was naked, and jumped into the sea. But the other disciples came in the boat, dragging the net full of fish, for they were not far from the land, only about a hundred yards off.

When they had gone ashore, they saw a charcoal fire there, with fish on it, and bread. Jesus said to them, "Bring some of the fish that you have just caught." So Simon Peter went aboard and hauled the net ashore, full of large fish, a hundred fifty-three of them; and though there were so many, the net was not torn. Jesus said to them, "Come and have breakfast." Now none of the disciples dared to ask him, "Who are you?" because they knew it was the Lord. Jesus came and took the bread and gave it to them, and did the same with the fish. This was now the third time that Jesus appeared to the disciples after he was raised from the dead.

Notice what you think and feel as you read the Gospel.

After three appearances, the disciples are starting to recognize the risen Jesus. He tells them how to fish and rewards their obedience. This man who washed their feet at the Last Supper now makes them breakfast on the beach.

Pray as you are led for yourself and others.

"What kind of man are you, Jesus? You are God, good and gentle among us. How may I serve you?" (Continue in your own words.)

Listen to Jesus.

Keep our moments close to you all day, dear servant. Draw strength from our love as you show love to others. What else is Jesus saying to you?

Ask God to show you how to live today.

"Show me where to fish, Lord. Help me obey you. Amen."

Saturday, April 2, 2016

Know that God is present with you and ready to converse.

"Banish all my unbelief and hardness of heart, Lord, and speak to me now."

Read the Gospel: Mark 16:9–15.

Now after he rose early on the first day of the week, Jesus appeared first to Mary Magdalene, from whom he had cast out seven demons. She went out and told those who had been with him, while they were mourning and weeping. But when they heard that he was alive and had been seen by her, they would not believe it.

After this he appeared in another form to two of them, as they were walking into the country. And they went back and told the rest, but they did not believe them.

Later he appeared to the eleven themselves as they were sitting at the table; and he upbraided them for their lack of faith and stubbornness, because they had not believed those who saw him after he had risen. And he said to them, "Go into all the world and proclaim the good news to the whole creation."

Notice what you think and feel as you read the Gospel.

The disciples are full of unbelief, even after the risen Jesus appears to them several times. These are the people to whom he gives the order to go into all the world to preach the Gospel.

Pray as you are led for yourself and others.

"You use frail human beings to do your work, Lord. Let me do my part . . ." (Continue in your own words.)

Listen to Jesus.

You are where I want you, beloved. I give you power to do what I want you to do. What are you afraid of? What else is Jesus saying to you?

Ask God to show you how to live today.

"Keep my eyes on the path that leads to you, Lord. Remain in my heart. Amen."

Sunday, April 3, 2016
Second Sunday of Easter

Know that God is present with you and ready to converse.

After his resurrection, the Lord appeared to his disciples many times and in many ways. Gradually they came to believe that he had been raised from the dead.

The light of Christ can dawn gradually upon us, too. When you are ready, open yourself to the light of the eternal Word of the Father: "You do not need my invitation to be here with me now, Lord. Let your bright Word dispel the darkness of my doubts."

Read the Gospel: John 20:19–31.

When it was evening on that day, the first day of the week, and the doors of the house where the disciples had met were locked for fear of the Jews, Jesus came and stood among them and said, "Peace be with you." After he said this, he showed them his hands and his side. Then the disciples rejoiced when they saw the Lord. Jesus said to them again, "Peace be with you. As the Father has sent me, so I send you." When he had said this, he breathed on them and said to them, "Receive the Holy Spirit. If you forgive the sins of any, they are forgiven them; if you retain the sins of any, they are retained."

But Thomas (who was called the Twin), one of the Twelve, was not with them when Jesus came. So the other disciples told him, "We have seen the Lord." But he said to them, "Unless I see the mark of the nails in his hands, and put my finger in the mark of the nails and my hand in his side, I will not believe."

A week later his disciples were again in the house, and Thomas was with them. Although the doors were shut, Jesus came and stood among them and said, "Peace be with you." Then he said to Thomas, "Put your finger here and see my hands. Reach out your hand and put it in my side. Do not doubt but believe." Thomas answered him, "My Lord and my God!" Jesus said to him, "Have you believed because you have seen me? Blessed are those who have not seen and yet have come to believe."

Now Jesus did many other signs in the presence of his disciples, which are not written in this book. But these are written so that you may come to believe that Jesus is the Messiah, the Son of God, and that through believing you may have life in his name.

Notice what you think and feel as you read the Gospel.

Jesus breathes on the disciples and says, "Receive the Holy Spirit." Later Jesus commands skeptical Thomas to put his finger into the wounds of his hands. Thomas proclaims, "My Lord and my God!"

Pray as you are led for yourself and others.

"Jesus, I claim your blessing upon those who have not seen you in your resurrected flesh but still believe in you. I believe in you. I need you to speak to me . . ." (Continue in your own words.)

Listen to Jesus.

What troubles you today, child? How may I help you? What else is Jesus saying to you?

Ask God to show you how to live today.

"Breathe your Holy Spirit upon me, Jesus. Show me how to work in your Spirit today. Amen."

Monday, April 4, 2016
The Annunciation of the Lord

Know that God is present with you and ready to converse.

"Lord, I give you myself today, to hear you and to obey."

Read the Gospel: Luke 1:26–38.

In the sixth month the angel Gabriel was sent by God to a town in Galilee called Nazareth, to a virgin engaged to a man whose name was Joseph, of the house of David. The virgin's name was Mary. And he came to her and said, "Greetings, favored one! The Lord is with you." But she was much perplexed by his words and pondered what sort of greeting this might be. The angel said to her, "Do not be afraid, Mary, for you have found favor with God. And now, you will conceive in your womb and bear a son, and you will name him Jesus. He will be great, and will be called the Son of the Most High, and the Lord God will give to him the throne of his ancestor David. He will reign over the house of Jacob forever, and of his kingdom there will be no end." Mary said to the angel, "How can this be, since I am a virgin?" The angel said to her, "The Holy Spirit will come upon you, and the power of the Most High will overshadow you; therefore the child to be born will be holy; he will be called Son of God. And now, your relative Elizabeth in her old age has also conceived a son; and this is the sixth month for her who was said to be barren. For nothing will be impossible with God." Then Mary said, "Here am I, the servant of the Lord; let it be with me according to your word." Then the angel departed from her.

Notice what you think and feel as you read the Gospel.

Mary considers in her mind what the angel says, and then she listens to the mighty prophesy about her Son. She has already given herself to God, so she beautifully says, "Let it be with me according to your word."

Pray as you are led for yourself and others.

"Let your plans for me be my plans, Lord, for I want to please you as Mary did. I know I can trust you in all matters . . ." (Continue in your own words.)

Listen to Jesus.

You can trust me, child. Give yourself to God each day. Look to God in large matters and small. What else is Jesus saying to you?

Ask God to show you how to live today.

"Lord, let it be to me according to your word. Amen."

Tuesday, April 5, 2016

Know that God is present with you and ready to converse.

"Let your Spirit stir within me, Lord. Your servant is listening."

Read the Gospel: John 3:7b–15.

Jesus said, "'You must be born from above.' The wind blows where it chooses, and you hear the sound of it, but you do not know where it comes from or where it goes. So it is with everyone who is born of the Spirit." Nicodemus said to him, "How can these things be?" Jesus answered him, "Are you a teacher of Israel, and yet you do not understand these things?

"Very truly, I tell you, we speak of what we know and testify to what we have seen; yet you do not receive our testimony. If I have told you about earthly things and you do not believe, how can you believe if I tell you about heavenly things? No one has ascended into heaven except the one who descended from heaven, the Son of Man. And just as Moses lifted up the serpent in the wilderness, so must the Son of Man be lifted up, that whoever believes in him may have eternal life."

Notice what you think and feel as you read the Gospel.

Jesus is talking to an earnest Pharisee named Nicodemus about spiritual rebirth. He says that rebirth comes by faith in him.

Pray as you are led for yourself and others.

"Lord, continuously renew your life within me. I want to walk in newness of life. I pray for the faith of those you have given me . . ." (Continue in your own words.)

Listen to Jesus.

I grant your prayers, beloved. You are mine. And so are those you have given to me in your prayer. What else is Jesus saying to you?

Ask God to show you how to live today.

"Let me do all things aware of your presence today. I love you, my God. Amen."

Wednesday, April 6, 2016

Know that God is present with you and ready to converse.

"Light of God, Lord Jesus, shine on me by your Word."

Read the Gospel: John 3:16–21.

Jesus said, "For God so loved the world that he gave his only Son, so that everyone who believes in him may not perish but may have eternal life.

"Indeed, God did not send the Son into the world to condemn the world, but in order that the world might be saved through him. Those who believe in him are not condemned; but those who do not believe are condemned already, because they have not believed in the name of the only Son of God. And this is the judgment, that the light has come into the world, and people loved darkness rather than light because their deeds were evil. For all who do evil hate the light and do not come to the light, so that their deeds may not be exposed. But those who do what is true come to the light, so that it may be clearly seen that their deeds have been done in God."

Notice what you think and feel as you read the Gospel.

God starts with love in his plan of salvation, sending his Son to be the light of the world. He knows that some will not come to the light because they love darkness, because their deeds are evil.

Pray as you are led for yourself and others.

"Lord, I am sorry that I, too, have harbored darkness. Shine your light in every corner of my being, so that I may be enlightened, true, and clean . . ." (Continue in your own words.)

Listen to Jesus.

You have come to me with a sincere heart. I forgive you and will continue to forgive as you strive for holiness. What else is Jesus saying to you?

Ask God to show you how to live today.

"Now light my way, Lord, to walk in the path of truth and love. Amen."

Thursday, April 7, 2016

Know that God is present with you and ready to converse.

"You are always near, wonderful Lord. Let me receive your truth today and take it to my heart."

Read the Gospel: John 3:31–36.

The one who comes from above is above all; the one who is of the earth belongs to the earth and speaks about earthly things. The one who comes from heaven is above all. He testifies to what he has seen and heard, yet no one accepts his testimony. Whoever has accepted his testimony has certified this, that God is true. He whom God has sent speaks the words of God, for he gives the Spirit without measure. The Father loves the Son and has placed all things in his hands. Whoever believes in the Son has eternal life; whoever disobeys the Son will not see life, but must endure God's wrath.

Notice what you think and feel as you read the Gospel.

Jesus describes how he shares love, power, and truth with his Father. That is his authority. He has his life to give us. God is true.

Pray as you are led for yourself and others.

"Jesus, I worship you in the great Trinity of Father, Son, and Holy Spirit. I long to know you better . . ." (Continue in your own words.)

Listen to Jesus.

Surrender yourself to God's will, beloved. Look for God in all your circumstances and seek to do God's will. What else is Jesus saying to you?

Ask God to show you how to live today.

"True God of true God, guide me into all your truth and love. Amen."

Friday, April 8, 2016

Know that God is present with you and ready to converse.

"Let me eat the bread of life, Jesus, for you are present in your Word."

Read the Gospel: John 6:1–15.

Jesus went to the other side of the Sea of Galilee, also called the Sea of Tiberias. A large crowd kept following him, because they saw the signs that he was doing for the sick. Jesus went up the mountain and sat down there with his disciples. Now the Passover, the festival of the Jews, was near. When he looked up and saw a large crowd coming toward him, Jesus said to Philip, "Where are we to buy bread for these people to eat?" He said this to test him, for he himself knew what he was going to do. Philip answered him, "Six months' wages would not buy enough bread for each of them to get a little." One of his disciples, Andrew, Simon Peter's brother, said to him, "There is a boy here who has five barley loaves and two fish. But what are they among so many people?" Jesus said, "Make the people sit down." Now there was a great deal of grass in the place; so they sat down, about five thousand in all. Then Jesus took the loaves, and when he had given thanks, he distributed them to those who were seated; so also the fish, as much as they wanted. When they were satisfied, he told his disciples, "Gather up the fragments left over, so that nothing may be lost." So they gathered them up, and from the fragments of the five barley loaves, left by those who had eaten, they filled twelve baskets. When the people saw the sign that he had done, they began to say, "This is indeed the prophet who is to come into the world."

When Jesus realized that they were about to come and take him by force to make him king, he withdrew again to the mountain by himself.

Notice what you think and feel as you read the Gospel.

Jesus calmly offers thanks and multiplies the five loaves and two fish to feed five thousand people, many of whom he healed. I can understand why they wanted to make him king. They do not understand his mission.

Pray as you are led for yourself and others.

"I do not always understand what is happening in my life, Lord. Help me to find you in it, and lead me in your way . . ." (Continue in your own words.)

Listen to Jesus.

Do not worry, child. Trust me. Pray for those who need your prayers. Do good to those in need. What else is Jesus saying to you?

Ask God to show you how to live today.

"Lord, I am praying now. Give me your Spirit to do good at every opportunity. Thank you. Amen."

Saturday, April 9, 2016

Know that God is present with you and ready to converse.

"I am in your presence, Lord. What have I to fear?"

Read the Gospel: John 6:16–21.

When evening came, his disciples went down to the sea, got into a boat, and started across the sea to Capernaum. It was now dark, and Jesus had not yet come to them. The sea became rough because a strong wind was blowing. When they had rowed about three or four miles, they saw Jesus walking on the sea and coming near the boat, and they were terrified. But he said to them, "It is I; do not be afraid." Then they wanted to take him into the boat, and immediately the boat reached the land toward which they were going.

Notice what you think and feel as you read the Gospel.

How astonished his disciples must have been as they watched Jesus walking toward them on the stormy sea. More than that, they were frightened. He simply says, "It is I; do not be afraid." When he gets into the boat, they immediately arrive at their destination.

Pray as you are led for yourself and others.

"Jesus, come to me when I am in the storm. Save me, Lord, so that I can serve you and others. I think about whom I might help . . ." (Continue in your own words.)

Listen to Jesus.

Yes, beloved, look for ways you can help others. Think about their needs. What else is Jesus saying to you?

Ask God to show you how to live today.

"If you stay with me, Jesus, I can find ways to help others today. I rejoice that you are my companion on the journey. Amen."

Sunday, April 10, 2016
Third Sunday of Easter

Know that God is present with you and ready to converse.

Jesus called himself the bread of life, offering himself to us as food to sustain us on our journey. He feeds us so that we can feed others.

When you are ready, open your heart and your mind and invite the Lord to feed you: "Risen Lord, feed me by your Word, the living Word of God."

Read the Gospel: John 21:1–19.

Jesus showed himself again to the disciples by the Sea of Tiberias; and he showed himself in this way. Gathered there together were Simon Peter, Thomas called the Twin, Nathanael of Cana in Galilee, the sons of Zebedee, and two others of his disciples. Simon Peter said to them, "I am going fishing." They said to him, "We will go with you." They went out and got into the boat, but that night they caught nothing.

Just after daybreak, Jesus stood on the beach; but the disciples did not know that it was Jesus. Jesus said to them, "Children, you have no fish, have you?" They answered him, "No." He said to them, "Cast the net to the right side of the boat, and you will find some." So they cast it, and now they were not able to haul it in because there were so many fish. That disciple whom Jesus loved said to Peter, "It is the Lord!" When Simon Peter heard that it was the Lord, he put on some clothes, for he was naked, and jumped into the sea. But the other disciples came in the boat, dragging the net full of fish, for they were not far from the land, only about a hundred yards off.

When they had gone ashore, they saw a charcoal fire there, with fish on it, and bread. Jesus said to them, "Bring some of the fish that you have just caught." So Simon Peter went aboard and hauled the net ashore, full of large fish, a hundred fifty-three of them; and though there were so many, the net was not torn. Jesus said to them, "Come and have breakfast." Now none of the disciples dared to ask him, "Who are you?" because they knew it was the Lord. Jesus came and took the bread and gave it to them, and did the same with the fish. This was now the third time that Jesus appeared to the disciples after he was raised from the dead.

When they had finished breakfast, Jesus said to Simon Peter, "Simon son of John, do you love me more than these?" He said to him, "Yes, Lord; you know that I love you." Jesus said to him, "Feed my lambs." A second time he said to him, "Simon son of John, do you love me?" He said to him, "Yes, Lord; you know that I love you." Jesus said to him, "Tend my sheep." He said to him the third time, "Simon son of John, do you love me?" Peter felt hurt because he said to him the third time, "Do you love me?" And he said to him, "Lord, you know everything; you know that I love you." Jesus said to him, "Feed my sheep. Very truly, I tell you, when you were younger, you used to fasten your own belt and to go wherever you wished. But when you grow old, you will stretch out your hands, and someone else will fasten a belt around you and take you where you do not wish to go." (He said this to indicate the kind of death by which Peter would glorify God.) After this he said to him, "Follow me."

Notice what you think and feel as you read the Gospel.

In this and in other appearances of the resurrected Jesus, even his own disciples do not immediately recognize him. Why is that?

Pray as you are led for yourself and others.

"Jesus, let me come to you as Peter did, urgently, for you are my life and my food. How may I obey your command to Peter to feed your lambs and your sheep?" (Continue in your own words.)

Listen to Jesus.

Follow me, dear disciple. Together we will practice loving others. Who needs to be fed? What else is Jesus saying to you?

Ask God to show you how to live today.

"I will follow you anywhere you lead me, Lord, today and all my life. Amen."

Monday, April 11, 2016

Know that God is present with you and ready to converse.

"Glory to you, Lord, for you alone are the bread of our eternal salvation. You are present in your Word."

Read the Gospel: John 6:22–29.

The day after the feeding of the five thousand the crowd that had stayed on the other side of the sea saw that there had been only one boat there. They also saw that Jesus had not gotten into the boat with his disciples, but that his disciples had gone away alone. Then some boats from Tiberias came near the place where they had eaten the bread after the Lord had given thanks. So when the crowd saw that neither Jesus nor his disciples were there, they themselves got into the boats and went to Capernaum looking for Jesus.

When they found him on the other side of the sea, they said to him, "Rabbi, when did you come here?" Jesus answered them, "Very truly, I tell you, you are looking for me, not because you saw signs, but because you ate your fill of the loaves. Do not work for the food that perishes, but for the food that endures for eternal life, which the Son of Man will give you. For it is on him that God the Father has set his seal." Then they said to him, "What must we do to perform the works of God?" Jesus answered them, "This is the work of God, that you believe in him whom he has sent."

Notice what you think and feel as you read the Gospel.

When the crowd is surprised to find Jesus on the other side of the lake with his disciples, he does not take the opportunity to glorify himself by speaking of the miracle. He urges them instead to seek the food that endures to eternal life, not the bread that perishes.

Pray as you are led for yourself and others.

"Jesus, sometimes I make things that perish my priority and neglect the food that you give to me. Help me do whatever is best to grow in your love and serve others . . ." (Continue in your own words.)

Listen to Jesus.

The food I give you is faith and love as you abide in me. Draw close to me often. Ask me for virtues, and I will give them to you. What else is Jesus saying to you?

Ask God to show you how to live today.

"Show yourself to me today in the faces of others, in the beauty of nature, and in the circumstances of my life. Thank you, Lord. Amen."

Tuesday, April 12, 2016

Know that God is present with you and ready to converse.

"Lord, give me the life-giving bread from heaven today and always."

Read the Gospel: John 6:30–35.

They said to him, "What sign are you going to give us then, so that we may see it and believe you? What work are you performing? Our ancestors ate the manna in the wilderness; as it is written, 'He gave them bread from heaven to eat.'" Then Jesus said to them, "Very truly, I tell you, it was not Moses who gave you the bread from heaven, but it is my Father who gives you the true bread from heaven. For the bread of God is that which comes down from heaven and gives life to the world." They said to him, "Sir, give us this bread always."

Jesus said to them, "I am the bread of life. Whoever comes to me will never be hungry, and whoever believes in me will never be thirsty."

Notice what you think and feel as you read the Gospel.

"Lord, give us this bread always." Do you ever hunger for God? That hunger is God working in you.

Pray as you are led for yourself and others.

"You yourself are the true miracle of manna falling into our wilderness, Lord. You give life to the whole world. I pray for the world, Lord, that it may seek and find your life, your peace . . ." (Continue in your own words.)

Listen to Jesus.

My hunger is for all souls in the whole world. You understand my heart. I long to gather all people of all time into my eternal kingdom. What else is Jesus saying to you?

Ask God to show you how to live today.

"I pray for your Church, for evangelization. Guide us with your Spirit. I volunteer to help in any way I can. Amen."

Wednesday, April 13, 2016

Know that God is present with you and ready to converse.

"Lord, let me see you now and believe."

Read the Gospel: John 6:35–40.

Jesus said to them, "I am the bread of life. Whoever comes to me will never be hungry, and whoever believes in me will never be thirsty. But I said to you that you have seen me and yet do not believe. Everything that the Father gives me will come to me, and anyone who comes to me I will never drive away; for I have come down from heaven, not to do my own will, but the will of him who sent me. And this is the will of him who sent me, that I should lose nothing of all that he has given me, but raise it up on the last day. This is indeed the will of my Father, that all who see the Son and believe in him may have eternal life; and I will raise them up on the last day."

Notice what you think and feel as you read the Gospel.

Jesus says those who come to him have been given to him by the Father, and he will never cast any out. God's will is that he should lose none of those who believe in him, but raise them on the last day.

Pray as you are led for yourself and others.

"Thank you for these beautiful promises. Keep them alive in my heart and let them increase my faith . . ." (Continue in your own words.)

Listen to Jesus.

Our love is the most important thing in your life, dear child. I have much to give you. What else is Jesus saying to you?

Ask God to show you how to live today.

"Let me eat the bread of life every day, Jesus, to strengthen me for your service. You are the Word of the Father. Amen."

Thursday, April 14, 2016

Know that God is present with you and ready to converse.

"Teach me, Jesus, and give me life by your Word."

Read the Gospel: John 6:44–51.

Jesus said, "No one can come to me unless drawn by the Father who sent me; and I will raise that person up on the last day. It is written in the prophets, 'And they shall all be taught by God.' Everyone who has heard and learned from the Father comes to me. Not that anyone has seen the Father except the one who is from God; he has seen the Father. Very truly, I tell you, whoever believes has eternal life. I am the bread of life. Your ancestors ate the manna in the wilderness, and they died. This is the bread that comes down from heaven, so that one may eat of it and not die. I am the living bread that came down from heaven. Whoever eats of this bread will live forever; and the bread that I will give for the life of the world is my flesh."

Notice what you think and feel as you read the Gospel.

The bread that Jesus gives for the world is his flesh. Jesus states emphatically that to eat this bread, and to receive his life within, is to live forever.

Pray as you are led for yourself and others.

"Living bread of heaven, feed me again today. I long to hear your voice . . ." (Continue in your own words.)

Listen to Jesus.

I am caring for you in every way, beloved disciple, but my chief concern is your spiritual life. I want you to walk in the new life I give you every day. What else is Jesus saying to you?

Ask God to show you how to live today.

"What specific things may I do for you and for others today, my Jesus? I wait to be taught by you. Amen."

Friday, April 15, 2016

Know that God is present with you and ready to converse.

"Son of Man, your Word is you, and you are flesh and blood. Be my food."

Read the Gospel: John 6:52–59.

The Jews then disputed among themselves, saying, "How can this man give us his flesh to eat?" So Jesus said to them, "Very truly, I tell you, unless you eat the flesh of the Son of Man and drink his blood, you have no life in you. Those who eat my flesh and drink my blood have eternal life, and I will raise them up on the last day; for my flesh is true food and my blood is true drink. Those who eat my flesh and drink my blood abide in me, and I in them. Just as the living Father sent me, and I live because of the Father, so whoever eats me will live because of me. This is the bread that came down from heaven, not like that which your ancestors ate, and they died. But the one who eats this bread will live forever." He said these things while he was teaching in the synagogue at Capernaum.

Notice what you think and feel as you read the Gospel.

Jesus seems to be speaking literally about his flesh and blood being the food of eternal life. Food indeed; drink indeed! To eat and drink them is to abide in him. How do I receive these words?

Pray as you are led for yourself and others.

"Lord, I believe you give us your flesh and blood in the Eucharist by the sacrament of the Mass. This is the teaching of the Church, and your Word concurs. Let those who do not see this truth grow in understanding and find you in the Eucharist . . ." (Continue in your own words.)

Listen to Jesus.

Beloved, my flesh and blood is my gift to the Church, my Body. I am present in the sacrament, but believers may eat my flesh and drink my blood in other ways, for I am in all things. What else is Jesus saying to you?

Ask God to show you how to live today.

"How may I eat your flesh and drink your blood today, Lord? As you offer yourself to me, I offer myself to you for the good of others. Amen."

Saturday, April 16, 2016

Know that God is present with you and ready to converse.

"As you are present in your Word, Lord, you are present in the Eucharist. Let me understand that."

Read the Gospel: John 6:60–69.

When many of his disciples heard it, they said, "This teaching is difficult; who can accept it?" But Jesus, being aware that his disciples were complaining about it, said to them, "Does this offend you? Then what if you were to see the Son of Man ascending to where he was before?

It is the spirit that gives life; the flesh is useless. The words that I have spoken to you are spirit and life. But among you there are some who do not believe." For Jesus knew from the first who were the ones that did not believe, and who was the one that would betray him. And he said, "For this reason I have told you that no one can come to me unless it is granted by the Father."

Because of this many of his disciples turned back and no longer went about with him. So Jesus asked the Twelve, "Do you also wish to go away?" Simon Peter answered him, "Lord, to whom can we go? You have the words of eternal life. We have come to believe and know that you are the Holy One of God."

Notice what you think and feel as you read the Gospel.

Jesus speaks boldly, knowing some will abandon him because of his "hard saying." The Twelve stay. I rejoice in the words of Peter, who expresses my own heart: "Lord, to whom shall we go? You have the words of eternal life . . ."

Pray as you are led for yourself and others.

"Jesus, let those who are skeptical of your Eucharistic presence feed on your Word, to increase their understanding . . ." (Continue in your own words.)

Listen to Jesus.

Many follow me in different ways, based on their own cultures, personal experiences, and dispositions. These are my sheep. This is my Church, my Body. Love them. Seek peace. What else is Jesus saying to you?

Ask God to show you how to live today.

"Lord, I do not want to judge my brother or sister or to stand in my own rightness or righteousness. Give me a spirit of true unity with all who follow you. Amen."

Sunday, April 17, 2016
Fourth Sunday of Easter

Know that God is present with you and ready to converse.

Jesus is the Good Shepherd, and we are the sheep of his pasture. He cares for us. He seeks us when we stray and carries us back to the fold. We hear his voice and rejoice at his goodness.

When you are ready, ask the Good Shepherd to speak to you today: "Lord of all, let me hear your voice."

Read the Gospel: John 10:27–30.

Jesus said, "My sheep hear my voice. I know them, and they follow me. I give them eternal life, and they will never perish. No one will snatch them out of my hand. What my Father has given me is greater than all else, and no one can snatch it out of the Father's hand. The Father and I are one."

Notice what you think and feel as you read the Gospel.

Jesus says his sheep hear his voice, and we are absolutely secure in him. We have eternal life. How great a salvation!

Pray as you are led for yourself and others.

"Lord, I don't have to wait until later to know you and love you. You speak to me now. I ask you today . . ." (Continue in your own words.)

Listen to Jesus.

Pour out all your heart to me, dear friend. I understand. I make all the difference in your life. What else is Jesus saying to you?

Ask God to show you how to live today.

"When I am uncertain or afraid, Good Shepherd, lead me to safety, lead me to you. Amen."

Monday, April 18, 2016

Know that God is present with you and ready to converse.

"Lord, my shepherd, you are with me. I worship you in your Word."

Read the Gospel: John 10:1–10.

Jesus continued, "Very truly, I tell you, anyone who does not enter the sheepfold by the gate but climbs in by another way is a thief and a bandit. The one who enters by the gate is the shepherd of the sheep. The gatekeeper opens the gate for him, and the sheep hear his voice. He calls his own sheep by name and leads them out. When he has brought out all his own, he goes ahead of them, and the sheep follow him because they know his voice. They will not follow a stranger, but they will run from him because they do not know the voice of strangers." Jesus used this figure of speech with them, but they did not understand what he was saying to them.

So again Jesus said to them, "Very truly, I tell you, I am the gate for the sheep. All who came before me are thieves and bandits; but the sheep did not listen to them. I am the gate. Whoever enters by me will be saved, and will come in and go out and find pasture. The thief comes only to steal and kill and destroy. I came that they may have life, and have it abundantly."

Notice what you think and feel as you read the Gospel.

Jesus calls himself the shepherd and the true door to salvation. His sheep hear his voice and follow him. His sheep do not hear the voices of strangers or thieves, only his.

Pray as you are led for yourself and others.

"It is wonderful to hear your voice, Lord. Speak to me every day, for I have needs, and those I love have needs . . ." (Continue in your own words.)

Listen to Jesus.

Tell me what you need, and tell me about those you love. I care about them, too. What else is Jesus saying to you?

Ask God to show you how to live today.

"Lord, show me what I can do for others today. Fill me with your love. Amen."

Tuesday, April 19, 2016

Know that God is present with you and ready to converse.

"I believe in you, Lord, for I hear you in your Word. Praise to you, Lord Jesus Christ."

Read the Gospel: John 10:22–30.

At that time the festival of the Dedication took place in Jerusalem. It was winter, and Jesus was walking in the Temple, in the portico of Solomon. So the Jews gathered around him and said to him, "How long will you keep us in suspense? If you are the Messiah, tell us plainly." Jesus answered, "I have told you, and you do not believe. The works that I do in my Father's name testify to me; but you do not believe, because you do not belong to my sheep. My sheep hear my voice. I know them, and they follow me. I give them eternal life, and they will never perish. No one will snatch them out of my hand. What my Father has given me is greater than all else, and no one can snatch it out of the Father's hand. The Father and I are one."

Notice what you think and feel as you read the Gospel.

Jesus again affirms his relationship with the Father. They are one. Those who believe are his sheep, secure in his hand, unto everlasting life.

Pray as you are led for yourself and others.

"Lord, I follow you. I listen for your voice. I thank you for your constant care. I pray for many others . . ." (Continue in your own words.)

Listen to Jesus.

I am with you always, child. What do you fear? What may I do for you? What else is Jesus saying to you?

Ask God to show you how to live today.

"You are good to me, Lord. How may I be good to someone else today? Amen."

Wednesday, April 20, 2016

Know that God is present with you and ready to converse.

"I am here with you, Lord, to receive your sayings and to obey them."

Read the Gospel: John 12:44–50.

Then Jesus cried aloud: "Whoever believes in me believes not in me but in him who sent me. And whoever sees me sees him who sent me. I have come as light into the world, so that everyone who believes in me should not remain in the darkness. I do not judge anyone who hears my words and does not keep them, for I came not to judge the world, but to save the world. The one who rejects me and does not receive my word has a judge; on the last day the word that I have spoken will serve as judge, for I have not spoken on my own, but the Father who sent me has himself given me a commandment about what to say and what to speak. And I know that his commandment is eternal life. What I speak, therefore, I speak just as the Father has told me."

Notice what you think and feel as you read the Gospel.

Jesus' word is the judge of humanity on the last day. Jesus is obedient to his Father in saying what he says. He asks us to believe and keep his sayings, and we will walk in his light.

Pray as you are led for yourself and others.

"You speak of the last day, Lord. You speak of judgment. Let me hide in the safety of you, full of your light, glorifying God the Father, Son, and Holy Spirit . . ." (Continue in your own words.)

Listen to Jesus.

Nothing will harm you, my friend, for you are mine, given to me by my Father. Rest in me. What else is Jesus saying to you?

Ask God to show you how to live today.

"As you care for me, Jesus, let me care for others. Let me give others the peace and rest that you give to me. Amen."

Thursday, April 21, 2016

Know that God is present with you and ready to converse.

"Master, speak. Your servant is listening."

Read the Gospel: John 13:16–20.

Jesus said, "Very truly, I tell you, servants are not greater than their master, nor are messengers greater than the one who sent them. If you know these things, you are blessed if you do them. I am not speaking of all of you; I know whom I have chosen. But it is to fulfill the scripture, 'The one who ate my bread has lifted his heel against me.' I tell you this now, before it occurs, so that when it does occur, you may believe that I am he. Very truly, I tell you, whoever receives one whom I send receives me; and whoever receives me receives him who sent me."

Notice what you think and feel as you read the Gospel.

Jesus reminds his followers that they must do as he does, for even as their master he has been their servant. He says we are blessed if we do the things we have learned to do from him.

Pray as you are led for yourself and others.

"Let me receive you and those you send to me, for in receiving them, I receive God, even the Father who sent you . . ." (Continue in your own words.)

Listen to Jesus.

Open your heart to others, and I will come in. What else is Jesus saying to you?

Ask God to show you how to live today.

"Show me opportunities to receive others into my life, and help me to serve them with true love. Amen."

Friday, April 22, 2016

Know that God is present with you and ready to converse.

"Lord, you are my all in all. I am lost apart from you. Let me know your truth."

Read the Gospel: John 14:1–6.

Jesus taught, "Do not let your hearts be troubled. Believe in God, believe also in me. In my Father's house there are many dwelling places. If it were not so, would I have told you that I go to prepare a place for you? And if I go and prepare a place for you, I will come again and will take you to myself, so that where I am, there you may be also. And you know the way to the place where I am going." Thomas said to him, "Lord, we do not know where you are going. How can we know the way?" Jesus said to him, "I am the way, and the truth, and the life. No one comes to the Father except through me."

Notice what you think and feel as you read the Gospel.

Jesus tells his disciples not to be troubled. He is going away, but he will return to take them to his Father's house. He is the way, the truth, and the life.

Pray as you are led for yourself and others.

"I want to come to your Father's house, Jesus. What can I do to please you today?" (Continue in your own words.)

Listen to Jesus.

You please me by your faith, dear disciple. You please me by your willingness to serve. What else is Jesus saying to you?

Ask God to show you how to live today.

"Give me your eyes, Jesus, and your heart of love, so that I can serve you in others. Amen."

Saturday, April 23, 2016

Know that God is present with you and ready to converse.

"In the name of the Father, the Son, and the Holy Spirit, I stand before you, ready to pray, ready to hear your holy Word."

Read the Gospel: John 14:7–14.

Jesus said, "If you know me, you will know my Father also. From now on you do know him and have seen him."

Philip said to him, "Lord, show us the Father, and we will be satisfied." Jesus said to him, "Have I been with you all this time, Philip, and you still do not know me? Whoever has seen me has seen the Father. How can you say, 'Show us the Father'? Do you not believe that I am in the Father and the Father is in me? The words that I say to you I do not speak on my own; but the Father who dwells in me does his works. Believe me that I am in the Father and the Father is in me; but if you do not, then believe me because of the works themselves. Very truly, I tell you, the one who believes in me will also do the works that I do and, in fact, will do greater works than these, because I am going to the Father. I will do whatever you ask in my name, so that the Father may be glorified in the Son. If in my name you ask me for anything, I will do it."

Notice what you think and feel as you read the Gospel.

Jesus, who is one with the Father, declares that those who believe in him will do the works that he did, and greater, to the glory of the Father.

Pray as you are led for yourself and others.

"Jesus, I can do nothing without you working through me and in me. I cast all my brokenness and weakness upon you. Can you use it for your Father's glory?" (Continue in your own words.)

Listen to Jesus.

By giving yourself to me, your Lord and master, you allow me to work. Do not strive in your own strength, but let go. That is how you will bear fruit to my Father's glory. What else is Jesus saying to you?

Ask God to show you how to live today.

"Lord, I am so full of myself. Fill me with your Spirit instead, so that I may do the works that you did. Amen."

Sunday, April 24, 2016
Fifth Sunday of Easter

Know that God is present with you and ready to converse.

God's ways are perfect, and God wills only our good. Abandon yourself into God's love, and invite God to speak to you: "God of love, I glorify you. Give me your Spirit to hear and obey your Word."

Read the Gospel: John 13:31–33a, 34–35.

When he had gone out, Jesus said, "Now the Son of Man has been glorified, and God has been glorified in him. If God has been glorified in him, God will also glorify him in himself and will glorify him at once. Little children, I am with you only a little longer. . . . I give you a new commandment, that you love one another. Just as I have loved you, you also should love one another. By this everyone will know that you are my disciples, if you have love for one another."

Notice what you think and feel as you read the Gospel.

Jesus speaks for his Father, commanding us to love one another. This is the great sign to the world: that we love one another.

Pray as you are led for yourself and others.

"Lord, how your disciples often fall short of your commandment to love one another! I myself fall short. How can I learn to love all who follow you?" (Continue in your own words.)

Listen to Jesus.

Open your heart to my heart, beloved disciple, and I will teach you how to love your brothers and sisters. Put aside judging, show mercy, and humble yourself. What else is Jesus saying to you?

Ask God to show you how to live today.

"Lord, give me your heart of love for all who believe in you, and help me show it in my actions. Amen."

Monday, April 25, 2016
Saint Mark, evangelist

Know that God is present with you and ready to converse.

"Lord Jesus, seated at the right hand of God and present with me now, help me to hear your Word."

Read the Gospel: Mark 16:15–20.

And Jesus said to them, "Go into all the world and proclaim the good news to the whole creation. The one who believes and is baptized will be saved; but the one who does not believe will be condemned. And these signs will accompany those who believe: by using my name they will cast out demons; they will speak in new tongues; they will pick up snakes in their hands, and if they drink any deadly thing, it will not hurt them; they will lay their hands on the sick, and they will recover."

So then the Lord Jesus, after he had spoken to them, was taken up into heaven and sat down at the right hand of God. And they went out and proclaimed the good news everywhere, while the Lord worked with them and confirmed the message by the signs that accompanied it.

Notice what you think and feel as you read the Gospel.

When the disciples obey Jesus' directive to preach the Gospel, the Lord works with them, confirming their message by signs.

Pray as you are led for yourself and others.

"Lord, protect me and the ones you have given me—family, friends, coworkers, and strangers—and work with us. Give us strength to declare your Gospel and to live it . . ." (Continue in your own words.)

Listen to Jesus.

Do not be afraid, child. No one can hurt you, for you are mine. Entrust yourself and your loved ones to me. What else is Jesus saying to you?

Ask God to show you how to live today.

"I believe you are present in all things, Lord. Open my eyes to see you in new ways today, and let me praise you before others. Amen."

Tuesday, April 26, 2016

Know that God is present with you and ready to converse.

"In your peace, Lord Jesus, I rejoice that you are with your Father, whom you love. You are also here with me."

Read the Gospel: John 14:27–31a.

Jesus said, "Peace I leave with you; my peace I give to you. I do not give to you as the world gives. Do not let your hearts be troubled, and do not let them be afraid. You heard me say to you, 'I am going away, and I am coming to you.' If you loved me, you would rejoice that I am going to the Father, because the Father is greater than I. And now I have told you this before it occurs, so that when it does occur, you may believe. I will no longer talk much with you, for the ruler of this world is coming. He has no power over me; but I do as the Father has commanded me, so that the world may know that I love the Father."

Notice what you think and feel as you read the Gospel.

Jesus tells his disciples not to let their hearts be troubled. He will go away from them, but he will return. He is always obedient to the Father, and he is always doing what is best for his followers.

Pray as you are led for yourself and others.

"Loving Lord, you are with me even when I do not sense it. How may I obey you today?" (Continue in your own words.)

Listen to Jesus.

If you love me, beloved servant, rejoice, giving glory to God in all you do and say. For you share in God's great victory over sin and death. What else is Jesus saying to you?

Ask God to show you how to live today.

"Open my heart and my lips to offer you sincere praise, Lord. Amen."

Wednesday, April 27, 2016

Know that God is present with you and ready to converse.

"Jesus, true vine abiding with me, wash me by your Word and let me bear much fruit to the glory of your Father and my Father."

Read the Gospel: John 15:1–8.

Jesus taught, "I am the true vine, and my Father is the vine grower. He removes every branch in me that bears no fruit. Every branch that bears fruit he prunes to make it bear more fruit. You have already been cleansed by the word that I have spoken to you. Abide in me as I abide in you. Just as the branch cannot bear fruit by itself unless it abides in the vine, neither can you unless you abide in me. I am the vine, you are the branches. Those who abide in me and I in them bear much fruit, because apart from me you can do nothing. Whoever does not abide in me is thrown away like a branch and withers; such branches are gathered, thrown into the fire, and burned. If you abide in me, and my words abide in you, ask for whatever you wish, and it will be done for you. My Father is glorified by this, that you bear much fruit and become my disciples."

Notice what you think and feel as you read the Gospel.

Without Jesus, the true vine, we wither and die. Abiding in Jesus, we bear fruit, for the Father himself prunes the vines.

Pray as you are led for yourself and others.

"Lord, prune me, that I may bear much fruit. Give me faithfulness to continue to abide in Jesus and his Word. Give me wisdom to ask for what is best . . ." (Continue in your own words.)

Listen to Jesus.

In me you grow in holiness, child. Growing is a process. So is bearing fruit. Abide in patience, and you will bear fruit even without knowing it. What else is Jesus saying to you?

Ask God to show you how to live today.

"Jesus, show me a time and place today where I can rejoin you and abide awhile in your gentle presence. Teach me how to abide constantly in you. Amen."

Thursday, April 28, 2016

Know that God is present with you and ready to converse.

"Give me the joy of your presence, Lord, as I attend to your Word."

Read the Gospel: John 15:9–11.

Jesus instructed, "As the Father has loved me, so I have loved you; abide in my love. If you keep my commandments, you will abide in my love, just as I have kept my Father's commandments and abide in his love. I have said these things to you so that my joy may be in you, and that your joy may be complete."

Notice what you think and feel as you read the Gospel.

Jesus' motive is love, his message is love, and his commandment is love. All this from his Father, who is love. What comes of this love? Joy.

Pray as you are led for yourself and others.

"Jesus, you want God's best things for us: love and joy. By receiving and living in love and joy, I can do your will . . ." (Continue in your own words.)

Listen to Jesus.

Loving is a divine art, beloved. I give you the power to love not just those you love already but also those you do not love. Who is that? What else is Jesus saying to you?

Ask God to show you how to live today.

"Lord, open my eyes to your path of love and help me to walk down it in your joy. Amen."

Friday, April 29, 2016

Know that God is present with you and ready to converse.

"Word of love, you call me and speak to me. Let me hear you in the depths of my soul."

Read the Gospel: John 15:12–17.

Jesus taught, saying, "This is my commandment, that you love one another as I have loved you. No one has greater love than this, to lay down one's life for one's friends. You are my friends if you do what I command you. I do not call you servants any longer, because the servant does not know what the master is doing; but I have called you friends, because I have made known to you everything that I have heard from my Father. You did not choose me but I chose you. And I appointed you to go and bear fruit, fruit that will last, so that the Father will give you whatever you ask him in my name. I am giving you these commands so that you may love one another."

Notice what you think and feel as you read the Gospel.

We are not hired servants but chosen and beloved friends of the Lord, who reveals to us everything he has heard from his Father.

Pray as you are led for yourself and others.

"Jesus, you are good and true. You chose me to love and to bear fruit. I ask the Father in your name . . ." (Continue in your own words.)

Listen to Jesus.

Yes, you are my chosen friend. Come closer to me. What else is Jesus saying to you?

Ask God to show you how to live today.

"How may I show love to you and to others today, Lord? Amen."

Saturday, April 30, 2016

Know that God is present with you and ready to converse.

"Creator God, let me know you by your Word, your Son and my Savior, Jesus Christ."

Read the Gospel: John 15:18–21.

Jesus said, "If the world hates you, be aware that it hated me before it hated you. If you belonged to the world, the world would love you as its own. Because you do not belong to the world, but I have chosen you out of the world—therefore the world hates you. Remember the word that I said to you, 'Servants are not greater than their master.' If they persecuted me, they will persecute you; if they kept my word, they will keep yours also. But they will do all these things to you on account of my name, because they do not know him who sent me."

Notice what you think and feel as you read the Gospel.

Jesus explains that his followers will experience the same resistance and even persecution that he did, simply because of the faith we profess. We cannot expect to be treated better than our master was treated.

Pray as you are led for yourself and others.

"Jesus, your Word is true. I have known mockery and rejection because of you. Let me not fear it but bear it while loving those who persecute me . . ." (Continue in your own words.)

Listen to Jesus.

There are those who do not know God. But you do, and I am with you. I bring good for you and for others out of the suffering you receive because you follow me. What else is Jesus saying to you?

Ask God to show you how to live today.

"Send your Spirit to help me be brave, gentle, and loving when someone turns on me. Amen."

Sunday, May 1, 2016
Sixth Sunday of Easter

Know that God is present with you and ready to converse.

The Holy Spirit proceeds from the eternal Father and the eternal Son, and the three persons are one.

"Holy Spirit, counselor, teach me now by the mighty Word, who is Jesus."

Read the Gospel: John 14:23–29.

Jesus answered Judas (not Iscariot), "Those who love me will keep my word, and my Father will love them, and we will come to them and make our home with them. Whoever does not love me does not keep my words; and the word that you hear is not mine, but is from the Father who sent me.

"I have said these things to you while I am still with you. But the Advocate, the Holy Spirit, whom the Father will send in my name, will teach you everything, and remind you of all that I have said to you. Peace I leave with you; my peace I give to you. I do not give to you as the world gives. Do not let your hearts be troubled, and do not let them be afraid. You heard me say to you, 'I am going away, and I am coming to you.' If you loved me, you would rejoice that I am going to the Father, because the Father is greater than I. And now I have told you this before it occurs, so that when it does occur, you may believe."

Notice what you think and feel as you read the Gospel.

If we love Jesus, we will keep his word. The Father will love us; Jesus and his Father will make their home in us; and the Holy Spirit will teach us all things.

Pray as you are led for yourself and others.

"Jesus, your promise of God in us inspires awe. Help me to keep your word . . ." (Continue in your own words.)

Listen to Jesus.

I teach you the way of love, dear one. My word to you is true. Trust God and walk in my Spirit. What else is Jesus saying to you?

Ask God to show you how to live today.

"Lord, give me your grace, the mighty Spirit, to guide me in obedience to your great commandment of love. Amen."

Monday, May 2, 2016

Know that God is present with you and ready to converse.

"Spirit of truth, you are witness to the Son of God. I long to know him and love him with all my heart."

Read the Gospel: John 15:26–16:4a.

Jesus said, "When the Advocate comes, whom I will send to you from the Father, the Spirit of truth who comes from the Father, he will testify on my behalf. You also are to testify because you have been with me from the beginning.

"I have said these things to you to keep you from stumbling. They will put you out of the synagogues. Indeed, an hour is coming when those who kill you will think that by doing so they are offering worship to God. And they will do this because they have not known the Father or me. But I have said these things to you so that when their hour comes you may remember that I told you about them."

Notice what you think and feel as you read the Gospel.

The Spirit not only witnesses to Jesus but also enables us to do the same. We need the Holy Spirit to strengthen us against persecution.

Pray as you are led for yourself and others.

"Lord, I pray for Christians who are experiencing persecution today. Strengthen their faith. Let them know you are close to them . . ." (Continue in your own words.)

Listen to Jesus.

I hear your prayers, beloved disciple. In me you are a member of a great Body of love, of lovers, and all their suffering—our suffering—is redeemed. It is holy. What else is Jesus saying to you?

Ask God to show you how to live today.

"When I suffer, Lord, remind me to offer it up for the good of others, especially those who are persecuted. Amen."

Tuesday, May 3, 2016
Saints Philip and James, apostles

Know that God is present with you and ready to converse.

"Jesus, if you would go away from me, I would be sorrowful. But you are present by your Spirit now. Alleluia."

Read the Gospel: John 14:6–14.

Jesus said to Philip, "I am the way, and the truth, and the life. No one comes to the Father except through me. If you know me, you will know my Father also. From now on you do know him and have seen him."

Philip said to him, "Lord, show us the Father, and we will be satisfied." Jesus said to him, "Have I been with you all this time, Philip, and you still do not know me? Whoever has seen me has seen the Father. How can you say, 'Show us the Father'? Do you not believe that I am in the Father and the Father is in me? The words that I say to you I do not speak on my own; but the Father who dwells in me does his works. Believe me that I am in the Father and the Father is in me; but if you do not, then believe me because of the works themselves. Very truly, I tell you, the one who believes in me will also do the works that I do and, in fact, will do greater works than these, because I am going to the Father. I will do whatever you ask in my name, so that the Father may be glorified in the Son. If in my name you ask me for anything, I will do it."

Notice what you think and feel as you read the Gospel.

Jesus says the Spirit will prove the world wrong about sin, righteousness, and judgment. He also says he has many more things to say to us. The Spirit will declare them to us.

Pray as you are led for yourself and others.

"I am listening, Lord. I am happy to sit in the silence and await your voice . . ." (Continue in your own words.)

Listen to Jesus.

I am happy with you, too, child. You are mine. I want you to understand what the world cannot understand. What else is Jesus saying to you?

Ask God to show you how to live today.

"Lord, I want to live by your truth as well as hear it. I need your Spirit for that, too. Amen."

Wednesday, May 4, 2016

Know that God is present with you and ready to converse.

"Almighty Trinity of love, you pour yourself out for me. Let my prayer please you."

Read the Gospel: John 16:12–15.

Jesus said to his disciples, "I still have many things to say to you, but you cannot bear them now. When the Spirit of truth comes, he will guide you into all the truth; for he will not speak on his own, but will speak whatever he hears, and he will declare to you the things that are to come. He will glorify me, because he will take what is mine and declare it to you. All that the Father has is mine. For this reason I said that he will take what is mine and declare it to you."

Notice what you think and feel as you read the Gospel.

Jesus sends the Spirit, the Spirit speaks of what belongs to Jesus, and Jesus has all that the Father has. What perfect unity among the three persons of the Trinity!

Pray as you are led for yourself and others.

"By your Spirit, Lord, I can know God, for God is one . . ." (Continue in your own words.)

Listen to Jesus.

God loves you, for you have believed my words and you follow me. What else is Jesus saying to you?

Ask God to show you how to live today.

"How may I live in your presence today, Lord? How may I serve? Amen."

Thursday, May 5, 2016

Know that God is present with you and ready to converse.

"Lord, I am slow of mind and heart. Help me understand your Word."

Read the Gospel: John 16:16–20.

Jesus said, "A little while, and you will no longer see me, and again a little while, and you will see me." Then some of his disciples said to one another, "What does he mean by saying to us, 'A little while, and you will no longer see me, and again a little while, and you will see me'; and 'Because I am going to the Father'?" They said, "What does he mean by this 'a little while'? We do not know what he is talking about." Jesus knew that they wanted to ask him, so he said to them, "Are you discussing among yourselves what I meant when I said, 'A little while, and you will no longer see me, and again a little while, and you will see me'? Very truly, I tell you, you will weep and mourn, but the world will rejoice; you will have pain, but your pain will turn into joy."

Notice what you think and feel as you read the Gospel.

Like me, the disciples sometimes do not understand the words of Jesus. He speaks of realities they cannot comprehend, because he speaks what his Father wills him to speak.

Pray as you are led for yourself and others.

"Lord, you encourage me to ask anything of the Father in your name. I ask for . . ." (Continue in your own words.)

Listen to Jesus.

You are safe in God, beloved disciple. I want to show you how to walk in God's way. What else is Jesus saying to you?

Ask God to show you how to live today.

"Lord, we want the same things. Guide me in God's way today and every day. Amen."

Friday, May 6, 2016

Know that God is present with you and ready to converse.

"Lord, in my pain, in my joy, you are always near me. I love you."

Read the Gospel: John 16:20–23.

Jesus said, "Very truly, I tell you, you will weep and mourn, but the world will rejoice; you will have pain, but your pain will turn into joy. When a woman is in labor, she has pain, because her hour has come. But when her child is born, she no longer remembers the anguish because of the joy of having brought a human being into the world. So you have pain now; but I will see you again, and your hearts will rejoice, and no one will take your joy from you. On that day you will ask nothing of me. Very truly, I tell you, if you ask anything of the Father in my name, he will give it to you."

Notice what you think and feel as you read the Gospel.

Jesus describes the pain of his disciples as being meaningful, producing a good result, just as a woman in labor has pain with a joyful result.

Pray as you are led for yourself and others.

"Jesus, I have pain and suffering in my life. I offer it to you for the good of those who are in need . . ." (Continue in your own words.)

Listen to Jesus.

Offer to God your whole self, all the thoughts, words, deeds, joys, and sufferings of your day. This is the way of blessing. What else is Jesus saying to you?

Ask God to show you how to live today.

"Jesus, let me give you thanks for all my joys and sorrows, for all things that come to me from the hand of God for my good. Help me live with this attitude and awareness today. Amen."

Saturday, May 7, 2016

Know that God is present with you and ready to converse.

"Almighty Father, you and I are one as you are one with Jesus, the holy Word of God."

Read the Gospel: John 16:23b–28.

Jesus taught, "Very truly, I tell you, if you ask anything of the Father in my name, he will give it to you. Until now you have not asked for anything in my name. Ask and you will receive, so that your joy may be complete.

"I have said these things to you in figures of speech. The hour is coming when I will no longer speak to you in figures, but will tell you plainly of the Father. On that day you will ask in my name. I do not say to you that I will ask the Father on your behalf; for the Father himself loves you, because you have loved me and have believed that I came from God. I came from the Father and have come into the world; again, I am leaving the world and am going to the Father."

Notice what you think and feel as you read the Gospel.

Jesus removes himself as the mediator between his disciples and his Father. He declares to them that they themselves have immediate access to his Father. The Father loves them because they have loved Jesus.

Pray as you are led for yourself and others.

"Jesus, you are so much more than a Savior to us. You free us from sin and death, yes, but you open to us direct relationship with the Father. So we say, 'Our Father' . . ." (Continue in your own words.)

Listen to Jesus.

I want your joy to be complete, beloved disciple. Believe in me. Rest in our Father. What else is Jesus saying to you?

Ask God to show you how to live today.

"I am your student, Lord. Teach me your lessons throughout this day. Amen."

Sunday, May 8, 2016
The Ascension of the Lord

Know that God is present with you and ready to converse.

In his ascension, Jesus leaves his disciples and returns to his Father, knowing that he will send the Holy Spirit upon his disciples to continue his work, preaching the gospel of salvation by the blood of the cross.

When you are ready, open yourself to the Lord with words such as these: "I look to you, Lord Jesus, as I continue the work you have given me."

Read the Gospel: Luke 24:46–53.

Jesus said to the disciples, "Thus it is written, that the Messiah is to suffer and to rise from the dead on the third day, and that repentance and forgiveness of sins is to be proclaimed in his name to all nations, beginning from Jerusalem. You are witnesses of these things. And see, I am sending upon you what my Father promised; so stay here in the city until you have been clothed with power from on high."

Then he led them out as far as Bethany, and, lifting up his hands, he blessed them. While he was blessing them, he withdrew from them and was carried up into heaven. And they worshiped him, and returned to Jerusalem with great joy; and they were continually in the Temple blessing God.

Notice what you think and feel as you read the Gospel.

Jesus commissions his followers for the great work of evangelization, promising them the power of the Holy Spirit. Then he goes with them to Bethany, blesses them, and ascends to heaven. They joyfully return to Jerusalem.

Pray as you are led for yourself and others.

"Alleluia! What a happy moment, Lord, when you returned to your Father. Your disciples are joyful, too. I bless God with them . . ." (Continue in your own words.)

Listen to Jesus.

My friend, thank you for joining us in our joy. Joy is a strength that witnesses to me. What else is Jesus saying to you?

Ask God to show you how to live today.

"Lord, allow me to detach myself from my own emotions and join myself to the joy of God, blissful in the Trinity. This is my future. Help me to commiserate with others, too, in their joys and in their sorrows. Amen."

Monday, May 9, 2016

Know that God is present with you and ready to converse.

"All-knowing Lord of heaven and earth, I gladly turn to you today."

Read the Gospel: John 16:29–33.

Jesus' disciples said, "Yes, now you are speaking plainly, not in any figure of speech! Now we know that you know all things, and do not need to have anyone question you; by this we believe that you came from God." Jesus answered them, "Do you now believe? The hour is coming, indeed it has come, when you will be scattered, each one to his home, and you will leave me alone. Yet I am not alone because the Father is with me. I have said this to you, so that in me you may have peace. In the world you face persecution. But take courage; I have conquered the world!"

Notice what you think and feel as you read the Gospel.

The disciples believe that Jesus came from God. And yet, Jesus admonishes them, they will be scattered. "But be of good cheer; I have overcome the world."

Pray as you are led for yourself and others.

"Jesus, thank you for helping me to overcome the tribulations of this world. I ask you . . ." (Continue in your own words.)

Listen to Jesus.

We can work together, child, and do things the right way. Don't be afraid, and don't rely on yourself. Give it all to me. What else is Jesus saying to you?

Ask God to show you how to live today.

"Jesus, I give you all my troubles, my will, and my whole self. Work your will in me and through me. Amen."

Tuesday, May 10, 2016

Know that God is present with you and ready to converse.

"Glory and honor to you, Lord Jesus Christ. Thank you for being with me, right here and now."

Read the Gospel: John 17:1–11a.

After Jesus had spoken these words, he looked up to heaven and said, "Father, the hour has come; glorify your Son so that the Son may glorify you, since you have given him authority over all people, to give eternal life to all whom you have given him. And this is eternal life, that they may know you, the only true God, and Jesus Christ whom you have sent. I glorified you on earth by finishing the work that you gave me to do. So now, Father, glorify me in your own presence with the glory that I had in your presence before the world existed.

"I have made your name known to those whom you gave me from the world. They were yours, and you gave them to me, and they have kept your word. Now they know that everything you have given me is from you; for the words that you gave to me I have given to them, and they have received them and know in truth that I came from you; and they have believed that you sent me. I am asking on their behalf; I am not asking on behalf of the world, but on behalf of those whom you gave me, because they are yours. All mine are yours, and yours are mine; and I have been glorified in them. And now I am no longer in the world, but they are in the world, and I am coming to you."

Notice what you think and feel as you read the Gospel.

Jesus speaks of the glory he shared with his Father before the world was made. He also says he is glorified in those the Father has given him.

Pray as you are led for yourself and others.

"Jesus, be glorified in me! What shall I do today to bring glory to you and to the Father?" (Continue in your own words.)

Listen to Jesus.

Keep your eyes on me, child. Join me in loving our Father. All things good in your life come out of this love. What else is Jesus saying to you?

Ask God to show you how to live today.

"Jesus, I cannot love you enough. Show me how I can glorify you today. Amen."

Wednesday, May 11, 2016

Know that God is present with you and ready to converse.

"Word of truth, sanctify me."

Read the Gospel: John 17:11b–19.

Jesus prayed, "Holy Father, protect them in your name that you have given me, so that they may be one, as we are one. While I was with them, I protected them in your name that you have given me. I guarded them, and not one of them was lost except the one destined to be lost, so that the scripture might be fulfilled. But now I am coming to you, and I speak these things in the world so that they may have my joy made complete in themselves. I have given them your word, and the world has hated them because they do not belong to the world, just as I do not belong to the world. I am not asking you to take them out of the world, but I ask you to protect them from the evil one. They do not belong to the world, just as I do not belong to the world. Sanctify them in the truth; your word is truth. As you have sent me into the world, so I have sent them into the world. And for their sakes I sanctify myself, so that they also may be sanctified in truth."

Notice what you think and feel as you read the Gospel.

Jesus prays for his disciples. He asks his Father not to take them out of the world, but to keep them "in your name" that they may be one and have his joy fulfilled. He prays to the Father to "sanctify them in the truth; your word is truth."

Pray as you are led for yourself and others.

"Thank you for keeping me safe, Lord. I seek you in your holy Word. I long to be one with you and the Father . . ." (Continue in your own words.)

Listen to Jesus.

The words of scripture I spoke for you. I speak these words now for you, beloved. What else is Jesus saying to you?

Ask God to show you how to live today.

"How may I demonstrate oneness with others who love and serve you? Amen."

Thursday, May 12, 2016

Know that God is present with you and ready to converse.

"Jesus, you are with me now. I long to be where you are, beholding your glory."

Read the Gospel: John 17:20–26.

Jesus prayed, "I ask not only on behalf of these, but also on behalf of those who will believe in me through their word, that they may all be one. As you, Father, are in me and I am in you, may they also be in us, so that the world may believe that you have sent me. The glory that you have given me I have given them, so that they may be one, as we are one, I in them and you in me, that they may become completely one, so that the world may know that you have sent me and have loved them even as you have loved me. Father, I desire that those also, whom you have given me, may be with me where I am, to see my glory, which you have given me because you loved me before the foundation of the world.

"Righteous Father, the world does not know you, but I know you; and these know that you have sent me. I made your name known to them, and I will make it known, so that the love with which you have loved me may be in them, and I in them."

Notice what you think and feel as you read the Gospel.

Jesus prays earnestly for unity among his followers, for by this unity the world will know that the Father loves us just as he loves Jesus.

Pray as you are led for yourself and others.

"Lord, I am not worthy that you should enter under my roof, but you are here, full of love for me. How may I return your love?" (Continue in your own words.)

Listen to Jesus.

Love others as you love me, child. Who is difficult to love? Love that person. Do it for me. What else is Jesus saying to you?

Ask God to show you how to live today.

"If you stay with me, Jesus, I can obey you today. Stay with me, Lord. Amen."

Friday, May 13, 2016

Know that God is present with you and ready to converse.

"You are here with love in your Word, Jesus. I will follow you."

Read the Gospel: John 21:15–19.

When they had finished breakfast, Jesus said to Simon Peter, "Simon son of John, do you love me more than these?" He said to him, "Yes, Lord; you know that I love you." Jesus said to him, "Feed my lambs." A second time he said to him, "Simon son of John, do you love me?" He said to him, "Yes, Lord; you know that I love you." Jesus said to him, "Tend my sheep." He said to him the third time, "Simon son of John, do you love me?" Peter felt hurt because he said to him the third time, "Do you love me?" And he said to him, "Lord, you know everything; you know that I love you." Jesus said to him, "Feed my sheep. Very truly, I tell you, when you were younger, you used to fasten your own belt and to go wherever you wished. But when you grow old, you will stretch out your hands, and someone else will fasten a belt around you and take you where you do not wish to go." (He said this to indicate the kind of death by which he would glorify God.) After this he said to him, "Follow me."

Notice what you think and feel as you read the Gospel.

Jesus questions Peter's love. When Peter affirms it, Jesus tells him to "feed my lambs and feed my sheep." Then the Lord warns Peter of what is in store before saying, "Follow me."

Pray as you are led for yourself and others.

"Jesus, Peter loved you and fed your lambs and sheep. He followed you even to the point of suffering and dying on a cross. Let me take up my cross and follow you, loving and feeding your lambs and sheep . . ." (Continue in your own words.)

Listen to Jesus.

My way looks hard sometimes, child, but I am with you. Do what I put before you to do today. What else is Jesus saying to you?

Ask God to show you how to live today.

"Let me see others with your eyes and with your heart, Lord. I pray for that grace today and always. Amen."

Saturday, May 14, 2016
Saint Matthias, apostle

Know that God is present with you and ready to converse.

"You love me, Lord, in this place. You have the words of life for me now."

Read the Gospel: John 15:9–17.

Jesus said, "As the Father has loved me, so I have loved you; abide in my love. If you keep my commandments, you will abide in my love, just as I have kept my Father's commandments and abide in his love. I have said these things to you so that my joy may be in you, and that your joy may be complete.

"This is my commandment, that you love one another as I have loved you. No one has greater love than this, to lay down one's life for one's friends. You are my friends if you do what I command you. I do not call you servants any longer, because the servant does not know what the master is doing; but I have called you friends, because I have made known to you everything that I have heard from my Father. You did not choose me but I chose you. And I appointed you to go and bear fruit, fruit that will last, so that the Father will give you whatever you ask him in my name. I am giving you these commands so that you may love one another."

Notice what you think and feel as you read the Gospel.

Jesus tells his disciples to love one another, even to be willing to lay down their lives for others. As his friends, Jesus' disciples are to do what he has done in the world.

Pray as you are led for yourself and others.

"Lord, your message is clear. Am I ready to lay down my life for my friends? I seek to die to myself . . ." (Continue in your own words.)

Listen to Jesus.

Dying to yourself, letting go of yourself, will give you joy, friend. Let it be for love of others. What else is Jesus saying to you?

Ask God to show you how to live today.

"What shall I ask the Father in your name, Lord? Amen."

Sunday, May 15, 2016
Pentecost

Know that God is present with you and ready to converse.

As the apostles gather in the upper room, the Holy Spirit falls upon them in a mighty way. The Holy Spirit is the driving power of the Church and of all believers.

When you are ready to pray, speak to the Lord: "Breathe on me, Jesus, and I will rejoice in your Spirit."

Read the Gospel: John 20:19–23.

When it was evening on that day, the first day of the week, and the doors of the house where the disciples had met were locked for fear of the Jews, Jesus came and stood among them and said, "Peace be with you." After he said this, he showed them his hands and his side. Then the disciples rejoiced when they saw the Lord. Jesus said to them again, "Peace be with you. As the Father has sent me, so I send you." When he had said this, he breathed on them and said to them, "Receive the Holy Spirit. If you forgive the sins of any, they are forgiven them; if you retain the sins of any, they are retained."

Notice what you think and feel as you read the Gospel.

The risen Lord visits his disciples in the room where they are shut in for fear. He shows them his hands and his side. Then he gives them his peace and tells them he is sending them out as the Father had sent him.

Pray as you are led for yourself and others.

"Holy Spirit, enlighten and guide me to forgive the sins of any I have not forgiven . . ." (Continue in your own words.)

Listen to Jesus.

Forgiving is your participation in the work of God. It is the mark of those who follow me. What else is Jesus saying to you?

Ask God to show you how to live today.

"Let your Spirit remain with me today; send me out to do your will. Amen."

Ordinary Time

INTRODUCTION

The second period of Ordinary Time begins immediately following Pentecost. The Holy Spirit has fallen upon the disciples while they prayed in the upper room. For the disciples personally, Pentecost was an event even more transforming than Easter, for the Holy Spirit gave them, as Jesus promised, power to carry the Good News to every nation on earth. So began the age of grace.

Our own journeys are similarly wrapped up with Christ's command to follow him every day. This is our own time of grace as we seek to do his work in today's world. By praying with the Word of God in this season, we may discover how we, too, can serve the Master. The last Sunday of Ordinary Time is the Feast of Christ the King, whose coming and kingdom we await.

Monday, May 16, 2016

Know that God is present with you and ready to converse.

"Word of God, my Jesus, take me by the hand and lead me to what you want for me."

Read the Gospel: Mark 9:14–29.

When Jesus, Peter, James, and John came to the disciples, they saw a great crowd around them, and some scribes arguing with them. When the whole crowd saw Jesus, they were immediately overcome with awe, and they ran forward to greet him. He asked them, "What are you arguing about with them?" Someone from the crowd answered him, "Teacher, I brought you my son; he has a spirit that makes him unable to speak; and whenever it seizes him, it dashes him down; and he foams and grinds his teeth and becomes rigid; and I asked your disciples to cast it out, but they could not do so." He answered them, "You faithless generation, how much longer must I be among you? How much longer must I put up with you? Bring him to me." And they brought the boy to him. When the spirit saw him, immediately it convulsed the boy, and he fell on the ground and rolled about, foaming at the mouth. Jesus asked the father, "How long has this been happening to him?" And he said, "From childhood. It has often cast him into the fire and into the water, to destroy him; but if you are able to do anything, have pity on us and help us." Jesus said to him, "If you are able! All things can be done for the one who believes." Immediately the father of the child cried out, "I believe; help my unbelief!" When Jesus saw that a crowd came running together, he rebuked the unclean spirit, saying to it, "You spirit that keeps this boy from speaking and hearing, I command you, come out of him, and never enter him again!" After crying out and convulsing him terribly, it came out, and the boy was like a corpse, so that most of them said, "He is dead." But Jesus took him by the hand and lifted him up, and he was able to stand. When he had entered the house, his disciples asked him privately, "Why could we not cast it out?" He said to them, "This kind can come out only through prayer."

Notice what you think and feel as you read the Gospel.

Jesus casts out a powerful evil spirit from the boy, even while he exhorts those standing by to believe, for "all things can be done for the one who believes."

Pray as you are led for yourself and others.

"Lord, I am often weak and disobedient; strengthen my faith so that I might please you . . ." (Continue in your own words.)

Listen to Jesus.

I do want you to believe in me, to trust my love for you in all your circumstances. What do you want me to do for you? What else is Jesus saying to you?

Ask God to show you how to live today.

"Do I know anyone who is suffering? Show me how to help someone today, doing unto him what I would want another to do unto me. Amen."

Tuesday, May 17, 2016

Know that God is present with you and ready to converse.

"Lord, you are real and want to instruct me by your Word. Let me be attentive."

Read the Gospel: Mark 9:30–37.

Jesus and his disciples went on from there and passed through Galilee. Jesus did not want anyone to know it; for he was teaching his disciples, saying to them, "The Son of Man is to be betrayed into human hands, and they will kill him, and three days after being killed, he will rise again." But they did not understand what he was saying and were afraid to ask him.

Then they came to Capernaum; and when he was in the house he asked them, "What were you arguing about on the way?" But they were silent, for on the way they had argued with one another who was the greatest. He sat down, called the Twelve, and said to them, "Whoever wants to be first must be last of all and servant of all." Then he took a little child and put it among them; and taking it in his arms, he said to them, "Whoever welcomes one such child in my name welcomes me, and whoever welcomes me welcomes not me but the one who sent me."

Notice what you think and feel as you read the Gospel.

The disciples do not understand Jesus' prophesy of his passion and death. They would rather discuss which of them is greatest. He patiently teaches them that the one who wishes to be greatest must be last of all and servant of all.

Pray as you are led for yourself and others.

"Jesus, I wish to be last of all and servant of all. Show me how to serve you today . . ." (Continue in your own words.)

Listen to Jesus.

If you seek blessedness and favor from God, give yourself to serving others, especially those in need. What else is Jesus saying to you?

Ask God to show you how to live today.

"Lord, help me to put aside my own self-interest and to think and do as your true servant. Let me see you in others. Amen."

Wednesday, May 18, 2016

Know that God is present with you and ready to converse.

"I open my heart and soul to you now, Word of the Father, light of the world. Scatter all my darkness."

Read the Gospel: Mark 9:38–40.

John said to Jesus, "Teacher, we saw someone casting out demons in your name, and we tried to stop him, because he was not following us." But Jesus said, "Do not stop him; for no one who does a deed of power in my name will be able soon afterward to speak evil of me. Whoever is not against us is for us."

Notice what you think and feel as you read the Gospel.

Even the stranger does mighty works in the name of Jesus. The master tells them to leave him alone and not to stop him.

Pray as you are led for yourself and others.

"Jesus, let me not harbor division in my heart. Let me honor all those who serve others in your name . . ." (Continue in your own words.)

Listen to Jesus.

Do not judge another's way. Follow me as closely as you can and leave your concerns about others to me. What else is Jesus saying to you?

Ask God to show you how to live today.

"Lord, I pray that all who work in your name may be one in you. Give us the Spirit of unity in you. Amen."

Thursday, May 19, 2016

Know that God is present with you and ready to converse.

"Teacher, I sit at your feet. Let me not just hear your Word but also act upon it."

Read the Gospel: Mark 9:41–50.

Jesus said, "For truly I tell you, whoever gives you a cup of water to drink because you bear the name of Christ will by no means lose the reward.

"If any of you put a stumbling block before one of these little ones who believe in me, it would be better for you if a great millstone were hung around your neck and you were thrown into the sea. If your hand causes you to stumble, cut it off; it is better for you to enter life maimed than to have two hands and to go to hell, to the unquenchable fire. And if your foot causes you to stumble, cut it off; it is better for you to enter life lame than to have two feet and to be thrown into hell. And if your eye causes you to stumble, tear it out; it is better for you to enter the kingdom of God with one eye than to have two eyes and to be thrown into hell, where their worm never dies, and the fire is never quenched.

"For everyone will be salted with fire. Salt is good; but if salt has lost its saltiness, how can you season it? Have salt in yourselves, and be at peace with one another."

Notice what you think and feel as you read the Gospel.

All who serve those who serve Christ will receive a reward. Those who cause others to sin bear responsibility. And we must be vigilant in turning away from our own sins. We are called to a high moral standard, and we can expect to be "salted with fire."

Pray as you are led for yourself and others.

"Lord, what can I do to serve those who serve in your name? Let me not lead others into sin, and let me welcome your grace to resist temptation . . ." (Continue in your own words.)

Listen to Jesus.

The little things I give you to do are great things when they are done in love. Find my love within your acts. Remind yourself of my words to you often. What else is Jesus saying to you?

Ask God to show you how to live today.

"I begin by praying for your servants. Cleanse me of my sins, especially my habitual sins, and let me replace them with acts of love. Amen."

Friday, May 20, 2016

Know that God is present with you and ready to converse.

"Lord, I hearken to your Word, for you have the words of truth for me."

Read the Gospel: Mark 10:1–12.

Jesus left that place and went to the region of Judea and beyond the Jordan. And crowds again gathered around him; and, as was his custom, he again taught them.

Some Pharisees came, and to test him they asked, "Is it lawful for a man to divorce his wife?" He answered them, "What did Moses command you?" They said, "Moses allowed a man to write a certificate of dismissal and to divorce her." But Jesus said to them, "Because of your hardness of heart he wrote this commandment for you. But from the beginning of creation, 'God made them male and female.' 'For this reason a man shall leave his father and mother and be joined to his wife, and the two shall become one flesh.' So they are no longer two, but one flesh. Therefore what God has joined together, let no one separate."

Then in the house the disciples asked him again about this matter. He said to them, "Whoever divorces his wife and marries another commits adultery against her; and if she divorces her husband and marries another, she commits adultery."

Notice what you think and feel as you read the Gospel.

Jesus sets a high standard for marriage. This unity is God's intention from creation, and humans should not set aside the purposes of God.

Pray as you are led for yourself and others.

"Jesus, this is a hard saying in our time. Let your Church uphold your ideal for marriage, even while we refrain from judging others . . ." (Continue in your own words.)

Listen to Jesus.

When I am present in a marriage, two can become one and grow in love for a lifetime. What else is Jesus saying to you?

Ask God to show you how to live today.

"Show me how I may grow in love today, Lord Jesus. Amen."

Saturday, May 21, 2016

Know that God is present with you and ready to converse.

"Bless me, Jesus. Hold me in your arms and lay your hands upon me, for I have come to you."

Read the Gospel: Mark 10:13–16.

People were bringing little children to Jesus in order that he might touch them; and the disciples spoke sternly to them. But when Jesus saw this, he was indignant and said to them, "Let the little children come to me; do not stop them; for it is to such as these that the kingdom of God belongs. Truly I tell you, whoever does not receive the kingdom of God as a little child will never enter it." And he took the children up in his arms, laid his hands on them, and blessed them.

Notice what you think and feel as you read the Gospel.

Jesus loves little children. He holds them up as examples to us, for to the childlike belongs the kingdom of God.

Pray as you are led for yourself and others.

"Make me your child, Jesus, simple and believing, open to receive all you have for me . . ." (Continue in your own words.)

Listen to Jesus.

Set yourself aside, child. Receive my blessings. What else is Jesus saying to you?

Ask God to show you how to live today.

"Let your simple purpose guide me, Lord, so that I may care about nothing other than following you and abiding in your presence. Amen."

Sunday, May 22, 2016
The Holy Trinity

Know that God is present with you and ready to converse.

Ours is a faith of many mysteries, beginning with God. God, the Creator of all, is infinite spirit, almighty, eternal, holy, and the fountain of every virtue. No one can understand God, but we can love God.

When you are ready, invite God to teach you by the Word: "Three persons, one God, speak your Word into my heart and soul."

Read the Gospel: John 16:12–15.

Jesus said, "I still have many things to say to you, but you cannot bear them now. When the Spirit of truth comes, he will guide you into all the truth; for he will not speak on his own, but will speak whatever he hears, and he will declare to you the things that are to come. He will glorify me, because he will take what is mine and declare it to you. All that the Father has is mine. For this reason I said that he will take what is mine and declare it to you."

Notice what you think and feel as you read the Gospel.

The disciples must have been baffled by Jesus' promise of the Spirit of truth who would come and declare the things of Jesus and the Father, and to speak of the infinite God who loves us beyond all human measure.

Pray as you are led for yourself and others.

"Spirit, declare to me the things of Jesus and the Father, that I may glorify God in my life . . ." (Continue in your own words.)

Listen to Jesus.

Keep listening in your heart to the words of the Spirit. We guide you in the ways of truth and love. What else is Jesus saying to you?

Ask God to show you how to live today.

"Remain with me, Jesus. Let me contemplate God's self and give God glory today and always. Amen."

Monday, May 23, 2016

Know that God is present with you and ready to converse.

"Lord, let me follow you and you alone. Teach me how."

Read the Gospel: Mark 10:17–27.

As Jesus was setting out on a journey, a man ran up and knelt before him, and asked him, "Good teacher, what must I do to inherit eternal life?" Jesus said to him, "Why do you call me good? No one is good but God alone. You know the commandments: 'You shall not murder; you shall not commit adultery; you shall not steal; you shall not bear false witness; you shall not defraud; honor your father and mother.'" He said to him, "Teacher, I have kept all these since my youth." Jesus, looking at him, loved him and said, "You lack one thing; go, sell what you own, and give the money to the poor, and you will have treasure in heaven; then come, follow me." When the man heard this, he was shocked and went away grieving, for he had many possessions.

Then Jesus looked around and said to his disciples, "How hard it will be for those who have wealth to enter the kingdom of God!" And the disciples were perplexed at these words. But Jesus said to them again, "Children, how hard it is to enter the kingdom of God! It is easier for a camel to go through the eye of a needle than for someone who is rich to enter the kingdom of God." They were greatly astounded and said to one another, "Then who can be saved?" Jesus looked at them and said, "For mortals it is impossible, but not for God; for God all things are possible."

Notice what you think and feel as you read the Gospel.

Jesus challenges the man's definition of "good," for the man believed himself to be good. Loving the man, Jesus offers him a unique opportunity to have treasure in heaven, inviting him to give it all away and follow him. Sadly, the man is not ready for that.

Pray as you are led for yourself and others.

"Lord, do not allow my possessions to come between us. Let me understand that all things are yours and that my real treasure is in trusting and following you . . ." (Continue in your own words.)

Listen to Jesus.

I take care of my own, my beloved. Possessions in your life have nothing to do with your life hereafter. What else is Jesus saying to you?

Ask God to show you how to live today.

"Lord, if things come between us, take those things from me. Let me steadfastly follow you, counting you my only treasure. Amen."

Tuesday, May 24, 2016

Know that God is present with you and ready to converse.

"I am present with the Word of God. What does the Spirit of truth say to me today?"

Read the Gospel: Mark 10:28–31.

Peter began to say to Jesus, "Look, we have left everything and followed you." Jesus said, "Truly I tell you, there is no one who has left house or brothers or sisters or mother or father or children or fields, for my sake and for the sake of the good news, who will not receive a hundredfold now in this age—houses, brothers and sisters, mothers and children, and fields, with persecutions—and in the age to come eternal life. But many who are first will be last, and the last will be first."

Notice what you think and feel as you read the Gospel.

Jesus confirms the great value of leaving everything and everyone to follow him. Our reward is not only in heaven but here, too, in the fellowship of believers. And in the age to come, eternal life!

Pray as you are led for yourself and others.

"Let me count what I have gained, Lord, in following you. Let me be unafraid to lose whatever I have because I gain God by losing myself . . ." (Continue in your own words.)

Listen to Jesus.

You make me joyful, friend. I have given you a heart for me. What else is Jesus saying to you?

Ask God to show you how to live today.

"Your truths are simple, Lord, but sometimes I am afraid to receive them in simple obedience. Show me how to do that. Amen."

Wednesday, May 25, 2016

Know that God is present with you and ready to converse.

"Lord, I sit in your presence, and I will speak to you. How I long to hear your voice rather than my own."

Read the Gospel: Mark 10:32–45.

The disciples were on the road, going up to Jerusalem, and Jesus was walking ahead of them; they were amazed, and those who followed were afraid. He took the Twelve aside again and began to tell them what was to happen to him, saying, "See, we are going up to Jerusalem, and the Son of Man will be handed over to the chief priests and the scribes, and they will condemn him to death; then they will hand him over to the Gentiles; they will mock him, and spit upon him, and flog him, and kill him; and after three days he will rise again."

James and John, the sons of Zebedee, came forward to him and said to him, "Teacher, we want you to do for us whatever we ask of you." And he said to them, "What is it you want me to do for you?" And they said to him, "Grant us to sit, one at your right hand and one at your left, in your glory." But Jesus said to them, "You do not know what you are asking. Are you able to drink the cup that I drink, or be baptized with the baptism that I am baptized with?" They replied, "We are able." Then Jesus said to them, "The cup that I drink you will drink; and with the baptism with which I am baptized, you will be baptized; but to sit at my right hand or at my left is not mine to grant, but it is for those for whom it has been prepared."

When the ten heard this, they began to be angry with James and John. So Jesus called them and said to them, "You know that among the Gentiles those whom they recognize as their rulers lord it over them, and their great ones are tyrants over them. But it is not so among you; but whoever wishes to become great among you must be your servant, and whoever wishes to be first among you must be slave of all. For the Son of Man came not to be served but to serve, and to give his life a ransom for many."

Notice what you think and feel as you read the Gospel.

People are people. Even the Twelve Jesus chose engage in petty vanity and dispute. They mean well, perhaps, but they do not seem to realize that to be great in the kingdom of heaven is to serve.

Pray as you are led for yourself and others.

"Lord, you put up with me in my whining and pleading for my own will. Forgive me. Align my heart, my will, to your own, for you want what is truly best . . ." (Continue in your own words.)

Listen to Jesus.

Becoming a servant is a beautiful thing, a blessed thing. My servants have the greatest master, my Father. What else is Jesus saying to you?

Ask God to show you how to live today.

"Give me opportunities to serve today, Jesus, and the grace to humble myself. Amen."

Thursday, May 26, 2016

Know that God is present with you and ready to converse.

"Jesus, as you are passing by, hear my prayer and let me follow you."

Read the Gospel: Mark 10:46–52.

They came to Jericho. As Jesus and his disciples and a large crowd were leaving Jericho, Bartimaeus son of Timaeus, a blind beggar, was sitting by the roadside. When he heard that it was Jesus of Nazareth, he began to shout out and say, "Jesus, Son of David, have mercy on me!" Many sternly ordered him to be quiet, but he cried out even more loudly, "Son of David, have mercy on me!" Jesus stood still and said, "Call him here." And they called the blind man, saying to him, "Take heart; get up, he is calling you." So throwing off his cloak, he sprang up and came to Jesus. Then Jesus said to him, "What do you want me to do for you?" The blind man said to him, "My teacher, let me see again." Jesus said to him, "Go; your faith has made you well." Immediately he regained his sight and followed him on the way.

Notice what you think and feel as you read the Gospel.

Blind Bar-Timaeus annoys others on the road where Jesus is passing by. He is too loud and keeps repeating, "Jesus, Son of David, have mercy on me!" Jesus hears him and stops, and the multitude witnesses another miracle. The blind man can see, and he follows Jesus.

Pray as you are led for yourself and others.

"Help me pray without ceasing, Lord, for my own needs and for the needs of others. I rely on your mercy . . ." (Continue in your own words.)

Listen to Jesus.

My hands are full of good gifts for you, child. Ask of me what you will. What else is Jesus saying to you?

Ask God to show you how to live today.

"Lord, as I leave this prayer today, let me follow you. Give me eyes to see you in others. Amen."

Friday, May 27, 2016

Know that God is present with you and ready to converse.

"Lord, when you are angry, the mountains quake. I come into your presence with holy fear."

Read the Gospel: Mark 11:11–26.

Then he entered Jerusalem and went into the Temple; and when Jesus had looked around at everything, as it was already late, he went out to Bethany with the Twelve.

On the following day, when they came from Bethany, he was hungry. Seeing in the distance a fig tree in leaf, he went to see whether perhaps he would find anything on it. When he came to it, he found nothing but leaves, for it was not the season for figs. He said to it, "May no one ever eat fruit from you again." And his disciples heard it.

Then they came to Jerusalem. And he entered the Temple and began to drive out those who were selling and those who were buying in the Temple, and he overturned the tables of the money changers and the seats of those who sold doves; and he would not allow anyone to carry anything through the Temple. He was teaching and saying, "Is it not written,

> 'My house shall be called a house of prayer for all the nations'?
> But you have made it a den of robbers."

And when the chief priests and the scribes heard it, they kept looking for a way to kill him; for they were afraid of him, because the whole crowd was spellbound by his teaching. And when evening came, Jesus and his disciples went out of the city.

In the morning as they passed by, they saw the fig tree withered away to its roots. Then Peter remembered and said to him, "Rabbi, look! The fig tree that you cursed has withered." Jesus answered them, "Have faith in God. Truly I tell you, if you say to this mountain, 'Be taken up and thrown into the sea,' and if you do not doubt in your heart, but believe that what you say will come to pass, it will be done for you. So I tell you, whatever you ask for in prayer, believe that you have received it, and it will be yours.

"Whenever you stand praying, forgive, if you have anything against anyone; so that your Father in heaven may also forgive you your trespasses."

Notice what you think and feel as you read the Gospel.

Pity the poor fig tree, cursed by the Lord for not bearing figs. Jesus is also angry at those who defile the Temple with buying and selling. The Temple is for prayer.

Pray as you are led for yourself and others.

"Lord, I begin by forgiving all persons I have not yet forgiven. Now teach me to pray with faith for what is good for myself and for others . . ." (Continue in your own words.)

Listen to Jesus.

Prayer is the way to be with God, beloved disciple. God works in and through prayers of the faithful. What else is Jesus saying to you?

Ask God to show you how to live today.

"Give me times of fruitful prayer throughout my day, Lord. Let my prayers bear fruit pleasing to you. Amen."

Saturday, May 28, 2016

Know that God is present with you and ready to converse.

"You are with me now, Lord. Your authority is from the Father."

Read the Gospel: Mark 11:27–33.

Again Jesus and his disciples came to Jerusalem. As he was walking in the Temple, the chief priests, the scribes, and the elders came to him and said, "By what authority are you doing these things? Who gave you this authority to do them?" Jesus said to them, "I will ask you one question; answer me, and I will tell you by what authority I do these things. Did the baptism of John come from heaven, or was it of human origin? Answer me." They argued with one another, "If we say, 'From heaven,' he will say, 'Why then did you not believe him?' But shall we say, 'Of human origin'?" They were afraid of the crowd, for all regarded John as truly a prophet. So they answered Jesus, "We do not know." And Jesus said to them, "Neither will I tell you by what authority I am doing these things."

Notice what you think and feel as you read the Gospel.

The chief priests, scribes, and elders question Jesus' authority. But they are too worried about the politics of their situation—their own authority—to reply honestly to his question about John.

Pray as you are led for yourself and others.

"Jesus, there are times when I fear others when I should be obeying and honoring you. Forgive me. But more than that, change me . . ." (Continue in your own words.)

Listen to Jesus.

I am washing you by my Word, friend. I send my Spirit into you. What else is Jesus saying to you?

Ask God to show you how to live today.

"Show me when my fear of others gets between you and me, Lord. Replace that fear with love. Amen."

Sunday, May 29, 2016
The Body and Blood of Christ

Know that God is present with you and ready to converse.

Out of compassion for the multitudes, Jesus multiplied the loaves and fish to feed them all. He feeds us still in the Eucharist, the food of eternal life. He is the bread of life.

When you are ready, ask the Lord to feed and heal you by his Word.

Read the Gospel: Luke 9:11b–17.

Jesus spoke to the crowd about the kingdom of God, and he healed those who needed to be cured.

The day was drawing to a close, and the Twelve came to him and said, "Send the crowd away, so that they may go into the surrounding villages and countryside, to lodge and get provisions; for we are here in a deserted place." But he said to them, "You give them something to eat." They said, "We have no more than five loaves and two fish—unless we are to go and buy food for all these people." For there were about five thousand men. And he said to his disciples, "Make them sit down in groups of about fifty each." They did so and made them all sit down. And taking the five loaves and the two fish, he looked up to heaven, and blessed and broke them, and gave them to the disciples to set before the crowd. And all ate and were filled. What was left over was gathered up, twelve baskets of broken pieces.

Notice what you think and feel as you read the Gospel.

The disciples worry about crowd management, but Jesus orders them to feed five thousand people with two fish and five loaves. They obey him, feed them all, and carry away twelve baskets of fragments.

Pray as you are led for yourself and others.

"Jesus, you constantly surprise your disciples with goodness. Open my eyes to your wonders, Lord, for I am your own . . ." (Continue in your own words.)

Listen to Jesus.

I feed you, child. I am your bread. What else is Jesus saying to you?

Ask God to show you how to live today.

"You are the bread of life to me, Jesus. Nourish me with yourself and let me be broken as bread for others. Amen."

Remain with Jesus as long as you can.

Monday, May 30, 2016

Know that God is present with you and ready to converse.

"Father, send your Son, your Word, into my heart and let me welcome him there."

Read the Gospel: Mark 12:1–12.

Then Jesus began to speak to them in parables. "A man planted a vineyard, put a fence around it, dug a pit for the wine press, and built a watchtower; then he leased it to tenants and went to another country. When the season came, he sent a slave to the tenants to collect from them his share of the produce of the vineyard. But they seized him, and beat him, and sent him away empty-handed. And again he sent another slave to them; this one they beat over the head and insulted. Then he sent another, and that one they killed. And so it was with many others; some they beat, and others they killed. He had still one other, a beloved son. Finally he sent him to them, saying, 'They will respect my son.' But those tenants said to one another, 'This is the heir; come, let us kill him, and the inheritance will be ours.' So they seized him, killed him, and threw him out of the vineyard. What then will the owner of the vineyard do? He will come and destroy the tenants and give the vineyard to others. Have you not read this scripture:

'The stone that the builders rejected
has become the cornerstone;
this was the Lord's doing,
and it is amazing in our eyes'?"

When they realized that he had told this parable against them, they wanted to arrest him, but they feared the crowd. So they left him and went away.

Notice what you think and feel as you read the Gospel.

God does not stop loving. He reaches out to sinners continuously, like the owner of the vineyard, hoping they will respond. Finally he sends his Son, who is killed. And yet the rejected one becomes the cornerstone of the building. How marvelous are God's ways!

Pray as you are led for yourself and others.

"Lord, I pray for those who reject you and who persecute those who follow you and serve you. Beginning with me, turn the hearts of sinners to you . . ." (Continue in your own words.)

Listen to Jesus.

Beloved, I am the light of the world. Whoever will come may come to the light. What else is Jesus saying to you?

Ask God to show you how to live today.

"How may I welcome you today? How may I be your light to others? Amen."

Tuesday, May 31, 2016
The Visitation of the Blessed Virgin Mary

Know that God is present with you and ready to converse.

"Holy Spirit, teach me true worship by your Word."

Read the Gospel: Luke 1:39–56.

In those days Mary set out and went with haste to a Judean town in the hill country, where she entered the house of Zechariah and greeted Elizabeth. When Elizabeth heard Mary's greeting, the child leaped in her womb. And Elizabeth was filled with the Holy Spirit and exclaimed with a loud cry, "Blessed are you among women, and blessed is the fruit of your womb. And why has this happened to me, that the mother of my

Lord comes to me? For as soon as I heard the sound of your greeting, the child in my womb leaped for joy. And blessed is she who believed that there would be a fulfillment of what was spoken to her by the Lord."

And Mary said,

"My soul magnifies the Lord,
    and my spirit rejoices in God my Savior,
for he has looked with favor on the lowliness of his servant.
    Surely, from now on all generations will call me
    blessed;
for the Mighty One has done great things for me,
    and holy is his name.
His mercy is for those who fear him
    from generation to generation.
He has shown strength with his arm;
    he has scattered the proud in the thoughts of their
    hearts.
He has brought down the powerful from their thrones,
    and lifted up the lowly;
he has filled the hungry with good things,
    and sent the rich away empty.
He has helped his servant Israel,
    in remembrance of his mercy,
according to the promise he made to our ancestors,
    to Abraham and to his descendants forever."

And Mary remained with her about three months and then returned to her home.

Notice what you think and feel as you read the Gospel.

Mary's inspired prayer of praise reveals the proper disposition to receiving the Holy Spirit: lowly surrender to the will of God and trust in God's salvation and faithfulness.

Pray as you are led for yourself and others.

"Lord, you will come to me if I receive you as Mary did, with humility and faith . . ." (Continue in your own words.)

Listen to Jesus.

I am with you, child, and I breathe my Spirit into your inner being. What else is Jesus saying to you?

Ask God to show you how to live today.

"Remind me of your presence with me as I live today. Show me how to let you work through me, especially as I am serving others. Amen."

Wednesday, June 1, 2016

Know that God is present with you and ready to converse.

"Living God, live in me. Illuminate my mind."

Read the Gospel: Mark 12:18–27.

Some Sadducees, who say there is no resurrection, came to Jesus and asked him a question, saying, "Teacher, Moses wrote for us that if a man's brother dies, leaving a wife but no child, the man shall marry the widow and raise up children for his brother. There were seven brothers; the first married and, when he died, left no children; and the second married the widow and died, leaving no children; and the third likewise; none of the seven left children. Last of all the woman herself died. In the resurrection whose wife will she be? For the seven had married her."

Jesus said to them, "Is not this the reason you are wrong, that you know neither the scriptures nor the power of God? For when they rise from the dead, they neither marry nor are given in marriage, but are like angels in heaven. And as for the dead being raised, have you not read in the book of Moses, in the story about the bush, how God said to him, 'I am the God of Abraham, the God of Isaac, and the God of Jacob'? He is God not of the dead, but of the living; you are quite wrong."

Notice what you think and feel as you read the Gospel.

The Sadducees try to trap Jesus in their elaborate question about the woman with seven husbands. They think they can force him to deny the resurrection of the dead and the afterlife. Jesus points out the error of their thinking and quotes Moses. The dead are alive in God.

Pray as you are led for yourself and others.

"My God and Savior, I can be slow to understand, slow to believe all you say to me. Work in my heart and mind . . ." (Continue in your own words.)

Listen to Jesus.

I am truly your teacher, beloved. Hear what I am saying to you now. What else is Jesus saying to you?

Ask God to show you how to live today.

"Shine light on my path today, Lord. Guide me in your way. Amen."

Thursday, June 2, 2016

Know that God is present with you and ready to converse.

"Lord, I am not far from your kingdom, for you are here and you give me your commandments for living well."

Read the Gospel: Mark 12:28–34.

One of the scribes came near and heard the Sadducees disputing with one another, and seeing that Jesus answered them well, he asked Jesus, "Which commandment is the first of all?" Jesus answered, "The first is, 'Hear, O Israel: the Lord our God, the Lord is one; you shall love the Lord your God with all your heart, and with all your soul, and with all your mind, and with all your strength.' The second is this, 'You shall love your neighbor as yourself.' There is no other commandment greater than these." Then the scribe said to him, "You are right, Teacher; you have truly said that 'he is one, and besides him there is no other'; and 'to love him with all the heart, and with all the understanding, and with all the strength,' and 'to love one's neighbor as oneself'—this is much more important than all whole burnt offerings and sacrifices." When Jesus saw that he answered wisely, he said to the scribe, "You are not far from the kingdom of God." After that no one dared to ask him any question.

Notice what you think and feel as you read the Gospel.

Jesus seems joyful to answer the scribe's question about the first commandment. God is one, and we are to love him with every part of our being and our neighbors as well. The scribe agrees with Jesus, happily repeating. Jesus tells him, "You are not far from the kingdom of God."

Pray as you are led for yourself and others.

"Jesus, let those great commandments penetrate and echo within me. This is all I need to know to live in God and with others . . ." (Continue in your own words.)

Listen to Jesus.

God is one. And you are one with God. Draw others into this oneness by loving them. What else is Jesus saying to you?

Ask God to show you how to live today.

"God, flood my heart, mind, soul, and spirit with your love, that I may please you and bear fruit to your glory. Amen."

Friday, June 3, 2016
Sacred Heart of Jesus

Know that God is present with you and ready to converse.

"Find me here, Lord. I am lost without you."

Read the Gospel: Luke 15:3–7.

So Jesus told them this parable: "Which one of you, having a hundred sheep and losing one of them, does not leave the ninety-nine in the wilderness and go after the one that is lost until he finds it? When he has found it, he lays it on his shoulders and rejoices. And when he comes home, he calls together his friends and neighbors, saying to them, 'Rejoice with me, for I have found my sheep that was lost.' Just so, I tell you, there will be more joy in heaven over one sinner who repents than over ninety-nine righteous persons who need no repentance."

Notice what you think and feel as you read the Gospel.

The shepherd seeks out the lost sheep and joyfully returns it to the fold. So is there joy in heaven when a sinner repents.

Pray as you are led for yourself and others.

"Lord, save me from my willful wandering away from you. Let my heart come to your heart and remain . . ." (Continue in your own words.)

Listen to Jesus.

I forgive you. I have given you my heart. I ask for yours. What else is Jesus saying to you?

Ask God to show you how to live today.

"Jesus, make my heart like yours so that I can do unto others what you ask of me. Amen."

Saturday, June 4, 2016
Immaculate Heart of the Blessed Virgin Mary

Know that God is present with you and ready to converse.

"Speak your truth into my heart, Jesus, and let it remain there always."

Read the Gospel: Luke 2:41–51.

Now every year Jesus' parents went to Jerusalem for the festival of the Passover. And when he was twelve years old, they went up as usual for the festival. When the festival was ended and they started to return, the boy Jesus stayed behind in Jerusalem, but his parents did not know it. Assuming that he was in the group of travelers, they went a day's journey. Then they started to look for him among their relatives and friends. When they did not find him, they returned to Jerusalem to search for him. After three days they found him in the Temple, sitting among the teachers, listening to them and asking them questions. And all who heard him were amazed at his understanding and his answers. When his parents saw him they were astonished; and his mother said to him, "Child, why have you treated us like this? Look, your father and I have been searching for you in great anxiety." He said to them, "Why were you searching for me? Did you not know that I must be in my Father's house?" But they did not understand what he said to them. Then he went down with them and came to Nazareth, and was obedient to them. His mother treasured all these things in her heart.

Notice what you think and feel as you read the Gospel.

Jesus remains in Jerusalem after his parents begin their journey home. When at last they find him conversing with the teachers in the Temple, what he says to his mother shows that he understands that his Father is God, and doing his Father's will is to be his sole focus. "His mother kept all these things in her heart."

Pray as you are led for yourself and others.

"Jesus, I honor your mother. Her humble heart surrendered to God like your own. She is a model for me. Pray for me, Mother of God . . ." (Continue in your own words.)

Listen to Jesus.

You are with us in the holy family of God, beloved. What else is Jesus saying to you?

Ask God to show you how to live today.

"Lead me in your way of peace, Jesus. Let my heart be quiet before you, like the immaculate heart of the Blessed Virgin Mary. Amen."

Sunday, June 5, 2016
Tenth Sunday in Ordinary Time

Know that God is present with you and ready to converse.

The Word of God has the power to speak to us no matter how many times we read it. Through the Word, God leads us to the next thing he wants from us.

When you are ready, call upon the Word of God: "Jesus, let me not be satisfied until I love God with all my heart, mind, soul, and strength."

Read the Gospel: Luke 7:11–17.

Soon afterwards Jesus went to a town called Nain, and his disciples and a large crowd went with him. As he approached the gate of the town, a man who had died was being carried out. He was his mother's only son, and she was a widow; and with her was a large crowd from the town. When the Lord saw her, he had compassion for her and said to her, "Do not weep." Then he came forward and touched the bier, and the bearers stood still. And he said, "Young man, I say to you, rise!" The dead man sat up and began to speak, and Jesus gave him to his mother. Fear seized all of them; and they glorified God, saying, "A great prophet has risen among us!" and "God has looked favorably on his people!" This word about him spread throughout Judea and all the surrounding country.

Notice what you think and feel as you read the Gospel.

Out of compassion for the grieving mother, Jesus raises her son from death. No wonder the crowd was seized by fear. "Truly God has visited his people."

Pray as you are led for yourself and others.

"Let your holy words perform your works within me, Lord, that I may live in you. Help me . . ." (Continue in your own words.)

Listen to Jesus.

I love to do things for you, friend. Ask of me good things for yourself and for those I have given you. What else is Jesus saying to you?

Ask God to show you how to live today.

"Let my thoughts, words, and deeds be true, Lord. I give them all to you. Amen."

Monday, June 6, 2016

Know that God is present with you and ready to converse.

"You are here to teach me the ways of happiness. Let me receive you, blessed Savior."

Read the Gospel: Matthew 5:1–12.

When Jesus saw the crowds, he went up the mountain; and after he sat down, his disciples came to him. Then he began to speak, and taught them, saying:

"Blessed are the poor in spirit, for theirs is the kingdom of heaven.

"Blessed are those who mourn, for they will be comforted.

"Blessed are the meek, for they will inherit the earth.

"Blessed are those who hunger and thirst for righteousness, for they will be filled.

"Blessed are the merciful, for they will receive mercy.

"Blessed are the pure in heart, for they will see God.

"Blessed are the peacemakers, for they will be called children of God.

"Blessed are those who are persecuted for righteousness' sake, for theirs is the kingdom of heaven.

"Blessed are you when people revile you and persecute you and utter all kinds of evil against you falsely on my account. Rejoice and be glad, for your reward is great in heaven, for in the same way they persecuted the prophets who were before you."

Notice what you think and feel as you read the Gospel.

The poor in spirit come first in this beautiful list of blessedness. What is this poverty of spirit? I feel it is opening the emptiness within me so that God can come in. The kingdom of heaven is within, it is here, and it is now. What in these words of Jesus most moves you?

Pray as you are led for yourself and others.

"I am poor, Jesus. Let me rejoice in that, for in my emptiness you fill me . . ." (Continue in your own words.)

Listen to Jesus.

The way of God is simple, child. Do you see how it resides in the heart? What else is Jesus saying to you?

Ask God to show you how to live today.

"Give me hunger for your blessed ways today, Lord, and every day of my life. Amen."

Tuesday, June 7, 2016

Know that God is present with you and ready to converse.

"Divine light, dispel my darkness and be the light in me."

Read the Gospel: Matthew 5:13–16.

Jesus said, "You are the salt of the earth; but if salt has lost its taste, how can its saltiness be restored? It is no longer good for anything, but is thrown out and trampled underfoot.

"You are the light of the world. A city built on a hill cannot be hid. No one after lighting a lamp puts it under the bushel basket, but on the lamp stand, and it gives light to all in the house. In the same way, let your light shine before others, so that they may see your good works and give glory to your Father in heaven."

Notice what you think and feel as you read the Gospel.

Jesus tells his followers that they are the salt of the earth: they preserve and improve the earth by their goodness. As the light of the world, their lives shine with love and truth so that others may see.

Pray as you are led for yourself and others.

"I long to do good works to the glory of your Father, Lord. How shall I proceed to be salt and light in this world?" (Continue in your own words.)

Listen to Jesus.

Begin with prayer, beloved, and I will guide your heart and hands in good works. What else is Jesus saying to you?

Ask God to show you how to live today.

"Keep me from all self-righteousness as I live in this world, Lord. Remind me that all I have and all I need is you. Amen."

Wednesday, June 8, 2016

Know that God is present with you and ready to converse.

"Jesus, open my heart and soul to your teaching, for I long for the kingdom of heaven."

Read the Gospel: Matthew 5:17–19.

Jesus said, "Do not think that I have come to abolish the law or the prophets; I have come not to abolish but to fulfill. For truly I tell you, until heaven and earth pass away, not one letter, not one stroke of a letter, will pass from the law until all is accomplished. Therefore, whoever breaks one of the least of these commandments, and teaches others to do the same, will be called least in the kingdom of heaven; but whoever does them and teaches them will be called great in the kingdom of heaven."

Notice what you think and feel as you read the Gospel.

Jesus affirms that the scriptures—the law and the prophets—contain enduring truth to believe and obey. Jesus says he does not abolish but fulfills the scripture. In him is the righteousness that exceeds that of the scribes and Pharisees.

Pray as you are led for yourself and others.

"Word of the Father, open my eyes to you in scripture, in the Old as well as the New Testament . . ." (Continue in your own words.)

Listen to Jesus.

I have much to teach you, beloved. Look to me to prepare you for my service. What else is Jesus saying to you?

Ask God to show you how to live today.

"Give me ears to hear your voice throughout my day. Wash me constantly by your Word, and I shall come into your kingdom. Amen."

Thursday, June 9, 2016

Know that God is present with you and ready to converse.

"You have the words of righteousness, Lord. Let me hear them now."

Read the Gospel: Matthew 5:20–26.

Jesus said, "For I tell you, unless your righteousness exceeds that of the scribes and Pharisees, you will never enter the kingdom of heaven.

"You have heard that it was said to those of ancient times, 'You shall not murder'; and 'whoever murders shall be liable to judgment.' But I say to you that if you are angry with a brother or sister, you will be liable to judgment; and if you insult a brother or sister, you will be liable to the council; and if you say, 'You fool,' you will be liable to the hell of fire. So when you are offering your gift at the altar, if you remember that your brother or sister has something against you, leave your gift there before the altar and go; first be reconciled to your brother or sister, and then come and offer your gift. Come to terms quickly with your accuser while you are on the way to court with him, or your accuser may hand you over to the judge, and the judge to the guard, and you will be thrown into prison. Truly I tell you, you will never get out until you have paid the last penny."

Notice what you think and feel as you read the Gospel.

Jesus fulfills the law by showing that sin is not just external acts against others but also unloving or unforgiving desires and attitudes. We must actively seek to be reconciled with all people who oppose us.

Pray as you are led for yourself and others.

"Lord, I need you to help me seek peace with some people in my life. I admit . . ." (Continue in your own words.)

Listen to Jesus.

You understand what I am saying to you, beloved disciple. Don't be afraid to obey me. I will be with you and bless you. What else is Jesus saying to you?

Ask God to show you how to live today.

"Give me the words to say when I need them, Lord. Thank you. Amen."

Friday, June 10, 2016

Know that God is present with you and ready to converse.

"Give me courage to hear and uphold your truth, Jesus. By your Word, mold me into the person you want me to be."

Read the Gospel: Matthew 5:27–32.

Jesus taught, "You have heard that it was said, 'You shall not commit adultery.' But I say to you that everyone who looks at a woman with lust has already committed adultery with her in his heart. If your right eye causes you to sin, tear it out and throw it away; it is better for you to lose one of your members than for your whole body to be thrown into hell. And if your right hand causes you to sin, cut it off and throw it away; it is better for you to lose one of your members than for your whole body to go into hell.

"It was also said, 'Whoever divorces his wife, let him give her a certificate of divorce.' But I say to you that anyone who divorces his wife, except on the ground of unchastity, causes her to commit adultery; and whoever marries a divorced woman commits adultery."

Notice what you think and feel as you read the Gospel.

Jesus does not flinch in his instructions for the righteousness that exceeds that of the scribes and Pharisees. Here he focuses on lust and its tragic consequences for marriage. We must be willing to deny ourselves and fight the sinful desires of the flesh in order to be holy in God and with others.

Pray as you are led for yourself and others.

"Lord, you know my sin. Forgive and cleanse me . . ." (Continue in your own words.)

Listen to Jesus.

I forgive you and give you grace to be pure and good. Come to me whenever you need me. What else is Jesus saying to you?

Ask God to show you how to live today.

"I need your Holy Spirit to transform me, Lord. Let me walk today in your Spirit, that I may please God, avoiding all offense. Amen."

Saturday, June 11, 2016

Know that God is present with you and ready to converse.

"Jesus, I need to hear your Word, for in you all the promises of God are fulfilled. Then by your grace I will say yes to you."

Read the Gospel: Matthew 5:33–37.

Jesus said, "Again, you have heard that it was said to those of ancient times, 'You shall not swear falsely, but carry out the vows you have made to the Lord.' But I say to you, Do not swear at all, either by heaven, for it is the throne of God, or by the earth, for it is his footstool, or by Jerusalem, for it is the city of the great King. And do not swear by your head, for you cannot make one hair white or black. Let your word be 'Yes, Yes' or 'No, No'; anything more than this comes from the evil one."

Notice what you think and feel as you read the Gospel.

Jesus expounds on a commandment Moses received from the Lord, that one must not swear falsely. Jesus says do not swear at all and do not swear by anything, for all things are God's and we have no control. A simple "yes" and "no" is enough.

Pray as you are led for yourself and others.

"Jesus, often I speak too much, promise too much, trust myself too much. Simplify my life. I put myself in your hands to lead me where you will. Here are some things I entrust to you . . ." (Continue in your own words.)

Listen to Jesus.

I hear your prayer, my good friend. We say yes to one another today. We belong to one another. What more do you need in this world or the next? What else is Jesus saying to you?

Ask God to show you how to live today.

"Jesus, show me how to speak and act aware of God's grandeur and my weakness. Help me value the simple ways today. Amen."

Sunday, June 12, 2016
Eleventh Sunday in Ordinary Time

Know that God is present with you and ready to converse.

Religion can be a trap. Jesus constantly preached against the legalism of the scribes and Pharisees. He revealed God's love and mercy in all that he said and did.

When you are ready, invite the Lord into your prayerful reading with words such as these: "Let me sit at your feet, merciful Savior, and love you in your Word."

Read the Gospel: Luke 7:36–8:3.

One of the Pharisees asked Jesus to eat with him, and he went into the Pharisee's house and took his place at the table. And a woman in the city, who was a sinner, having learned that he was eating in the Pharisee's house, brought an alabaster jar of ointment. She stood behind him at his feet, weeping, and began to bathe his feet with her tears and to dry them with her hair. Then she continued kissing his feet and anointing them with the ointment. Now when the Pharisee who had invited him saw it, he said to himself, "If this man were a prophet, he would have known who and what kind of woman this is who is touching him—that she is a sinner." Jesus spoke up and said to him, "Simon, I have something to say to you." "Teacher," he replied, "speak." "A certain creditor had two debtors; one owed five hundred denarii, and the other fifty. When they could not pay, he canceled the debts for both of them. Now which of them will love him more?" Simon answered, "I suppose the one for whom he canceled the greater debt." And Jesus said to him, "You have judged rightly." Then turning toward the woman, he said to Simon, "Do you see this woman? I entered your house; you gave me no water for my feet, but she has bathed my feet with her tears and dried them with her hair. You gave me no kiss, but from the time I came in she has not stopped kissing my feet. You did not anoint my head with oil, but she has anointed my feet with ointment. Therefore, I tell you, her sins, which were many, have been forgiven; hence she has shown great love. But the one to whom little is forgiven, loves little." Then he said to her, "Your sins are forgiven." But those who were at the table with him began to say among themselves, "Who is this who even forgives sins?" And he said to the woman, "Your faith has saved you; go in peace."

Soon afterward he went on through cities and villages, proclaiming and bringing the good news of the kingdom of God. The Twelve were with him, as well as some women who had been cured of evil spirits and infirmities: Mary, called Magdalene, from whom seven demons had gone out, and Joanna, the wife of Herod's steward Chuza, and Susanna, and many others, who provided for them out of their resources.

Notice what you think and feel as you read the Gospel.

Jesus reads the judgmental heart of Simon and gently teaches him about love and gratitude for God's forgiveness. The woman forgiven of many sins loves Jesus extravagantly. He gives her his peace.

Pray as you are led for yourself and others.

"Help me not to judge others, Lord, for my own sins are many. Let me respond to your forgiveness with extravagant love for you . . ." (Continue in your own words.)

Listen to Jesus.

You are on the path of joy, my child. We walk together in loving conversation. What else is Jesus saying to you?

Ask God to show you how to live today.

"You have forgiven me much, Jesus. Is there an extravagant way that I can show you my love today? Amen."

Monday, June 13, 2016

Know that God is present with you and ready to converse.

"Lord, I embrace my freedom to hear and obey your Word."

Read the Gospel: Matthew 5:38–42.

Jesus said, "You have heard that it was said, 'An eye for an eye and a tooth for a tooth.' But I say to you, do not resist an evildoer. But if anyone strikes you on the right cheek, turn the other also; and if anyone wants to sue you and take your coat, give your cloak as well; and if anyone forces you to go one mile, go also the second mile. Give to everyone who begs from you, and do not refuse anyone who wants to borrow from you."

Notice what you think and feel as you read the Gospel.

Jesus gives his followers a way to retain freedom in harmful or hurtful circumstances: by choosing to give generously, out of love for God, rather than demanding "an eye for an eye."

Pray as you are led for yourself and others.

"Jesus, I want to love my enemies as you did. Who seeks to force, oppress, or hurt me?" (Continue in your own words.)

Listen to Jesus.

I give you my peace, beloved. Are you following me today? What else is Jesus saying to you?

Ask God to show you how to live today.

"In situations of potential conflict, Lord, help me to step aside from my own point of view and empathize with whoever opposes me. Then let me act as you would. Amen."

Tuesday, June 14, 2016

Know that God is present with you and ready to converse.

"Father, I stand in your presence seeking your grace to hear and do your will."

Read the Gospel: Matthew 5:43–48.

Jesus taught, "You have heard that it was said, 'You shall love your neighbor and hate your enemy.' But I say to you, love your enemies and pray for those who persecute you, so that you may be children of your Father in heaven; for he makes his sun rise on the evil and on the good, and sends rain on the righteous and on the unrighteous. For if you love those who love you, what reward do you have? Do not even the tax collectors do the same? And if you greet only your brothers and sisters, what more are you doing than others? Do not even the Gentiles do the same? Be perfect, therefore, as your heavenly Father is perfect."

Notice what you think and feel as you read the Gospel.

Only by God's grace can we become perfect as he is perfect or learn to love our enemies as Jesus does. Jesus participates in the love of his Father, and he asks us to do the same.

Pray as you are led for yourself and others.

"God, you are love. I hunger and thirst to be in you so that I may do your will in loving others . . ." (Continue in your own words.)

Listen to Jesus.

You are understanding what is needed, child. That is why I say, "Deny yourself and follow me." What else is Jesus saying to you?

Ask God to show you how to live today.

"The tasks you give me are far above my ability, Lord. Help me to work patiently within your grace. Amen."

Wednesday, June 15, 2016

Know that God is present with you and ready to converse.

"Father, you see me here. I seek you in your Word."

Read the Gospel: Matthew 6:1–6, 16–18.

Jesus said, "Beware of practicing your piety before others in order to be seen by them; for then you have no reward from your Father in heaven.

"So whenever you give alms, do not sound a trumpet before you, as the hypocrites do in the synagogues and in the streets, so that they may be praised by others. Truly I tell you, they have received their reward. But when you give alms, do not let your left hand know what your right hand is doing, so that your alms may be done in secret; and your Father who sees in secret will reward you.

"And whenever you pray, do not be like the hypocrites; for they love to stand and pray in the synagogues and at the street corners, so that they may be seen by others. Truly I tell you, they have received their reward. But whenever you pray, go into your room and shut the door and pray to your Father who is in secret; and your Father who sees in secret will reward you. . . .

"And whenever you fast, do not look dismal, like the hypocrites, for they disfigure their faces so as to show others that they are fasting. Truly I tell you, they have received their reward. But when you fast, put oil on your head and wash your face, so that your fasting may be seen not by others but by your Father who is in secret; and your Father who sees in secret will reward you."

Notice what you think and feel as you read the Gospel.

God sees our secrets. Jesus says we should keep God in mind when we fast, pray, give alms, and do good deeds. The pious acts that please God most are those that escape the attention of others.

Pray as you are led for yourself and others.

"Jesus, you fasted, prayed, and did much good with no thought for yourself or for what opinion others had of you. Give me that mind . . ." (Continue in your own words.)

Listen to Jesus.

Your journey is one of constant change. Keep your mind on me, and you will come through it victorious. What else is Jesus saying to you?

Ask God to show you how to live today.

"Make me aware of moments, Lord—moments to pray, deny myself, and do good to someone else. Let me do all things unto God. Amen."

Thursday, June 16, 2016

Know that God is present with you and ready to converse.

"Holy Lord, I reach out to you with my heart. Let my words of prayer be true. Lead me by your Word."

Read the Gospel: Matthew 6:7–15.

Jesus said, "When you are praying, do not heap up empty phrases as the Gentiles do; for they think that they will be heard because of their many words. Do not be like them, for your Father knows what you need before you ask him.

"Pray then in this way:

Our Father in heaven,
hallowed be your name.
Your kingdom come.
Your will be done,
  on earth as it is in heaven.
Give us this day our daily bread.
And forgive us our debts,
  as we also have forgiven our debtors.
And do not bring us to the time of trial,
  but rescue us from the evil one.

"For if you forgive others their trespasses, your heavenly Father will also forgive you; but if you do not forgive others, neither will your Father forgive your trespasses."

Notice what you think and feel as you read the Gospel.

Jesus tells the people to avoid heaping up empty phrases when they pray. God knows what we need before we ask.

Pray as you are led for yourself and others.

"Let my prayer glorify you, Lord. Whom may I forgive?" (Continue in your own words.)

Listen to Jesus.

We have a relationship of hearts, beloved. We love to be together as we are now. What else is Jesus saying to you?

Ask God to show you how to live today.

"Teach me how to pray throughout my day. Keep me close to you, Lord. Amen."

Friday, June 17, 2016

Know that God is present with you and ready to converse.

"Master, the universe and all things within it are yours. Teach me about yourself by the light of your Word."

Read the Gospel: Matthew 6:19–23.

Jesus said, "Do not store up for yourselves treasures on earth, where moth and rust consume and where thieves break in and steal; but store up for yourselves treasures in heaven, where neither moth nor rust consumes and where thieves do not break in and steal. For where your treasure is, there your heart will be also.

"The eye is the lamp of the body. So, if your eye is healthy, your whole body will be full of light; but if your eye is unhealthy, your whole body will be full of darkness. If then the light in you is darkness, how great is the darkness!"

Notice what you think and feel as you read the Gospel.

Jesus removes our focus from worldly treasures and urges us to store up treasures in heaven. What we look at determines whether we walk in the light or in the darkness.

Pray as you are led for yourself and others.

"Jesus, give me a heart for heaven and eyes for only you . . ." (Continue in your own words).

Listen to Jesus.

I have called you to your desires for me, beloved. I am pleased to give you the kingdom. What else is Jesus saying to you?

Ask God to show you how to live today.

"Jesus, break me out of my ordinary way of seeing and loving you. Let me draw very near and please you. Amen."

Saturday, June 18, 2016

Know that God is present with you and ready to converse.

"I am in this moment with you, Father; with you, Holy Spirit; and with you, Jesus Christ. Word of God, fill me."

Read the Gospel: Matthew 6:24–34.

Jesus taught, "No one can serve two masters; for a slave will either hate the one and love the other, or be devoted to the one and despise the other. You cannot serve God and wealth.

"Therefore I tell you, do not worry about your life, what you will eat or what you will drink, or about your body, what you will wear. Is not life more than food, and the body more than clothing? Look at the birds of the air; they neither sow nor reap nor gather into barns, and yet your heavenly Father feeds them. Are you not of more value than they? And can any of you by worrying add a single hour to your span of life? And why do you worry about clothing? Consider the lilies of the field, how they grow; they neither toil nor spin, yet I tell you, even Solomon in all his glory was not clothed like one of these. But if God so clothes the grass of the field, which is alive today and tomorrow is thrown into the oven, will he not much more clothe you—you of little faith? Therefore do not worry, saying, 'What will we eat?' or 'What will we drink?' or 'What will we wear?' For it is the Gentiles who strive for all these things; and indeed your heavenly Father knows that you need all these things. But strive first for the kingdom of God and his righteousness, and all these things will be given to you as well.

"So do not worry about tomorrow, for tomorrow will bring worries of its own. Today's trouble is enough for today."

Notice what you think and feel as you read the Gospel.

Jesus understands human anxieties, our striving for necessities, our worries about tomorrow. He teaches the people to put anxiety, worry, and fear aside. God will provide what we truly need.

Pray as you are led for yourself and others.

"Jesus, I admit I worry . . ." (Continue in your own words.)

Listen to Jesus.

Receive my peace, child. You have your trials. Give them to me. What else is Jesus saying to you?

Ask God to show you how to live today.

"Thank you, Jesus. I give you all that I possess, all that I am, and all my joys and sufferings of this day. As anxieties arise in me, take them, too. Amen."

Sunday, June 19, 2016
Twelfth Sunday in Ordinary Time

Know that God is present with you and ready to converse.

The Cross of Christ, the instrument of Jesus' terrible death, is also the symbol of his glory—and ours.

When you are ready, ask Jesus to help you follow him with words such as these: "Risen Lord, reveal yourself to me now in your holy Word."

Read the Gospel: Luke 9:18–24.

Once when Jesus was praying alone, with only the disciples near him, he asked them, "Who do the crowds say that I am?" They answered, "John the Baptist; but others, Elijah; and still others, that one of the ancient prophets has arisen." He said to them, "But who do you say that I am?" Peter answered, "The Messiah of God."

He sternly ordered and commanded them not to tell anyone, saying, "The Son of Man must undergo great suffering, and be rejected by the elders, chief priests, and scribes, and be killed, and on the third day be raised."

Then he said to them all, "If any want to become my followers, let them deny themselves and take up their cross daily and follow me. For those who want to save their life will lose it, and those who lose their life for my sake will save it."

Notice what you think and feel as you read the Gospel.

Jesus knows who he is, and where he is going—to violent death, then resurrection. His disciples will understand it only in time, when they, too, take up their crosses and follow him.

Pray as you are led for yourself and others.

"Today I take up my cross and follow you, Lord . . ." (Continue in your own words.)

Listen to Jesus.

You follow me with your cross, and you are following me to resurrection. I am raising you to my life. What else is Jesus saying to you?

Ask God to show you how to live today.

"Show me how to lose my life for your sake, Jesus, for I want to live in your life. Amen."

Monday, June 20, 2016

Know that God is present with you and ready to converse.

"Speak to my heart, Word of God, so that I may walk in your truth."

Read the Gospel: Matthew 7:1–5.

Jesus taught, "Do not judge, so that you may not be judged. For with the judgment you make you will be judged, and the measure you give will be the measure you get. Why do you see the speck in your neighbor's eye, but do not notice the log in your own eye? Or how can you say to your neighbor, 'Let me take the speck out of your eye,' while the log is in your own eye? You hypocrite, first take the log out of your own eye, and then you will see clearly to take the speck out of your neighbor's eye."

Notice what you think and feel as you read the Gospel.

Jesus commands us not to judge others, warning us that by doing so we bring judgment upon ourselves. By his metaphor, Jesus says that our own faults blind us to the faults of others, and perhaps the greatest fault is the pride that leads us to judge a brother.

Pray as you are led for yourself and others.

"No one has ever spoken as you have, Jesus! I love you, for you challenge me . . ." (Continue in your own words.)

Listen to Jesus.

I am pleased that you seek me with all your heart, beloved disciple. What else is Jesus saying to you?

Ask God to show you how to live today.

"When I am tempted to judge another today, let me see my error and remember your mercy. Amen."

Tuesday, June 21, 2016

Know that God is present with you and ready to converse.

"Lead me to you through the narrow gate, Lord, for I long for your life."

Read the Gospel: Matthew 7:6, 12–14.

Jesus said, "Do not give what is holy to dogs; and do not throw your pearls before swine, or they will trample them underfoot and turn and maul you. . . .

"In everything do to others as you would have them do to you; for this is the law and the prophets.

"Enter through the narrow gate; for the gate is wide and the road is easy that leads to destruction, and there are many who take it. For the gate is narrow and the road is hard that leads to life, and there are few who find it."

Notice what you think and feel as you read the Gospel.

This is the golden rule that sums up the law and the prophets. Jesus knows it is not easy. The way that leads to life is hard, "and there are few who find it."

Pray as you are led for yourself and others.

"Jesus, I know you do not wish that any should perish. I pray for others, that many will find the way to eternal life . . ." (Continue in your own words.)

Listen to Jesus.

I hear your prayers for those I have given you. Pray and do not fear. What else is Jesus saying to you?

Ask God to show you how to live today.

"Make me aware of a situation in my day where I may do unto others what I wish that others would do unto me. Then give me grace to do it, Lord. Amen."

Wednesday, June 22, 2016

Know that God is present with you and ready to converse.

"Lord of love, I approach you now in awe of your Word, the Word of God. Help me to hear your voice."

Read the Gospel: Matthew 7:15–20.

Jesus instructed, "Beware of false prophets, who come to you in sheep's clothing but inwardly are ravenous wolves. You will know them by their fruits. Are grapes gathered from thorns, or figs from thistles? In the same way, every good tree bears good fruit, but the bad tree bears bad fruit. A good tree cannot bear bad fruit, nor can a bad tree bear good fruit. Every tree that does not bear good fruit is cut down and thrown into the fire. Thus you will know them by their fruits."

Notice what you think and feel as you read the Gospel.

Jesus warns us about false prophets. They put on a good show but have selfish and destructive motives. They will be destroyed, for they cannot bear fruit. But a sound tree bears good fruit. Look to the fruits.

Pray as you are led for yourself and others.

"Lord, give me discernment in choosing my teachers. Never let me be led astray . . ." (Continue in your own words.)

Listen to Jesus.

I am your shepherd, child. Live close to me and you yourself will bear good fruit. What else is Jesus saying to you?

Ask God to show you how to live today.

"You are good to me, Lord Jesus. I praise you. How may I bring glory to you today? Amen."

Thursday, June 23, 2016

Know that God is present with you and ready to converse.

"Be my rock, Word of God, and let me build my house upon you."

Read the Gospel: Matthew 7:21–29.

Jesus taught, "Not everyone who says to me, 'Lord, Lord,' will enter the kingdom of heaven, but only the one who does the will of my Father in heaven. On that day many will say to me, 'Lord, Lord, did we not prophesy in your name, and cast out demons in your name, and do many deeds of power in your name?' Then I will declare to them, 'I never knew you; go away from me, you evildoers.'

"Everyone then who hears these words of mine and acts on them will be like a wise man who built his house on rock. The rain fell, the floods came, and the winds blew and beat on that house, but it did not fall, because it had been founded on rock. And everyone who hears these words of mine and does not act on them will be like a foolish man who built his house on sand. The rain fell, and the floods came, and the winds blew and beat against that house, and it fell—and great was its fall!"

Now when Jesus had finished saying these things, the crowds were astounded at his teaching, for he taught them as one having authority, and not as their scribes.

Notice what you think and feel as you read the Gospel.

Jesus wants those who act in his name to have a close relationship with him. Only by knowing him can a person do the will of his Father. We build that friendship with Jesus on his words, hearing and doing them. That's the rock of safety.

Pray as you are led for yourself and others.

"Let me draw close to you by your words and do the will of your Father. Guide me . . ." (Continue in your own words.)

Listen to Jesus.

You are safe in me, beloved. You are listening to my words. What else is Jesus saying to you?

Ask God to show you how to live today.

"I pray today for those who are building upon sand. Let them realize their mistake and make you their rock. Amen."

Friday, June 24, 2016
Nativity of John the Baptist

Know that God is present with you and ready to converse.

"Lord of hosts, heavenly King, you are near me now and feed me by your Word."

Read the Gospel: Luke 1:57–66, 80.

Now the time came for Elizabeth to give birth, and she bore a son. Her neighbors and relatives heard that the Lord had shown his great mercy to her, and they rejoiced with her.

On the eighth day they came to circumcise the child, and they were going to name him Zechariah after his father. But his mother said, "No; he is to be called John." They said to her, "None of your relatives has this name." Then they began motioning to his father to find out what name he wanted to give him. He asked for a writing tablet and wrote, "His name is John." And all of them were amazed. Immediately his mouth was opened and his tongue freed, and he began to speak, praising God. Fear came over all their neighbors, and all these things were talked about throughout the entire hill country of Judea. All who heard them pondered them and said, "What then will this child become?" For, indeed, the hand of the Lord was with him. . . .

The child grew and became strong in spirit, and he was in the wilderness until the day he appeared publicly to Israel.

Notice what you think and feel as you read the Gospel.

God does his will through the elderly couple, parents of the infant John. The neighbors wonder, "What will this child be?" For the hand of the Lord was with him.

Pray as you are led for yourself and others.

"May your hand be with me, Lord. I need you . . ." (Continue in your own words.)

Listen to Jesus.

I'm glad you come to me with your needs. I am with you and helping you. What else is Jesus saying to you?

Ask God to show you how to live today.

"How may I become strong in Spirit to do your will and serve others? Amen."

Saturday, June 25, 2016

Know that God is present with you and ready to converse.

"I am unworthy to be in your presence, holy Son of God, but you invite me to enter your Word. Let it cleanse and heal me."

Read the Gospel: Matthew 8:5–17.

When Jesus entered Capernaum, a centurion came to him, appealing to him and saying, "Lord, my servant is lying at home paralyzed, in terrible distress." And he said to him, "I will come and cure him." The centurion answered, "Lord, I am not worthy to have you come under my roof; but only speak the word, and my servant will be healed. For I also am a man under authority, with soldiers under me; and I say to one, 'Go,' and he goes, and to another, 'Come,' and he comes, and to my slave, 'Do this,' and the slave does it." When Jesus heard him, he was amazed and said to those who followed him, "Truly I tell you, in no one in Israel have I found such faith. I tell you, many will come from east and west and will eat with Abraham and Isaac and Jacob in the kingdom of heaven, while the heirs of the kingdom will be thrown into the outer darkness, where there will be weeping and gnashing of teeth." And to the centurion Jesus said, "Go; let it be done for you according to your faith." And the servant was healed in that hour.

When Jesus entered Peter's house, he saw his mother-in-law lying in bed with a fever; he touched her hand, and the fever left her, and she got up and began to serve him. That evening they brought to him many who were possessed with demons; and he cast out the spirits with a word, and cured all who were sick. This was to fulfill what had been spoken through the prophet Isaiah, "He took our infirmities and bore our diseases."

Notice what you think and feel as you read the Gospel.

Jesus marvels at the faith of the centurion and heals his paralyzed servant without even going to him. He then heals Peter's mother of a fever. How? Isaiah said, "He took our infirmities and bore our diseases."

Pray as you are led for yourself and others.

"Jesus, thank you for bearing my infirmities and diseases in your own flesh. You are a great Savior . . ." (Continue in your own words.)

Listen to Jesus.

Believe in my power. Your faith in me pleases me. What else is Jesus saying to you?

Ask God to show you how to live today.

"I know people who need your healing touch and helping hand, Lord. I place them before you now. Amen."

Sunday, June 26, 2016
Thirteenth Sunday in Ordinary Time

Know that God is present with you and ready to converse.

God is merciful, and he asks us to show mercy to others. Forgiveness is our watchword now that we follow him.

When you are ready, invite the Lord to speak to you: "I open my heart to hear your Word. Let it transform me utterly."

Read the Gospel: Luke 9:51–62.

When the days drew near for him to be taken up, Jesus set his face to go to Jerusalem. And he sent messengers ahead of him. On their way they entered a village of the Samaritans to make ready for him; but they did not receive him, because his face was set toward Jerusalem. When his disciples James and John saw it, they said, "Lord, do you want us to command fire to come down from heaven and consume them?" But he turned and rebuked them. Then they went on to another village.

As they were going along the road, someone said to him, "I will follow you wherever you go." And Jesus said to him, "Foxes have holes, and birds of the air have nests; but the Son of Man has nowhere to lay his head." To another he said, "Follow me." But he said, "Lord, first let me go and bury my father." But Jesus said to him, "Let the dead bury their own dead; but as for you, go and proclaim the kingdom of God." Another said, "I will follow you, Lord; but let me first say farewell to those at my home." Jesus said to him, "No one who puts a hand to the plow and looks back is fit for the kingdom of God."

Notice what you think and feel as you read the Gospel.

Jesus sets his face to go to Jerusalem as activity swirls around him, and he speaks hard truth to some would-be followers: "No one who . . . looks back is fit for the kingdom of God."

Pray as you are led for yourself and others.

"Jesus, my hand is on the plow and my face is set for the kingdom of God. Be my strength . . ." (Continue in your own words.)

Listen to Jesus.

I know your heart, beloved. Give me your all and follow me. What else is Jesus saying to you?

Ask God to show you how to live today.

"Glory to you, Lord. Your kingdom come. Your will be done in me and in those you have given me to love and serve. Amen."

Monday, June 27, 2016

Know that God is present with you and ready to converse.

"Master, you have the words of eternal life. Speak to me now."

Read the Gospel: Matthew 8:18–22.

Now when Jesus saw great crowds around him, he gave orders to go over to the other side. A scribe then approached and said, "Teacher, I will follow you wherever you go." And Jesus said to him, "Foxes have holes, and birds of the air have nests; but the Son of Man has nowhere to lay his head." Another of his disciples said to him, "Lord, first let me go and bury my father." But Jesus said to him, "Follow me, and let the dead bury their own dead."

Notice what you think and feel as you read the Gospel.

Some people set conditions before they are willing to follow Jesus. But the Lord insists, "Follow me."

Pray as you are led for yourself and others.

"You are the life, Jesus. Help me put aside my conditions and excuses and follow you now . . ." (Continue in your own words.)

Listen to Jesus.

Beloved, you make me happy when you come to me. Stay with me and listen to what else I am saying. What else is Jesus saying to you?

Ask God to show you how to live today.

"Let me hear your words all day, Lord. Let me walk very close to you. Amen."

Tuesday, June 28, 2016

Know that God is present with you and ready to converse.

"You are present with me even in the storms of my life. What do you have for me today, Lord?"

Read the Gospel: Matthew 8:23–27.

When Jesus got into the boat, his disciples followed him. A windstorm arose on the sea, so great that the boat was being swamped by the waves; but he was asleep. And they went and woke him up, saying, "Lord, save us! We are perishing!" And he said to them, "Why are you afraid, you of little faith?" Then he got up and rebuked the winds and the sea; and there was a dead calm. They were amazed, saying, "What sort of man is this, that even the winds and the sea obey him?"

Notice what you think and feel as you read the Gospel.

The disciples are frightened in the storm as Jesus sleeps. He questions their fears and calls them "men of little faith." They marvel when he calms the storm: "What sort of man is this?"

Pray as you are led for yourself and others.

"I am like one of your disciples, Lord, afraid of many things . . ." (Continue in your own words.)

Listen to Jesus.

Spend time with me in prayer, child, and I will take away your fear. What else is Jesus saying to you?

Ask God to show you how to live today.

"At every stormy moment, Lord, great or small, remind me to turn to you for calm and help. Then let me marvel at your power and love. Amen."

Wednesday, June 29, 2016
Saints Peter and Paul, apostles

Know that God is present with you and ready to converse.

"Father, reveal your Son to me by your Word."

Read the Gospel: Matthew 16:13–19.

Now when Jesus came into the district of Caesarea Philippi, he asked his disciples, "Who do people say that the Son of Man is?" And they said, "Some say John the Baptist, but others Elijah, and still others Jeremiah or one of the prophets." He said to them, "But who do you say that I am?" Simon Peter answered, "You are the Messiah, the Son of the living God." And Jesus answered him, "Blessed are you, Simon son of Jonah! For flesh and blood has not revealed this to you, but my Father in heaven. And I tell you, you are Peter, and on this rock I will build my Church, and the gates of Hades will not prevail against it. I will give you the keys of the kingdom of heaven, and whatever you bind on earth will be bound in heaven, and whatever you loose on earth will be loosed in heaven."

Notice what you think and feel as you read the Gospel.

Peter proclaims Jesus the Christ, Son of the living God. Jesus blesses him for it and establishes his Church upon that rock. He gives Peter authority over things in heaven and on earth and the promise that the power of death will not prevail against his Church.

Pray as you are led for yourself and others.

"How your great Church rolls on, Lord! Thank you for being with us to the end of the world. Help us be faithful and worthy of your kingdom . . ." (Continue in your own words.)

Listen to Jesus.

I love my Church, my Bride, my own Body. What else is Jesus saying to you?

Ask God to show you how to live today.

"What can I do for your Church, Lord? I am ready to serve in my own small way. Amen."

Thursday, June 30, 2016

Know that God is present with you and ready to converse.

"Almighty Father, Jesus is your Word. Plant him in my heart today."

Read the Gospel: Matthew 9:1–8.

And after getting into a boat Jesus crossed the sea and came to his own town.

And just then some people were carrying a paralyzed man lying on a bed. When Jesus saw their faith, he said to the paralytic, "Take heart, son; your sins are forgiven." Then some of the scribes said to themselves, "This man is blaspheming." But Jesus, perceiving their thoughts, said, "Why do you think evil in your hearts? For which is easier, to say, 'Your sins are forgiven,' or to say, 'Stand up and walk'? But so that you may know that the Son of Man has authority on earth to forgive sins"—he then said to the paralytic—"Stand up, take your bed and go to your home." And he stood up and went to his home. When the crowds saw it, they were filled with awe, and they glorified God, who had given such authority to human beings.

Notice what you think and feel as you read the Gospel.

The scribes are scandalized when Jesus forgives the sins of the paralytic before healing him. Jesus rebukes them and tells them plainly that the

Son of Man has authority to forgive sins on earth. The crowds glorify God when the man is healed.

Pray as you are led for yourself and others.

"Sometimes I come to you asking favors when I should be seeking forgiveness . . ." (Continue in your own words.)

Listen to Jesus.

Take heart, child; your sins are forgiven. Ask of me whatever you want. What else is Jesus saying to you?

Ask God to show you how to live today.

"Thank you, Jesus. Let your grace remain with me today so that I may be merciful to others and show them your peace. Amen."

Friday, July 1, 2016

Know that God is present with you and ready to converse.

"Merciful Savior, I hear your call and come to the table of your Word."

Read the Gospel: Matthew 9:9–13.

As Jesus was walking along, he saw a man called Matthew sitting at the tax booth; and he said to him, "Follow me." And he got up and followed him.

And as he sat at dinner in the house, many tax collectors and sinners came and were sitting with him and his disciples. When the Pharisees saw this, they said to his disciples, "Why does your teacher eat with tax collectors and sinners?" But when he heard this, he said, "Those who are well have no need of a physician, but those who are sick. Go and learn what this means, 'I desire mercy, not sacrifice.' For I have come to call not the righteous but sinners."

Notice what you think and feel as you read the Gospel.

Jesus does not care what the Pharisees think. He eats with tax collectors and sinners because they need him. He is merciful. He says that God desires mercy, not sacrifice.

Pray as you are led for yourself and others.

"Let me rise and follow you as Matthew does, Jesus. For I need your mercy, too . . ." (Continue in your own words.)

Listen to Jesus.

You are dear to me, child. Let us make plans together. What else is Jesus saying to you?

Ask God to show you how to live today.

"I thank you for your forgiveness, Lord. How may I show mercy toward others today? Amen."

Saturday, July 2, 2016

Know that God is present with you and ready to converse.

"Let me receive your grace and truth by your Word, Lord. Jesus, you are full of grace and truth."

Read the Gospel: Matthew 9:14–17.

Then the disciples of John came to Jesus, saying, "Why do we and the Pharisees fast often, but your disciples do not fast?" And Jesus said to them, "The wedding guests cannot mourn as long as the bridegroom is with them, can they? The days will come when the bridegroom is taken away from them, and then they will fast. No one sews a piece of unshrunk cloth on an old cloak, for the patch pulls away from the cloak, and a worse tear is made. Neither is new wine put into old wineskins; otherwise, the skins burst, and the wine is spilled, and the skins are destroyed; but new wine is put into fresh wineskins, and so both are preserved."

Notice what you think and feel as you read the Gospel.

Jesus explains in parables to the disciples of John the Baptist how he is bringing something new. His disciples do not fast because the Bridegroom is with them. He is the wine of new life.

Pray as you are led for yourself and others.

"Pour me new wine, Lord, and make of me a new wineskin to preserve it into eternal life . . ." (Continue in your own words.)

Listen to Jesus.

Not just I but all the souls in heaven rejoice in your faith and love. We will welcome you at the marriage supper of the Lamb. What else is Jesus saying to you?

Ask God to show you how to live today.

"I cannot serve others, Lord, unless you give me what I need to do so. Please help me do something good today and avoid evil. Amen."

Sunday, July 3, 2016
Fourteenth Sunday in Ordinary Time

Know that God is present with you and ready to converse.

Jesus commissioned his disciples to preach the Gospel and gave them power to heal and cast out demons. They would be rejected by many, but the Holy Spirit would lead them and strengthen them.

When you are ready, invite the Holy Spirit into your reading and your prayer: "Holy Spirit, always present everywhere, I give myself to you now. Teach me by the Word of God."

Read the Gospel: Luke 10:1–12, 17–20.

After this the Lord appointed seventy others and sent them on ahead of him in pairs to every town and place where he himself intended to go. He said to them, "The harvest is plentiful, but the laborers are few; therefore ask the Lord of the harvest to send out laborers into his harvest. Go on your way. See, I am sending you out like lambs into the midst of wolves. Carry no purse, no bag, no sandals; and greet no one on the road. Whatever house you enter, first say, 'Peace to this house!' And if anyone is there who shares in peace, your peace will rest on that person; but if not, it will return to you. Remain in the same house, eating and drinking whatever they provide, for the laborer deserves to be paid. Do not move about from house to house. Whenever you enter a town and its people welcome you, eat what is set before you; cure the sick who are there, and say to them, 'The kingdom of God has come near to you.' But whenever you enter a town and they do not welcome you, go out into its streets and say, 'Even the dust of your town that clings to our feet, we wipe off in protest against you. Yet know this: the kingdom of God has come near.' I tell you, on that day it will be more tolerable for Sodom than for that town." . . .

The seventy returned with joy, saying, "Lord, in your name even the demons submit to us!" He said to them, "I watched Satan fall from heaven like a flash of lightning. See, I have given you authority to tread on snakes and scorpions, and over all the power of the enemy; and nothing will hurt you. Nevertheless, do not rejoice at this, that the spirits submit to you, but rejoice that your names are written in heaven."

Notice what you think and feel as you read the Gospel.

Jesus commissions seventy disciples, sending them out two by two with instructions for ministry. They are to bring his peace, healing, and help to all who will receive. The seventy return with joy, marveling at the power they have in his name.

Pray as you are led for yourself and others.

"Jesus, give me the power I need to meet my responsibilities to those you have given me. Let me see needs beyond my own . . ." (Continue in your own words.)

Listen to Jesus.

You are my servant, beloved. You serve me when you serve others. What else is Jesus saying to you?

Ask God to show you how to live today.

"I want to spend more time with you throughout my day. Teach me how to find you more often in others. Amen."

Monday, July 4, 2016

Know that God is present with you and ready to converse.

"Lord, I reach out to you. Touch me and raise me to your life."

Read the Gospel: Matthew 9:18–26.

While Jesus was saying these things to them, suddenly a leader of the synagogue came in and knelt before him, saying, "My daughter has just died; but come and lay your hand on her, and she will live." And Jesus got up and followed him, with his disciples. Then suddenly a woman who had been suffering from hemorrhages for twelve years came up behind him and touched the fringe of his cloak, for she said to herself, "If I only touch his cloak, I will be made well." Jesus turned, and seeing her he said, "Take heart, daughter; your faith has made you well." And instantly the woman was made well. When Jesus came to the leader's house and saw the flute players and the crowd making a commotion, he said, "Go away; for the girl is not dead but sleeping." And they laughed at him. But when the crowd had been put outside, he went in and took her by the hand, and the girl got up. And the report of this spread throughout that district.

Notice what you think and feel as you read the Gospel.

Jesus is willing to heal the ruler's daughter and follows him. On the way a sick woman touches the fringe of his garment and receives healing, too.

Pray as you are led for yourself and others.

"Mighty Savior, you reward faith. All your ways are just and loving. I give myself to you now . . ." (Continue in your own words.)

Listen to Jesus.

Pray for faith, friend. Faith in me gives you peace and power to serve. What else is Jesus saying to you?

Ask God to show you how to live today.

"Whom may I touch with your love today, Lord? Amen."

Tuesday, July 5, 2016

Know that God is present with you and ready to converse.

"Loving Lord, I am lost without you. Let me hear your voice."

Read the Gospel: Matthew 9:32–38.

After they had gone away, a demoniac who was mute was brought to him. And when the demon had been cast out, the one who had been mute spoke; and the crowds were amazed and said, "Never has anything like this been seen in Israel." But the Pharisees said, "By the ruler of the demons he casts out the demons."

Then Jesus went about all the cities and villages, teaching in their synagogues, and proclaiming the good news of the kingdom, and curing every disease and every sickness. When he saw the crowds, he had compassion for them, because they were harassed and helpless, like sheep without a shepherd. Then he said to his disciples, "The harvest is plentiful, but the laborers are few; therefore ask the Lord of the harvest to send out laborers into his harvest."

Notice what you think and feel as you read the Gospel.

The Pharisees accuse Jesus of casting out demons by the power of the devil. But Jesus continues to preach the kingdom and heal, for he sees humanity as "harassed and helpless, like sheep without a shepherd." There is a plentiful harvest of souls, he says, but we are to pray to God to send laborers into his harvest.

Pray as you are led for yourself and others.

"When you ask me to pray for laborers, Lord, you involve me in the work of your Father . . ." (Continue in your own words.)

Listen to Jesus.

I give you my heart to pray that my Father's will be done. As you come to know me better, you will continuously pray that my Father's will be done on earth. What else is Jesus saying to you?

Ask God to show you how to live today.

"Our Father, who art in heaven, hallowed be thy name. Thy kingdom come, thy will be done . . . Amen."

Wednesday, July 6, 2016

Know that God is present with you and ready to converse.

"Your Word is the kingdom of heaven, Lord. I invite you in."

Read the Gospel: Matthew 10:1–7.

Then Jesus summoned his twelve disciples and gave them authority over unclean spirits, to cast them out, and to cure every disease and every sickness. These are the names of the twelve apostles: first, Simon, also known as Peter, and his brother Andrew; James son of Zebedee, and his brother John; Philip and Bartholomew; Thomas and Matthew the tax collector; James son of Alphaeus, and Thaddaeus; Simon the Cananaean, and Judas Iscariot, the one who betrayed him.

These twelve Jesus sent out with the following instructions: "Go nowhere among the Gentiles, and enter no town of the Samaritans, but go rather to the lost sheep of the house of Israel. As you go, proclaim the good news, 'The kingdom of heaven has come near.'"

Notice what you think and feel as you read the Gospel.

Jesus gives the apostles his own powers. Their first mission is to the "lost sheep of Israel."

Pray as you are led for yourself and others.

"Jesus, you loved your own. Give me the love I need to care for my own . . ." (Continue in your own words.)

Listen to Jesus.

The kingdom of heaven is at hand for you, too, dear disciple. What else is Jesus saying to you?

Ask God to show you how to live today.

"Today, like every day, I do not know how to serve. But I trust you to show me, Lord, and give me power to speak and do as you would have me. Amen."

Thursday, July 7, 2016

Know that God is present with you and ready to converse.

"Holy Lord, I worship you with every breath of my being; I am your servant."

Read the Gospel: Matthew 10:7–15.

Jesus instructed, "As you go, proclaim the good news, 'The kingdom of heaven has come near.' Cure the sick, raise the dead, cleanse the lepers, cast out demons. You received without payment; give without payment. Take no gold, or silver, or copper in your belts, no bag for your journey, or two tunics, or sandals, or a staff; for laborers deserve their food. Whatever town or village you enter, find out who in it is worthy, and stay there until you leave. As you enter the house, greet it. If the house is worthy, let your peace come upon it; but if it is not worthy, let your peace return to you. If anyone will not welcome you or listen to your words, shake off the dust from your feet as you leave that house or town. Truly I tell you, it will be more tolerable for the land of Sodom and Gomorrah on the day of judgment than for that town."

Notice what you think and feel as you read the Gospel.

Jesus instructs his followers, reminding them that since they "received without payment" they are to "give without payment." And if anyone will not receive you, just leave.

Pray as you are led for yourself and others.

"Lord, I pray for those who do not receive you. I know people who refuse to hear or, hearing, refuse to come to you . . ." (Continue in your own words.)

Listen to Jesus.

Your heart and mine mourn for those who reject me and the gift of life. What else is Jesus saying to you?

Ask God to show you how to live today.

"Jesus, help me to do what I can do—and to leave the rest to you. Amen."

Friday, July 8, 2016

Know that God is present with you and ready to converse.

"Spirit of the Father, speak to me through the holy Word of today's Gospel. Open my ears and heart to every word."

Read the Gospel: Matthew 10:16–23.

Jesus said, "See, I am sending you out like sheep into the midst of wolves; so be wise as serpents and innocent as doves. Beware of them, for they will hand you over to councils and flog you in their synagogues; and you will be dragged before governors and kings because of me, as a testimony to them and the Gentiles. When they hand you over, do not worry about how you are to speak or what you are to say; for what you are to say will be given to you at that time; for it is not you who speak, but the Spirit of your Father speaking through you. Brother will betray brother to death, and a father his child, and children will rise against parents and have them put to death; and you will be hated by all because of my name. But the one who endures to the end will be saved. When they persecute you in one town, flee to the next; for truly I tell you, you will not have gone through all the towns of Israel before the Son of Man comes."

Notice what you think and feel as you read the Gospel.

Jesus prepares his disciples for rejection and persecution, advising them to be "wise as serpents and innocent as doves." There are wolves out there, yes, but the disciples need not be anxious, for the Spirit will be with them to help them endure to the end.

Pray as you are led for yourself and others.

"I know wolves, Lord. I have anxieties in dealing with those who oppose me . . ." (Continue in your own words.)

Listen to Jesus.

No one can do you any harm, beloved, as long as you cling to me. Love and forgive those who seek to harm you in any way. What else is Jesus saying to you?

Ask God to show you how to live today.

"Lord, give me grace to endure. I need you today, Jesus. Amen."

Saturday, July 9, 2016

Know that God is present with you and ready to converse.

"Teacher, you are with me now. Let me learn from your Word."

Read the Gospel: Matthew 10:24–33.

Jesus said, "A disciple is not above the teacher, nor a slave above the master; it is enough for the disciple to be like the teacher, and the slave like the master. If they have called the master of the house Beelzebul, how much more will they malign those of his household!

"So have no fear of them; for nothing is covered up that will not be uncovered, and nothing secret that will not become known. What I say to you in the dark, tell in the light; and what you hear whispered, proclaim from the housetops. Do not fear those who kill the body but cannot kill the soul; rather fear him who can destroy both soul and body in hell. Are not two sparrows sold for a penny? Yet not one of them will fall to the ground apart from your Father. And even the hairs of your head are all counted. So do not be afraid; you are of more value than many sparrows.

"Everyone therefore who acknowledges me before others, I also will acknowledge before my Father in heaven; but whoever denies me before others, I also will deny before my Father in heaven."

Notice what you think and feel as you read the Gospel.

Jesus tells his disciples they have nothing to fear from people who hate and malign them. Those who kill your body cannot kill your soul. Don't be afraid. Acknowledge Jesus as Lord, and trust the Father.

Pray as you are led for yourself and others.

"Master, let me be like you. Let me be unafraid and acknowledge you as Lord among others . . ." (Continue in your own words.)

Listen to Jesus.

Why should you be afraid when I am with you, child? I speak of you to my Father. What else is Jesus saying to you?

Ask God to show you how to live today.

"I offer myself to you today—all my thoughts, words, and deeds—for the good of others. Amen."

Sunday, July 10, 2016
Fifteenth Sunday in Ordinary Time

Know that God is present with you and ready to converse.

Jesus taught love: love of God, love of neighbor, and love of enemy. He demonstrated his teaching extravagantly in his passion and death on the cross.

When you are ready, open yourself to hear the Word of God: "Teacher, what must I do to inherit eternal life?"

Read the Gospel: Luke 10:25–37.

Just then a lawyer stood up to test Jesus. "Teacher," he said, "what must I do to inherit eternal life?" He said to him, "What is written in the law? What do you read there?" He answered, "You shall love the Lord your God with all your heart, and with all your soul, and with all your strength, and with all your mind; and your neighbor as yourself." And he said to him, "You have given the right answer; do this, and you will live."

But wanting to justify himself, he asked Jesus, "And who is my neighbor?" Jesus replied, "A man was going down from Jerusalem to Jericho, and fell into the hands of robbers, who stripped him, beat him, and went away, leaving him half dead. Now by chance a priest was going down that road; and when he saw him, he passed by on the other side. So likewise a Levite, when he came to the place and saw him, passed by on the other side. But a Samaritan while traveling came near him; and when he saw him, he was moved with pity. He went to him and bandaged his wounds, having poured oil and wine on them. Then he put him on his own animal, brought him to an inn, and took care of him. The next day he took out two denarii, gave them to the innkeeper, and said, 'Take care of him; and when I come back, I will repay you whatever more you spend.' Which of these three, do you think, was a neighbor to the man who fell into the hands of the robbers?" He said, "The one who showed him mercy." Jesus said to him, "Go and do likewise."

Notice what you think and feel as you read the Gospel.

Jesus tells the story of the priest, the Levite, and the Samaritan. Only the Samaritan gets involved, showing compassion to the man half dead on the road. Jesus says, "Go and do likewise." This is the way to inherit eternal life.

Pray as you are led for yourself and others.

"Give me a generous heart, Lord . . ." (Continue in your own words.)

Listen to Jesus.

When you love, you give, and you can give only what you have received from God. Now I give you the gift of freedom to give to those in need. What else is Jesus saying to you?

Ask God to show you how to live today.

"You call me to your own moral nobility, Lord. Help me to act worthy of you, for I bear your name. Amen."

Monday, July 11, 2016

Know that God is present with you and ready to converse.

"I come into your presence rejoicing, Lord, for your Word is my light and my law."

Read the Gospel: Matthew 10:34–11:1.

Jesus said, "Do not think that I have come to bring peace to the earth; I have not come to bring peace, but a sword.

For I have come to set a man against his father,
and a daughter against her mother,
and a daughter-in-law against her mother-in-law;
and one's foes will be members of one's own household.

"Whoever loves father or mother more than me is not worthy of me; and whoever loves son or daughter more than me is not worthy of me; and whoever does not take up the cross and follow me is not worthy of me. Those who find their life will lose it, and those who lose their life for my sake will find it.

"Whoever welcomes you welcomes me, and whoever welcomes me welcomes the one who sent me. Whoever welcomes a prophet in the name of a prophet will receive a prophet's reward; and whoever welcomes a righteous person in the name of a righteous person will receive the reward of the righteous; and whoever gives even a cup of cold water to one of these little ones in the name of a disciple—truly I tell you, none of these will lose their reward."

Now when Jesus had finished instructing his twelve disciples, he went on from there to teach and proclaim his message in their cities.

Notice what you think and feel as you read the Gospel.

Faith in Christ causes divisions, even among families. But loving Jesus is most important—denying self, taking up one's cross, and following him.

Pray as you are led for yourself and others.

"Lord, I pray that all in my family will draw close to you. Show mercy and bring healing . . ." (Continue in your own words.)

Listen to Jesus.

Continue to pray for those I have given you, beloved disciple. I love them, too. What else is Jesus saying to you?

Ask God to show you how to live today.

"Help us to grow as family, Lord, in faith and love for you. Amen."

Tuesday, July 12, 2016

Know that God is present with you and ready to converse.

"Mighty Lord, with me now, you will come in glory to judge the living and the dead. Open my heart to your Word."

Read the Gospel: Matthew 11:20–24.

Then Jesus began to reproach the cities in which most of his deeds of power had been done, because they did not repent. "Woe to you, Chorazin! Woe to you, Bethsaida! For if the deeds of power done in you had been done in Tyre and Sidon, they would have repented long ago in sackcloth and ashes. But I tell you, on the day of judgment it will be more tolerable for Tyre and Sidon than for you. And you, Capernaum,

will you be exalted to heaven?
No, you will be brought down to Hades.

"For if the deeds of power done in you had been done in Sodom, it would have remained until this day. But I tell you that on the day of judgment it will be more tolerable for the land of Sodom than for you."

Notice what you think and feel as you read the Gospel.

Jesus upbraids the cities in which he has done most of his mighty works because they do not repent. He warns them of the judgment.

Pray as you are led for yourself and others.

"Lord, I pray for those in my own community, nation, and world. Give us the grace to repent of all our wickedness and turn to you . . ." (Continue in your own words.)

Listen to Jesus.

I have mercy in my hand. I will reward those who turn from sin and seek righteousness. What else is Jesus saying to you?

Ask God to show you how to live today.

"Lord, what can I do to help reverse wrongdoing where I live? Amen."

Wednesday, July 13, 2016

Know that God is present with you and ready to converse.

"Father, you reveal your truths to children. Give me ears to hear you now."

Read the Gospel: Matthew 11:25–27.

At that time Jesus said, "I thank you, Father, Lord of heaven and earth, because you have hidden these things from the wise and the intelligent and have revealed them to infants; yes, Father, for such was your gracious will. All things have been handed over to me by my Father; and no one knows the Son except the Father, and no one knows the Father except the Son and anyone to whom the Son chooses to reveal him."

Notice what you think and feel as you read the Gospel.

Jesus thanks his Father that he hides truth from those who are wise and reveals it to babes. No one knows the Father except those to whom the Son chooses to reveal him.

Pray as you are led for yourself and others.

"Let me drop all pretense of wisdom, Lord. I stand before you as a child . . ." (Continue in your own words.)

Listen to Jesus.

You know me, child. My Father and I are one, and you are one with us. What else is Jesus saying to you?

Ask God to show you how to live today.

"Lead me in the simple way today, Lord of heaven and earth. Amen."

Thursday, July 14, 2016

Know that God is present with you and ready to converse.

"Let me learn from you, Jesus, Word of God. I seek rest for my soul."

Read the Gospel: Matthew 11:28–30.

Jesus taught, "Come to me, all you that are weary and are carrying heavy burdens, and I will give you rest. Take my yoke upon you, and learn from me; for I am gentle and humble in heart, and you will find rest for your souls. For my yoke is easy, and my burden is light."

Notice what you think and feel as you read the Gospel.

Gentle and lowly in heart, Jesus calls to souls, offering rest. His yoke is easy and his burden is light.

Pray as you are led for yourself and others.

"Lord, how often do I labor under my own burdens? Let me take up yours . . ." (Continue in your own words.)

Listen to Jesus.

Pray to have a heart like mine, child. There is your perfect rest. What else is Jesus saying to you?

Ask God to show you how to live today.

"Jesus, I pray that I may look upon others with your heart and that my actions will follow. Amen."

Friday, July 15, 2016

Know that God is present with you and ready to converse.

"I join you now, Lord, ready to hear your holy Word."

Read the Gospel: Matthew 12:1–8.

At that time Jesus went through the cornfields on the Sabbath; his disciples were hungry, and they began to pluck heads of grain and to eat. When the Pharisees saw it, they said to him, "Look, your disciples are doing what is not lawful to do on the Sabbath." He said to them, "Have you not read what David did when he and his companions were hungry? He entered the house of God and ate the bread of the Presence, which it was not lawful for him or his companions to eat, but only for the priests. Or have you not read in the law that on the Sabbath the priests in the Temple break the Sabbath and yet are guiltless? I tell you, something greater than the Temple is here. But if you had known what this means, 'I desire mercy and not sacrifice,' you would not have condemned the guiltless. For the Son of Man is lord of the Sabbath."

Notice what you think and feel as you read the Gospel.

Jesus uses scripture to defend himself against the legalistic accusations of the Pharisees. They need to understand that God desires mercy, not sacrifice. The Son of Man is Lord of the Sabbath.

Pray as you are led for yourself and others.

"Jesus, I have sometimes judged by human standards the freedom of others. Give me your mercy . . ." (Continue in your own words.)

Listen to Jesus.

You are learning, my friend. Continue to turn your heart toward mercy. What else is Jesus saying to you?

Ask God to show you how to live today.

"Make me aware in the moments of my day when I have opportunities to withhold judgment and show mercy. Then let me obey you in this, Lord. Amen."

Saturday, July 16, 2016

Know that God is present with you and ready to converse.

"Proclaim justice and hope to my soul through your Spirit and your Word. I am listening, Lord."

Read the Gospel: Matthew 12:14–21.

But the Pharisees went out and conspired against Jesus, how to destroy him.

When Jesus became aware of this, he departed. Many crowds followed him, and he cured all of them, and he ordered them not to make him known. This was to fulfill what had been spoken through the prophet Isaiah:

"Here is my servant, whom I have chosen,
    my beloved, with whom my soul is well pleased.
I will put my Spirit upon him,
    and he will proclaim justice to the Gentiles.
He will not wrangle or cry aloud,
    nor will anyone hear his voice in the streets.
He will not break a bruised reed
    or quench a smoldering wick
until he brings justice to victory.
    And in his name the Gentiles will hope."

Notice what you think and feel as you read the Gospel.

Jesus withdraws from the plotting Pharisees and heals all who come to him, asking them not to make him known. He is the fulfillment of Isaiah's servant messiah, favored by God, full of the Spirit, quietly proclaiming justice to the Gentiles.

Pray as you are led for yourself and others.

"Lord, bring justice to victory. I hope . . ." (Continue in your own words.)

Listen to Jesus.

I hear your prayers, chosen servant. Seek justice on earth and you will see it triumph. What else is Jesus saying to you?

Ask God to show you how to live today.

"Help me to be just and fair in my own dealings, Lord. Amen."

Sunday, July 17, 2016
Sixteenth Sunday in Ordinary Time

Know that God is present with you and ready to converse.

This is the day of rest. We are so busy with our business every day—even Sundays. It takes effort to stop and pray. When we do, we are easily distracted. Let us settle ourselves to listen to Jesus. He is near.

When you are ready, let Jesus know you want to hear his words: "Lord, you have come into my house. Let me sit at your feet and listen to your teaching."

Read the Gospel: Luke 10:38–42.

Now as they went on their way, Jesus entered a certain village, where a woman named Martha welcomed him into her home. She had a sister named Mary, who sat at the Lord's feet and listened to what he was saying. But Martha was distracted by her many tasks; so she came to him and asked, "Lord, do you not care that my sister has left me to do all the work by myself? Tell her then to help me." But the Lord answered her, "Martha, Martha, you are worried and distracted by many things; there is need of only one thing. Mary has chosen the better part, which will not be taken away from her."

Notice what you think and feel as you read the Gospel.

Martha complains to Jesus that she is serving the company while her sister just sits there at his feet. He gently admonishes her for being anxious. Mary has made the better choice.

Pray as you are led for yourself and others.

"Lord, let me spend more time with you. I, too, can be anxious and troubled . . ." (Continue in your own words.)

Listen to Jesus.

If you wish to be mine, come to me, beloved. Take time to sit in my presence. What else is Jesus saying to you?

Ask God to show you how to live today.

"Let me find you often during my day, Lord, to bask in your love, your peace, your wisdom, and to praise you, thank you, and worship you. Amen."

Monday, July 18, 2016

Know that God is present with you and ready to converse.

"Son of God, Word of the Father, I long to hear you."

Read the Gospel: Matthew 12:38–42.

Then some of the scribes and Pharisees said to Jesus, "Teacher, we wish to see a sign from you." But he answered them, "An evil and adulterous generation asks for a sign, but no sign will be given to it except the sign of the prophet Jonah. For just as Jonah was three days and three nights in the belly of the sea monster, so for three days and three nights the Son of Man will be in the heart of the earth. The people of Nineveh will rise up at the judgment with this generation and condemn it, because they repented at the proclamation of Jonah, and see, something greater than Jonah is here! The queen of the south will rise up at the judgment with this generation and condemn it, because she came from the ends of the earth to listen to the wisdom of Solomon, and see, something greater than Solomon is here!"

Notice what you think and feel as you read the Gospel.

Jesus rebukes the Pharisees for asking for a sign, declaring that the only sign they will see is his resurrection after three days in the earth. This evil generation neither repents, as did Nineveh, nor receives Jesus' preaching, as did Solomon's visitor.

Pray as you are led for yourself and others.

"I offer myself to you, Lord, repenting now of my sins and open to what you have to say to me . . ." (Continue in your own words.)

Listen to Jesus.

My mercy is a constant stream for you to drink. My Spirit speaks to you what you need to hear. What else is Jesus saying to you?

Ask God to show you how to live today.

"Let me never underestimate your power, Lord. All things are possible in you. Work in me and through me today. Amen."

Tuesday, July 19, 2016

Know that God is present with you and ready to converse.

"Jesus, Savior, you call me to do God's will."

Read the Gospel: Matthew 12:46–50.

While Jesus was still speaking to the crowds, his mother and his brothers were standing outside, wanting to speak to him. Someone told him, "Look, your mother and your brothers are standing outside, wanting to speak to you." But to the one who had told him this, Jesus replied, "Who is my mother, and who are my brothers?" And pointing to his disciples, he said, "Here are my mother and my brothers! For whoever does the will of my Father in heaven is my brother and sister and mother."

Notice what you think and feel as you read the Gospel.

Jesus' mother and brethren are outside asking to speak to him. Jesus turns to his disciples and pronounces them his mother and his brethren, for they do the will of God by following him.

Pray as you are led for yourself and others.

"Jesus, thank you for adopting me into your family. As God's child, let me bring you glory today . . ." (Continue in your own words.)

Listen to Jesus.

I love you, child. You, too, are begotten of the Father. What do you ask from God today? What else is Jesus saying to you?

Ask God to show you how to live today.

"Give me a clear sense of God's will for me, Lord, and then the grace to do it. Glory be to the Father . . . Amen."

Wednesday, July 20, 2016

Know that God is present with you and ready to converse.

"Sow the seeds of divine life deep in my soul, Lord, that they may bear fruit to your glory."

Read the Gospel: Matthew 13:1–9.

That same day Jesus went out of the house and sat beside the sea. Such great crowds gathered around him that he got into a boat and sat there, while the whole crowd stood on the beach. And he told them many things in parables, saying: "Listen! A sower went out to sow. And as he sowed, some seeds fell on the path, and the birds came and ate them up. Other seeds fell on rocky ground, where they did not have much soil, and they sprang up quickly, since they had no depth of soil. But when the sun rose, they were scorched; and since they had no root, they withered away. Other seeds fell among thorns, and the thorns grew up and choked them. Other seeds fell on good soil and brought forth grain, some a hundredfold, some sixty, some thirty. Let anyone with ears listen!"

Notice what you think and feel as you read the Gospel.

Jesus describes a sower sowing seeds. The seeds grow or do not grow according to the condition of the soil they fall upon. Most seeds fail, but the ones that fall on good soil yield much grain.

Pray as you are led for yourself and others.

"I will bear fruit as I take your Word deep into my being. Help me to do so every day, Lord . . ." (Continue in your own words.)

Listen to Jesus.

What is the condition of your heart, beloved? Give me your whole heart. What else is Jesus saying to you?

Ask God to show you how to live today.

"Grow in me, Lord, day and night, that I may be as you in the world. Amen."

Thursday, July 21, 2016

Know that God is present with you and ready to converse.

"You have given me much, Word of God. I open my heart to your abundance."

Read the Gospel: Matthew 13:10–17.

Then Jesus' disciples came and asked him, "Why do you speak to them in parables?" He answered, "To you it has been given to know the secrets of the kingdom of heaven, but to them it has not been given. For to those who have, more will be given, and they will have an abundance; but from those who have nothing, even what they have will be taken away. The reason I speak to them in parables is that 'seeing they do not perceive, and hearing they do not listen, nor do they understand.' With them indeed is fulfilled the prophecy of Isaiah that says:

'You will indeed listen, but never understand,
and you will indeed look, but never perceive.
For this people's heart has grown dull,
and their ears are hard of hearing,

and they have shut their eyes;
so that they might not look with their eyes,
and listen with their ears,
and understand with their heart and turn—
and I would heal them.'

"But blessed are your eyes, for they see, and your ears, for they hear. Truly I tell you, many prophets and righteous people longed to see what you see, but did not see it, and to hear what you hear, but did not hear it."

Notice what you think and feel as you read the Gospel.

Jesus tells his disciples that they have been given to know the secrets of the kingdom, and they will be given even more. But others will not hear or understand. He quotes from Isaiah to identify the reason: "This people's heart has grown dull."

Pray as you are led for yourself and others.

"Lord, soften the hearts of those who do not understand and let them turn to you . . ." (Continue in your own words.)

Listen to Jesus.

I long to heal the hardhearted, beloved disciple. I speak to them in many ways. What else is Jesus saying to you?

Ask God to show you how to live today.

"May I have the privilege of sowing a seed today, Lord? Let me share with another a secret of your kingdom—its peace, its love, its mercy, its healing, its joy. Amen."

Friday, July 22, 2016
Saint Mary Magdalene

Know that God is present with you and ready to converse.

"Be with me and speak, Lord, as you did to Mary outside your open tomb."

Read the Gospel: John 20:1–2, 11–18.

Early on the first day of the week, while it was still dark, Mary Magdalene came to the tomb and saw that the stone had been removed from the tomb. So she ran and went to Simon Peter and the other disciple, the one whom Jesus loved, and said to them, "They have taken the Lord out of the tomb, and we do not know where they have laid him." . . .

But Mary stood weeping outside the tomb. As she wept, she bent over to look into the tomb; and she saw two angels in white, sitting where the body of Jesus had been lying, one at the head and the other at the feet. They said to her, "Woman, why are you weeping?" She said to them, "They have taken away my Lord, and I do not know where they have laid him." When she had said this, she turned around and saw Jesus standing there, but she did not know that it was Jesus. Jesus said to her, "Woman, why are you weeping? Whom are you looking for?" Supposing him to be the gardener, she said to him, "Sir, if you have carried him away, tell me where you have laid him, and I will take him away." Jesus said to her, "Mary!" She turned and said to him in Hebrew, "Rabbouni!" (which means teacher). Jesus said to her, "Do not hold on to me, because I have not yet ascended to the Father. But go to my brothers and say to them, 'I am ascending to my Father and your Father, to my God and your God.'" Mary Magdalene went and announced to the disciples, "I have seen the Lord"; and she told them that he had said these things to her.

Notice what you think and feel as you read the Gospel.

Mary has the privilege of seeing the risen Lord before the other disciples even understand that he was to rise on the third day. Jesus gently charges her to bring the news of his resurrection to the others and to let them know he is ascending to "my Father and your Father, to my God and your God."

Pray as you are led for yourself and others.

"You turn weeping into joy by your presence, Lord. You know the sorrows that are on my heart . . ." (Continue in your own words.)

Listen to Jesus.

I am with you, beloved. All your sorrows will give way to rejoicing. These things shall be well. What else is Jesus saying to you?

Ask God to show you how to live today.

"Lord, I offer all my joys and sorrows of this day to God for the good of all those you have given me, especially those most in need of your touch. Amen."

Saturday, July 23, 2016

Know that God is present with you and ready to converse.

"Father, you do not sleep, but you constantly work to accomplish your loving purposes. Work in me today by your holy Word."

Read the Gospel: Matthew 13:24–30.

Jesus put before them another parable: "The kingdom of heaven may be compared to someone who sowed good seed in his field; but while everybody was asleep, an enemy came and sowed weeds among the wheat, and then went away. So when the plants came up and bore grain, then the weeds appeared as well. And the slaves of the householder came and said to him, 'Master, did you not sow good seed in your field? Where, then, did these weeds come from?' He answered, 'An enemy has done this.' The slaves said to him, 'Then do you want us to go and gather them?' But he replied, 'No; for in gathering the weeds you would uproot the wheat along with them. Let both of them grow together until the harvest; and at harvest time I will tell the reapers, collect the weeds first and bind them in bundles to be burned, but gather the wheat into my barn.'"

Notice what you think and feel as you read the Gospel.

Jesus tells the story of a farmer who sows wheat, but at night an enemy sows weeds among the wheat. When the farmer discovers it, he decides to do nothing. At the harvest he will separate the weeds from the wheat. The former he will burn; the latter he will gather into the barn. This is a parable of the kingdom.

Pray as you are led for yourself and others.

"You allow evils to continue in the world, Lord. I rest in your patience until the harvest is ready . . ." (Continue in your own words.)

Listen to Jesus.

My Father works and I work in the world. In the triumph of love, if you remain faithful, you will be among those gathered into the kingdom of heaven. What else is Jesus saying to you?

Ask God to show you how to live today.

"Help me to trust you to work all things for good, even wrongdoing and injustice. Keep me from being choked by the weeds. Amen."

Sunday, July 24, 2016
Seventeenth Sunday in Ordinary Time

Know that God is present with you and ready to converse.

Prayer is the way we build our friendship with God. God tells us to seek, to praise, to love, to ask, and to worship. God promises to guide, to forgive, to heal, and to help us. Jesus even teaches us to pray.

When you are ready, read the Gospel with fresh eyes and an open heart. "As I seek you today, Lord, you are already present with me. Teach me how to pray by your Word."

Read the Gospel: Luke 11:1–13.

Jesus was praying in a certain place, and after he had finished, one of his disciples said to him, "Lord, teach us to pray, as John taught his disciples." He said to them, "When you pray, say:

> Father, hallowed be your name.
> Your kingdom come.
> Give us each day our daily bread.
> And forgive us our sins,
> for we ourselves forgive everyone indebted to us.
> And do not bring us to the time of trial."

And he said to them, "Suppose one of you has a friend, and you go to him at midnight and say to him, 'Friend, lend me three loaves of bread; for a friend of mine has arrived, and I have nothing to set before him.' And he answers from within, 'Do not bother me; the door has already been locked, and my children are with me in bed; I cannot get up and give you anything.' I tell you, even though he will not get up and give him anything because he is his friend, at least because of his persistence he will get up and give him whatever he needs.

"So I say to you, ask, and it will be given you; search, and you will find; knock, and the door will be opened for you. For everyone who asks receives, and everyone who searches finds, and for everyone who knocks, the door will be opened. Is there anyone among you who, if your child asks for a fish, will give a snake instead of a fish? Or if the child asks for an egg, will give a scorpion? If you then, who are evil, know how to give good gifts to your children, how much more will the heavenly Father give the Holy Spirit to those who ask him!"

Notice what you think and feel as you read the Gospel.

After praying, Jesus responds to a disciple's request by teaching them the Our Father and telling them the parable of the persistent friend. God will give to those who ask persistently.

Pray as you are led for yourself and others.

"Give me the Holy Spirit, Lord, so that I can love you and live, serve, and pray as you want . . ." (Continue in your own words.)

Listen to Jesus.

In your seeking is your finding. Let your hunger for God grow. You will receive what you truly long for. What else is Jesus saying to you?

Ask God to show you how to live today.

"Lord, keep me knocking on your door all day long. I believe you will open doors for me and for those I pray for. Amen."

Monday, July 25, 2016
Saint James, apostle

Know that God is present with you and ready to converse.

"I love your living Word, Lord. Let me drink of it deeply."

Read the Gospel: Matthew 20:20–28.

Then the mother of the sons of Zebedee came to Jesus with her sons, and kneeling before him, she asked a favor of him. And he said to her, "What do you want?" She said to him, "Declare that these two sons of mine will sit, one at your right hand and one at your left, in your kingdom." But Jesus answered, "You do not know what you are asking. Are you able to drink the cup that I am about to drink?" They said to him, "We are able." He said to them, "You will indeed drink my cup, but to sit at my right hand and at my left, this is not mine to grant, but it is for those for whom it has been prepared by my Father."

When the ten heard it, they were angry with the two brothers. But Jesus called them to him and said, "You know that the rulers of the Gentiles lord it over them, and their great ones are tyrants over them. It will not be so among you; but whoever wishes to be great among you must be your servant, and whoever wishes to be first among you must be your slave; just as the Son of Man came not to be served but to serve, and to give his life a ransom for many."

Notice what you think and feel as you read the Gospel.

Jesus seems to approve of the sons of Zebedee when they say they are able to drink the cup that Jesus is to drink. Yet, he reminds the Twelve that the way to true greatness is to be a servant.

Pray as you are led for yourself and others.

"I offer myself to you as a servant, Lord. Show me what you want me to do . . ." (Continue in your own words.)

Listen to Jesus.

I accept your offer, beloved servant. I will show you what to do. What else is Jesus saying to you?

Ask God to show you how to live today.

"Help me to be unselfish, Lord, and to give generously of my time, my work, my possessions, and my money. For all I have is yours. Amen."

Tuesday, July 26, 2016

Know that God is present with you and ready to converse.

"Lord God of hosts, Father of the kingdom, let me hear your voice in your Word."

Read the Gospel: Matthew 13:36–43.

Then Jesus left the crowds and went into the house. And his disciples approached him, saying, "Explain to us the parable of the weeds of the field." He answered, "The one who sows the good seed is the Son of Man; the field is the world, and the good seed are the children of the kingdom; the weeds are the children of the evil one, and the enemy who sowed them is the devil; the harvest is the end of the age, and the reapers are angels. Just as the weeds are collected and burned up with fire, so will it be at the end of the age. The Son of Man will send his angels, and they will collect out of his kingdom all causes of sin and all evildoers, and they will throw them into the furnace of fire, where there will be weeping and gnashing of teeth. Then the righteous will shine like the sun in the kingdom of their Father. Let anyone with ears listen!"

Notice what you think and feel as you read the Gospel.

Jesus himself will come again in the company of his angels to gather up and destroy all causes of sin and all evildoers. "Then the righteous will shine like the sun in the kingdom of their Father."

Pray as you are led for yourself and others.

"Jesus, let me be among the righteous shining like the sun in your Father's kingdom. I have some things I would like to talk with you about . . ." (Continue in your own words.)

Listen to Jesus.

I am glad you bring these things to me, child. With God all things are possible. Listen to me. What else is Jesus saying to you?

Ask God to show you how to live today.

"Help me to do good without self-righteousness, Lord. Keep me from pride. Keep me in your humble love. Amen."

Wednesday, July 27, 2016

Know that God is present with you and ready to converse.

"I seek you and your kingdom, Lord. Let me find you and it in your Word."

Read the Gospel: Matthew 13:44–46.

Jesus said, "The kingdom of heaven is like treasure hidden in a field, which someone found and hid; then in his joy he goes and sells all that he has and buys that field.

"Again, the kingdom of heaven is like a merchant in search of fine pearls; on finding one pearl of great value, he went and sold all that he had and bought it."

Notice what you think and feel as you read the Gospel.

Jesus illustrates how a person should respond to finding the kingdom of heaven. One should sell all one has to buy it. It is the pearl of great value.

Pray as you are led for yourself and others.

"You use worldly pictures to speak of a spiritual thing. You yourself are the kingdom of heaven, and you live within me now. Let me value you within me more than everything else I have or am or want . . ." (Continue in your own words.)

Listen to Jesus.

Let go of yourself and all the things you cherish so that my love can flood your heart. This is the kingdom that will last forever. What else is Jesus saying to you?

Ask God to show you how to live today.

"Show me what I can sell today so that you can replace it. Show me day by day how to let go of myself and to live more and more simply in you. Amen."

Thursday, July 28, 2016

Know that God is present with you and ready to converse.

"As I listen to your Word, Holy Spirit, quicken my heart to understand and obey."

Read the Gospel: Matthew 13:47–53.

Jesus taught, "Again, the kingdom of heaven is like a net that was thrown into the sea and caught fish of every kind; when it was full, they drew it ashore, sat down, and put the good into baskets but threw out the bad. So it will be at the end of the age. The angels will come out and separate the evil from the righteous and throw them into the furnace of fire, where there will be weeping and gnashing of teeth.

"Have you understood all this?" They answered, "Yes." And he said to them, "Therefore every scribe who has been trained for the kingdom of heaven is like the master of a household who brings out of his treasure what is new and what is old." When Jesus had finished these parables, he left that place.

Notice what you think and feel as you read the Gospel.

Jesus compares the kingdom to a net that catches both good and bad. The good is preserved; the bad is thrown away. So it will be at the end of the age. He says everyone trained in the kingdom of heaven possesses treasure both old and new.

Pray as you are led for yourself and others.

"Jesus, continue to train me in your kingdom so that I may gather spiritual treasures both old and new . . ." (Continue in your own words.)

Listen to Jesus.

The three great treasures of my kingdom are faith, hope, and love. Ask for them and all other virtues will follow—humility, patience, prudence, mercy, and justice. What else is Jesus saying to you?

Ask God to show you how to live today.

"Lord, all virtues come by the Holy Spirit, not by me. As I receive them, let me live and be in this world to the glory of almighty God. Amen."

Friday, July 29, 2016
Saint Martha

Know that God is present with you and ready to converse.

"Lord, I am often distracted and anxious as I rush through my days. Let me begin with a fervent desire for you."

Read the Gospel: Luke 10:38–42.

Now as they went on their way, Jesus entered a certain village, where a woman named Martha welcomed him into her home. She had a sister named Mary, who sat at the Lord's feet and listened to what he was saying. But Martha was distracted by her many tasks; so she came to him and asked, "Lord, do you not care that my sister has left me to do all the work by myself? Tell her then to help me." But the Lord answered her, "Martha, Martha, you are worried and distracted by many things; there is need of only one thing. Mary has chosen the better part, which will not be taken away from her."

Notice what you think and feel as you read the Gospel.

Martha is busy serving. Who can fault her for that? Someone needs to take care of things. But she has lost perspective, for the Lord is in her house. She complains that Mary doesn't help her, and Jesus lovingly corrects Martha.

Pray as you are led for yourself and others.

"Jesus, correct me when I forget that you are first in my life, when I lose proper perspective. For example . . ." (Continue in your own words.)

Listen to Jesus.

I will continue to draw you back to myself when you wander, for you are my beloved servant. I will continue to teach you by my words. What else is Jesus saying to you?

Ask God to show you how to live today.

"Give me order in my life, Lord. Show me how to manage my affairs so that you are glorified while I do what needs to be done for the sake of myself and others. Amen."

Saturday, July 30, 2016

Know that God is present with you and ready to converse.

"Lord, this is a world of sin. Keep me mindful that you work all things for good for those you love. I praise you, almighty Father."

Read the Gospel: Matthew 14:1–12.

At that time Herod the ruler heard reports about Jesus; and he said to his servants, "This is John the Baptist; he has been raised from the dead, and for this reason these powers are at work in him." For Herod had arrested John, bound him, and put him in prison on account of Herodias, his brother Philip's wife, because John had been telling him, "It is not lawful for you to have her." Though Herod wanted to put him to death, he feared the crowd, because they regarded him as a prophet. But when Herod's birthday came, the daughter of Herodias danced before the company, and she pleased Herod so much that he promised on oath to grant her whatever she might ask. Prompted by her mother, she said, "Give me the head of John the Baptist here on a platter." The king was grieved, yet out of regard for his oaths and for the guests, he commanded it to be given; he sent and had John beheaded in the prison. The head was brought on a platter and given to the girl, who brought it to her mother. His disciples came and took the body and buried it; then they went and told Jesus.

Notice what you think and feel as you read the Gospel.

King Herod is wicked, vain, cowardly, adulterous, and foolish. Herodias's daughter dances lewdly before the guests, then demands John the Baptist's head be brought to her on a platter. Herod orders it done. John's disciples bury the body and go tell Jesus.

Pray as you are led for yourself and others.
"This is the world, Lord. Such evil goes on constantly. Let me have no part in it. Let me be one who works for justice and peace . . ." (Continue in your own words.)

Listen to Jesus.
Evil is appalling, friend, but justice will prevail. I am your peace. Walk with me today. What else is Jesus saying to you?

Ask God to show you how to live today.
"Deliver me from evil, Lord. Help me to be brave as I walk even through the valley of death, for you are with me. Thank you, blessed Savior. Amen."

Sunday, July 31, 2016
Eighteenth Sunday in Ordinary Time

Know that God is present with you and ready to converse.
We cannot trust in wealth. It will not save us; we cannot take it with us. Our hearts must be rich in the things of God.

When you are ready to hear his words, approach the Lord and speak to him: "Holy Lord, God of hosts, I draw near to you now. Purify my heart by your Word."

Read the Gospel: Luke 12:13–21.
Someone in the crowd said to Jesus, "Teacher, tell my brother to divide the family inheritance with me." But he said to him, "Friend, who set me to be a judge or arbitrator over you?" And he said to them, "Take care! Be on your guard against all kinds of greed; for one's life does not consist in the abundance of possessions." Then he told them a parable: "The land of a rich man produced abundantly. And he thought to himself, 'What should I do, for I have no place to store my crops?' Then he said, 'I will do this: I will pull down my barns and build larger ones, and there I will store all my grain and my goods. And I will say to my soul, soul, you have ample goods laid up for many years; relax, eat, drink, be merry.' But God said to him, 'You fool! This very night your life is being demanded of you. And the things you have prepared, whose will they be?' So it is with those who store up treasures for themselves but are not rich toward God."

Notice what you think and feel as you read the Gospel.

Jesus tells a parable of a rich man who foolishly relies on his possessions, planning to take his ease to eat, drink, and be merry. But that night his soul is taken from him, and he never gets a chance to enjoy his riches. Jesus says we should be rich toward God.

Pray as you are led for yourself and others.

"How may I be prudent about earthly possessions, Lord, while I grow rich in the things of God? Give me wisdom and . . ." (Continue in your own words.)

Listen to Jesus.

I know what you need, beloved. Come and spend time with me often. I will bless you beyond your imagining. What else is Jesus saying to you?

Ask God to show you how to live today.

"Jesus, I sense my detachment from possessions originates in a heart fixed on you, full of love and trust. Shine light into my darkness as I follow you today. Amen."

Monday, August 1, 2016

Know that God is present with you and ready to converse.

"Feed me by your Word, Bread of Life."

Read the Gospel: Matthew 14:13–21.

Now when Jesus heard this, he withdrew from there in a boat to a deserted place by himself. But when the crowds heard it, they followed him on foot from the towns. When he went ashore, he saw a great crowd; and he had compassion for them and cured their sick. When it was evening, the disciples came to him and said, "This is a deserted place, and the hour is now late; send the crowds away so that they may go into the villages and buy food for themselves." Jesus said to them, "They need not go away; you give them something to eat." They replied, "We have nothing here but five loaves and two fish." And he said, "Bring them here to me." Then he ordered the crowds to sit down on the grass. Taking the five loaves and the two fish, he looked up to heaven, and blessed and broke the loaves, and gave them to the disciples, and the disciples gave them to the crowds. And all ate and were filled; and they took up what was left over of the broken pieces, twelve baskets full. And those who ate were about five thousand men, besides women and children.

Notice what you think and feel as you read the Gospel.

Jesus feels compassion for the crowd following him and heals their sick. The disciples worry about the people becoming hungry in this lonely place and suggest to Jesus that he send them away to the town where they can buy food. Jesus takes the opportunity to multiply the loaves and fishes to feed them all.

Pray as you are led for yourself and others.

"I hunger for you, Lord. Give me your bread so that I can feed others as the disciples did . . ." (Continue in your own words.)

Listen to Jesus.

The more you eat this bread, the more you will hunger for it. The hunger I put within you is a great gift. What else is Jesus saying to you?

Ask God to show you how to live today.

"I thank you and give you glory, Lord. Let me remain in your presence today. Open my eyes to see God working in my life and in the lives of others. Amen."

Tuesday, August 2, 2016

Know that God is present with you and ready to converse.

"Lord, save me, for I have little faith, and truly you are the Son of God."

Read the Gospel: Matthew 14:22–36.

Immediately Jesus made the disciples get into the boat and go on ahead to the other side, while he dismissed the crowds. And after he had dismissed the crowds, he went up the mountain by himself to pray. When evening came, he was there alone, but by this time the boat, battered by the waves, was far from the land, for the wind was against them. And early in the morning he came walking toward them on the sea. But when the disciples saw him walking on the sea, they were terrified, saying, "It is a ghost!" And they cried out in fear. But immediately Jesus spoke to them and said, "Take heart, it is I; do not be afraid."

Peter answered him, "Lord, if it is you, command me to come to you on the water." He said, "Come." So Peter got out of the boat, started walking on the water, and came toward Jesus. But when he noticed the strong wind, he became frightened, and beginning to sink, he cried out, "Lord, save me!" Jesus immediately reached out his hand and caught him, saying to him, "You of little faith, why did you doubt?" When they got into the boat, the wind ceased. And those in the boat worshiped him, saying, "Truly you are the Son of God."

When they had crossed over, they came to land at Gennesaret. After the people of that place recognized him, they sent word throughout the region and brought all who were sick to him, and begged him that they might touch even the fringe of his cloak; and all who touched it were healed.

Notice what you think and feel as you read the Gospel.

Jesus sends his disciples off in the boat and goes up into the hills to be alone and pray. Meanwhile the boat is making poor progress against the wind. Jesus approaches the boat by walking on the water. The disciples are frightened until he says, "Take heart, it is I; do not be afraid." That's when Peter gets into the act . . .

Pray as you are led for yourself and others.

"Jesus, help me to do as you did—go off alone to pray. For I need grace to believe during the storms of my life . . ." (Continue in your own words.)

Listen to Jesus.

Walk to me, dear disciple. Take my hand. You are safe with me. What else is Jesus saying to you?

Ask God to show you how to live today.

"Reveal to me opportunities in my day to reach out in faith to you. Help me to be willing to share my faith with others. Amen."

Wednesday, August 3, 2016

Know that God is present with you and ready to converse.

"Jesus, I sometimes wander and am sometimes lost. But I look to you now in faith."

Read the Gospel: Matthew 15:21–28.

Jesus left that place and went away to the district of Tyre and Sidon. Just then a Canaanite woman from that region came out and started shouting, "Have mercy on me, Lord, Son of David; my daughter is tormented by a demon." But he did not answer her at all. And his disciples came and urged him, saying, "Send her away, for she keeps shouting after us." He answered, "I was sent only to the lost sheep of the house of Israel." But she came and knelt before him, saying, "Lord, help me." He answered, "It is not fair to take the children's food and throw it to the dogs." She said, "Yes, Lord, yet even the dogs eat the crumbs that fall from their masters' table." Then Jesus answered her, "Woman, great is your faith! Let it be done for you as you wish." And her daughter was healed instantly.

Notice what you think and feel as you read the Gospel.

The encounter with the Canaanite woman is an opportunity for Jesus to show how he loves and heals people of every nation. He grants her desire because of her great faith. The woman's daughter is healed immediately.

Pray as you are led for yourself and others.

"Lord, I persist in asking you for healing for myself and for others. Increase my faith and answer my prayers . . ." (Continue in your own words.)

Listen to Jesus.

I do answer your prayer. Pray from the heart. Pray for those I give you. What else is Jesus saying to you?

Ask God to show you how to live today.

"Give me compassion for those on the margins of society who have serious needs. Help me to help them, for I can do nothing without you, Lord. Amen."

Thursday, August 4, 2016

Know that God is present with you and ready to converse.

"Father, reveal your Son to me by your Word and by your Spirit."

Read the Gospel: Matthew 16:13–23.

Now when Jesus came into the district of Caesarea Philippi, he asked his disciples, "Who do people say that the Son of Man is?" And they said, "Some say John the Baptist, but others Elijah, and still others Jeremiah or one of the prophets." He said to them, "But who do you say that I am?" Simon Peter answered, "You are the Messiah, the Son of the living God." And Jesus answered him, "Blessed are you, Simon son of Jonah! For flesh and blood has not revealed this to you, but my Father in heaven. And I tell you, you are Peter, and on this rock I will build my Church, and the gates of Hades will not prevail against it. I will give you the keys of the kingdom of heaven, and whatever you bind on earth will be bound in heaven, and whatever you loose on earth will be loosed in heaven." Then he sternly ordered the disciples not to tell anyone that he was the Messiah.

From that time on, Jesus began to show his disciples that he must go to Jerusalem and undergo great suffering at the hands of the elders and chief priests and scribes, and be killed, and on the third day be raised. And Peter took him aside and began to rebuke him, saying, "God forbid it, Lord! This must never happen to you." But he turned and said to Peter, "Get behind me, Satan! You are a stumbling block to me; for you are setting your mind not on divine things but on human things."

Notice what you think and feel as you read the Gospel.

When Peter declares that Jesus is the Christ, the Son of the living God, Jesus pronounces him the rock upon which he will build his Church. The power of death will not prevail against the Church until the end of time.

Pray as you are led for yourself and others.

"Jesus, thank you for your Church, your Body. I pray for all bishops, priests, religious, and lay people in your service, especially for . . ." (Continue in your own words.)

Listen to Jesus.

Do not fear the powers of the world, beloved. Seek to do good, to love, and to serve, and you will build up the Church. What else is Jesus saying to you?

Ask God to show you how to live today.

"Show me the good to do today, Lord. Let me do it truly in your Spirit, lovingly, humbly, peacefully. Glory be to God, Father, Son, and Holy Spirit. Amen."

Friday, August 5, 2016

Know that God is present with you and ready to converse.

"Jesus, I now turn away from all that I am and have and look to you in your holy Word."

Read the Gospel: Matthew 16:24–28.

Then Jesus told his disciples, "If any want to become my followers, let them deny themselves and take up their cross and follow me. For those who want to save their life will lose it, and those who lose their life for my sake will find it. For what will it profit them if they gain the whole world but forfeit their life? Or what will they give in return for their life?

"For the Son of Man is to come with his angels in the glory of his Father, and then he will repay everyone for what has been done. Truly I tell you, there are some standing here who will not taste death before they see the Son of Man coming in his kingdom."

Notice what you think and feel as you read the Gospel.

Jesus tells his disciples that they must deny themselves, lose themselves, take up their crosses, and follow him. At the end of time he will come in glory and repay every person for what he or she has done.

Pray as you are led for yourself and others.

"Jesus, give me singleness of heart to follow you as you ask. Let me do no evil, but give me power to do good . . ." (Continue in your own words.)

Listen to Jesus.

My life is in you, beloved. I give you what you ask for. What else can I do for you? What else is Jesus saying to you?

Ask God to show you how to live today.

"My spirit is willing but my flesh is weak, Lord, so I rely on you to help me serve you and others as I should. Be my strength, Lord. Amen."

Saturday, August 6, 2016
The Transfiguration of the Lord

Know that God is present with you and ready to converse.

"Jesus, you prayed in the company of your disciples; I pray in your company, Lord. I will listen now to the voice of God."

Read the Gospel: Luke 9:28b–36.

Jesus took with him Peter and John and James, and went up on the mountain to pray. And while he was praying, the appearance of his face changed, and his clothes became dazzling white. Suddenly they saw two men, Moses and Elijah, talking to him. They appeared in glory and were speaking of his departure, which he was about to accomplish at Jerusalem. Now Peter and his companions were weighed down with sleep; but since they had stayed awake, they saw his glory and the two men who stood with him. Just as they were leaving him, Peter said to Jesus, "Master, it is good for us to be here; let us make three dwellings, one for you, one for Moses, and one for Elijah"—not knowing what he said. While he was saying this, a cloud came and overshadowed them; and they were terrified as they entered the cloud. Then from the cloud came a voice that said, "This is my Son, my Chosen; listen to him!" When the voice had spoken, Jesus was found alone. And they kept silent and in those days told no one any of the things they had seen.

Notice what you think and feel as you read the Gospel.

Jesus gives his disciples a glimpse of his glory; his appearance is altered and his clothing becomes dazzling white. How the disciples marvel to see Moses and Elijah consulting with Jesus about the events that will happen to him in Jerusalem. As the prophets are departing, a cloud overshadows all of them and the Father speaks: "This is my Son, my Chosen; listen to him!"

Pray as you are led for yourself and others.

"Lord, great is your glory. I glorify you with all my heart. And I listen . . ." (Continue in your own words.)

Listen to Jesus.

I share the glory of my Father, beloved. You share my glory, for you are my beloved disciple and you hear my voice. One day and forever you will fully share in the glory of God. What else is Jesus saying to you?

Ask God to show you how to live today.

"Jesus, I cannot take in your amazing love for me. You have given me eternal life. Show me how to take up my cross today, following you. Thank you. Amen."

Sunday, August 7, 2016
Nineteenth Sunday in Ordinary Time

Know that God is present with you and ready to converse.

Jesus is the truth and the way to God. We believe, we trust, we turn away from evil, and we care for those in need. Our reward is to be received by God.

When you are ready, invite God into your prayer with words such as these: "Father, it is your good pleasure to give me the kingdom. Let me treasure your Word in my heart and do it."

Read the Gospel: Luke 12:32–48.

Jesus said, "Do not be afraid, little flock, for it is your Father's good pleasure to give you the kingdom. Sell your possessions, and give alms. Make purses for yourselves that do not wear out, an unfailing treasure in heaven, where no thief comes near and no moth destroys. For where your treasure is, there your heart will be also.

"Be dressed for action and have your lamps lit; be like those who are waiting for their master to return from the wedding banquet, so that they may open the door for him as soon as he comes and knocks. Blessed are those slaves whom the master finds alert when he comes; truly I tell you, he will fasten his belt and have them sit down to eat, and he will come and serve them. If he comes during the middle of the night, or near dawn, and finds them so, blessed are those slaves.

"But know this: if the owner of the house had known at what hour the thief was coming, he would not have let his house be broken into. You also must be ready, for the Son of Man is coming at an unexpected hour."

Peter said, "Lord, are you telling this parable for us or for everyone?" And the Lord said, "Who then is the faithful and prudent manager whom his master will put in charge of his slaves, to give them their allowance of food at the proper time? Blessed is that slave whom his master will find at work when he arrives. Truly I tell you, he will put that one in charge of all his possessions. But if that slave says to himself, 'My master is delayed in coming,' and if he begins to beat the other slaves, men and women, and to eat and drink and get drunk, the master of that slave will come on a day when he does not expect him and at an hour that he does not know, and will cut him in pieces, and put him with the unfaithful. That slave who knew what his master wanted, but did not prepare himself or do what was wanted, will receive a severe beating. But the one who did not know and did what deserved a beating will receive a light beating. From everyone to whom much has been given, much will be required; and from the one to whom much has been entrusted, even more will be demanded."

Notice what you think and feel as you read the Gospel.

In parable, Jesus tells his disciples to provide themselves with treasure in heaven by selling their possessions, giving alms, awaiting his return, serving justly in earthly affairs, and persevering in good. He says when the master comes and finds his servants doing his will, he himself will sit them at his table and serve them. What humility in Jesus!

Pray as you are led for yourself and others.

"Lord, you have given me much, and you promise much more. What do you require of me?" (Continue in your own words.)

Listen to Jesus.

You already know many things I ask of you, dear servant. Do them and I will open your eyes to more. What else is Jesus saying to you?

Ask God to show you how to live today.

"Lord, I know that in my own power I cannot succeed, but I can do all things if you are with me. Let me serve others in the strength of your Holy Spirit. Amen."

Monday, August 8, 2016

Know that God is present with you and ready to converse.

"Jesus, you provide for all my needs. Thank you. Now I need you and the wisdom of your Word."

Read the Gospel: Matthew 17:22–27.

As they were gathering in Galilee, Jesus said to them, "The Son of Man is going to be betrayed into human hands, and they will kill him, and on the third day he will be raised." And they were greatly distressed.

When they reached Capernaum, the collectors of the Temple tax came to Peter and said, "Does your teacher not pay the Temple tax?" He said, "Yes, he does." And when he came home, Jesus spoke of it first, asking, "What do you think, Simon? From whom do kings of the earth take toll or tribute? From their children or from others?" When Peter said, "From others," Jesus said to him, "Then the children are free. However, so that we do not give offense to them, go to the sea and cast a hook; take the first fish that comes up; and when you open its mouth, you will find a coin; take that and give it to them for you and me."

Notice what you think and feel as you read the Gospel.

Jesus distresses his disciples by telling them plainly of his death and resurrection on the third day. Surely they put his words out of their minds. The Lord then instructs Peter how to pay their taxes. He sends him out to catch a fish with a shekel in its mouth.

Pray as you are led for yourself and others.

"Your ways are marvelous, Jesus. You saved my soul by your cross and resurrection, you give me eternal life, and you also meet my needs here and now . . ." (Continue in your own words.)

Listen to Jesus.

"I delight to give you the kingdom, child, and all things on heaven and earth. Ask me for what you need." What else is Jesus saying to you?

Ask God to show you how to live today.

"Thank you, generous Lord and Master. What can I do for you today and tomorrow? Amen."

Tuesday, August 9, 2016

Know that God is present with you and ready to converse.

"I am before you, Lord; let me be as a child, humbly learning from your Word."

Read the Gospel: Matthew 18:1–5, 10, 12–14.

At that time the disciples came to Jesus and asked, "Who is the greatest in the kingdom of heaven?" He called a child, whom he put among them, and said, "Truly I tell you, unless you change and become like children, you will never enter the kingdom of heaven. Whoever becomes humble like this child is the greatest in the kingdom of heaven. Whoever welcomes one such child in my name welcomes me. . . .

"Take care that you do not despise one of these little ones; for, I tell you, in heaven their angels continually see the face of my Father in heaven. . . .

"What do you think? If a shepherd has a hundred sheep, and one of them has gone astray, does he not leave the ninety-nine on the mountains and go in search of the one that went astray? And if he finds it, truly I tell you, he rejoices over it more than over the ninety-nine that never went astray. So it is not the will of your Father in heaven that one of these little ones should be lost."

Notice what you think and feel as you read the Gospel.

Jesus tells his disciples they must become like children to enter the kingdom of heaven. He identifies with the children. The shepherd seeks for his one lost sheep and returns it to the flock rejoicing. It is the will of his Father that not one of these little ones be lost.

Pray as you are led for yourself and others.

"Jesus, forgive me when I am wise in my own eyes. I know nothing without you. Let me pray for children . . ." (Continue in your own words.)

Listen to Jesus.

Yes, child of my Father, humility is putting others before yourself. Constantly thinking about yourself leads you away from humility. What else is Jesus saying to you?

Ask God to show you how to live today.

"I turn to you, Teacher. Let me see others through your eyes. Thank you. Amen."

Wednesday, August 10, 2016

Know that God is present with you and ready to converse.

"You alone are worthy, Lord. You gave your life for me. I want to follow you."

Read the Gospel: John 12:24–26.

Jesus said, "Very truly, I tell you, unless a grain of wheat falls into the earth and dies, it remains just a single grain; but if it dies, it bears much fruit. Those who love their life lose it, and those who hate their life in this world will keep it for eternal life. Whoever serves me must follow me, and where I am, there will my servant be also. Whoever serves me, the Father will honor."

Notice what you think and feel as you read the Gospel.

Jesus says that, to be fruitful, the grain of wheat must die. So in this life we must die to enter into eternal life. Following Jesus, the servant will receive honor from the Father.

Pray as you are led for yourself and others.

"Lord, free me from fear of death, for I want take up my cross and follow you, bearing much fruit . . ." (Continue in your own words.)

Listen to Jesus.

You bear fruit by abiding in me, beloved servant and friend. You cannot know how much. Be faithful in little things. What else is Jesus saying to you?

Ask God to show you how to live today.

"Give me the proper attitude toward my life, Lord. Let me value you more than life. Give me grace to serve you today. Amen."

Thursday, August 11, 2016

Know that God is present with you and ready to converse.

"Justice is yours, everlasting Father. But I live by your mercy. Open my heart to your Word."

Read the Gospel: Matthew 18:21–19:1.

Then Peter came and said to Jesus, "Lord, if another member of the church sins against me, how often should I forgive? As many as seven times?" Jesus said to him, "Not seven times, but, I tell you, seventy-seven times.

"For this reason the kingdom of heaven may be compared to a king who wished to settle accounts with his slaves. When he began the reckoning, one who owed him ten thousand talents was brought to him; and, as he could not pay, his lord ordered him to be sold, together with his wife and children and all his possessions, and payment to be made. So the slave fell on his knees before him, saying, 'Have patience with me, and I will pay you everything.' And out of pity for him, the lord of that slave released him and forgave him the debt. But that same slave, as he went out, came upon one of his fellow slaves who owed him a hundred denarii; and seizing him by the throat, he said, 'Pay what you owe.' Then his fellow slave fell down and pleaded with him, 'Have patience with me, and I will pay you.' But he refused; then he went and threw him into prison until he would pay the debt. When his fellow slaves saw what had happened, they were greatly distressed, and they went and reported to their lord all that had taken place. Then his lord summoned him and said to him, 'You wicked slave! I forgave you all that debt because you pleaded with me. Should you not have had mercy on your fellow slave, as I had mercy on you?' And in anger his lord handed him over to be tortured until he would pay his entire debt. So my heavenly Father will also do to every one of you, if you do not forgive your brother or sister from your heart."

When Jesus had finished saying these things, he left Galilee and went to the region of Judea beyond the Jordan.

Notice what you think and feel as you read the Gospel.

Jesus tells the parable of the king who out of pity forgave one of his servants a large debt. Later, when the king hears that the servant refused to forgive a fellow servant a much smaller debt, even putting him in prison, he is angry and throws the unmerciful servant in jail.

Pray as you are led for yourself and others.

"Lord, I receive your mercy every day. Let me forgive from my heart all who have offended me in the past and all who offend me now . . ." (Continue in your own words.)

Listen to Jesus.

Seventy times seven I give you grace to forgive. Do not judge others. Walk in my mercy. What else is Jesus saying to you?

Ask God to show you how to live today.

"Lord, I am often unaware of my judgmental attitudes toward others. Help me see when I am judgmental, and help me to show mercy in place of judgment. Amen."

Friday, August 12, 2016

Know that God is present with you and ready to converse.

"Lord, give me grace to receive your Word."

Read the Gospel: Matthew 19:3–12.

Some Pharisees came to Jesus, and to test him they asked, "Is it lawful for a man to divorce his wife for any cause?" He answered, "Have you not read that the one who made them at the beginning 'made them male and female,' and said, 'For this reason a man shall leave his father and mother and be joined to his wife, and the two shall become one flesh'? So they are no longer two, but one flesh. Therefore what God has joined together, let no one separate." They said to him, "Why then did Moses command us to give a certificate of dismissal and to divorce her?" He said to them, "It was because you were so hardhearted that Moses allowed you to divorce your wives, but from the beginning it was not so. And I say to you, whoever divorces his wife, except for unchastity, and marries another commits adultery."

His disciples said to him, "If such is the case of a man with his wife, it is better not to marry." But he said to them, "Not everyone can accept this teaching, but only those to whom it is given. For there are eunuchs who have been so from birth, and there are eunuchs who have been made eunuchs by others, and there are eunuchs who have made themselves eunuchs for the sake of the kingdom of heaven. Let anyone accept this who can."

Notice what you think and feel as you read the Gospel.

Jesus replies to the Pharisees' questions about divorce by affirming the oneness of a married couple ordained by God. The Mosaic institution of divorce, Jesus says, is an accommodation to human "hardness of heart." When the disciples suggest that it would be better not to marry, Jesus says that not all people can live the single life.

Pray as you are led for yourself and others.

"Lord, you have called me to my state in life. Help me to be faithful and chaste . . ." (Continue in your own words.)

Listen to Jesus.

My Church is my bride, and you and I are one. Walk in this love. What else is Jesus saying to you?

Ask God to show you how to live today.

"My Jesus, I love you, and I give you everything I am, for you give yourself to me without withholding anything. Amen."

Saturday, August 13, 2016

Know that God is present with you and ready to converse.

"Lay your hands on me, Lord, and let me receive your blessing."

Read the Gospel: Matthew 19:13–15.

Then little children were being brought to Jesus in order that he might lay his hands on them and pray. The disciples spoke sternly to those who brought them; but Jesus said, "Let the little children come to me, and do not stop them; for it is to such as these that the kingdom of heaven belongs." And he laid his hands on them and went on his way.

Notice what you think and feel as you read the Gospel.

Jesus tells his disciples to let the children come to him, for the kingdom of heaven belongs to the childlike. He lays his hands on the children.

Pray as you are led for yourself and others.

"Make me childlike, Lord, in faith and love and openness to you . . ." (Continue in your own words.)

Listen to Jesus.

A child does not pretend to be something he or she is not. I ask you to be authentic. You will find me in your truest self. What else is Jesus saying to you?

Ask God to show you how to live today.

"Lord, I long for authenticity in all my relationships, especially my relationship with you. Show me how to be real. May I bring you glory. Amen."

Sunday, August 14, 2016
Twentieth Sunday in Ordinary Time

Know that God is present with you and ready to converse.

Following Christ is costly. Jesus requires we give him all we are and all we have. No wonder many do not follow him. But if we follow him, the rewards in this life and in the next are immense. We receive eternal life in the presence of our loving God. Let us take up our cross today.

When you are ready, speak to Jesus: "God made flesh, you have disrupted history by coming among us. You have disrupted my life, too, in saving me from death. I thank you, Lord, and I need you again today."

Read the Gospel: Luke 12:49–53.

Jesus said, "I came to bring fire to the earth, and how I wish it were already kindled! I have a baptism with which to be baptized, and what stress I am under until it is completed! Do you think that I have come to bring peace to the earth? No, I tell you, but rather division! From now on, five in one household will be divided, three against two and two against three; they will be divided:

> father against son
> and son against father,
> mother against daughter
> and daughter against mother,
> mother-in-law against her daughter-in-law
> and daughter-in-law against mother-in-law."

Notice what you think and feel as you read the Gospel.

Jesus says he came to cast fire upon the earth. He knows he will be the cause of division, even within families, for not all will follow him.

Pray as you are led for yourself and others.

"Jesus, I, too, experience strife in relationships because I follow you. Help me to deal with others as you would . . ." (Continue in your own words.)

Listen to Jesus.

There is a time to yield and a time to speak up. Ask me what to do, and I will show you. What else is Jesus saying to you?

Ask God to show you how to live today.

"Lord, give me your wisdom as I seek to heal division. Help me make peace with those who oppose me. Thank you for your presence today. Amen."

Monday, August 15, 2016
The Assumption of the Blessed Virgin Mary

Know that God is present with you and ready to converse.

"Let me magnify you, Lord, for you have done great things for me."

Read the Gospel: Luke 1:39–56.

In those days Mary set out and went with haste to a Judean town in the hill country, where she entered the house of Zechariah and greeted Elizabeth. When Elizabeth heard Mary's greeting, the child leaped in her womb. And Elizabeth was filled with the Holy Spirit and exclaimed with a loud cry, "Blessed are you among women, and blessed is the fruit

of your womb. And why has this happened to me, that the mother of my Lord comes to me? For as soon as I heard the sound of your greeting, the child in my womb leaped for joy. And blessed is she who believed that there would be a fulfillment of what was spoken to her by the Lord."
And Mary said,

"My soul magnifies the Lord,
 and my spirit rejoices in God my Savior,
for he has looked with favor on the lowliness of his servant.
 Surely, from now on all generations will call me blessed;
for the Mighty One has done great things for me,
 and holy is his name.
His mercy is for those who fear him
 from generation to generation.
He has shown strength with his arm;
 he has scattered the proud in the thoughts of their hearts.
He has brought down the powerful from their thrones,
 and lifted up the lowly;
he has filled the hungry with good things,
 and sent the rich away empty.
He has helped his servant Israel,
 in remembrance of his mercy,
according to the promise he made to our ancestors,
 to Abraham and to his descendants forever."

And Mary remained with her about three months and then returned to her home.

Notice what you think and feel as you read the Gospel.

Mary rejoices in her Savior in a beautiful prayer. She speaks of God's great mercy upon those who are lowly and hungry, while he scatters the proud in the imagination of their hearts.

Pray as you are led for yourself and others.

"Lord, Mary spoke in the illumination of your Spirit. She understands your loving ways and your loving purposes . . ." (Continue in your own words.)

Listen to Jesus.

I have honored my mother. Love her, because she is your mother, too. What else is Jesus saying to you?

Ask God to show you how to live today.

"Lord, I seek to know and do your will today. I seek to be worthy of you and your blessed mother. Mary, pray for me now and at the hour of my death. Amen."

Tuesday, August 16, 2016

Know that God is present with you and ready to converse.

"Lord, you have blessed me with riches. Let them not come between us. Let me find true riches in your Word."

Read the Gospel: Matthew 19:23–30.

Then Jesus said to his disciples, "Truly I tell you, it will be hard for a rich person to enter the kingdom of heaven. Again I tell you, it is easier for a camel to go through the eye of a needle than for someone who is rich to enter the kingdom of God." When the disciples heard this, they were greatly astounded and said, "Then who can be saved?" But Jesus looked at them and said, "For mortals it is impossible, but for God all things are possible."

Then Peter said in reply, "Look, we have left everything and followed you. What then will we have?" Jesus said to them, "Truly I tell you, at the renewal of all things, when the Son of Man is seated on the throne of his glory, you who have followed me will also sit on twelve thrones, judging the twelve tribes of Israel. And everyone who has left houses or brothers or sisters or father or mother or children or fields, for my name's sake, will receive a hundredfold, and will inherit eternal life. But many who are first will be last, and the last will be first."

Notice what you think and feel as you read the Gospel.

Jesus tells his disciples that it is hard for a rich man to enter the kingdom of heaven, harder than for a camel to go through the eye of a needle. This is a serious warning against relying on one's wealth. Yet Jesus assures Peter that all who abandon their former lives for him will receive a hundredfold in the kingdom and eternal life.

Pray as you are led for yourself and others.

"Lord, I do not know if I am rich or poor. I ask you to help me understand whether I displease you by covetousness or by anxiety about obtaining what I need—or think I need—to live . . ." (Continue in your own words.)

Listen to Jesus.

I love you very much, dear disciple. I understand your confusions. I want to guide you through. What else is Jesus saying to you?

Ask God to show you how to live today.

"Jesus, risen Lord, whether I am rich or poor, I want to be yours alone. I do not wish to depend upon what I have for a secure future. Let me depend only on you. Amen."

Wednesday, August 17, 2016

Know that God is present with you and ready to converse.

"Generous Lord, you grant me mercy, not justice. I receive your mercy as I receive you in your Word."

Read the Gospel: Matthew 20:1–16.

Jesus taught, "For the kingdom of heaven is like a landowner who went out early in the morning to hire laborers for his vineyard. After agreeing with the laborers for the usual daily wage, he sent them into his vineyard. When he went out about nine o'clock, he saw others standing idle in the marketplace; and he said to them, 'You also go into the vineyard, and I will pay you whatever is right.' So they went. When he went out again about noon and about three o'clock, he did the same. And about five o'clock he went out and found others standing around; and he said to them, 'Why are you standing here idle all day?' They said to him, 'Because no one has hired us.' He said to them, 'You also go into the vineyard.' When evening came, the owner of the vineyard said to his manager, 'Call the laborers and give them their pay, beginning with the last and then going to the first.' When those hired about five o'clock came, each of them received the usual daily wage. Now when the first came, they thought they would receive more; but each of them also received the usual daily wage. And when they received it, they grumbled against the landowner, saying, 'These last worked only one hour, and you have made them equal to us who have borne the burden of the day and the scorching heat.' But he replied to one of them, 'Friend, I am doing you no wrong; did you not agree with me for the usual daily wage? Take what belongs to you and go; I choose to give to this last the same as I give to you. Am I not allowed to do what I choose with what belongs to me? Or are you envious because I am generous?' So the last will be first, and the first will be last."

Notice what you think and feel as you read the Gospel.

All who work in the householder's vineyard receive a single denarius, whether they worked all day or an hour. Those who worked all day complain, though they had agreed to work for the pay they received. The householder chides them for begrudging his generosity.

Pray as you are led for yourself and others.

"Lord, I am grateful because I have not served you long, yet you give me eternal life . . ." (Continue in your own words.)

Listen to Jesus.

It is my pleasure to give you the kingdom, friend. I rejoice in your love for me. What else is Jesus saying to you?

Ask God to show you how to live today.

"Jesus, it pleases me to make you happy. You are good to me. Let me do something for you. Thank you. Amen."

Thursday, August 18, 2016

Know that God is present with you and ready to converse.

"Lord, you have called me. Choose me, too. Clothe me with the righteousness of your Word."

Read the Gospel: Matthew 22:1–14.

Once more Jesus spoke to them in parables, saying: "The kingdom of heaven may be compared to a king who gave a wedding banquet for his son. He sent his slaves to call those who had been invited to the wedding banquet, but they would not come. Again he sent other slaves, saying, 'Tell those who have been invited: Look, I have prepared my dinner, my oxen and my fat calves have been slaughtered, and everything is ready; come to the wedding banquet.' But they made light of it and went away, one to his farm, another to his business, while the rest seized his slaves, mistreated them, and killed them. The king was enraged. He sent his troops, destroyed those murderers, and burned their city. Then he said to his slaves, 'The wedding is ready, but those invited were not worthy. Go therefore into the main streets, and invite everyone you find to the wedding banquet.' Those slaves went out into the streets and gathered all whom they found, both good and bad; so the wedding hall was filled with guests.

"But when the king came in to see the guests, he noticed a man there who was not wearing a wedding robe, and he said to him, 'Friend, how did you get in here without a wedding robe?' And he was speechless. Then the king said to the attendants, 'Bind him hand and foot, and throw him into the outer darkness, where there will be weeping and gnashing of teeth.' For many are called, but few are chosen."

Notice what you think and feel as you read the Gospel.

The invited guests do not come to the marriage feast that a king has prepared for his son. In fact, they kill the king's servants. Angry, the king sends his troops to destroy their city, and he invites strangers off the streets to the wedding feast. The king notices one man without a wedding garment, and casts him into the outer darkness. Many are called, but few are chosen.

Pray as you are led for yourself and others.

"Lord, this parable frightens me, for I am not prepared for your feast . . ." (Continue in your own words.)

Listen to Jesus.

Servant, my blood washes you. You shine before God in my righteousness. Remain in me. What else is Jesus saying to you?

Ask God to show you how to live today.

"Lord, let me never take for granted your grace. Let me take all my strength from you, knowing my own unworthiness. Amen."

Friday, August 19, 2016

Know that God is present with you and ready to converse.

"Command me, Lord, by your Word. Your servant listens."

Read the Gospel: Matthew 22:34–40.

When the Pharisees heard that Jesus had silenced the Sadducees, they gathered together, and one of them, a lawyer, asked him a question to test him. "Teacher, which commandment in the law is the greatest?" He said to him, "'You shall love the Lord your God with all your heart, and with all your soul, and with all your mind.' This is the greatest and first commandment. And a second is like it: 'You shall love your neighbor as yourself.' On these two commandments hang all the law and the prophets."

Notice what you think and feel as you read the Gospel.

Jesus passes the lawyer's test, declaring the greatest commandment. You shall love the Lord with all your heart, soul, and mind, and your neighbor as yourself. This sums up all the teaching of the law and the prophets.

Pray as you are led for yourself and others.

"Lord, I offer you my heart, soul, and mind. Fill them with love for you . . ." (Continue in your own words.)

Listen to Jesus.

I grant your prayer, beloved. Come to me often for renewal. How will you show your love to those I have given you? What else is Jesus saying to you?

Ask God to show you how to live today.

"Lord, I don't know what will happen today or tomorrow. Lead me through. I offer my hands and my heart in your service. Amen."

Saturday, August 20, 2016

Know that God is present with you and ready to converse.

"Lord and master, Jesus Christ, I am your servant, here to understand your Word in my heart."

Read the Gospel: Matthew 23:1–12.

Then Jesus said to the crowds and to his disciples, "The scribes and the Pharisees sit on Moses's seat; therefore, do whatever they teach you and follow it; but do not do as they do, for they do not practice what they teach. They tie up heavy burdens, hard to bear, and lay them on the shoulders of others; but they themselves are unwilling to lift a finger to move them. They do all their deeds to be seen by others; for they make their phylacteries broad and their fringes long. They love to have the place of honor at banquets and the best seats in the synagogues, and to be greeted with respect in the marketplaces, and to have people call them rabbi. But you are not to be called rabbi, for you have one teacher, and you are all students. And call no one your father on earth, for you have one Father—the one in heaven. Nor are you to be called instructors, for you have one instructor, the Messiah. The greatest among you will be your servant. All who exalt themselves will be humbled, and all who humble themselves will be exalted."

Notice what you think and feel as you read the Gospel.

Jesus tells the people not to act like religious people who do not practice what they preach. Do not seek places of honor or titles. He who is greatest among you shall be your servant. The one who is humble shall be exalted.

Pray as you are led for yourself and others.

"Jesus, I have not always been immune to the good opinion of others. Give me true humility . . ." (Continue in your own words.)

Listen to Jesus.

I, your master, am your servant, beloved. I wash your feet. I give you what you ask. What else is Jesus saying to you?

Ask God to show you how to live today.

"Son of the Father, meek and lowly of heart, teach me how to walk in true humility today and every day, for I am nothing without you. Amen."

Sunday, August 21, 2016
Twenty-First Sunday in Ordinary Time

Know that God is present with you and ready to converse.

How many will inherit the kingdom of God? We cannot know. But we know God does not will that anyone be lost. We know there shall be great multitudes from the east and west and north and south. With God all things are possible.

Approach the Word of God with reverence and in prayer: "Lord, let me be among those who sit at your table. By your Word, feed my hunger to know you and to love you."

Read the Gospel: Luke 13:22–30.

Jesus went through one town and village after another, teaching as he made his way to Jerusalem. Someone asked him, "Lord, will only a few be saved?" He said to them, "Strive to enter through the narrow door; for many, I tell you, will try to enter and will not be able. When once the owner of the house has got up and shut the door, and you begin to stand outside and to knock at the door, saying, 'Lord, open to us,' then in reply he will say to you, 'I do not know where you come from.' Then you will begin to say, 'We ate and drank with you, and you taught in our streets.' But he will say, 'I do not know where you come from; go away from me, all you evildoers!' There will be weeping and gnashing of teeth when you see Abraham and Isaac and Jacob and all the prophets in the kingdom of God, and you yourselves thrown out. Then people will come from east and west, from north and south, and will eat in the kingdom of God. Indeed, some are last who will be first, and some are first who will be last."

Notice what you think and feel as you read the Gospel.

Jesus exhorts the people to enter the kingdom by the narrow door, for many will seek to enter but will not be able. The householder will shut the door on those who think they have the right to enter.

Pray as you are led for yourself and others.

"Lord, let my love for you be genuine. Let me turn away from all iniquity and serve you from my heart . . ." (Continue in your own words.)

Listen to Jesus.

Do not be afraid, beloved disciple. I have called and chosen you to sit at my table. What else is Jesus saying to you?

Ask God to show you how to live today.

"How may I follow you today, Savior? I give myself to whatever you would have me do. Amen."

Monday, August 22, 2016

Know that God is present with you and ready to converse.

"Lord, I stand before you today seeking simplicity and integrity in my worship of you."

Read the Gospel: Matthew 23:13–22.

Jesus warned, "But woe to you, scribes and Pharisees, hypocrites! For you lock people out of the kingdom of heaven. For you do not go in yourselves, and when others are going in, you stop them. Woe to you, scribes and Pharisees, hypocrites! For you cross sea and land to make a single convert, and you make the new convert twice as much a child of hell as yourselves.

"Woe to you, blind guides, who say, 'Whoever swears by the sanctuary is bound by nothing, but whoever swears by the gold of the sanctuary is bound by the oath.' You blind fools! For which is greater, the gold or the sanctuary that has made the gold sacred? And you say, 'Whoever swears by the altar is bound by nothing, but whoever swears by the gift that is on the altar is bound by the oath.' How blind you are! For which is greater, the gift or the altar that makes the gift sacred? So whoever swears by the altar, swears by it and by everything on it; and whoever swears by the sanctuary, swears by it and by the one who dwells in it; and whoever swears by heaven, swears by the throne of God and by the one who is seated upon it."

Notice what you think and feel as you read the Gospel.

Jesus rails against hypocrites, particularly the powerful religious leaders of his day. He hates their petty and wrongheaded human rules. He hates the way they mislead others. He declares that they are blind fools.

Pray as you are led for yourself and others.

"Lord, forgive me all my hypocrisy. Forgive me the times I have misled others . . ." (Continue in your own words.)

Listen to Jesus.

I desire truth in the inner heart. Commune with me. I will not mislead you. What else is Jesus saying to you?

Ask God to show you how to live today.

"Jesus, let me do something good and true today to make amends. Give me your truth, your heart, your grace, and I will do your will. I praise you. Amen."

Tuesday, August 23, 2016

Know that God is present with you and ready to converse.

"Lord, I seek to observe the weighty matters of the law. I will hear your voice with all my senses."

Read the Gospel: Matthew 23:23–26.

Jesus warned, "Woe to you, scribes and Pharisees, hypocrites! For you tithe the mint, dill, and cumin, and have neglected the weightier matters of the law: justice and mercy and faith. It is these you ought to have practiced without neglecting the others. You blind guides! You strain out a gnat but swallow a camel!

"Woe to you, scribes and Pharisees, hypocrites! For you clean the outside of the cup and of the plate, but inside they are full of greed and self-indulgence. You blind Pharisee! First clean the inside of the cup, so that the outside also may become clean."

Notice what you think and feel as you read the Gospel.

Jesus pronounces woe over the scribes and Pharisees for their little observances of the law while they neglect the weightier matters, namely, justice, mercy, and faith.

Pray as you are led for yourself and others.

"Lord, give me hunger and capacity for justice, mercy, and faith. I celebrate your goodness and want to do as you do . . ." (Continue in your own words.)

Listen to Jesus.

Beloved, I have my hand on your shoulder. I know your heart. We walk together. What else is Jesus saying to you?

Ask God to show you how to live today.

"Lord, may I ask you again for deeper faith, greater mercy, and a godly sense of justice? I do not wish my prayers to be mere lip service. I want to speak to your heart from my heart. Thank you. Amen."

Wednesday, August 24, 2016
Saint Bartholomew, apostle

Know that God is present with you and ready to converse.

"Jesus, you see me here, praying in secret. You are the Son of God."

Read the Gospel: John 1:45–51.

Philip found Nathanael and said to him, "We have found him about whom Moses in the law and also the prophets wrote, Jesus son of Joseph from Nazareth." Nathanael said to him, "Can anything good come out of Nazareth?" Philip said to him, "Come and see." When Jesus saw Nathanael coming toward him, he said of him, "Here is truly an Israelite in whom there is no deceit!" Nathanael asked him, "Where did you get to know me?" Jesus answered, "I saw you under the fig tree before Philip called you." Nathanael replied, "Rabbi, you are the Son of God! You are the king of Israel!" Jesus answered, "Do you believe because I told you that I saw you under the fig tree? You will see greater things than these." And he said to him, "Very truly, I tell you, you will see heaven opened and the angels of God ascending and descending upon the Son of Man."

Notice what you think and feel as you read the Gospel.

Philip tells Nathaniel that they have found the promised Messiah. Doubtful, Nathaniel nevertheless follows Philip to see Jesus and hears the Lord say of him, "Here is truly an Israelite in whom there is no deceit!" In Church tradition, Nathaniel became the apostle Bartholomew.

Pray as you are led for yourself and others.

"You promised Nathaniel a vision of heaven, with angels ascending and descending on the Son of Man. I long to see you in your glory, Lord . . ." (Continue in your own words.)

Listen to Jesus.

In a little while you shall see me as I am. All waiting, all of time, will pass away, and you shall be as I am in my Father's kingdom. What else is Jesus saying to you?

Ask God to show you how to live today.

"Lord, give me strength to resist the temptations of the day and grace to do what is right and good. Amen."

Thursday, August 25, 2016

Know that God is present with you and ready to converse.

"Lord, I am ready to hear your holy Word. Thank you."

Read the Gospel: Matthew 24:42–51.

Jesus instructed, "Keep awake therefore, for you do not know on what day your Lord is coming. But understand this: if the owner of the house had known in what part of the night the thief was coming, he would have stayed awake and would not have let his house be broken into. Therefore you also must be ready, for the Son of Man is coming at an unexpected hour.

"Who then is the faithful and wise slave, whom his master has put in charge of his household, to give the other slaves their allowance of food at the proper time? Blessed is that slave whom his master will find at work when he arrives. Truly I tell you, he will put that one in charge of all his possessions. But if that wicked slave says to himself, 'My master is delayed,' and he begins to beat his fellow slaves, and eats and drinks with drunkards, the master of that slave will come on a day when he does not expect him and at an hour that he does not know. He will cut him in pieces and put him with the hypocrites, where there will be weeping and gnashing of teeth."

Notice what you think and feel as you read the Gospel.

Jesus tells his disciples to wait and watch for his return. He exhorts them to be faithful and wise servants, caring for the master's household.

Pray as you are led for yourself and others.

"Lord, I believe your return will be unexpected. Let me live as though you are coming today or tomorrow. Let me be faithful and wise in meeting my responsibilities . . ." (Continue in your own words.)

Listen to Jesus.

You have heard my words. I give you grace to act in obedience to them. Turn to me when you fail. I will lift you up. What else is Jesus saying to you?

Ask God to show you how to live today.

"Lord, I have faith in you. I now seek an increase of faithfulness. Help me to be steadily attentive in my service to you and to all those you have given me. You are good to me. Amen."

Friday, August 26, 2016

Know that God is present with you and ready to converse.

"Lord, I watch and wait for you, and now you are here. Teach me wisdom by your Word."

Read the Gospel: Matthew 25:1–13.

Jesus said, "Then the kingdom of heaven will be like this. Ten bridesmaids took their lamps and went to meet the bridegroom. Five of them were foolish, and five were wise. When the foolish took their lamps, they took no oil with them; but the wise took flasks of oil with their lamps. As the bridegroom was delayed, all of them became drowsy and slept. But at midnight there was a shout, 'Look! Here is the bridegroom! Come out to meet him.' Then all those bridesmaids got up and trimmed their lamps. The foolish said to the wise, 'Give us some of your oil, for our lamps are going out.' But the wise replied, 'No! There will not be enough for you and for us; you had better go to the dealers and buy some for yourselves.' And while they went to buy it, the bridegroom came, and those who were ready went with him into the wedding banquet; and the door was shut. Later the other bridesmaids came also, saying, 'Lord, lord, open to us.' But he replied, 'Truly I tell you, I do not know you.' Keep awake therefore, for you know neither the day nor the hour."

Notice what you think and feel as you read the Gospel.

This is Jesus' parable of the ten maidens. The five foolish maidens neglect to bring oil for their lamps and miss the bridegroom when he arrives at midnight. The wise go with the bridegroom into the marriage feast.

Pray as you are led for yourself and others.

"I am saddened by this parable, Lord. I don't know if I have a flask of oil to hold me over while I wait for you. I suspect many do not have this oil . . ." (Continue in your own words.)

Listen to Jesus.

The oil comes by knowing me. If you love me and pray and hear my words, you have the oil you need to enter the marriage feast. What else is Jesus saying to you?

Ask God to show you how to live today.

"Let your imminent return be present in my mind today, Lord. How can I know you better? Amen."

Saturday, August 27, 2016

Know that God is present with you and ready to converse.

"Lord, when you come in glory, I long to hear you say 'Well done, good and faithful servant.' What do you have to say to me now?"

Read the Gospel: Matthew 25:14–30.

Jesus said, "For it is as if a man, going on a journey, summoned his slaves and entrusted his property to them; to one he gave five talents, to another two, to another one, to each according to his ability. Then he went away. The one who had received the five talents went off at once and traded with them, and made five more talents. In the same way, the one who had the two talents made two more talents. But the one who had received the one talent went off and dug a hole in the ground and hid his master's money. After a long time the master of those slaves came and settled accounts with them. Then the one who had received the five talents came forward, bringing five more talents, saying, 'Master, you handed over to me five talents; see, I have made five more talents.' His master said to him, 'Well done, good and trustworthy slave; you have been trustworthy in a few things, I will put you in charge of many things; enter into the joy of your master.' And the one with the two talents also came forward, saying, 'Master, you handed over to me two talents; see, I have made two more talents.' His master said to him, 'Well done, good and trustworthy slave; you have been trustworthy in a few things, I will put you in charge of many things; enter into the joy of your master.' Then the one who had received the one talent also came forward, saying, 'Master, I knew that you were a harsh man, reaping where you did not sow, and gathering where you did not scatter seed; so I was afraid, and I went and hid your talent in the ground. Here you have what is yours.' But his master replied, 'You wicked and lazy slave! You knew, did you, that I reap where I did not sow, and gather where I did not scatter? Then you ought to have invested my money with the bankers, and on my return I would have received what was my own with interest. So take the talent from him, and give it to the one with the ten talents. For to all those who have, more will be given, and they will have an abundance; but from those who have nothing, even what they have will be taken away. As for this worthless slave, throw him into the outer darkness, where there will be weeping and gnashing of teeth.'"

Notice what you think and feel as you read the Gospel.

Jesus tells the parable of the talents—the servants who invest the money entrusted to them and the servant who does not. Jesus says that to one who has, more will be given, but the one who has not will lose even what he has.

Pray as you are led for yourself and others.

"What have you given me, Lord? What talents do I have? How may I increase them for your glory?" (Continue in your own words.)

Listen to Jesus.

Do not minimize the gifts I have given you, dear servant. Do not be afraid to take risks in my service and in the service of others. I will bless you and prosper your efforts. What else is Jesus saying to you?

Ask God to show you how to live today.

"Lord, give me the courage I need today and always. All I have is yours. I seek nothing for myself but you. You will not abandon me. Amen."

Sunday, August 28, 2016
Twenty-Second Sunday in Ordinary Time

Know that God is present with you and ready to converse.

Jesus humbled himself to be born in human flesh, and he asks us to do good in secret and for no reward. Our true reward is spiritual: the resurrection to eternal life.

When you are ready, ask God to give you Jesus' understanding of value: "Jesus, you are present with me in your Word and by your Spirit. Let me hear and obey."

Read the Gospel: Luke 14:1, 7–14.

On one occasion when Jesus was going to the house of a leader of the Pharisees to eat a meal on the Sabbath, they were watching him closely. . . .

When Jesus noticed how the guests chose the places of honor, he told them a parable. "When you are invited by someone to a wedding banquet, do not sit down at the place of honor, in case someone more distinguished than you has been invited by your host; and the host who invited both of you may come and say to you, 'Give this person your place,' and then in disgrace you would start to take the lowest place. But when you are invited, go and sit down at the lowest place, so that when your host comes, he may say to you, 'Friend, move up higher'; then you will be honored in the presence of all who sit at the table with you. For all who exalt themselves will be humbled, and those who humble themselves will be exalted."

He said also to the one who had invited him, "When you give a luncheon or a dinner, do not invite your friends or your brothers or your relatives or rich neighbors, in case they may invite you in return, and you would be repaid. But when you give a banquet, invite the poor, the crippled, the lame, and the blind. And you will be blessed, because they cannot repay you, for you will be repaid at the resurrection of the righteous."

Notice what you think and feel as you read the Gospel.

Jesus teaches that the one who humbles himself or herself will be exalted, and the one who does good things for those who can reciprocate misses out on true blessedness. It is better to do good to those who cannot repay in order to receive your reward at the resurrection of the just.

Pray as you are led for yourself and others.

"Jesus, I wish to do good to those in need who cannot repay me. Give me opportunities for true generosity . . ." (Continue in your own words.)

Listen to Jesus.

I am present with the poor. Look for me and you will see me. Do justice. What else is Jesus saying to you?

Ask God to show you how to live today.

"Jesus, I give myself to you today so that you can make me the kind of person who serves the poor and does justice with a loving heart. Praise you, Savior. Amen."

Monday, August 29, 2016
Martyrdom of Saint John the Baptist

Know that God is present with you and ready to converse.

"Lord, you are here with me now. You are in all the circumstances of my life. Let me see you in your Word."

Read the Gospel: Mark 6:17–29.

Herod himself had sent men who arrested John, bound him, and put him in prison on account of Herodias, his brother Philip's wife, because Herod had married her. For John had been telling Herod, "It is not lawful for you to have your brother's wife." And Herodias had a grudge against him, and wanted to kill him. But she could not, for Herod feared John, knowing that he was a righteous and holy man, and he protected him. When he heard him, he was greatly perplexed; and yet he liked to listen to him. But an opportunity came when Herod on his birthday gave a banquet for his courtiers and officers and for the leaders of Galilee. When his daughter Herodias came in and danced, she pleased Herod and his guests; and the king said to the girl, "Ask me for whatever you wish, and I will give it." And he solemnly swore to her, "Whatever you ask me, I will give you, even half of my kingdom." She went out and said to her mother, "What should I ask for?" She replied, "The head of John the baptizer." Immediately she rushed back to the king and requested, "I want you to give me at once the head of John the Baptist on a platter." The king was deeply grieved; yet out of regard for his oaths and for the guests, he did not want to refuse her. Immediately the king sent a soldier of the guard with orders to bring John's head. He went and beheaded him in the prison, brought his head on a platter, and gave it to the girl. Then the girl gave it to her mother. When his disciples heard about it, they came and took his body, and laid it in a tomb.

Notice what you think and feel as you read the Gospel.

John the Baptist is beheaded on the command of Herod, who knows John to be a holy man. Yet he is also intent on pleasing Herodias, who hates John for denouncing their adulterous union. Poor Herod, caught between his integrity and his pride, no doubt regrets his foolish vows, and yet he murders John the Baptist.

Pray as you are led for yourself and others.

"Lord, keep me from acting today out of pride, like Herod. Keep my gaze steadily upon you . . ." (Continue in your own words.)

Listen to Jesus.

Child, servant, friend, I am with you. Love me with all your heart, and I will light your way. What else is Jesus saying to you?

Ask God to show you how to live today.

"Lord, reveal to me pressures in my life—things that influence me to do things I should not do or things that prevent me from doing things I should. Then help me separate myself from those pressures. May you receive honor and glory forever. Amen."

Tuesday, August 30, 2016

Know that God is present with you and ready to converse.

"Son of God, you sit at the right hand of the Father, who has given you authority over everything in heaven and on earth. I bow before you. I seek you in your Word."

Read the Gospel: Luke 4:31–37.

Jesus went down to Capernaum, a city in Galilee, and was teaching them on the Sabbath. They were astounded at his teaching, because he spoke with authority. In the synagogue there was a man who had the spirit of an unclean demon, and he cried out with a loud voice, "Let us alone! What have you to do with us, Jesus of Nazareth? Have you come to destroy us? I know who you are, the Holy One of God." But Jesus rebuked him, saying, "Be silent, and come out of him!" When the demon had thrown him down before them, he came out of him without having done him any harm. They were all amazed and kept saying to one another, "What kind of utterance is this? For with authority and power he commands the unclean spirits, and out they come!" And a report about him began to reach every place in the region.

Notice what you think and feel as you read the Gospel.

Jesus speaks with authority, amazing those who hear him. Jesus works miracles, casting out the demon, amazing those who witness it. The news of him spreads.

Pray as you are led for yourself and others.

"Lord, I give you authority over my heart, mind, soul, spirit, and will. Rule me, Lord, for your rule is all love . . ." (Continue in your own words.)

Listen to Jesus.

I receive you, beloved. You give me joy. Let us walk closely together today. What else is Jesus saying to you?

Ask God to show you how to live today.

"Dear Lord, if there are areas of my life that I withhold from you, show them to me so that I may be completely yours. Amen."

Wednesday, August 31, 2016

Know that God is present with you and ready to converse.

"Strong Son of God, I need your touch, your healing, your care. I am here with you now."

Read the Gospel: Luke 4:38–44.

After leaving the synagogue Jesus entered Simon's house. Now Simon's mother-in-law was suffering from a high fever, and they asked him about her. Then he stood over her and rebuked the fever, and it left her. Immediately she got up and began to serve them.

As the sun was setting, all those who had any who were sick with various kinds of diseases brought them to him; and he laid his hands on each of them and cured them. Demons also came out of many, shouting, "You are the Son of God!" But he rebuked them and would not allow them to speak, because they knew that he was the Messiah.

At daybreak he departed and went into a deserted place. And the crowds were looking for him; and when they reached him, they wanted to prevent him from leaving them. But he said to them, "I must proclaim the good news of the kingdom of God to the other cities also; for I was sent for this purpose." So he continued proclaiming the message in the synagogues of Judea.

Notice what you think and feel as you read the Gospel.

Jesus heals Simon's mother-in-law and other sick and possessed people in the community. Even the demons know that he is the Son of God, the Christ. Jesus does not allow them to speak of it.

Pray as you are led for yourself and others.

"Jesus, I think of those I love who need your touch. I bring them to you now . . ." (Continue in your own words.)

Listen to Jesus.

In God your prayers have power to help and heal, dear servant. Prayer is work that I have assigned you. What else is Jesus saying to you?

Ask God to show you how to live today.

"Lord, help me to pray more often during my days. In every situation of joy, fear, confusion, or labor, let my heart speak to you, and let me hear you and be guided by your words. Amen."

Thursday, September 1, 2016

Know that God is present with you and ready to converse.

"Lord, this sinner comes to you now to hear the Word of God. Wash and heal me by your Word."

Read the Gospel: Luke 5:1–11.

Once while Jesus was standing beside the lake of Gennesaret, and the crowd was pressing in on him to hear the Word of God, he saw two boats there at the shore of the lake; the fishermen had gone out of them and were washing their nets. He got into one of the boats, the one belonging to Simon, and asked him to put out a little way from the shore. Then he sat down and taught the crowds from the boat. When he had finished speaking, he said to Simon, "Put out into the deep water and let down your nets for a catch." Simon answered, "Master, we have worked all night long but have caught nothing. Yet if you say so, I will let down the nets." When they had done this, they caught so many fish that their nets were beginning to break. So they signaled their partners in the other boat to come and help them. And they came and filled both boats, so that they began to sink. But when Simon Peter saw it, he fell down at Jesus' knees, saying, "Go away from me, Lord, for I am a sinful man!" For he and all who were with him were amazed at the catch of fish that they had taken; and so also were James and John, sons of Zebedee, who were partners with Simon. Then Jesus said to Simon, "Do not be afraid; from now on you will be catching people." When they had brought their boats to shore, they left everything and followed him.

Notice what you think and feel as you read the Gospel.

The people want to hear the Word of God from Jesus. He teaches them from Simon's boat. Later he commands Simon to let down his nets into the deep. Simon obeys, even though he and the other disciples have caught nothing all night. They now catch fish enough to fill both boats, and Simon falls down before the Lord, exclaiming, "Go away from me, Lord, for I am a sinful man!" Jesus tells them that in the future they will be catching men.

Pray as you are led for yourself and others.

"Lord, can you use me? How can I help others to find you and follow you?" (Continue in your own words.)

Listen to Jesus.

Seek God first. Set your heart on me, loving me. Then you will be able to speak my words and do my works for others. What else is Jesus saying to you?

Ask God to show you how to live today.

"Lord, only in you can I speak your words and do your works. Let me abide in you and see opportunities to serve and honor you. Amen."

Friday, September 2, 2016

Know that God is present with you and ready to converse.

"Lord, I desire you, your new wine, your new garment, for you make all things new. Renew me by your Word."

Read the Gospel: Luke 5:33–39.

Then the Pharisees said to Jesus, "John's disciples, like the disciples of the Pharisees, frequently fast and pray, but your disciples eat and drink." Jesus said to them, "You cannot make wedding guests fast while the bridegroom is with them, can you? The days will come when the bridegroom will be taken away from them, and then they will fast in those days." He also told them a parable: "No one tears a piece from a new garment and sews it on an old garment; otherwise the new will be torn, and the piece from the new will not match the old. And no one puts new wine into old wineskins; otherwise the new wine will burst the skins and will be spilled, and the skins will be destroyed. But new wine must be put into fresh wineskins. And no one after drinking old wine desires new wine, but says, 'The old is good.'"

Notice what you think and feel as you read the Gospel.

Jesus defends his disciples against the Pharisees' observation that they do not fast but eat and drink. He says his disciples will fast, but not while he, the Bridegroom, is with them. His parable of the new and the old suggests that he brings something entirely new. He does. Never before has God come to humanity in the flesh to make us children of God.

Pray as you are led for yourself and others.

"I adore you, Son of the Father, and I surrender all of myself to you. Give me your heart and mind. Let me do your will . . ." (Continue in your own words.)

Listen to Jesus.

I love it when you come to me seeking renewal. I grant you grace, my child. What else is Jesus saying to you?

Ask God to show you how to live today.

"Lord, show me something new to do today that will glorify you, especially if it is some good deed done in secret. Amen."

Saturday, September 3, 2016

Know that God is present with you and ready to converse.

"I lift up my heart to you, Lord. Order my priorities by your holy Word."

Read the Gospel: Luke 6:1–5.

One Sabbath while Jesus was going through the cornfields, his disciples plucked some heads of grain, rubbed them in their hands, and ate them. But some of the Pharisees said, "Why are you doing what is not lawful on the Sabbath?" Jesus answered, "Have you not read what David did when he and his companions were hungry? He entered the house of God and took and ate the bread of the Presence, which it is not lawful for any but the priests to eat, and gave some to his companions?" Then he said to them, "The Son of Man is lord of the Sabbath."

Notice what you think and feel as you read the Gospel.

Jesus refutes the Pharisees' legalism by scripture. Are disciples breaking the Sabbath by eating grain from fields? He proclaims that the Son of Man is Lord of the Sabbath. Were they frustrated? Angry? Baffled? Did any understand?

Pray as you are led for yourself and others.

"Lord, my God, let me walk in your freedom, full of your love, seeking to do your will, not my own . . ." (Continue in your own words.)

Listen to Jesus.

Beloved, I have called you in love. God seeks your worship. That is my will. What else is Jesus saying to you?

Ask God to show you how to live today.

"I have many choices, Lord. Open my eyes to see the best use of my time and efforts in service to you and those you have given me. Thank you. Amen."

Sunday, September 4, 2016
Twenty-Third Sunday in Ordinary Time

Know that God is present with you and ready to converse.

How committed are we to God? Are we willing to pay the price? Do we long for God and his kingdom?

When you are ready to hear God's Word, invite Jesus to speak to you in a personal way: "Jesus, teach me by your Word. Penetrate my heart and mind. Make me your own."

Read the Gospel: Luke 14:25–33.

Now large crowds were traveling with Jesus; and he turned and said to them, "Whoever comes to me and does not hate father and mother, wife and children, brothers and sisters, yes, and even life itself, cannot be my disciple. Whoever does not carry the cross and follow me cannot be my disciple. For which of you, intending to build a tower, does not first sit down and estimate the cost, to see whether he has enough to complete it? Otherwise, when he has laid a foundation and is not able to finish, all who see it will begin to ridicule him, saying, 'This fellow began to build and was not able to finish.' Or what king, going out to wage war against another king, will not sit down first and consider whether he is able with ten thousand to oppose the one who comes against him with twenty thousand? If he cannot, then, while the other is still far away, he sends a delegation and asks for the terms of peace. So therefore, none of you can become my disciple if you do not give up all your possessions."

Notice what you think and feel as you read the Gospel.

Jesus asks his followers for complete renunciation of all things and all people, even family. He wants them to do it in a calculating manner, counting the cost of such commitment. We must bear our own crosses and come after him to be worthy of discipleship.

Pray as you are led for yourself and others.

"Lord, teach me the art of renouncing myself in following you. I am sometimes so full of myself . . ." (Continue in your own words.)

Listen to Jesus.

Turning away from self and toward me is a simple act of the heart. Understand that all your value, all your blessedness, and all your fruitfulness are in me. What else is Jesus saying to you?

Ask God to show you how to live today.

"Turn my heart from all improper affections of people or things. Then help me to count the cost and with all my heart come after you. Amen."

Monday, September 5, 2016

Know that God is present with you and ready to converse.

"Jesus, you suffered much for doing good. Let me love you, Word of God."

Read the Gospel: Luke 6:6–11.

On another Sabbath Jesus entered the synagogue and taught, and there was a man there whose right hand was withered. The scribes and the Pharisees watched him to see whether he would cure on the Sabbath, so that they might find an accusation against him. Even though he knew what they were thinking, he said to the man who had the withered hand, "Come and stand here." He got up and stood there. Then Jesus said to them, "I ask you, is it lawful to do good or to do harm on the Sabbath, to save life or to destroy it?" After looking around at all of them, he said to him, "Stretch out your hand." He did so, and his hand was restored. But they were filled with fury and discussed with one another what they might do to Jesus.

Notice what you think and feel as you read the Gospel.

Jesus knows the thoughts of the Pharisees and the scribes. They are looking for ways to accuse him of being a lawbreaker. It is the Sabbath. He asks them whether it's lawful to do good on the Sabbath. They cannot answer. He heals the man with the withered hand. They are filled with fury.

Pray as you are led for yourself and others.

"Jesus, those you loved and came to save hated you. I pray for all those who hate you, who oppose you, who flee from you, who ignore you . . ." (Continue in your own words.)

Listen to Jesus.

When you pray for my enemies, you share my heart, beloved disciple. Do any oppose you? How will you love them? What else is Jesus saying to you?

Ask God to show you how to live today.

"Lord, help me turn away anger with gentleness. Make me aware in the moment. All glory to God. Amen."

Tuesday, September 6, 2016

Know that God is present with you and ready to converse.

"Powerful Word of God, you are with me to reveal God's goodness and mercy."

Read the Gospel: Luke 6:12–19.

Now during those days Jesus went out to the mountain to pray; and he spent the night in prayer to God. And when day came, he called his disciples and chose twelve of them, whom he also named apostles: Simon, whom he named Peter, and his brother Andrew, and James, and John, and Philip, and Bartholomew, and Matthew, and Thomas, and James son of Alphaeus, and Simon, who was called the Zealot, and Judas son of James, and Judas Iscariot, who became a traitor.

He came down with them and stood on a level place, with a great crowd of his disciples and a great multitude of people from all Judea, Jerusalem, and the coast of Tyre and Sidon. They had come to hear him and to be healed of their diseases; and those who were troubled with unclean spirits were cured. And all in the crowd were trying to touch him, for power came out from him and healed all of them.

Notice what you think and feel as you read the Gospel.

Jesus prays all night. Then he works, naming the twelve Apostles. He goes to speak to the large crowd that has gathered. He speaks, heals them, and casts out unclean spirits.

Pray as you are led for yourself and others.

"No man ever did the works that you did, Lord. I offer myself to your work now . . ." (Continue in your own words.)

Listen to Jesus.

To bear fruit in me, child, give yourself to prayer. In prayer I will lead, guide, and strengthen you. What else is Jesus saying to you?

Ask God to show you how to live today.

"Lord, I adore you. Show me how to please you in all that I think, say, and do. Amen."

Wednesday, September 7, 2016

Know that God is present with you and ready to converse.

"Jesus, I seek the path of blessedness. Let your Word speak to my heart."

Read the Gospel: Luke 6:20–26.

Then Jesus looked up at his disciples and said:

"Blessed are you who are poor,
for yours is the kingdom of God.
"Blessed are you who are hungry now,
for you will be filled.
"Blessed are you who weep now,
for you will laugh.

"Blessed are you when people hate you, and when they exclude you, revile you, and defame you on account of the Son of Man. Rejoice in that day and leap for joy, for surely your reward is great in heaven; for that is what their ancestors did to the prophets.

"But woe to you who are rich,
for you have received your consolation.
"Woe to you who are full now,
for you will be hungry.
"Woe to you who are laughing now,
for you will mourn and weep.

"Woe to you when all speak well of you, for that is what their ancestors did to the false prophets."

Notice what you think and feel as you read the Gospel.

Jesus declares that the hungry will be satisfied, those weeping will laugh, and those reviled will be rewarded in heaven. Those who are rich now, full now, laugh now, and are spoken well of now will experience woe.

Pray as you are led for yourself and others.

"Jesus, I am hungry for God, and I weep for my sins. Help me to be single-minded in your service and in serving others . . ." (Continue in your own words.)

Listen to Jesus.

Do not trust in possessions or attainments, dear servant. Trust in me. I care for you. What else is Jesus saying to you?

Ask God to show you how to live today.

"Lord, show me the things that come between us and help me turn away from them. I need you hour by hour. Amen."

Thursday, September 8, 2016
Nativity of the Blessed Virgin Mary

Know that God is present with you and ready to converse.

"God, you exist. You are above all and in all. You are with Mary. You are with me now. I praise you."

Read the Gospel: Matthew 1:1–16, 18–23

An account of the genealogy of Jesus the Messiah, the son of David, the son of Abraham.

Abraham was the father of Isaac, and Isaac the father of Jacob, and Jacob the father of Judah and his brothers, and Judah the father of Perez and Zerah by Tamar, and Perez the father of Hezron, and Hezron the father of Aram, and Aram the father of Aminadab, and Aminadab the father of Nahshon, and Nahshon the father of Salmon, and Salmon the father of Boaz by Rahab, and Boaz the father of Obed by Ruth, and Obed the father of Jesse, and Jesse the father of King David.

And David was the father of Solomon by the wife of Uriah, and Solomon the father of Rehoboam, and Rehoboam the father of Abijah, and Abijah the father of Asaph, and Asaph the father of Jehoshaphat, and Jehoshaphat the father of Joram, and Joram the father of Uzziah, and Uzziah the father of Jotham, and Jotham the father of Ahaz, and Ahaz the father of Hezekiah, and Hezekiah the father of Manasseh, and Manasseh the father of Amos, and Amos the father of Josiah, and Josiah the father of Jechoniah and his brothers, at the time of the deportation to Babylon.

And after the deportation to Babylon: Jechoniah was the father of Salathiel, and Salathiel the father of Zerubbabel, and Zerubbabel the father of Abiud, and Abiud the father of Eliakim, and Eliakim the father of Azor, and Azor the father of Zadok, and Zadok the father of Achim, and Achim the father of Eliud, and Eliud the father of Eleazar, and Eleazar the father of Matthan, and Matthan the father of Jacob, and Jacob the father of Joseph the husband of Mary, of whom Jesus was born, who is called the Messiah. . . .

Now the birth of Jesus the Messiah took place in this way. When his mother Mary had been engaged to Joseph, but before they lived together, she was found to be with child from the Holy Spirit. Her husband, Joseph, being a righteous man and unwilling to expose her to public disgrace, planned to dismiss her quietly. But just when he had resolved to do this, an angel of the Lord appeared to him in a dream and said, "Joseph, son of David, do not be afraid to take Mary as your wife, for the child conceived in her is from the Holy Spirit. She will bear a son, and you are to name him Jesus, for he will save his people from their sins." All this took place to fulfill what had been spoken by the Lord through the prophet:

> "Look, the virgin shall conceive and bear a son,
> and they shall name him Emmanuel,
> which means, 'God is with us.'"

Notice what you think and feel as you read the Gospel.

Jesus has a long human lineage, but his mother was found to be with child by the Holy Spirit. As the prophet had said, "A virgin shall conceive and bear a son and his name shall be Emmanuel, God with us."

Pray as you are led for yourself and others.

"Jesus, I offer you my heart. Fill it with your Spirit and be born in me . . ." (Continue in your own words.)

Listen to Jesus.

I came to save people from their sins. Give me your sins now, and I will forgive them. What else is Jesus saying to you?

Ask God to show you how to live today.

"Thank you, merciful Savior. Be with me as I make amends by doing good and giving to those in need—my time, my work, and my money. Amen."

Friday, September 9, 2016

Know that God is present with you and ready to converse.

"Teacher, Son of God who is present with me now, let me learn to love you by your Word."

Read the Gospel: Luke 6:39–42.

Jesus also told his disciples a parable: "Can a blind person guide a blind person? Will not both fall into a pit? A disciple is not above the teacher, but everyone who is fully qualified will be like the teacher. Why do you see the speck in your neighbor's eye, but do not notice the log in your own eye? Or how can you say to your neighbor, 'Friend, let me take out the speck in your eye,' when you yourself do not see the log in your own eye? You hypocrite, first take the log out of your own eye, and then you will see clearly to take the speck out of your neighbor's eye."

Notice what you think and feel as you read the Gospel.

When a person is fully taught, Jesus says, he or she will be like the teacher. Jesus teaches against finding fault in others. He directs us to look to our own faults and fix them first.

Pray as you are led for yourself and others.

"Help me to obey you in this, Lord. Let me not see others' faults but only my own, so that you may cleanse and heal me . . ." (Continue in your own words.)

Listen to Jesus.

It is a great blessing to see yourself as you are—a person with faults. I work in you and through you, true servant. What else is Jesus saying to you?

Ask God to show you how to live today.

"So lead me Lord, my light, my way. Without you I stumble in the dark. Glory to you, Lord Jesus Christ. Amen."

Saturday, September 10, 2016

Know that God is present with you and ready to converse.

"Lord, make my heart good, that I may do your will and bear fruit to your glory. I listen to your Word."

Read the Gospel: Luke 6:43–49.

Jesus said, "No good tree bears bad fruit, nor again does a bad tree bear good fruit; for each tree is known by its own fruit. Figs are not gathered from thorns, nor are grapes picked from a bramble bush. The good person out of the good treasure of the heart produces good, and the evil person out of evil treasure produces evil; for it is out of the abundance of the heart that the mouth speaks.

"Why do you call me 'Lord, Lord,' and do not do what I tell you? I will show you what someone is like who comes to me, hears my words, and acts on them. That one is like a man building a house, who dug deeply and laid the foundation on rock; when a flood arose, the river burst against that house but could not shake it, because it had been well built. But the one who hears and does not act is like a man who built a house on the ground without a foundation. When the river burst against it, immediately it fell, and great was the ruin of that house."

Notice what you think and feel as you read the Gospel.

Jesus speaks of the heart, the source of good or evil in a person. Those who hear and do the words of Jesus will bear fruit and be secure always in every storm. Jesus is the rock of safety.

Pray as you are led for yourself and others.

"Lord, I often mean well, but I do not do what you ask me to do. How may I be a doer as well as a hearer of your word?" (Continue in your own words.)

Listen to Jesus.

I give you my Spirit, servant. Even in your failings, you are learning faithfulness. Your efforts are not wasted. What else is Jesus saying to you?

Ask God to show you how to live today.

"Without your constant presence, Lord, I can do nothing. Thank you for your Spirit. Teach me how to be true to you. Amen."

Sunday, September 11, 2016
Twenty-Fourth Sunday in Ordinary Time

Know that God is present with you and ready to converse.

In the Lord is joy. We have tears, but we also have joys. The source of our joy is the goodness of the Lord, who loves us and saves us. Even the angels rejoice in that.

When you are ready, invite the Lord into your prayer: "Lord, I have been lost, but now I rejoice in you. Let me know you in your holy Word."

Read the Gospel: Luke 15:1–32.

Now all the tax collectors and sinners were coming near to listen to him. And the Pharisees and the scribes were grumbling and saying, "This fellow welcomes sinners and eats with them."

So Jesus told them this parable: "Which one of you, having a hundred sheep and losing one of them, does not leave the ninety-nine in the wilderness and go after the one that is lost until he finds it? When he has found it, he lays it on his shoulders and rejoices. And when he comes home, he calls together his friends and neighbors, saying to them, 'Rejoice with me, for I have found my sheep that was lost.' Just so, I tell you, there will be more joy in heaven over one sinner who repents than over ninety-nine righteous persons who need no repentance.

"Or what woman having ten silver coins, if she loses one of them, does not light a lamp, sweep the house, and search carefully until she finds it? When she has found it, she calls together her friends and neighbors, saying, 'Rejoice with me, for I have found the coin that I had lost.'

Just so, I tell you, there is joy in the presence of the angels of God over one sinner who repents."

Then Jesus said, "There was a man who had two sons. The younger of them said to his father, 'Father, give me the share of the property that will belong to me.' So he divided his property between them. A few days later the younger son gathered all he had and traveled to a distant country, and there he squandered his property in dissolute living. When he had spent everything, a severe famine took place throughout that country, and he began to be in need. So he went and hired himself out to one of the citizens of that country, who sent him to his fields to feed the pigs. He would gladly have filled himself with the pods that the pigs were eating; and no one gave him anything. But when he came to himself he said, 'How many of my father's hired hands have bread enough and to spare, but here I am dying of hunger! I will get up and go to my father, and I will say to him, "Father, I have sinned against heaven and before you; I am no longer worthy to be called your son; treat me like one of your hired hands."' So he set off and went to his father. But while he was still far off, his father saw him and was filled with compassion; he ran and put his arms around him and kissed him. Then the son said to him, 'Father, I have sinned against heaven and before you; I am no longer worthy to be called your son.' But the father said to his slaves, 'Quickly, bring out a robe—the best one—and put it on him; put a ring on his finger and sandals on his feet. And get the fatted calf and kill it, and let us eat and celebrate; for this son of mine was dead and is alive again; he was lost and is found!' And they began to celebrate.

"Now his elder son was in the field; and when he came and approached the house, he heard music and dancing. He called one of the slaves and asked what was going on. He replied, 'Your brother has come, and your father has killed the fatted calf, because he has got him back safe and sound.' Then he became angry and refused to go in. His father came out and began to plead with him. But he answered his father, 'Listen! For all these years I have been working like a slave for you, and I have never disobeyed your command; yet you have never given me even a young goat so that I might celebrate with my friends. But when this son of yours came back, who has devoured your property with prostitutes, you killed the fatted calf for him!' Then the father said to him, 'Son, you are always with me, and all that is mine is yours. But we had to celebrate and rejoice, because this brother of yours was dead and has come to life; he was lost and has been found.'"

Notice what you think and feel as you read the Gospel.

Jesus tells parables about God finding the lost. The shepherd rejoices to find the lost sheep; the woman rejoices to find the lost coin. The angels rejoice over one sinner who repents. And the father of the prodigal son rejoices at his return.

Pray as you are led for yourself and others.

"Lord, let me be a cause of rejoicing to you and to the angels of heaven . . ." (Continue in your own words.)

Listen to Jesus.

You do give me joy, beloved disciple. Will you find time for me again today? What else is Jesus saying to you?

Ask God to show you how to live today.

"Lord, awaken my heart to you during moments of my day. Let me be your traveling companion. Amen."

Monday, September 12, 2016

Know that God is present with you and ready to converse.

"Jesus, let me approach you with faith, trusting that your Word will work your will in me."

Read the Gospel: Luke 7:1–10.

After Jesus had finished all his sayings in the hearing of the people, he entered Capernaum. A centurion there had a slave whom he valued highly, and who was ill and close to death. When he heard about Jesus, he sent some Jewish elders to him, asking him to come and heal his slave. When they came to Jesus, they appealed to him earnestly, saying, "He is worthy of having you do this for him, for he loves our people, and it is he who built our synagogue for us." And Jesus went with them, but when he was not far from the house, the centurion sent friends to say to him, "Lord, do not trouble yourself, for I am not worthy to have you come under my roof; therefore I did not presume to come to you. But only speak the word, and let my servant be healed. For I also am a man set under authority, with soldiers under me; and I say to one, 'Go,' and he goes, and to another, 'Come,' and he comes, and to my slave, 'Do this,' and the slave does it." When Jesus heard this he was amazed at him, and turning to the crowd that followed him, he said, "I tell you, not even in Israel have I found such faith." When those who had been sent returned to the house, they found the slave in good health.

Notice what you think and feel as you read the Gospel.

The good centurion never does speak directly to Jesus. He sends elders and friends to speak for him. He feels unworthy to speak to Jesus or to have Jesus come into his house. Yet he wants Jesus to heal a beloved slave who is sick. Jesus marvels at the centurion's faith and heals his slave from a distance.

Pray as you are led for yourself and others.

"Jesus, you love faith and you love humility. Increase them in me so that I may please you more . . ." (Continue in your own words.)

Listen to Jesus.

You ask me for good things, and I grant them to you. What else would you like me to do for you? What else is Jesus saying to you?

Ask God to show you how to live today.

"Lord, show me what I may do for you today, for others. Let me be your slave. Amen."

Tuesday, September 13, 2016

Know that God is present with you and ready to converse.

"God, you visited people in the flesh of your Christ. You are with me now in your Word and by your Spirit. Let me glorify you."

Read the Gospel: Luke 7:11–17.

Soon afterward Jesus went to a town called Nain, and his disciples and a large crowd went with him. As he approached the gate of the town, a man who had died was being carried out. He was his mother's only son, and she was a widow; and with her was a large crowd from the town. When the Lord saw her, he had compassion for her and said to her, "Do not weep." Then he came forward and touched the bier, and the bearers stood still. And he said, "Young man, I say to you, rise!" The dead man sat up and began to speak, and Jesus gave him to his mother. Fear seized all of them; and they glorified God, saying, "A great prophet has risen among us!" and "God has looked favorably on his people!" This word about him spread throughout Judea and all the surrounding country.

Notice what you think and feel as you read the Gospel.

Jesus feels compassion for the widow weeping as her dead son is being carried out of the city. He touches the bier and commands the young man to arise, then gives him to his mother. The crowd glorifies God and believes Jesus is God.

Pray as you are led for yourself and others.

"Jesus, I mourn those I love who have died. I pray for . . ." (Continue in your own words.)

Listen to Jesus.

I am life, beloved disciple. You will be united with your loved ones forever in heaven. What else is Jesus saying to you?

Ask God to show you how to live today.

"Lord, what shall I do to glorify you today? How may I honor my dead? Amen."

Wednesday, September 14, 2016
Exaltation of the Holy Cross

Know that God is present with you and ready to converse.

"God of love, open to me the Word of love."

Read the Gospel: John 3:13–17.

Jesus taught, "No one has ascended into heaven except the one who descended from heaven, the Son of Man. And just as Moses lifted up the serpent in the wilderness, so must the Son of Man be lifted up, that whoever believes in him may have eternal life.

"For God so loved the world that he gave his only Son, so that everyone who believes in him may not perish but may have eternal life.

"Indeed, God did not send the Son into the world to condemn the world, but in order that the world might be saved through him."

Notice what you think and feel as you read the Gospel.

Jesus says he, the Son of Man, will be lifted up as Moses lifted up the serpent in the wilderness to heal the people. Whoever believes in the Son will have eternal life. Jesus is the Savior of the world, the revelation of God's love for us.

Pray as you are led for yourself and others.

"Strengthen me in faith, Lord, that I may know your love and act upon it . . ." (Continue in your own words.)

Listen to Jesus.

Beloved, simply look to me, my cross. When you take up your own cross and follow me, you declare my love to the world. What else is Jesus saying to you?

Ask God to show you how to live today.

"Let me share in the glory of your cross, Lord. I thank you for your great love for me and for all those you have given me. Amen."

Thursday, September 15, 2016
Our Lady of Sorrows

Know that God is present with you and ready to converse.

"Jesus, give me your love for your mother, Our Lady of Sorrows."

Read the Gospel: John 19:25b–27.

Meanwhile, standing near the cross of Jesus were his mother, and his mother's sister, Mary the wife of Clopas, and Mary Magdalene. When Jesus saw his mother and the disciple whom he loved standing beside her, he said to his mother, "Woman, here is your son." Then he said to the disciple, "Here is your mother." And from that hour the disciple took her into his own home.

Notice what you think and feel as you read the Gospel.

The mother of Jesus, other faithful women, and the apostle John are standing at the foot of the cross. Jesus speaks to Mary, "Mother, behold, your son." Then he says to John, "Behold, your mother!" From that day the disciple takes her to his own home.

Pray as you are led for yourself and others.

"Jesus, you never stop caring for others. You honor your mother. I thank you for giving her to me . . ." (Continue in your own words.)

Listen to Jesus.

You may speak to my mother, for you are her child, too. She speaks to me on your behalf. What else is Jesus saying to you?

Ask God to show you how to live today.

"Lord, let me be close to your mother today. Let me turn to her to pray for me and those I care for. Thank you, dear Jesus. Amen."

Friday, September 16, 2016

Know that God is present with you and ready to converse.

"Lord, you are here with me now. I bless you. Let me remain in your company all day."

Read the Gospel: Luke 8:1–3.

Soon afterward Jesus went on through cities and villages, proclaiming and bringing the good news of the kingdom of God. The Twelve were with him, as well as some women who had been cured of evil spirits and infirmities: Mary, called Magdalene, from whom seven demons had gone out, and Joanna, the wife of Herod's steward Chuza, and Susanna, and many others, who provided for them out of their resources.

Notice what you think and feel as you read the Gospel.

The Gospel reading recognizes and honors those who traveled with Jesus: the Twelve, Mary Magdalene, Joanna, Susanna, and many others who provided for Jesus and his disciples.

Pray as you are led for yourself and others.

"Lord, how may I support those who bring the Good News of the kingdom of God to others?" (Continue in your own words.)

Listen to Jesus.

Bless those who serve me, and pray for them, beloved servant and friend. Support them in their work. What else is Jesus saying to you?

Ask God to show you how to live today.

"I say again, Lord: let me remain in your company all day, following you closely and serving. Thank you for that privilege. Amen."

Saturday, September 17, 2016

Know that God is present with you and ready to converse.

"Ever-present Lord, God of hosts, give me a heart to hear your Word and hold it fast."

Read the Gospel: Luke 8:4–15.

When a great crowd gathered and people from town after town came to him, Jesus said in a parable: "A sower went out to sow his seed; and as he sowed, some fell on the path and was trampled on, and the birds of the air ate it up. Some fell on the rock; and as it grew up, it withered for lack of moisture. Some fell among thorns, and the thorns grew with it and choked it. Some fell into good soil, and when it grew, it produced a hundredfold." As he said this, he called out, "Let anyone with ears to hear listen!"

Then his disciples asked him what this parable meant. He said, "To you it has been given to know the secrets of the kingdom of God; but to others I speak in parables, so that

> 'looking they may not perceive,
> and listening they may not understand.'

"Now the parable is this: The seed is the word of God. The ones on the path are those who have heard; then the devil comes and takes away the word from their hearts, so that they may not believe and be saved. The ones on the rock are those who, when they hear the word, receive it with joy. But these have no root; they believe only for a while and in a time of testing fall away. As for what fell among the thorns, these are the ones who hear; but as they go on their way, they are choked by the cares and riches and pleasures of life, and their fruit does not mature. But as for that in the good soil, these are the ones who, when they hear the word, hold it fast in an honest and good heart, and bear fruit with patient endurance."

Notice what you think and feel as you read the Gospel.

Jesus tells the familiar parable of the sower. The seed is the Word of God, the ground it lands upon is the hearers of the Word. Depending on the condition of the ground, some seeds don't germinate, some spring up only briefly, some are choked by thorns, but some grow. The Word bears fruit in those who hold it fast in an honest and good heart.

Pray as you are led for yourself and others.

"Jesus, do not let me presume that my heart is right and ready for you. I need you to create in me an honest and good heart. Make it like your own . . ." (Continue in your own words.)

Listen to Jesus.

I love to sanctify your heart with truth and goodness. Turn to me often. What else is Jesus saying to you?

Ask God to show you how to live today.

"Lord, I am not worthy of your blessings. Let me share them with others today. Thank you for allowing me to serve you. Amen."

Sunday, September 18, 2016
Twenty-Fifth Sunday in Ordinary Time

Know that God is present with you and ready to converse.

The Lord leads us into his ways by our circumstances, the direction of others, reason, common sense, conscience, our desires, and wisdom. The Holy Spirit is present with us at all times, within and without. We offer him our freedom to do his will.

When you are ready, invite the Lord to speak with you today by his Word: "Lord, let me understand what you are saying to me by your Word. Let it speak to my heart by your Spirit."

Read the Gospel: Luke 16:1–13.

Then Jesus said to the disciples, "There was a rich man who had a manager, and charges were brought to him that this man was squandering his property. So he summoned him and said to him, 'What is this that I hear about you? Give me an accounting of your management, because you cannot be my manager any longer.' Then the manager said to himself, 'What will I do, now that my master is taking the position away from me? I am not strong enough to dig, and I am ashamed to beg. I have decided what to do so that, when I am dismissed as manager, people may welcome me into their homes.' So, summoning his master's debtors one by one, he asked the first, 'How much do you owe my master?' He answered, 'A hundred jugs of olive oil.' He said to him, 'Take your bill, sit down quickly, and make it fifty.' Then he asked another, 'And how much do you owe?' He replied, 'A hundred containers of wheat.' He said to him, 'Take your bill and make it eighty.' And his master commended the dishonest manager because he had acted shrewdly; for the children of this age are more shrewd in dealing with their own generation than are the children of light. And I tell you, make friends for yourselves by means of dishonest wealth so that when it is gone, they may welcome you into the eternal homes.

"Whoever is faithful in a very little is faithful also in much; and whoever is dishonest in a very little is dishonest also in much. If then you have not been faithful with the dishonest wealth, who will entrust to you the true riches? And if you have not been faithful with what belongs to another, who will give you what is your own? No slave can serve two masters; for a slave will either hate the one and love the other, or be devoted to the one and despise the other. You cannot serve God and wealth."

Notice what you think and feel as you read the Gospel.
Jesus tells the parable of the dishonest servant who, learning he is about to be fired, negotiates generously with those who owe the master money. Learning of this, the master commends the steward for his prudence. Jesus urges his own, people of light, to use worldly wisdom and unrighteous mammon to receive eternal life.

Pray as you are led for yourself and others.
"Lord, I pray for prudence, light, and wisdom, that I may manage my affairs and property for the benefit of my soul . . ." (Continue in your own words.)

Listen to Jesus.
Remind yourself that all you have comes from the hand of your master. God wants you to use it and distribute it to others but not to rely on it. What else is Jesus saying to you?

Ask God to show you how to live today.
"Give me the proper attitude toward unrighteous mammon, Lord. Let me see the traps in it and overcome them by your Spirit. Amen."

Monday, September 19, 2016

Know that God is present with you and ready to converse.
"Word of God, you proceed from the Father; speak to my heart by your Spirit now.

Read the Gospel: Luke 8:16–18.
Jesus taught, "No one after lighting a lamp hides it under a jar, or puts it under a bed, but puts it on a lamp stand, so that those who enter may see the light. For nothing is hidden that will not be disclosed, nor is anything secret that will not become known and come to light. Then pay attention to how you listen; for to those who have, more will be given; and from those who do not have, even what they seem to have will be taken away."

Notice what you think and feel as you read the Gospel.

Jesus speaks in parables. The one who lights a lamp puts it on a stand. All hidden things will be revealed, all secrets will come to light. Hear carefully, he says, for those who have will be given more. Those who have little will have it taken away.

Pray as you are led for yourself and others.

"Lord, you know my secrets. Wash me, that I may receive your light and your words . . ." (Continue in your own words.)

Listen to Jesus.

Do not be afraid of the light, beloved. This light is the love of God for you. What else is Jesus saying to you?

Ask God to show you how to live today.

"Lord, how may I walk in your light today, open and true to all the world? Amen."

Tuesday, September 20, 2016

Know that God is present with you and ready to converse.

"Word of the Father, be present and let me hear you in my deepest being."

Read the Gospel: Luke 8:19–21.

Then Jesus' mother and his brothers came to him, but they could not reach him because of the crowd. And he was told, "Your mother and your brothers are standing outside, wanting to see you." But he said to them, "My mother and my brothers are those who hear the word of God and do it."

Notice what you think and feel as you read the Gospel.

Jesus tells the crowd how they can become his mother or his brothers and sisters. Hear the Word of God and do it, he says.

Pray as you are led for yourself and others.

"Jesus, you honor me by allowing me to be one in your family, even with your mother. Let me do my part . . ." (Continue in your own words.)

Listen to Jesus.

Some have died for God's Word, beloved. Honor them. What else is Jesus saying to you?

Ask God to show you how to live today.

"Lord, take away from me the fear of death and fear of suffering. Let me trust in your providence. Amen."

Wednesday, September 21, 2016
Saint Matthew, apostle and evangelist

Know that God is present with you and ready to converse.

"Lord, you call to me, a sinner. Let me hear your Word."

Read the Gospel: Matthew 9:9–13.

As Jesus was walking along, he saw a man called Matthew sitting at the tax booth; and he said to him, "Follow me." And he got up and followed him.

And as he sat at dinner in the house, many tax collectors and sinners came and were sitting with him and his disciples. When the Pharisees saw this, they said to his disciples, "Why does your teacher eat with tax collectors and sinners?" But when he heard this, he said, "Those who are well have no need of a physician, but those who are sick. Go and learn what this means, 'I desire mercy, not sacrifice.' For I have come to call not the righteous but sinners."

Notice what you think and feel as you read the Gospel.

Jesus calls Matthew away from his work as tax collector. Then in the house he sits down with many tax collectors and sinners. These, he tells the Pharisees who question his choice of companions, are the ones who need him. Those who think they are righteous need to learn to show and receive mercy.

Pray as you are led for yourself and others.

"Jesus, Matthew risked everything to follow you, and you gave him the task of writing the Gospel. Call me and let me serve you, too . . ." (Continue in your own words.)

Listen to Jesus.

I have called you, beloved servant. I am preparing you for fruitfulness. What else is Jesus saying to you?

Ask God to show you how to live today.

"How may I cooperate with your work in me and in the lives of those you have given me? Amen."

Thursday, September 22, 2016

Know that God is present with you and ready to converse.

"You are with me here and now, Lord. Let me seek you in your Word."

Read the Gospel: Luke 9:7–9.

Now Herod the ruler heard about all that had taken place, and he was perplexed, because it was said by some that John had been raised from the dead, by some that Elijah had appeared, and by others that one of the ancient prophets had arisen. Herod said, "John I beheaded; but who is this about whom I hear such things?" And he tried to see him.

Notice what you think and feel as you read the Gospel.

Herod, who beheaded John the Baptist, hears about Jesus and is perplexed. Who is this man who preaches and heals? Herod then seeks to see Jesus.

Pray as you are led for yourself and others.

"Jesus, I do not want to seek you out of fear or for favors. I want to seek you and love you for yourself . . ." (Continue in your own words.)

Listen to Jesus.

I love you for yourself, friend. I receive your love with joy. Let us continue in this love. What else is Jesus saying to you?

Ask God to show you how to live today.

"I pray for those who do not walk in your friendship, Lord. How may I help them find you? Amen."

Friday, September 23, 2016

Know that God is present with you and ready to converse.

"Crucified Savior, I adore you. Speak to me by your holy Word."

Read the Gospel: Luke 9:18–22.

Once when Jesus was praying alone, with only the disciples near him, he asked them, "Who do the crowds say that I am?" They answered, "John the Baptist; but others, Elijah; and still others, that one of the ancient prophets has arisen." He said to them, "But who do you say that I am?" Peter answered, "The Messiah of God."

He sternly ordered and commanded them not to tell anyone, saying, "The Son of Man must undergo great suffering, and be rejected by the elders, chief priests, and scribes, and be killed, and on the third day be raised."

Notice what you think and feel as you read the Gospel.

Jesus confirms to his disciples that he is the Christ of God. He charges them to tell no one. Then he speaks about his own destiny to suffer, be rejected by the Jewish authorities, and be killed, but on the third day be raised. The disciples must have wondered why he asked them to keep his secret. What must they have thought of his prophesy?

Pray as you are led for yourself and others.

"Risen Lord, I give you all of myself today for the good of others. Show me how to serve in your Spirit . . ." (Continue in your own words.)

Listen to Jesus.

Many need love like ours, dear one. There are many ways to give it to them. Open your eyes and your heart. What else is Jesus saying to you?

Ask God to show you how to live today.

"Jesus, I am often slow to see and afraid to act when I do. Please take away these defects that dishonor you. Amen."

Saturday, September 24, 2016

Know that God is present with you and ready to converse.

"You will that your words may sink into my ears, Lord. So be it."

Read the Gospel: Luke 9:43b–45.

While everyone was amazed at all that he was doing, Jesus said to his disciples, "Let these words sink into your ears: The Son of Man is going to be betrayed into human hands." But they did not understand this saying; its meaning was concealed from them, so that they could not perceive it. And they were afraid to ask him about this saying.

Notice what you think and feel as you read the Gospel.

While the crowds marvel at Jesus' powerful works, he tells his disciples the hard truth. He will be delivered into the hands of men. They don't understand, but they are afraid to ask him what he means.

Pray as you are led for yourself and others.

"Help me understand whatever you want me to know, Lord. Help me to apply your words . . ." (Continue in your own words.)

Listen to Jesus.

I enable you to understand. You know me and love me. What else is Jesus saying to you?

Ask God to show you how to live today.

"Let me see you in everything today, Lord—or at least in some things. You are everywhere. Be strong in me. Amen."

Sunday, September 25, 2016
Twenty-Sixth Sunday in Ordinary Time

Know that God is present with you and ready to converse.

It is easy for us to be so busy and stressed in our daily lives that we forget about the ultimate purpose and goal of life. Our goal is to find eternal life in the kingdom of God, glorifying God forever. We must ask God to prepare us for heaven, to make us worthy by God's grace.

When you are ready, speak to the Lord with an open and receptive heart: "Jesus, risen from the dead, present with me now, let me hear and obey your Word."

Read the Gospel: Luke 16:19–31.

Jesus said, "There was a rich man who was dressed in purple and fine linen and who feasted sumptuously every day. And at his gate lay a poor man named Lazarus, covered with sores, who longed to satisfy his hunger with what fell from the rich man's table; even the dogs would come and lick his sores. The poor man died and was carried away by the angels to be with Abraham. The rich man also died and was buried. In Hades, where he was being tormented, he looked up and saw Abraham far away with Lazarus by his side. He called out, 'Father Abraham, have mercy on me, and send Lazarus to dip the tip of his finger in water and cool my tongue; for I am in agony in these flames.' But Abraham said, 'Child, remember that during your lifetime you received your good things, and Lazarus in like manner evil things; but now he is comforted here, and you are in agony. Besides all this, between you and us a great chasm has been fixed, so that those who might want to pass from here to you cannot do so, and no one can cross from there to us.' He said, 'Then, father, I beg you to send him to my father's house—for I have five brothers—that he may warn them, so that they will not also come into this place of torment.' Abraham replied, 'They have Moses and the prophets; they should listen to them.' He said, 'No, father Abraham; but if someone goes to them from the dead, they will repent.' He said to him, 'If they do not listen to Moses and the prophets, neither will they be convinced even if someone rises from the dead.'"

Notice what you think and feel as you read the Gospel.

Jesus tells the story of the rich man and poor Lazarus, who after his miserable life goes to his heavenly reward in Abraham's bosom. The tormented rich man begs Abraham for relief, or to send Lazarus to go warn his brothers. Abraham refuses.

Pray as you are led for yourself and others.

"Jesus, you understand our hearts. Give me eyes to see every Lazarus in this world and to alleviate that suffering . . ." (Continue in your own words.)

Listen to Jesus.

I love the poor, who suffer as I did. You can minister to them in my love. What else is Jesus saying to you?

Ask God to show you how to live today.

"May the hearts of the wealthy be open to see the poor of the earth and to provide for them. Let the wealthy avoid the rich man's fate. Amen."

Monday, September 26, 2016

Know that God is present with you and ready to converse.

"Lord, let me receive you in your Word."

Read the Gospel: Luke 9:46–50.

An argument arose among the disciples as to which one of them was the greatest. But Jesus, aware of their inner thoughts, took a little child and put it by his side, and said to them, "Whoever welcomes this child in my name welcomes me, and whoever welcomes me welcomes the one who sent me; for the least among all of you is the greatest."

John answered, "Master, we saw someone casting out demons in your name, and we tried to stop him, because he does not follow with us." But Jesus said to him, "Do not stop him; for whoever is not against you is for you."

Notice what you think and feel as you read the Gospel.

As the disciples argue among themselves about who is the greatest, Jesus uses a child to illustrate that the least among them is the greatest. Whoever receives the child, he says, receives him, and whoever receives him receives the one who sent him, God.

Pray as you are led for yourself and others.

"Jesus, I aspire to be the least and to receive you as a child. Transform me, Lord, to be and do what you will . . ." (Continue in your own words.)

Listen to Jesus.

Do not forget the children, beloved disciple. They need me. They need you. What else is Jesus saying to you?

Ask God to show you how to live today.

"Show me how I can help, Lord. Strengthen me in your service. May you receive all honor and glory forever. Amen."

Tuesday, September 27, 2016

Know that God is present with you and ready to converse.

"Merciful Savior, let me walk with you in your Word."

Read the Gospel: Luke 9:51–56.

When the days drew near for him to be taken up, Jesus set his face to go to Jerusalem. And he sent messengers ahead of him. On their way they entered a village of the Samaritans to make ready for him; but they did not receive him, because his face was set toward Jerusalem. When his disciples James and John saw it, they said, "Lord, do you want us to command fire to come down from heaven and consume them?" But he turned and rebuked them. Then they went on to another village.

Notice what you think and feel as you read the Gospel.

Jesus deals with prejudice, for he is a Jew in Samaria. He is not allowed to stay there. His disciples James and John are angry and want to punish the Samaritans with fire from heaven. Jesus rebukes them, and they move on to another village.

Pray as you are led for yourself and others.

"Lord, have I discriminated against you? You are present in the poor, the oppressed, the marginalized . . ." (Continue in your own words.)

Listen to Jesus.

My child, love them all with the love I have given you. What you do for love is great, however small. What else is Jesus saying to you?

Ask God to show you how to live today.

"Lord, sometimes I feel I walk through my day blind to you. Wake me up and let me see you in those I tend to turn away from. Lead me, Lord. Amen."

Wednesday, September 28, 2016

Know that God is present with you and ready to converse.

"Father, Son, and Holy Spirit, you are all present in the Word. You are here with me now. Let me receive you in my heart."

Read the Gospel: Luke 9:57–62.

As they were going along the road, someone said to Jesus, "I will follow you wherever you go." And Jesus said to him, "Foxes have holes, and birds of the air have nests; but the Son of Man has nowhere to lay his head." To another he said, "Follow me." But he said, "Lord, first let me go and bury my father." But Jesus said to him, "Let the dead bury their own dead; but as for you, go and proclaim the kingdom of God."

Another said, "I will follow you, Lord; but let me first say farewell to those at my home." Jesus said to him, "No one who puts a hand to the plow and looks back is fit for the kingdom of God."

Notice what you think and feel as you read the Gospel.

Jesus encounters several who would delay following him because of the sacrifices that it will entail. He calls them, but they make excuses. He says, "No one who . . . looks back is fit for the kingdom of God."

Pray as you are led for yourself and others.

"Jesus, help me to keep my hand on the plow and not look back. Strip away all my excuses to commit to you all that I have and all that I am . . ." (Continue in your own words.)

Listen to Jesus.

Beloved disciple, you hear my words and seek to obey. I love you for that. What else is Jesus saying to you?

Ask God to show you how to live today.

"Lord, let me see my weaknesses and give them over to you today. Let me rely entirely on you in all I do. I give you glory, Holy Trinity. Amen."

Thursday, September 29, 2016
Saints Michael, Gabriel, and Raphael, archangels

Know that God is present with you and ready to converse.

"Lord, God of hosts, I long to see your face. I am here with you now to find you in your Word."

Read the Gospel: John 1:47–51.

When Jesus saw Nathanael coming toward him, Jesus said of him, "Here is truly an Israelite in whom there is no deceit!" Nathanael asked him, "Where did you get to know me?" Jesus answered, "I saw you under the fig tree before Philip called you." Nathanael replied, "Rabbi, you are the Son of God! You are the King of Israel!" Jesus answered, "Do you believe because I told you that I saw you under the fig tree? You will see greater things than these." And he said to him, "Very truly, I tell you, you will see heaven opened and the angels of God ascending and descending upon the Son of Man."

Notice what you think and feel as you read the Gospel.

When Jesus tells Nathanael that he saw him under the fig tree, Nathanael believes Jesus is the Son of God. Yet Jesus tells him he will see still greater things: "heaven opened, and the angels of God ascending and descending upon the Son of Man."

Pray as you are led for yourself and others.

"Son of God, let me glorify you as the angels do. Give me a heart full of worship . . ." (Continue in your own words.)

Listen to Jesus.

Your love for me gives me joy, friend. Ask of me whatever you will. What else is Jesus saying to you?

Ask God to show you how to live today.

"I ask for more love for you and for all those you have given me. Guide me to act as you would have me act. Amen."

Friday, September 30, 2016

Know that God is present with you and ready to converse.

"Lord, I prepare in your presence to hear your Word."

Read the Gospel: Luke 10:13–16.

Jesus warned, "Woe to you, Chorazin! Woe to you, Bethsaida! For if the deeds of power done in you had been done in Tyre and Sidon, they would have repented long ago, sitting in sackcloth and ashes. But at the judgment it will be more tolerable for Tyre and Sidon than for you. And you, Capernaum,

will you be exalted to heaven?
No, you will be brought down to Hades.

"Whoever listens to you listens to me, and whoever rejects you rejects me, and whoever rejects me rejects the one who sent me."

Notice what you think and feel as you read the Gospel.

Jesus reproaches the people who had seen his mighty works and heard his preaching yet refused to repent. They wish to be exalted, but they will be brought low.

Pray as you are led for yourself and others.

"Jesus, you speak of repentance. I repent of my sins. I seek not to be exalted but to find you in humble sorrow for my sins . . ." (Continue in your own words.)

Listen to Jesus.

Pride often blinds people, even my servants. Look to your heart and root out all pride and arrogance. What else is Jesus saying to you?

Ask God to show you how to live today.

"Shine your light into my soul, dear Jesus, and cast out all that is not pleasing to you. I abandon myself to you. Amen."

Saturday, October 1, 2016

Know that God is present with you and ready to converse.

"I come into your presence rejoicing, Lord, for you give me yourself in your Word."

Read the Gospel: Luke 10:17–24.

The seventy returned with joy, saying, "Lord, in your name even the demons submit to us!" Jesus said to them, "I watched Satan fall from heaven like a flash of lightning. See, I have given you authority to tread on snakes and scorpions, and over all the power of the enemy; and nothing will hurt you. Nevertheless, do not rejoice at this, that the spirits submit to you, but rejoice that your names are written in heaven."

At that same hour Jesus rejoiced in the Holy Spirit and said, "I thank you, Father, Lord of heaven and earth, because you have hidden these things from the wise and the intelligent and have revealed them to infants; yes, Father, for such was your gracious will. All things have been handed over to me by my Father; and no one knows who the Son is except the Father, or who the Father is except the Son and anyone to whom the Son chooses to reveal him."

Then turning to the disciples, Jesus said to them privately, "Blessed are the eyes that see what you see! For I tell you that many prophets and kings desired to see what you see, but did not see it, and to hear what you hear, but did not hear it."

Notice what you think and feel as you read the Gospel.

The seventy Jesus sent out return with joy because of the powers Jesus gave them to work wonders among the people. Yet Jesus tells them that the source of their joy should be that their names are written in heaven.

Pray as you are led for yourself and others.

"Jesus, your message is always that this life is only a prelude to the next, which is everlasting life in your glorious kingdom. Stay my mind and heart on that truth as I do my duty every day . . ." (Continue in your own words.)

Listen to Jesus.

Continue in my love, chosen disciple. Nothing will harm you when you remain in me. What else is Jesus saying to you?

Ask God to show you how to live today.

"Make me aware of all the reasons I have for rejoicing, especially your great promises to those who remain faithful to the end. Amen."

Sunday, October 2, 2016
Twenty-Seventh Sunday in Ordinary Time

Know that God is present with you and ready to converse.

The Lord knows our imperfections, yet he demands that we strive for holiness. Holiness comes as we let the Holy Spirit work in us, transforming us inwardly in the image of Christ Jesus.

When you are ready, place yourself before the Lord with words such as these: "Almighty Word of the Father, I bow before you and listen with my heart."

Read the Gospel: Luke 17:5–10.

The apostles said to the Lord, "Increase our faith!" The Lord replied, "If you had faith the size of a mustard seed, you could say to this mulberry tree, 'Be uprooted and planted in the sea,' and it would obey you.

"Who among you would say to your slave who has just come in from plowing or tending sheep in the field, 'Come here at once and take your place at the table'? Would you not rather say to him, 'Prepare supper for me, put on your apron and serve me while I eat and drink; later you may eat and drink'? Do you thank the slave for doing what was commanded? So you also, when you have done all that you were ordered to do, say, 'We are worthless slaves; we have done only what we ought to have done!'"

Notice what you think and feel as you read the Gospel.
The disciples want more faith. Jesus tells them of the power of even a little faith. Then he tells them that a servant who does whatever the master requires still must consider himself unworthy, for he has done only his duty.

Pray as you are led for yourself and others.
"Help me to act on the little faith I have, Lord, to serve you as you will. How may I go above and beyond my duty?" (Continue in your own words.)

Listen to Jesus.
Remember that I am always with you, beloved servant. With God all things are possible. Believe me. What else is Jesus saying to you?

Ask God to show you how to live today.
"Let it be you working through me today, Jesus. I do not trust myself. I trust only you. Amen."

Monday, October 3, 2016

Know that God is present with you and ready to converse.
"I delight in your Word, dear Lord. Let it teach my heart and guide my steps."

Read the Gospel: Luke 10:25–37.
Just then a lawyer stood up to test Jesus. "Teacher," he said, "what must I do to inherit eternal life?" Jesus said to him, "What is written in the law? What do you read there?" He answered, "You shall love the Lord your God with all your heart, and with all your soul, and with all your strength, and with all your mind; and your neighbor as yourself." And Jesus said to him, "You have given the right answer; do this, and you will live."

But wanting to justify himself, he asked Jesus, "And who is my neighbor?" Jesus replied, "A man was going down from Jerusalem to Jericho, and fell into the hands of robbers, who stripped him, beat him, and went away, leaving him half dead. Now by chance a priest was going down that road; and when he saw him, he passed by on the other side. So likewise a Levite, when he came to the place and saw him, passed by on the other side. But a Samaritan while traveling came near him; and when he saw him, he was moved with pity. He went to him and bandaged his wounds, having poured oil and wine on them. Then he put him on his own animal, brought him to an inn, and took care of him. The next day he took out two denarii, gave them to the innkeeper, and said, 'Take care of him; and when I come back, I will repay you whatever more you spend.' Which of these three, do you think, was a neighbor to the man who fell into the hands of the robbers?" He said, "The one who showed him mercy." Jesus said to him, "Go and do likewise."

Notice what you think and feel as you read the Gospel.

The lawyer answers Jesus' question well. But, upon hearing the great parable of the good Samaritan, the man could no longer justify himself, caught in his own question.

Pray as you are led for yourself and others.

"Give me what the Samaritan had, Lord: true and generous compassion for his neighbor . . ." (Continue in your own words.)

Listen to Jesus.

Love is always the path to eternal life, beloved. You grow in love for God and neighbor as you exercise it by your works. What else is Jesus saying to you?

Ask God to show you how to live today.

"Help me to practice compassion today. Be my strength, Lord. Amen."

Tuesday, October 4, 2016

Know that God is present with you and ready to converse.

"Almighty Father, let me know your gentle Son by my reading of your holy Word."

Read the Gospel: Luke 10:38–42.

Now as they went on their way, Jesus entered a certain village, where a woman named Martha welcomed him into her home. She had a sister named Mary, who sat at the Lord's feet and listened to what he was saying. But Martha was distracted by her many tasks; so she came to him and asked, "Lord, do you not care that my sister has left me to do all the work by myself? Tell her then to help me." But the Lord answered her, "Martha, Martha, you are worried and distracted by many things; there is need of only one thing. Mary has chosen the better part, which will not be taken away from her."

Notice what you think and feel as you read the Gospel.

Jesus doesn't say Martha is wrong to be serving the guests, but he does say that Mary has chosen the better part.

Pray as you are led for yourself and others.

"Help me to be close to you and learn from you, Jesus, so I may better serve others . . ." (Continue in your own words.)

Listen to Jesus.

Without me you can do nothing, beloved disciple. In me and through me, you will bear much fruit to the glory of God. What else is Jesus saying to you?

Ask God to show you how to live today.

"Lord, as I give all to you today, prosper the works of my hands according to your gracious will. Amen."

Wednesday, October 5, 2016

Know that God is present with you and ready to converse.

"Jesus, teach me to pray."

Read the Gospel: Luke 11:1–4.

Jesus was praying in a certain place, and after he had finished, one of his disciples said to him, "Lord, teach us to pray, as John taught his disciples." He said to them, "When you pray, say:

> Father, hallowed be your name.
> Your kingdom come.
> Give us each day our daily bread.
> And forgive us our sins,
> for we ourselves forgive everyone indebted to us.
> And do not bring us to the time of trial."

Notice what you think and feel as you read the Gospel.

Jesus responds to his disciples' request to teach them to pray. This is Luke's version of the Our Father, which emphasizes forgiveness. Jesus puts his Father's glory first and the kingdom second.

Pray as you are led for yourself and others.

"Fill me with the desire to glorify you, Lord, Father, Son, and Holy Spirit. You are everything to me . . ." (Continue in your own words.)

Listen to Jesus.

By prayer you grow in the knowledge of God, beloved. Be faithful in it. What else is Jesus saying to you?

Ask God to show you how to live today.

"Lord, I give you all my thoughts, words, deeds, joys, and sorrows for the good of others—especially the poor, the sick, the lost, and the lonely. Let my entire day be an unceasing prayer for them. Amen."

Thursday, October 6, 2016

Know that God is present with you and ready to converse.

"Lord, you know what I need before I ask. You find me before I seek you. Guide me by your Word."

Read the Gospel: Luke 11:5–13.

And Jesus said to the disciples, "Suppose one of you has a friend, and you go to him at midnight and say to him, 'Friend, lend me three loaves of bread; for a friend of mine has arrived, and I have nothing to set before him.' And he answers from within, 'Do not bother me; the door has already been locked, and my children are with me in bed; I cannot get up and give you anything.' I tell you, even though he will not get up and give him anything because he is his friend, at least because of his persistence he will get up and give him whatever he needs.

"So I say to you, ask, and it will be given you; search, and you will find; knock, and the door will be opened for you. For everyone who asks receives, and everyone who searches finds, and for everyone who knocks, the door will be opened. Is there anyone among you who, if your child asks for a fish, will give a snake instead of a fish? Or if the child asks for an egg, will give a scorpion? If you then, who are evil, know how to give good gifts to your children, how much more will the heavenly Father give the Holy Spirit to those who ask him!"

Notice what you think and feel as you read the Gospel.

Jesus has to be aware of the humor in this parable. He compares God to a friend who is irritated by being disturbed at midnight. Even though they are friends, he doesn't want to get out of bed and give his friend bread. But he does it just to get rid of him. So Jesus urges us to persevere in asking God for whatever we need.

Pray as you are led for yourself and others.

"Lord, keep me coming back to you. I ask for many things for myself and for those you ask me to pray for . . ." (Continue in your own words.)

Listen to Jesus.

By praying, you allow me to work in you and in your life, beloved. Continue in your desire for the good things of God. Continue praying for others. What else is Jesus saying to you?

Ask God to show you how to live today.

"You say that God will give the Holy Spirit to those who ask, Lord. I ask. I desire. I need. I persist in asking according to your Word. Amen."

Friday, October 7, 2016

Know that God is present with you and ready to converse.

"Lord, open to me the mysteries of your Word. Let it do its deep work in me to your glory."

Read the Gospel: Luke 11:15–26.

But some of crowd said, "He casts out demons by Beelzebul, the ruler of the demons." Others, to test him, kept demanding from him a sign from heaven. But he knew what they were thinking and said to them, "Every kingdom divided against itself becomes a desert, and house falls on house. If Satan also is divided against himself, how will his kingdom stand? For you say that I cast out the demons by Beelzebul. Now if I cast out the demons by Beelzebul, by whom do your exorcists cast them out? Therefore they will be your judges. But if it is by the finger of God that I cast out the demons, then the kingdom of God has come to you. When a strong man, fully armed, guards his castle, his property is safe. But when one stronger than he attacks him and overpowers him, he takes away his armor in which he trusted and divides his plunder. Whoever is not with me is against me, and whoever does not gather with me scatters.

"When the unclean spirit has gone out of a person, it wanders through waterless regions looking for a resting place, but not finding any, it says, 'I will return to my house from which I came.' When it comes, it finds it swept and put in order. Then it goes and brings seven other spirits more evil than itself, and they enter and live there; and the last state of that person is worse than the first."

Notice what you think and feel as you read the Gospel.

Some people find fault with the good Jesus does, accusing him of casting out demons by the prince of demons. Jesus points out the absurdity of their accusation.

Pray as you are led for yourself and others.

"Jesus, your words chill me. You have saved me from sin. Do not let me return to a life of sin . . ." (Continue in your own words.)

Listen to Jesus.

Do not trust yourself, friend. Look to God for safety and security. What else is Jesus saying to you?

Ask God to show you how to live today.

"Lord, teach me to walk in this fear of the Lord today. Let me not be ungrateful for your mercies. Keep me from taking your mercy and my safety for granted. Amen."

Saturday, October 8, 2016

Know that God is present with you and ready to converse.

"I seek your blessing, Lord of all. And I seek to commune with you in the reading of your Word. Thank you for being with me now."

Read the Gospel: Luke 11:27–28.

While Jesus was saying this, a woman in the crowd raised her voice and said to him, "Blessed is the womb that bore you and the breasts that nursed you!" But he said, "Blessed rather are those who hear the word of God and obey it!"

Notice what you think and feel as you read the Gospel.

A woman in the crowd pronounces blessing on Jesus' mother. She could not know about the Blessed Virgin Mary as we do, that all generations would call her blessed.

Pray as you are led for yourself and others.

"Lord, I have heard. Now let me keep your Word . . ." (Continue in your own words.)

Listen to Jesus.

I give you my grace to obey my word. Your works will declare your love for me and for your neighbor. What else is Jesus saying to you?

Ask God to show you how to live today.

"Lord, you have honored your mother and given her to me as my mother. Thank you. I bless her, too. Amen."

Sunday, October 9, 2016
Twenty-Eighth Sunday in Ordinary Time

Know that God is present with you and ready to converse.

The saints of God learn gratitude on the journey. We learn to notice our blessings more and more and, as we put greater trust in our Father, we give thanks even for our trials, for we know they will work for our good.

When you are ready, open yourself to gratitude and to the work of Jesus within you. "Jesus, you are passing by now. Master, have mercy on me."

Read the Gospel: Luke 17:11–19.

On the way to Jerusalem Jesus was going through the region between Samaria and Galilee. As he entered a village, ten lepers approached him. Keeping their distance, they called out, saying, "Jesus, master, have mercy on us!" When he saw them, he said to them, "Go and show yourselves to the priests." And as they went, they were made clean. Then one of them, when he saw that he was healed, turned back, praising God with a loud voice. He prostrated himself at Jesus' feet and thanked him. And he was a Samaritan. Then Jesus asked, "Were not ten made clean? But the other nine, where are they? Was none of them found to return and give praise to God except this foreigner?" Then he said to him, "Get up and go on your way; your faith has made you well."

Notice what you think and feel as you read the Gospel.

Jesus cleanses ten lepers on his way to Jerusalem. One, a Samaritan, returns to thank him. Jesus seems dismayed that only one of ten returns to thank him, but he commends the faith of the one who did.

Pray as you are led for yourself and others.

"Lord, you do so much for me and mine. I thank you . . ." (Continue in your own words.)

Listen to Jesus.

Be content with all you have and all your circumstances, and give thanks to God. Do not be anxious, but trust God with all your needs. What else is Jesus saying to you?

Ask God to show you how to live today.

"Lord, help me be grateful today. Let my mouth be full of thanksgiving. You made me, you care for me and those I love, and you have chosen me to live in your everlasting kingdom. Your goodness is measureless. I praise you and thank you. Amen."

Monday, October 10, 2016

Know that God is present with you and ready to converse.

"Lord, what a privilege to stand in the presence of the Most High. Let me study your Word and learn from it."

Read the Gospel: Luke 11:29–32.

When the crowds were increasing, Jesus began to say, "This generation is an evil generation; it asks for a sign, but no sign will be given to it except the sign of Jonah. For just as Jonah became a sign to the people of Nineveh, so the Son of Man will be to this generation. The queen of the south will rise at the judgment with the people of this generation and condemn them, because she came from the ends of the earth to listen to the wisdom of Solomon, and see, something greater than Solomon is here! The people of Nineveh will rise up at the judgment with this generation and condemn it, because they repented at the proclamation of Jonah, and see, something greater than Jonah is here!"

Notice what you think and feel as you read the Gospel.

Jesus speaks harshly to those who follow him to see his mighty works. He preaches repentance. Their sign, he says, will be the sign of Jonah, who foreshadows his own resurrection. But Jesus focuses on the repentance of the people of Nineveh. This generation will not repent even though something greater than Jonah is here!

Pray as you are led for yourself and others.

"Jesus, people are still seeking signs, still slow to repent. I pray for them. May I offer you true repentance . . ." (Continue in your own words.)

Listen to Jesus.

I wash you by my words and by my Spirit, beloved disciple. What else is Jesus saying to you?

Ask God to show you how to live today.

"Thank you, Savior, for your mercy. Grant me your Spirit to resist temptations. Help me overcome my habitual faults. Amen."

Tuesday, October 11, 2016

Know that God is present with you and ready to converse.

"God, you created all things by your Word. I ask you to create a new heart in me by your Word. I desire a heart like yours, Jesus."

Read the Gospel: Luke 11:37–41.

While Jesus was speaking, a Pharisee invited him to dine with him; so he went in and took his place at the table.

The Pharisee was amazed to see that he did not first wash before dinner. Then the Lord said to him, "Now you Pharisees clean the outside of the cup and of the dish, but inside you are full of greed and wickedness. You fools! Did not the one who made the outside make the inside also? So give for alms those things that are within; and see, everything will be clean for you."

Notice what you think and feel as you read the Gospel.

Jesus instructs the Pharisee in matters of ceremonial washing before meals. The Pharisees are concerned about outer cleanliness, says Jesus, but not inner wickedness. What God wants is inner cleanliness. That will make all things clean.

Pray as you are led for yourself and others.

"Jesus, I long for goodness within. Only by your transforming Spirit can I be clean and good . . ." (Continue in your own words.)

Listen to Jesus.

What you do, servant, do with all your heart unto the Lord, not for show before others. What else is Jesus saying to you?

Ask God to show you how to live today.

"Savior, reveal to me ways in which I can live today more truly with a clean heart and clean hands. I invite you to dine with me, Lord. Amen."

Wednesday, October 12, 2016

Know that God is present with you and ready to converse.

"Lord, I look to you now. I want to see the world with eyes of truth. Your Word is truth."

Read the Gospel: Luke 11:42–46.

Jesus warned, "But woe to you Pharisees! For you tithe mint and rue and herbs of all kinds, and neglect justice and the love of God; it is these you ought to have practiced, without neglecting the others. Woe to you Pharisees! For you love to have the seat of honor in the synagogues and to be greeted with respect in the marketplaces. Woe to you! For you are like unmarked graves, and people walk over them without realizing it."

One of the lawyers answered him, "Teacher, when you say these things, you insult us too." And he said, "Woe also to you lawyers! For you load people with burdens hard to bear, and you yourselves do not lift a finger to ease them."

Notice what you think and feel as you read the Gospel.

Jesus reproaches the Pharisees and the lawyers for petty religious observance done for the sake of appearance and to receive honor from others. They neglect justice and the love of God. They are like unmarked graves, he says.

Pray as you are led for yourself and others.

"Lord, I desire to be just in all my affairs . . ." (Continue in your own words.)

Listen to Jesus.

Justice reigns in the kingdom of heaven, servant. Do justice and pray for the coming of the kingdom. God will mete out perfect justice. What else is Jesus saying to you?

Ask God to show you how to live today.

"I will strive to act justly. Show me how I can work for justice for others. Praise to your name, just Lord. Amen."

Thursday, October 13, 2016

Know that God is present with you and ready to converse.

"Your Word is true, Lord. You know my heart. Let me hear your Word of truth now and take it to heart."

Read the Gospel: Luke 11:47–54.

Jesus warned, "Woe to you! For you build the tombs of the prophets whom your ancestors killed. So you are witnesses and approve of the deeds of your ancestors; for they killed them, and you build their tombs. Therefore also the wisdom of God said, 'I will send them prophets and apostles, some of whom they will kill and persecute,' so that this generation may be charged with the blood of all the prophets shed since the foundation of the world, from the blood of Abel to the blood of Zechariah, who perished between the altar and the sanctuary. Yes, I tell you, it will be charged against this generation. Woe to you lawyers! For you have taken away the key of knowledge; you did not enter yourselves, and you hindered those who were entering."

When he went outside, the scribes and the Pharisees began to be very hostile toward him and to cross-examine him about many things, lying in wait for him, to catch him in something he might say.

Notice what you think and feel as you read the Gospel.

Jesus continues to speak woe upon the Pharisees, scribes, and lawyers. He threatens them with judgment. He tells them they are complicit in their fathers' killing of the prophets sent by God. He says they have hindered learning. The scribes and the Pharisees now begin to press him, to provoke him, lying in wait to catch him in something.

Pray as you are led for yourself and others.

"Merciful Lord, I pray for your enemies. They are miserable, though they may think they are not . . ." (Continue in your own words.)

Listen to Jesus.

People will always oppose what is right and just, wise and good. You will make enemies when you strive to do my will. What else is Jesus saying to you?

Ask God to show you how to live today.

"Make me valiant, Jesus—wise and brave in the causes of righteousness. Is there something I can do today? Amen."

Friday, October 14, 2016

Know that God is present with you and ready to converse.

"Word of God, breathe on me now. Make me wise in the ways of God."

Read the Gospel: Luke 12:1–7.

Meanwhile, when the crowd gathered by the thousands so that they trampled on one another, Jesus began to speak first to his disciples, "Beware of the yeast of the Pharisees, that is, their hypocrisy. Nothing is covered up that will not be uncovered, and nothing secret that will not become known. Therefore whatever you have said in the dark will be heard in the light, and what you have whispered behind closed doors will be proclaimed from the housetops.

"I tell you, my friends, do not fear those who kill the body, and after that can do nothing more. But I will warn you whom to fear: fear him who, after he has killed, has authority to cast into hell. Yes, I tell you, fear him! Are not five sparrows sold for two pennies? Yet not one of them is forgotten in God's sight. But even the hairs of your head are all counted. Do not be afraid; you are of more value than many sparrows."

Notice what you think and feel as you read the Gospel.

Mobbed by thousands, Jesus takes a moment to warn his disciples to beware of hypocrisy, for all hidden and secret things will be revealed. Don't fear those who can kill your body; fear only him who has the power to cast into hell. God greatly values each person.

Pray as you are led for yourself and others.

"Lord, let me live with your ordered priorities, fearless of men but walking before you with fear and trembling, lest I offend you . . ." (Continue in your own words.)

Listen to Jesus.

Cling to my mercy, beloved disciple. Offer to God all that you are, and God will receive you. What else is Jesus saying to you?

Ask God to show you how to live today.

"I give you all my secrets, Lord. Uncover in me all that I seek to hide even from myself. Amen."

Saturday, October 15, 2016

Know that God is present with you and ready to converse.

"Holy Spirit, give me ears to hear your Word. Prepare me, Lord."

Read the Gospel: Luke 12:8–12.

Jesus instructed, "And I tell you, everyone who acknowledges me before others, the Son of Man also will acknowledge before the angels of God; but whoever denies me before others will be denied before the angels of God. And everyone who speaks a word against the Son of Man will be forgiven; but whoever blasphemes against the Holy Spirit will not be forgiven. When they bring you before the synagogues, the rulers, and the authorities, do not worry about how you are to defend yourselves or what you are to say; for the Holy Spirit will teach you at that very hour what you ought to say."

Notice what you think and feel as you read the Gospel.

Jesus understands that some will be ashamed to acknowledge their allegiance to him in public. Yet he insists upon being acknowledged, and he warns that those who deny him will be denied before the angels of God. He speaks of the work of the Spirit to give us the words to say to those who challenge and persecute us.

Pray as you are led for yourself and others.

"You ask great courage, Lord, but you provide your Spirit to help us witness to your Gospel. Help me abandon myself to your Spirit . . ." (Continue in your own words.)

Listen to Jesus.

You have nothing to fear, beloved disciple, as long as you are following me. What else is Jesus saying to you?

Ask God to show you how to live today.

"Jesus, I rely on your mercy. Spirit, I rely on your inspiration. Give me an opportunity today to acknowledge Jesus. Amen."

Sunday, October 16, 2016
Twenty-Ninth Sunday in Ordinary Time

Know that God is present with you and ready to converse.

Prayer is our communion with God. To desire God is prayer, to seek God is prayer. To love, to praise, to thank, to ask—all are prayer. The Lord wants us to persist in prayer, for through it God works.

When you are ready, join the Lord in prayer: "Lord, I come to you again today to pray over your Word. I know that you hear me. Let me hear you."

Read the Gospel: Luke 18:1–8.

Then Jesus told his disciples a parable about their need to pray always and not to lose heart. He said, "In a certain city there was a judge who neither feared God nor had respect for people. In that city there was a widow who kept coming to him and saying, 'Grant me justice against my opponent.' For a while he refused; but later he said to himself, 'Though I have no fear of God and no respect for anyone, yet because this widow keeps bothering me, I will grant her justice, so that she may not wear me out by continually coming.'" And the Lord said, "Listen to what the unjust judge says. And will not God grant justice to his chosen ones who cry to him day and night? Will he delay long in helping them? I tell you, he will quickly grant justice to them. And yet, when the Son of Man comes, will he find faith on earth?"

Notice what you think and feel as you read the Gospel.

Jesus' parable says we should always pray and not lose heart. Even the unrighteous judge will do justice for one who persists in asking. So God will vindicate his elect, who cry out to him day and night. Then Jesus asks, "When the Son of Man comes, will he find faith on earth?"

Pray as you are led for yourself and others.

"Lord, I pray that you will find faith on earth. You came to save us. You call us to your kingdom. I have many things to pray for . . ." (Continue in your own words.)

Listen to Jesus.

I grant you patience, beloved, for all shall be done in God's time. It pleases God that you ask and ask again with all your heart. What else is Jesus saying to you?

Ask God to show you how to live today.

"What do your elect cry to you day and night, Lord? What vindication do they seek? Teach me to pray as they do. Amen."

Monday, October 17, 2016

Know that God is present with you and ready to converse.

"Reveal to me the riches of your Word, Lord God, for I long to know you, love you, serve you, and glorify you."

Read the Gospel: Luke 12:13–21.

Someone in the crowd said to Jesus, "Teacher, tell my brother to divide the family inheritance with me." But he said to him, "Friend, who set me to be a judge or arbitrator over you?" And he said to them, "Take care! Be on your guard against all kinds of greed; for one's life does not consist in the abundance of possessions." Then he told them a parable: "The land of a rich man produced abundantly. And he thought to himself, 'What should I do, for I have no place to store my crops.' Then he said, 'I will do this: I will pull down my barns and build larger ones, and there I will store all my grain and my goods. And I will say to my soul, soul, you have ample goods laid up for many years; relax, eat, drink, be merry.' But God said to him, 'You fool! This very night your life is being demanded of you. And the things you have prepared, whose will they be?' So it is with those who store up treasures for themselves but are not rich toward God."

Notice what you think and feel as you read the Gospel.

Jesus teaches his followers to beware of all covetousness. He tells the parable of the rich man who becomes richer and so thinks it is time to relax, eat, drink, and be merry. That's the night he dies. Who knows who will inherit his treasure? Rather, strive to be rich toward God, Jesus says.

Pray as you are led for yourself and others.

"Lord, I confess I have longed for earthly riches. Turn my heart wholly toward you. Let me trust in your care rather than in what I own . . ." (Continue in your own words.)

Listen to Jesus.

I give you my peace, beloved servant. I provide you all the things that you need. Grow in virtue by my grace. That is your wealth. What else is Jesus saying to you?

Ask God to show you how to live today.

"Give me prudence in managing all my affairs, and let me be generous knowing that all I have comes from you. Blessed be your name, Lord. Amen."

Tuesday, October 18, 2016
Saint Luke, evangelist

Know that God is present with you and ready to converse.

"You are here with me, gracious Lord. Grant me peace to receive your Word."

Read the Gospel: Luke 10:1–9.

After this the Lord appointed seventy others and sent them on ahead of him in pairs to every town and place where he himself intended to go. He said to them, "The harvest is plentiful, but the laborers are few; therefore ask the Lord of the harvest to send out laborers into his harvest. Go on your way. See, I am sending you out like lambs into the midst of wolves. Carry no purse, no bag, no sandals; and greet no one on the road. Whatever house you enter, first say, 'Peace to this house!' And if anyone is there who shares in peace, your peace will rest on that person; but if not, it will return to you. Remain in the same house, eating and drinking whatever they provide, for the laborer deserves to be paid. Do not move about from house to house. Whenever you enter a town and its people welcome you, eat what is set before you; cure the sick who are there, and say to them, 'The kingdom of God has come near to you.'"

Notice what you think and feel as you read the Gospel.

Jesus sends out the seventy ahead of him two by two to heal the sick in his name and to preach the good news of the kingdom. He gives them instructions. The first is to pray for the Lord to provide laborers for this plentiful harvest. They are to be as lambs in the midst of wolves, peaceful, comfortable about receiving hospitality, and respectful of others.

Pray as you are led for yourself and others.

"Lord, I pray for more laborers in your vineyard. Call and commission many in your service . . ." (Continue in your own words.)

Listen to Jesus.

Let every disciple know that he or she is called to heal the world's ills and announce my kingdom. What else is Jesus saying to you?

Ask God to show you how to live today.

"I hear your call, Lord. Give me power to be faithful to your service. I, too, desire the salvation of all. Amen."

Wednesday, October 19, 2016

Know that God is present with you and ready to converse.

"Lord, your servant stands before you. I long to do your will. Teach me by your holy Word."

Read the Gospel: Luke 12:39–48.

Jesus taught, "But know this: if the owner of the house had known at what hour the thief was coming, he would not have let his house be broken into. You also must be ready, for the Son of Man is coming at an unexpected hour."

Peter said, "Lord, are you telling this parable for us or for everyone?" And the Lord said, "Who then is the faithful and prudent manager whom his master will put in charge of his slaves, to give them their allowance of food at the proper time? Blessed is that slave whom his master will find at work when he arrives. Truly I tell you, he will put that one in charge of all his possessions. But if that slave says to himself, 'My master is delayed in coming,' and if he begins to beat the other slaves, men and women, and to eat and drink and get drunk, the master of that slave will come on a day when he does not expect him and at an hour that he does not know, and will cut him in pieces, and put him with the unfaithful. That slave who knew what his master wanted, but did not prepare himself or do what was wanted, will receive a severe beating. But the one who did not know and did what deserved a beating will receive a light beating. From everyone to whom much has been given, much will be required; and from the one to whom much has been entrusted, even more will be demanded."

Notice what you think and feel as you read the Gospel.

Jesus speaks of his return at an unannounced time, and he speaks of being a faithful servant of the master's household. The faithful servant the master will reward upon his return; unfaithful servants will be beaten according to their understanding of the master's will.

Pray as you are led for yourself and others.

"Lord, I want to serve you for love of you, not fear. How may I be faithful and wise in your service today?" (Continue in your own words.)

Listen to Jesus.

Use what I give you, and be faithful over little. Seek God every day, and you will grow rich in the things of God. What else is Jesus saying to you?

Ask God to show you how to live today.

"Forgive my failings, Lord, and give me wisdom to know your will and power to do it faithfully. May my service glorify you. Amen."

Thursday, October 20, 2016

Know that God is present with you and ready to converse.

"Almighty Father, Holy Spirit, and Son of God, Word of God, I worship you and glorify you. I invite you to transform me in your image."

Read the Gospel: Luke 12:49–53.

Jesus said, "I came to bring fire to the earth, and how I wish it were already kindled! I have a baptism with which to be baptized, and what stress I am under until it is completed! Do you think that I have come to bring peace to the earth? No, I tell you, but rather division! From now on five in one household will be divided, three against two and two against three; they will be divided:

father against son
and son against father,
mother against daughter
and daughter against mother,
mother-in-law against her daughter-in-law
and daughter-in-law against mother-in-law."

Notice what you think and feel as you read the Gospel.

Jesus takes the long view of history stretching forward after his crucifixion, which he calls a baptism. He says he came to cast fire on the earth, great division and conflict, even within families.

Pray as you are led for yourself and others.

"I have witnessed these divisions, Lord. Yet I seek to make peace . . ." (Continue in your own words.)

Listen to Jesus.

Yes, strive to be at peace with all people, beloved. Even in the midst of strife and opposition, I am your peace. What else is Jesus saying to you?

Ask God to show you how to live today.

"Jesus, I pray for members of my own family. Touch them with your grace and your peace. Amen."

Friday, October 21, 2016

Know that God is present with you and ready to converse.

"Great judge of all, I seek mercy and redemption in your Word."

Read the Gospel: Luke 12:54–59.

Jesus also said to the crowds, "When you see a cloud rising in the west, you immediately say, 'It is going to rain'; and so it happens. And when you see the south wind blowing, you say, 'There will be scorching heat'; and it happens. You hypocrites! You know how to interpret the appearance of earth and sky, but why do you not know how to interpret the present time?

"And why do you not judge for yourselves what is right? Thus, when you go with your accuser before a magistrate, on the way make an effort to settle the case, or you may be dragged before the judge, and the judge hand you over to the officer, and the officer throw you in prison. I tell you, you will never get out until you have paid the very last penny."

Notice what you think and feel as you read the Gospel.

Jesus accuses the multitudes of hypocrisy, for they can read the signs of the weather to predict it, but they do not read the signs about what is right. He urges them to settle quickly with their accusers to avoid prison.

Pray as you are led for yourself and others.

"Jesus, help me understand what these words mean for me . . ." (Continue in your own words.)

Listen to Jesus.

I am Lord of your life, child. Look to your circumstances and find me in them. I will guide you to do my will. What else is Jesus saying to you?

Ask God to show you how to live today.

"Lord, I submit to your will and your providence. You are all I have. I place my trust in you. Amen."

Saturday, October 22, 2016

Know that God is present with you and ready to converse.

"Almighty Creator, you are everywhere at all times. Let me be present for you now as I read your Word."

Read the Gospel: Luke 13:1–9.

At that very time there were some present who told Jesus about the Galileans whose blood Pilate had mingled with their sacrifices. He asked them, "Do you think that because these Galileans suffered in this way they were worse sinners than all other Galileans? No, I tell you; but unless you repent, you will all perish as they did. Or those eighteen who were killed when the tower of Siloam fell on them—do you think that they were worse offenders than all the others living in Jerusalem? No, I tell you; but unless you repent, you will all perish just as they did."

Then he told this parable: "A man had a fig tree planted in his vineyard; and he came looking for fruit on it and found none. So he said to the gardener, 'See here! For three years I have come looking for fruit on this fig tree, and still I find none. Cut it down! Why should it be wasting the soil?' He replied, 'Sir, let it alone for one more year, until I dig around it and put manure on it. If it bears fruit next year, well and good; but if not, you can cut it down.'"

Notice what you think and feel as you read the Gospel.

As now, people in Jesus' time tend to blame the victims when disaster befalls them. Those who suffer must be sinners. Jesus says no. All are sinners. All are at risk of dying in their sins. He tells the parable of the unproductive fig tree. The vinedresser persuades the master to spare it and give it another year to produce fruit.

Pray as you are led for yourself and others.

"Lord, how may I be more fruitful, more pleasing to you?" (Continue in your own words.)

Listen to Jesus.

You are my own, beloved disciple. You bear fruit by staying close to me. I am your fruitfulness. What else is Jesus saying to you?

Ask God to show you how to live today.

"Jesus, when my heart strays from you, bring me back. Impress upon me how completely I depend on you for all happiness and fruitfulness. Amen."

Sunday, October 23, 2016
Thirtieth Sunday in Ordinary Time

Know that God is present with you and ready to converse.

What is the trait or attitude most pleasing to God? We know from the example of the Blessed Virgin Mary, as well as her Son, that it is humility.

When you are ready, humble yourself before the eternal Word of the Father: "Lord, give me a lowly heart to approach you. Hear my prayer and let me hear you."

Read the Gospel: Luke 18:9–14.

Jesus also told this parable to some who trusted in themselves that they were righteous and regarded others with contempt: "Two men went up to the Temple to pray, one a Pharisee and the other a tax collector. The Pharisee, standing by himself, was praying thus, 'God, I thank you that I am not like other people: thieves, rogues, adulterers, or even like this tax collector. I fast twice a week; I give a tenth of all my income.' But the tax collector, standing far off, would not even look up to heaven, but was beating his breast and saying, 'God, be merciful to me, a sinner!' I tell you, this man went down to his home justified rather than the other; for all who exalt themselves will be humbled, but all who humble themselves will be exalted."

Notice what you think and feel as you read the Gospel.

Jesus tells the story of the Pharisee and the tax collector praying in the Temple. The Pharisee thanks God for his righteousness compared with other people. The tax collector beats his breast and asks God for mercy, for he is a sinner. Jesus approves the prayer of the tax collector and the way of humility.

Pray as you are led for yourself and others.

"My God, have mercy upon me, a sinner. Give me true sorrow for my sins so that you can cleanse me . . ." (Continue in your own words.)

Listen to Jesus.

Your sins are forgiven, dear one. I will be your companion all day long. Ask of me whatever you desire. What else is Jesus saying to you?

Ask God to show you how to live today.

"I desire true humility, Lord, for I know that is the way to please you. Teach me your humility, Jesus. Amen."

Monday, October 24, 2016

Know that God is present with you and ready to converse.

"Lord, I rejoice in your power and your goodness. You are here with me now. You love me by your Word."

Read the Gospel: Luke 13:10–17.

Now Jesus was teaching in one of the synagogues on the Sabbath. And just then there appeared a woman with a spirit that had crippled her for eighteen years. She was bent over and was quite unable to stand up straight. When Jesus saw her, he called her over and said, "Woman, you are set free from your ailment." When he laid his hands on her, immediately she stood up straight and began praising God. But the leader of the synagogue, indignant because Jesus had cured on the Sabbath, kept saying to the crowd, "There are six days on which work ought to be done; come on those days and be cured, and not on the Sabbath day." But the Lord answered him and said, "You hypocrites! Does not each of you on the Sabbath untie his ox or his donkey from the manger, and lead it away to give it water? And ought not this woman, a daughter of Abraham whom Satan bound for eighteen long years, be set free from this bondage on the Sabbath day?" When he said this, all his opponents were put to shame; and the entire crowd was rejoicing at all the wonderful things that he was doing.

Notice what you think and feel as you read the Gospel.

Jesus heals the woman who could not stand up straight. She praises God. But the ruler of the synagogue objects to the healings Jesus performed on the Sabbath. Jesus points out the absurdity of his indignation, and all the people rejoice.

Pray as you are led for yourself and others.

"Jesus, there are many who need your healing of body, mind, heart, and soul. The Spirit brings these people to mind . . ." (Continue in your own words.)

Listen to Jesus.

Have faith in what you have prayed, beloved. I, too, love those for whom you pray. What else is Jesus saying to you?

Ask God to show you how to live today.

"Lord, I get impatient. Give me eyes to see you work today. Give me grace to work with you. Amen."

Tuesday, October 25, 2016

Know that God is present with you and ready to converse.

"Lord, let your Word be sown in my heart and grow mighty."

Read the Gospel: Luke 13:18–21.

Jesus said therefore, "What is the kingdom of God like? And to what should I compare it? It is like a mustard seed that someone took and sowed in the garden; it grew and became a tree, and the birds of the air made nests in its branches."

And again he said, "To what should I compare the kingdom of God? It is like yeast that a woman took and mixed in with three measures of flour until all of it was leavened."

Notice what you think and feel as you read the Gospel.

Jesus compares the kingdom of God to a mustard seed that grows huge, like yeast that leavens the whole batch of meal. Out of something small can come something great, for this is the kingdom of God. God uses small, ordinary things to do his holy will.

Pray as you are led for yourself and others.

"Lord, I am small and ordinary. Let me receive your kingdom within, and let it transform me . . ." (Continue in your own words.)

Listen to Jesus.

You desire me, my beloved, and I desire you. How may I serve you today? What else is Jesus saying to you?

Ask God to show you how to live today.

"Jesus, give me the grace to walk in your way: humble, peaceful, and loving toward all. Amen."

Wednesday, October 26, 2016

Know that God is present with you and ready to converse.

"Lord, let me know you by your Word. Your Word is life."

Read the Gospel: Luke 13:22–30.

Jesus went through one town and village after another, teaching as he made his way to Jerusalem. Someone asked him, "Lord, will only a few be saved?" He said to them, "Strive to enter through the narrow door; for many, I tell you, will try to enter and will not be able. When once the owner of the house has got up and shut the door, and you begin to stand outside and to knock at the door, saying, 'Lord, open to us,' then in reply he will say to you, 'I do not know where you come from.' Then you will begin to say, 'We ate and drank with you, and you taught in our streets.' But he will say, 'I do not know where you come from; go away from me, all you evildoers!' There will be weeping and gnashing of teeth when you see Abraham and Isaac and Jacob and all the prophets in the kingdom of God, and you yourselves thrown out. Then people will come from east and west, from north and south, and will eat in the kingdom of God. Indeed, some are last who will be first, and some are first who will be last."

Notice what you think and feel as you read the Gospel.

Someone asks Jesus whether those who are saved are few. Jesus turns the man's focus back onto himself: strive to enter by the narrow door, Jesus says.

Pray as you are led for yourself and others.

"Lord, you are my door to the kingdom. Let me stay true to you. I pray for those who do not know you yet . . ." (Continue in your own words.)

Listen to Jesus.

Whoever will may come to me. Pray that hearts may hear my call and come to me. I will give them eternal life. What else is Jesus saying to you?

Ask God to show you how to live today.

"Jesus, there is so much at stake for souls in this life. So many are in jeopardy. How may I help? I offer myself today. Amen."

Thursday, October 27, 2016

Know that God is present with you and ready to converse.

"Lord God of hosts, gather me under your wings that I may be safe forever."

Read the Gospel: Luke 13:31–35.

At that very hour some Pharisees came and said to Jesus, "Get away from here, for Herod wants to kill you." He said to them, "Go and tell that fox for me, 'Listen, I am casting out demons and performing cures today and tomorrow, and on the third day I finish my work. Yet today, tomorrow, and the next day I must be on my way, because it is impossible for a prophet to be killed outside of Jerusalem.' Jerusalem, Jerusalem, the city that kills the prophets and stones those who are sent to it! How often have I desired to gather your children together as a hen gathers her brood under her wings, and you were not willing! See, your house is left to you. And I tell you, you will not see me until the time comes when you say, 'Blessed is the one who comes in the name of the Lord.'"

Notice what you think and feel as you read the Gospel.

The Pharisees tell Jesus that Herod wants to kill him. He says he has to do what he has to do today, tomorrow, and the next day. He is heading toward Jerusalem, where he knows he will be put to death. He laments because he would have gathered the children of Jerusalem under his wings, but they were not willing.

Pray as you are led for yourself and others.

"Jesus, you were resolved to do your Father's will, to die at the hands of men. Yet your sadness was not for yourself but for those who would not come to you . . ." (Continue in your own words.)

Listen to Jesus.

People still refuse to come to me. It grieves me. I thank you, dear disciple, for heeding my call. Let us walk together in love. What else is Jesus saying to you?

Ask God to show you how to live today.

"My Lord and my Savior, Jesus Christ, let me walk with you to Jerusalem. I, too, have a cross to bear. Amen."

Friday, October 28, 2016
Saints Simon and Jude, apostles

Know that God is present with you and ready to converse.

"Jesus, you prepared for your work by prayer. I seek to do as you did. I will pray with you, Word of God."

Read the Gospel: Luke 6:12–16.

Now during those days Jesus went out to the mountain to pray; and he spent the night in prayer to God. And when day came, he called his disciples and chose twelve of them, whom he also named apostles: Simon, whom he named Peter, and his brother Andrew, and James, and John, and Philip, and Bartholomew, and Matthew, and Thomas, and James son of Alphaeus, and Simon, who was called the Zealot, and Judas son of James, and Judas Iscariot, who became a traitor.

Notice what you think and feel as you read the Gospel.

Jesus prays all night alone in the hills. The next day he calls his disciples, including Simon and Jude. Judas Iscariot, the traitor, was among them.

Pray as you are led for yourself and others.

"Jesus, you chose ordinary men, not even the best men. You allowed a traitor in. Help me understand your ways, Lord . . ." (Continue in your own words.)

Listen to Jesus.

Let the saving power of God work in you, my child. I have work for you that only you can do. What else is Jesus saying to you?

Ask God to show you how to live today.

"Lord, it would be my joy to do something for you, for others. Tell me what to do and how to go about it. I want to do it in the way that pleases you. Amen."

Saturday, October 29, 2016

Know that God is present with you and ready to converse.

"Lord, let me come to you with true humility. Let me not presume or exalt myself with you or with others. I am a sinner, saved by your grace."

Read the Gospel: Luke 14:1, 7–11.

On one occasion when Jesus was going to the house of a leader of the Pharisees to eat a meal on the Sabbath, they were watching him closely. . . .

When he noticed how the guests chose the places of honor, he told them a parable. "When you are invited by someone to a wedding banquet, do not sit down at the place of honor, in case someone more distinguished than you has been invited by your host; and the host who invited both of you may come and say to you, 'Give this person your place,' and then in disgrace you would start to take the lowest place. But when you are invited, go and sit down at the lowest place, so that when your host comes, he may say to you, 'Friend, move up higher'; then you will be honored in the presence of all who sit at the table with you. For all who exalt themselves will be humbled, and those who humble themselves will be exalted."

Notice what you think and feel as you read the Gospel.

Jesus tells the parable of the wedding guests who choose to sit at the places of honor, but then have to move to the lowest places when they are asked to give way. Jesus says to choose the lowest places. By humility you will be exalted.

Pray as you are led for yourself and others.

"Jesus, your ways are often upside down. You yourself humbled yourself and gave yourself for sinners. May I follow you?" (Continue in your own words.)

Listen to Jesus.

Love will lead you, child. Love gives, love dies, and love lives forever in God. What else is Jesus saying to you?

Ask God to show you how to live today.

"Lord, give me your own pure heart of love. Let me lose myself and not count the cost. Amen."

Sunday, October 30, 2016
Thirty-First Sunday in Ordinary Time

Know that God is present with you and ready to converse.

Jesus is our salvation, God becoming man to suffer and die for sinners, putting death to death by his death, and conferring upon us everlasting life in the kingdom of God. How can we not be joyful?

When you are ready, place yourself in the presence of the Lord, inviting him to enter and stay with you: "Jesus, you are passing by. Stop and visit in the house of this sinner today."

Read the Gospel: Luke 19:1–10.

Jesus entered Jericho and was passing through it. A man was there named Zacchaeus; he was a chief tax collector and was rich. He was trying to see who Jesus was, but on account of the crowd he could not, because he was short in stature. So he ran ahead and climbed a sycamore tree to see him, because he was going to pass that way. When Jesus came to the place, he looked up and said to him, "Zacchaeus, hurry and come down; for I must stay at your house today." So he hurried down and was happy to welcome him. All who saw it began to grumble and said, "He has gone to be the guest of one who is a sinner." Zacchaeus stood there and said to the Lord, "Look, half of my possessions, Lord, I will give to the poor; and if I have defrauded anyone of anything, I will pay back four times as much." Then Jesus said to him, "Today salvation has come to this house, because he too is a son of Abraham. For the Son of Man came to seek out and to save the lost."

Notice what you think and feel as you read the Gospel.

Zacchaeus climbs a tree to get a better look at Jesus passing by. Jesus invites himself to stay at Zacchaeus' house. Zacchaeus is eager to make amends for his sins. Jesus loves him, saying, "Salvation has come to this house today."

Pray as you are led for yourself and others.

"Jesus, you love to save the lost. Save me today. Save me from myself . . ." (Continue in your own words.)

Listen to Jesus.

You see how easy it is to be with me, beloved? I long to spend more time with you. We have much to talk about. What else is Jesus saying to you?

Ask God to show you how to live today.

"Master, let me respond to your invitation to be with you more often. I want to know you and you to know me. Amen."

Monday, October 31, 2016

Know that God is present with you and ready to converse.

"Merciful God, I must be among the poor, the maimed, the lame, and the blind, for you have called me to your banquet. I praise you."

Read the Gospel: Luke 14:12–14.

Jesus said also to the one who had invited him, "When you give a luncheon or a dinner, do not invite your friends or your brothers or your relatives or rich neighbors, in case they may invite you in return, and you would be repaid. But when you give a banquet, invite the poor, the crippled, the lame, and the blind. And you will be blessed, because they cannot repay you, for you will be repaid at the resurrection of the righteous."

Notice what you think and feel as you read the Gospel.

Jesus advises his host how to throw a party. Don't invite your kin, your friends, or your wealthy neighbors, for they will return the favor. Instead invite those who cannot repay you, the excluded. Then you will be blessed. You will receive repayment at the resurrection of the just.

Pray as you are led for yourself and others.

"Jesus Christ, I long for the resurrection of the just, that I may be worthy . . ." (Continue in your own words.)

Listen to Jesus.

Look for ways to do good to those who cannot repay you, servant. I have lifted you. How may you lift someone else in need? What else is Jesus saying to you?

Ask God to show you how to live today.

"Savior, let me see opportunities to obey you today, to love and give to those who cannot repay me. Give me a generous spirit to do it. Amen."

Tuesday, November 1, 2016
All Saints' Day

Know that God is present with you and ready to converse.

"Lord, I seek the blessedness that is you. I offer you all that I am."

Read the Gospel: Matthew 5:1–12a.

When Jesus saw the crowds, he went up the mountain; and after he sat down, his disciples came to him. Then he began to speak, and taught them, saying:

"Blessed are the poor in spirit, for theirs is the kingdom of heaven.
"Blessed are those who mourn, for they will be comforted.
"Blessed are the meek, for they will inherit the earth.
"Blessed are those who hunger and thirst for righteousness, for they will be filled.
"Blessed are the merciful, for they will receive mercy.
"Blessed are the pure in heart, for they will see God.
"Blessed are the peacemakers, for they will be called children of God.
"Blessed are those who are persecuted for righteousness' sake, for theirs is the kingdom of heaven.
"Blessed are you when people revile you and persecute you and utter all kinds of evil against you falsely on my account. Rejoice and be glad, for your reward is great in heaven."

Notice what you think and feel as you read the Gospel.

Jesus tells the crowd how to enter into the blessedness, the happiness, of God. It's not what the world thinks. God's way is poverty, humility, righteousness, mercy, purity of heart, peace, and suffering persecution. This is what he asks of his followers, promising great rewards.

Pray as you are led for yourself and others.

"Jesus, give me the courage to turn away from myself and embrace your values. I have far to go. Only by your Spirit can I follow you as you ask . . ." (Continue in your own words.)

Listen to Jesus.

Gladly I give you my Spirit, beloved. Do not be afraid of my calling you. Abandon yourself to my care, my words, and my guidance. What else is Jesus saying to you?

Ask God to show you how to live today.

"You seem to ask so much, my God, but you provide everything. Will you give me opportunities today to show mercy, make peace, become meek, and suffer persecution? Be with me, Holy Spirit, and help me pass the test. Amen."

Wednesday, November 2, 2016
All Souls' Day

Know that God is present with you and ready to converse.

"Jesus, you come from the Father to love us, to save us from death, to lead us by your Word. I give you thanks."

Read the Gospel: John 6:37–40.

Jesus said, "Everything that the Father gives me will come to me, and anyone who comes to me I will never drive away; for I have come down from heaven, not to do my own will, but the will of him who sent me. And this is the will of him who sent me, that I should lose nothing of all that he has given me, but raise it up on the last day. This is indeed the will of my Father, that all who see the Son and believe in him may have eternal life; and I will raise them up on the last day."

Notice what you think and feel as you read the Gospel.

Jesus talks of all those the Father has given to him. These people will come to him and be safe. For he came down from heaven to do his Father's will. The Father wills that he lose none, but that he would raise them up at the last day; all those who believe in the Son have eternal life.

Pray as you are led for yourself and others.

"Your love and mercy for sinners is infinite, Lord. I believe in you. I thank you . . ." (Continue in your own words.)

Listen to Jesus.

I have ransomed your soul, my child. In this world you will have trials and you will have joys, but by your faithfulness you will be with me in the end. What else is Jesus saying to you?

Ask God to show you how to live today.

"Lord, teach me how to embrace the will of your Father, to rejoice in all my circumstances, knowing that your Father has allowed them for my good. Amen."

Thursday, November 3, 2016

Know that God is present with you and ready to converse.

"God, let me be one who gives you joy by listening to and loving your Word, my Lord and Savior, Jesus Christ."

Read the Gospel: Luke 15:1–10.

Now all the tax collectors and sinners were coming near to listen to Jesus. And the Pharisees and the scribes were grumbling and saying, "This fellow welcomes sinners and eats with them."

So he told them this parable: "Which one of you, having a hundred sheep and losing one of them, does not leave the ninety-nine in the wilderness and go after the one that is lost until he finds it? When he has found it, he lays it on his shoulders and rejoices. And when he comes home, he calls together his friends and neighbors, saying to them, 'Rejoice with me, for I have found my sheep that was lost.' Just so, I tell you, there will be more joy in heaven over one sinner who repents than over ninety-nine righteous persons who need no repentance.

"Or what woman having ten silver coins, if she loses one of them, does not light a lamp, sweep the house, and search carefully until she finds it? When she has found it, she calls together her friends and neighbors, saying, 'Rejoice with me, for I have found the coin that I had lost.' Just so, I tell you, there is joy in the presence of the angels of God over one sinner who repents."

Notice what you think and feel as you read the Gospel.

Jesus tells parables about the joy of finding the lost—a sheep and a coin. The man and woman spare no efforts to find what they have lost, and when they do, they rejoice, and they invite others to rejoice with them. So the angels rejoice when one sinner repents.

Pray as you are led for yourself and others.

"Jesus, have mercy on me . . ." (Continue in your own words.)

Listen to Jesus.

Rise, beloved disciple, and walk with me today. Look upon the world with my love. Rejoice with me, for I have found you. What else is Jesus saying to you?

Ask God to show you how to live today.

"I am ready, Savior, to do whatever you ask me to do. Let me hear your voice in my heart all day long. Amen."

Friday, November 4, 2016

Know that God is present with you and ready to converse.

"Your Word is light to my path, Lord. I come into your presence with joy."

Read the Gospel: Luke 16:1–8.

Then Jesus said to the disciples, "There was a rich man who had a manager, and charges were brought to him that this man was squandering his property. So he summoned him and said to him, 'What is this that I hear about you? Give me an accounting of your management, because you cannot be my manager any longer.' Then the manager said to himself, 'What will I do, now that my master is taking the position away from me? I am not strong enough to dig, and I am ashamed to beg. I have decided what to do so that, when I am dismissed as manager, people may welcome me into their homes.' So, summoning his master's debtors one by one, he asked the first, 'How much do you owe my master?' He answered, 'A hundred jugs of olive oil.' He said to him, 'Take your bill, sit down quickly, and make it fifty.' Then he asked another, 'And how much do you owe?' He replied, 'A hundred containers of wheat.' He said to him, 'Take your bill and make it eighty.' And his master commended the dishonest manager because he had acted shrewdly; for the children of this age are more shrewd in dealing with their own generation than are the children of light."

Notice what you think and feel as you read the Gospel.

Jesus tells the parable of the dishonest steward who, when he is relieved of his duties, settles up with the master's debtors by giving them discounts. The master commends the steward for his prudence. Jesus says that the sons of the world are wiser than the sons of light.

Pray as you are led for yourself and others.

"Jesus, how may I practice prudence in all my affairs, worldly and spiritual?" (Continue in your own words.)

Listen to Jesus.

I give you understanding, beloved servant. What do you seek to do? What will your master approve? What else is Jesus saying to you?

Ask God to show you how to live today.

"Master, you give me freedom. I offer it to you. Let my actions be worthy of you and give you glory. Amen."

Saturday, November 5, 2016

Know that God is present with you and ready to converse.

"Lord God, almighty Father, I am your servant. Let my heart receive your Word and obey you."

Read the Gospel: Luke 16:9–15.

Jesus instructed, "And I tell you, make friends for yourselves by means of dishonest wealth so that when it is gone, they may welcome you into the eternal homes.

"Whoever is faithful in a very little is faithful also in much; and whoever is dishonest in a very little is dishonest also in much. If then you have not been faithful with the dishonest wealth, who will entrust to you the true riches? And if you have not been faithful with what belongs to another, who will give you what is your own? No slave can serve two masters; for a slave will either hate the one and love the other, or be devoted to the one and despise the other. You cannot serve God and wealth."

The Pharisees, who were lovers of money, heard all this, and they ridiculed him. So he said to them, "You are those who justify yourselves in the sight of others; but God knows your hearts; for what is prized by human beings is an abomination in the sight of God."

Notice what you think and feel as you read the Gospel.

Jesus talks about the convergence of worldly honesty and spiritual honesty. Faithfulness in worldly affairs is part of faithfulness in godly affairs. Trustworthiness with worldly riches entitles one to heavenly riches. But while we live in the world, we do not love it. We are to serve only God.

Pray as you are led for yourself and others.

"Jesus, let me be faithful in my worldly affairs while I give all my devotion to God. There are things I need to do . . ." (Continue in your own words.)

Listen to Jesus.

All the little things you do matter to me, beloved. You please me when you are fair, honest, generous, and kind. What else is Jesus saying to you?

Ask God to show you how to live today.

"Let me discover ways in which I can obey you today, dear Jesus. Thank you for opening my heart and mind to you today. Amen."

Sunday, November 6, 2016
Thirty-Second Sunday in Ordinary Time

Know that God is present with you and ready to converse.

We cannot know what heaven will be, for it is beyond imagining. We shall be as Jesus is, glorified, and know God as we are known by God. Heaven is a world of perfect love to the glory of God forever and ever.

When you are ready, turn your attention to the living God and ask for what you need: "Lord, God of Abraham, Isaac, and Jacob, let my heart be turned to you. I hunger for your Word."

Read the Gospel: Luke 20:27–38.

Some Sadducees, those who say there is no resurrection, came to Jesus and asked him a question, "Teacher, Moses wrote for us that if a man's brother dies, leaving a wife but no children, the man shall marry the widow and raise up children for his brother. Now there were seven brothers; the first married, and died childless; then the second and the third married her, and so in the same way all seven died childless. Finally the woman also died. In the resurrection, therefore, whose wife will the woman be? For the seven had married her."

Jesus said to them, "Those who belong to this age marry and are given in marriage; but those who are considered worthy of a place in that age and in the resurrection from the dead neither marry nor are given in marriage. Indeed they cannot die anymore, because they are like angels and are children of God, being children of the resurrection. And the fact that the dead are raised Moses himself showed, in the story about the bush, where he speaks of the Lord as the God of Abraham, the God of Isaac, and the God of Jacob. Now he is God not of the dead, but of the living; for to him all of them are alive."

Notice what you think and feel as you read the Gospel.

The Sadducees devise a far-fetched question to challenge Jesus' teaching about the resurrection. He says that marriage bonds are irrelevant in the resurrection, for all who attain it are alive forever in God.

Pray as you are led for yourself and others.

"I seek your life, Lord, for without you I have no life. I offer my life to you. Use me as you will . . ." (Continue in your own words.)

Listen to Jesus.

I receive you, dear friend. I love you. What do you ask from me today? What else is Jesus saying to you?

Ask God to show you how to live today.

"Your words are sweet to me, Jesus. I want them to permeate all I do and say. I want to live in God today. Amen."

Monday, November 7, 2016

Know that God is present with you and ready to converse.

"Lord, increase my faith to hear your Word and do your will. I turn to you with your praises in my heart."

Read the Gospel: Luke 17:1–6.

Jesus said to his disciples, "Occasions for stumbling are bound to come, but woe to anyone by whom they come! It would be better for you if a millstone were hung around your neck and you were thrown into the sea than for you to cause one of these little ones to stumble. Be on your guard! If another disciple sins, you must rebuke the offender, and if there is repentance, you must forgive. And if the same person sins against you seven times a day, and turns back to you seven times and says, 'I repent,' you must forgive."

The apostles said to the Lord, "Increase our faith!" The Lord replied, "If you had faith the size of a mustard seed, you could say to this mulberry tree, 'Be uprooted and planted in the sea,' and it would obey you."

Notice what you think and feel as you read the Gospel.

Jesus is realistic about temptations. But woe to him who causes one of these little ones to sin! Rebuke the sinner, but forgive him seven times a day when he repents. The disciples ask the Lord for more faith. He says they can do great things with even a grain of faith.

Pray as you are led for yourself and others.

"Lord, I am sometimes tempted to sin against you and others. I repent and ask for your Spirit to resist temptations . . ." (Continue in your own words.)

Listen to Jesus.

You are right to fear sin, for sin is death. You are called to be a child of light. Follow me. What else is Jesus saying to you?

Ask God to show you how to live today.

"How may I act in faith today, Jesus? I long to do something good for you. Amen."

Tuesday, November 8, 2016

Know that God is present with you and ready to converse.

"You, Lord, are one in Father, Son, and Holy Spirit. Let me unite with you now by your Word."

Read the Gospel: Luke 17:7–10.

Jesus asked, "Who among you would say to your slave who has just come in from plowing or tending sheep in the field, 'Come here at once and take your place at the table'? Would you not rather say to him, 'Prepare supper for me, put on your apron and serve me while I eat and drink; later you may eat and drink'? Do you thank the slave for doing what was commanded? So you also, when you have done all that you were ordered to do, say, 'We are worthless slaves; we have done only what we ought to have done!'"

Notice what you think and feel as you read the Gospel.

Jesus talks common sense about the master-servant relationship. The master simply expects the servant to do all that he commands. So we, when we have done all that our master commands, should say, "We are unworthy, for we have done only our duty."

Pray as you are led for yourself and others.

"Lord, you know my shortcomings in serving you. Forgive and strengthen me to do all that you ask . . ." (Continue in your own words.)

Listen to Jesus.

You are doing what I ask, beloved servant, spending this time with me. I want you to reflect our love to the world. What else is Jesus saying to you?

Ask God to show you how to live today.

"Spirit of Jesus Christ, work in me and through me that I may do all my duty today. Amen."

Wednesday, November 9, 2016
Dedication of the Lateran Basilica in Rome

Know that God is present with you and ready to converse.

"God of love, I am your temple. Quicken me by your holy Word."

Read the Gospel: John 2:13–22.

The Passover of the Jews was near, and Jesus went up to Jerusalem. In the Temple he found people selling cattle, sheep, and doves, and the money-changers seated at their tables. Making a whip of cords, he drove all of them out of the Temple, both the sheep and the cattle. He also poured out the coins of the money-changers and overturned their tables. He told those who were selling the doves, "Take these things out of here! Stop making my Father's house a marketplace!" His disciples remembered that it was written, "Zeal for your house will consume me." The Jews then said to him, "What sign can you show us for doing this?" Jesus answered them, "Destroy this temple, and in three days I will raise it up." The Jews then said, "This temple has been under construction for forty-six years, and will you raise it up in three days?" But he was speaking of the temple of his body. After he was raised from the dead, his disciples remembered that he had said this; and they believed the scripture and the word that Jesus had spoken.

Notice what you think and feel as you read the Gospel.

In anger, Jesus casts the merchants out of the Temple in Jerusalem, driving out the livestock and pouring out the coins of the money-changers. They were defiling his Father's house with trade. When the Jews ask for a sign, Jesus tells them that when they destroy this temple, his body, he will raise it up in three days. They do not understand.

Pray as you are led for yourself and others.

"I offer you my whole self, Lord, to be your habitation. All that I value is of you . . ." (Continue in your own words.)

Listen to Jesus.

I am near to you always, inside and outside, my beloved. Give yourself to me a hundred times a day. I give myself to you. What else is Jesus saying to you?

Ask God to show you how to live today.

"Dear Jesus, I thank you for your self. You forgive, you wash, you light my way. I have no one but you. Amen."

Thursday, November 10, 2016
Saint Leo the Great, pope and doctor of the Church

Know that God is present with you and ready to converse.

"Lord, your kingdom is within me, and yet I wait for your coming. Give me patience to hear and await you."

Read the Gospel: Luke 17:20–25.

Once Jesus was asked by the Pharisees when the kingdom of God was coming, and he answered, "The kingdom of God is not coming with things that can be observed; nor will they say, 'Look, here it is!' or 'There it is!' For, in fact, the kingdom of God is among you."

Then he said to the disciples, "The days are coming when you will long to see one of the days of the Son of Man, and you will not see it. They will say to you, 'Look there!' or 'Look here!' Do not go, do not set off in pursuit. For as the lightning flashes and lights up the sky from one side to the other, so will the Son of Man be in his day. But first he must endure much suffering and be rejected by this generation."

Notice what you think and feel as you read the Gospel.

Jesus tells the Pharisees that the kingdom of God is in their midst. He tells his disciples to wait patiently for his return and not be distracted by reports. The Son of Man will come as the lightning flashes and lights up the sky from one side to the other.

Pray as you are led for yourself and others.

"Lord, I too long for your return. But for now let me see you and know you in the midst of my life . . ." (Continue in your own words.)

Listen to Jesus.

Where you look for me, you will find me, beloved disciple. I am present in all matter, all spirit, all people, and all souls. Look for me. What else is Jesus saying to you?

Ask God to show you how to live today.

"I want to honor and praise you whenever I recognize you, my God. Let me please you today. Amen."

Friday, November 11, 2016

Know that God is present with you and ready to converse.

"Lord, I want to be ready. Prepare me now to welcome you in your Word."

Read the Gospel: Luke 17:26–37.

Jesus said, "Just as it was in the days of Noah, so too it will be in the days of the Son of Man. They were eating and drinking, and marrying and being given in marriage, until the day Noah entered the ark, and the flood came and destroyed all of them. Likewise, just as it was in the days of Lot: they were eating and drinking, buying and selling, planting and building, but on the day that Lot left Sodom, it rained fire and sulfur from heaven and destroyed all of them—it will be like that on the day that the Son of Man is revealed. On that day, anyone on the housetop who has belongings in the house must not come down to take them away; and likewise anyone in the field must not turn back. Remember Lot's wife. Those who try to make their life secure will lose it, but those who lose their life will keep it. I tell you, on that night there will be two in one bed; one will be taken and the other left. There will be two women grinding meal together; one will be taken and the other left." Then they asked him, "Where, Lord?" He said to them, "Where the corpse is, there the vultures will gather."

Notice what you think and feel as you read the Gospel.

Jesus speaks of the surprise ending, his return. He advises his disciples not to try to save anything, not to turn back. Those who try to preserve their lives will lose them; those who lose their lives will find them. Where will this happen? Jesus says the vultures will gather where the body is.

Pray as you are led for yourself and others.

"Lord, who can understand these prophesies of your return? I ask only that you make of me one of those who abandon their lives for your sake . . ." (Continue in your own words.)

Listen to Jesus.

You understand what you need to understand, dear friend. Do not be afraid of the end, but pray that the hearts of people turn to me before that day. What else is Jesus saying to you?

Ask God to show you how to live today.

"I know many who do not seem to think about you, Lord. I pray today for all those who ignore you or push you aside. Show yourself to them and let them turn to you. Amen."

Saturday, November 12, 2016

Know that God is present with you and ready to converse.

"Lord, you are coming to vindicate your chosen who cry to you day and night. I cry to you now."

Read the Gospel: Luke 18:1–8.

Then Jesus told them a parable about their need to pray always and not to lose heart. He said, "In a certain city there was a judge who neither feared God nor had respect for people. In that city there was a widow who kept coming to him and saying, 'Grant me justice against my opponent.' For a while he refused; but later he said to himself, 'Though I have no fear of God and no respect for anyone, yet because this widow keeps bothering me, I will grant her justice, so that she may not wear me out by continually coming.'" And the Lord said, "Listen to what the unjust judge says. And will not God grant justice to his chosen ones who cry to him day and night? Will he delay long in helping them? I tell you, he will quickly grant justice to them. And yet, when the Son of Man comes, will he find faith on earth?"

Notice what you think and feel as you read the Gospel.

Jesus tells a parable of a judge who grants a request simply to be free of a widow's constant pleading. How much more will God vindicate the elect who cry to him day and night? Nevertheless, when the Son of Man comes, will he find faith on earth?

Pray as you are led for yourself and others.

"Your final question is chilling, Lord. Faith comes by hearing the Word of God. Let faith grow in the hearts of people, Lord . . ." (Continue in your own words.)

Listen to Jesus.

I am here to be found, child. I am always knocking. Tell others of our joy. What else is Jesus saying to you?

Ask God to show you how to live today.

"How may I show others that you are real, that you wish them to know and love you? Give me grace to speak of it, to live it. Amen."

Sunday, November 13, 2016
Thirty-Third Sunday in Ordinary Time

Know that God is present with you and ready to converse.

Time as we know it is linear. God dwells in eternity, an infinite present. When time shall be no more, after Jesus returns and establishes his kingdom, we shall worship and praise him for his unspeakable goodness.

When you are ready, approach the Lord: "I come to you surrounded by a violent world. As I pass my days on earth, be my shelter, Lord. I await your glorious coming."

Read the Gospel: Luke 21:5–19.

When some were speaking about the Temple, how it was adorned with beautiful stones and gifts dedicated to God, Jesus said, "As for these things that you see, the days will come when not one stone will be left upon another; all will be thrown down."

They asked him, "Teacher, when will this be, and what will be the sign that this is about to take place?" And he said, "Beware that you are not led astray; for many will come in my name and say, 'I am he!' and, 'The time is near!' Do not go after them."

"When you hear of wars and insurrections, do not be terrified; for these things must take place first, but the end will not follow immediately." Then he said to them, "Nation will rise against nation, and kingdom against kingdom; there will be great earthquakes, and in various places famines and plagues; and there will be dreadful portents and great signs from heaven.

"But before all this occurs, they will arrest you and persecute you; they will hand you over to synagogues and prisons, and you will be brought before kings and governors because of my name. This will give you an opportunity to testify. So make up your minds not to prepare your defense in advance; for I will give you words and a wisdom that none of your opponents will be able to withstand or contradict. You will be betrayed even by parents and brothers, by relatives and friends; and they will put some of you to death. You will be hated by all because of my name. But not a hair of your head will perish. By your endurance you will gain your souls."

Notice what you think and feel as you read the Gospel.

Jesus predicts the destruction of the great Temple in Jerusalem, which later comes to pass. He tells his disciples not to be fooled by false Christs or to be terrified by wars and tumults. They are inevitable signs.

Pray as you are led for yourself and others.

"Keep my gaze on you, my God, in the midst of all tumult. If I lose my life, I gain everlasting life . . ." (Continue in your own words.)

Listen to Jesus.

I thirst for souls, beloved servant. I thirst to save all I call. Pray for those who resist my call. What else is Jesus saying to you?

Ask God to show you how to live today.

"Jesus, I know many think that faith in you is foolish. I am blessed to be a fool for you. I want others to know you and to be born into your life. What do you want me to do? Amen."

Monday, November 14, 2016

Know that God is present with you and ready to converse.

"Jesus, as you are passing by, I cry to you, 'Have mercy on me.'"

Read the Gospel: Luke 18:35–43.

As Jesus approached Jericho, a blind man was sitting by the roadside begging. When he heard a crowd going by, he asked what was happening. They told him, "Jesus of Nazareth is passing by." Then he shouted, "Jesus, Son of David, have mercy on me!" Those who were in front sternly ordered him to be quiet; but he shouted even more loudly, "Son of David, have mercy on me!" Jesus stood still and ordered the man to be brought to him; and when he came near, he asked him, "What do you want me to do for you?" He said, "Lord, let me see again." Jesus said to him, "Receive your sight; your faith has saved you." Immediately he regained his sight and followed him, glorifying God; and all the people, when they saw it, praised God.

Notice what you think and feel as you read the Gospel.

The blind man cries out to Jesus and persists until Jesus stops and heals him. He and all those present glorify God.

Pray as you are led for yourself and others.

"Jesus, let me receive my sight. I long to see you in others . . ." (Continue in your own words.)

Listen to Jesus.

Receive your sight by faith in me. Glorify God. Be my witness among the people. What else is Jesus saying to you?

Ask God to show you how to live today.

"Your glory is above the heavens. You are the almighty, the God of love. You are truth. You are holiness. Let me see your glory and reflect it in my life. Thank you, Lord. Amen."

Tuesday, November 15, 2016

Know that God is present with you and ready to converse.

"Jesus, let me seek you and find you in your Word. Let it change my life and deepen my love for you."

Read the Gospel: Luke 19:1–10.

Jesus entered Jericho and was passing through it. A man was there named Zacchaeus; he was a chief tax collector and was rich. He was trying to see who Jesus was, but on account of the crowd he could not, because he was short in stature. So he ran ahead and climbed a sycamore tree to see him, because he was going to pass that way. When Jesus came to the place, he looked up and said to him, "Zacchaeus, hurry and come down; for I must stay at your house today." So he hurried down and was happy to welcome him. All who saw it began to grumble and said, "He has gone to be the guest of one who is a sinner." Zacchaeus stood there and said to the Lord, "Look, half of my possessions, Lord, I will give to the poor; and if I have defrauded anyone of anything, I will pay back four times as much." Then Jesus said to him, "Today salvation has come to this house, because he too is a son of Abraham. For the Son of Man came to seek out and to save the lost."

Notice what you think and feel as you read the Gospel.

Zacchaeus, a rich man, wants to see Jesus passing by, so he climbs a tree. Jesus sees him up there, knows him, and calls him down because Zacchaeus will be his host. When people disapprove of Jesus being the guest of a sinner, Zacchaeus speaks of amending his sinful ways. Jesus says that today salvation has come to this house.

Pray as you are led for yourself and others.

"You came to save the lost, Jesus. Many seem lost . . ." (Continue in your own words.)

Listen to Jesus.

Do not lose heart, beloved. I am still among the people seeking and saving the lost. I will lose nothing of what my Father has given me. What else is Jesus saying to you?

Ask God to show you how to live today.

"I offer myself for your service, Lord. What can I do today for you? Amen."

Wednesday, November 16, 2016

Know that God is present with you and ready to converse.

"Jesus, great king over all, give me what I need to serve you. Speak to me by your Word."

Read the Gospel: Luke 19:11–28.

As the people were listening to this, Jesus went on to tell a parable, because he was near Jerusalem, and because they supposed that the kingdom of God was to appear immediately. So he said, "A nobleman went to a distant country to get royal power for himself and then return. He summoned ten of his slaves, and gave them ten pounds, and said to them, 'Do business with these until I come back.' But the citizens of his country hated him and sent a delegation after him, saying, 'We do not want this man to rule over us.' When he returned, having received royal power, he ordered these slaves, to whom he had given the money, to be summoned so that he might find out what they had gained by trading. The first came forward and said, 'Lord, your pound has made ten more pounds.' He said to him, 'Well done, good slave! Because you have been trustworthy in a very small thing, take charge of ten cities.' Then the second came, saying, 'Lord, your pound has made five pounds.' He said to him, 'And you, rule over five cities.' Then the other came, saying, 'Lord, here is your pound. I wrapped it up in a piece of cloth, for I was afraid of you, because you are a harsh man; you take what you did not deposit, and reap what you did not sow.' He said to him, 'I will judge you by your own words, you wicked slave! You knew, did you, that I was a harsh man, taking what I did not deposit and reaping what I did not sow? Why then did you not put my money into the bank? Then when I returned, I could have collected it with interest.' He said to the bystanders, 'Take the pound from him and give it to the one who has ten pounds.' (And they said to him, 'Lord, he has ten pounds!') 'I tell you, to all those who have, more will be given; but from those who have nothing, even what they have will be taken away. But as for these enemies of mine who did not want me to be king over them—bring them here and slaughter them in my presence.'" After he had said this, he went on ahead, going up to Jerusalem.

Notice what you think and feel as you read the Gospel.

As Jesus heads toward Jerusalem, the people expect the kingdom of God to appear immediately. So he tells a parable about a nobleman who is called away to be made king over all the people, even though the people do not want it. When he returns, he dispenses just rewards and punishments.

Pray as you are led for yourself and others.

"Lord, let me not be a servant who hides his pound, afraid to invest it in your service . . ." (Continue in your own words.)

Listen to Jesus.

Step out in faith, servant and friend. You will learn and grow, and I will be with you at all times. What else is Jesus saying to you?

Ask God to show you how to live today.

"Give me ideas, new ways and old ways, to please you. How may I serve those who need the most? Amen."

Thursday, November 17, 2016

Know that God is present with you and ready to converse.

"Jesus, let me join you in your sorrow for the people who do not know you."

Read the Gospel: Luke 19:41–44.

As Jesus came near and saw the city, he wept over it, saying, "If you, even you, had only recognized on this day the things that make for peace! But now they are hidden from your eyes. Indeed, the days will come upon you, when your enemies will set up ramparts around you and surround you, and hem you in on every side. They will crush you to the ground, you and your children within you, and they will not leave within you one stone upon another; because you did not recognize the time of your visitation from God."

Notice what you think and feel as you read the Gospel.

Jesus weeps for Jerusalem, for the people there do not know what makes for peace. He laments the coming destruction of the city because, he says, its people did not know the time of his visitation.

Pray as you are led for yourself and others.

"Jesus Christ, Savior, open the eyes of all peoples to your lordship, your mercy, your salvation . . ." (Continue in your own words.)

Listen to Jesus.

I call souls in tears. When they come to me, I rejoice with the saints and the angels. This is also what I ask of you, beloved disciple. What else is Jesus saying to you?

Ask God to show you how to live today.

"Give me your heart for people, Lord. Let me despair of no one. I offer you myself today. Use me as you will. Amen."

Friday, November 18, 2016

Know that God is present with you and ready to converse.

"My faith wavers, Son of God. Take my hand."

Read the Gospel: Matthew 14:22–33.

Immediately Jesus made the disciples get into the boat and go on ahead to the other side, while he dismissed the crowds. And after he had dismissed the crowds, he went up the mountain by himself to pray. When evening came, he was there alone, but by this time the boat, battered by the waves, was far from the land, for the wind was against them. And early in the morning he came walking toward them on the sea. But when the disciples saw him walking on the sea, they were terrified, saying, "It is a ghost!" And they cried out in fear. But immediately Jesus spoke to them and said, "Take heart, it is I; do not be afraid."

Peter answered him, "Lord, if it is you, command me to come to you on the water." He said, "Come." So Peter got out of the boat, started walking on the water, and came toward Jesus. But when he noticed the strong wind, he became frightened, and beginning to sink, he cried out, "Lord, save me!" Jesus immediately reached out his hand and caught him, saying to him, "You of little faith, why did you doubt?" When they got into the boat, the wind ceased. And those in the boat worshiped him, saying, "Truly you are the Son of God."

Notice what you think and feel as you read the Gospel.

Jesus spends a night alone in prayer while his disciples go by boat to the other side. A storm comes up and hinders their progress. Then Jesus comes, walking toward them on the water, saying, "Do not be afraid," for they are terrified. Jesus grants Peter's request to walk to him on the water. Jesus saves him when he starts to sink. Back in the boat, the disciples worship.

Pray as you are led for yourself and others.

"Lord, teach me to pray as you did. Teach me to trust you in everything . . ." (Continue in your own words.)

Listen to Jesus.

Prayer is of the heart, beloved. Desire God with all your heart, for all that is good is of God. What else is Jesus saying to you?

Ask God to show you how to live today.

"I have heard your Word today, Lord. Let me be a doer of it, trusting in you. Amen."

Saturday, November 19, 2016

Know that God is present with you and ready to converse.

"Lord of life, I am silent in your presence, listening to your Word."

Read the Gospel: Luke 20:27–40.

Some Sadducees, those who say there is no resurrection, came to Jesus and asked him a question, "Teacher, Moses wrote for us that if a man's brother dies, leaving a wife but no children, the man shall marry the widow and raise up children for his brother. Now there were seven brothers; the first married, and died childless; then the second and the third married her, and so in the same way all seven died childless. Finally the woman also died. In the resurrection, therefore, whose wife will the woman be? For the seven had married her."

Jesus said to them, "Those who belong to this age marry and are given in marriage; but those who are considered worthy of a place in that age and in the resurrection from the dead neither marry nor are given in marriage. Indeed they cannot die anymore, because they are like angels and are children of God, being children of the resurrection. And the fact that the dead are raised Moses himself showed, in the story about the bush, where he speaks of the Lord as the God of Abraham, the God of Isaac, and the God of Jacob. Now he is God not of the dead, but of the living; for to him all of them are alive." Then some of the scribes answered, "Teacher, you have spoken well." For they no longer dared to ask him another question.

Notice what you think and feel as you read the Gospel.

Jesus affirms the resurrection to those who do not believe in it. They ask him a trick question to trap him, but he refutes them with scripture. God is God of the living, and all live to God. They approve his answer and do not dare ask more questions.

Pray as you are led for yourself and others.

"So let me learn from scripture, Jesus. Let the world know that God is eternal life . . ." (Continue in your own words.)

Listen to Jesus.

I have revealed the resurrection of the body by rising from the dead. Be witness to that, friend. What else is Jesus saying to you?

Ask God to show you how to live today.

"I put all that I am and all that I have at your service today. For you are the risen Lord, glorious on your throne. Draw us into your kingdom, Jesus Christ. Amen."

Sunday, November 20, 2016
Christ the King

Know that God is present with you and ready to converse.

Jesus Christ is the king of glory, high and lifted up. The Lamb of God sits on his throne, triumphant, worthy of all praise.

When you are ready, address him, for he waits to hear you: "Does the king humble himself to speak to me? Lord, I listen, trembling with joy and fear."

Read the Gospel: Luke 23:35–43.

And the people stood by, watching; but the leaders scoffed at Jesus, saying, "He saved others; let him save himself if he is the Messiah of God, his chosen one!" The soldiers also mocked him, coming up and offering him sour wine, and saying, "If you are the King of the Jews, save yourself!" There was also an inscription over him, "This is the King of the Jews."

One of the criminals who were hanged there kept deriding him and saying, "Are you not the Messiah? Save yourself and us!" But the other rebuked him, saying, "Do you not fear God, since you are under the same sentence of condemnation? And we indeed have been condemned justly, for we are getting what we deserve for our deeds, but this man has done nothing wrong." Then he said, "Jesus, remember me when you come into your kingdom." He replied, "Truly I tell you, today you will be with me in paradise."

Notice what you think and feel as you read the Gospel.

Jesus hangs on the cross while people mock him, saying, "Save yourself if you are the Christ, the king of the Jews." Even one of those being crucified with him rails at him to save them all. But the other criminal rebukes him and asks Jesus to remember him when he comes into his kingly power. Jesus tells him that today he will be with him in paradise.

Pray as you are led for yourself and others.

"Jesus, your words are truth. You suffered and died to make me a child of God . . ." (Continue in your own words.)

Listen to Jesus.

Reflect upon my cross, beloved. It is the narrow gate into my kingdom. What else is Jesus saying to you?

Ask God to show you how to live today.

"I take up my cross, crucified Savior. I am not worthy of you, but I follow you. Remember me, Christ, my king. Amen."

Monday, November 21, 2016

Know that God is present with you and ready to converse.

"Father, all that I have you have given me. Give me a heart to give it all back to you, for you are all I need."

Read the Gospel: Luke 21:1–4.

He looked up and saw rich people putting their gifts into the treasury; he also saw a poor widow put in two small copper coins. He said, "Truly I tell you, this poor widow has put in more than all of them; for all of them have contributed out of their abundance, but she out of her poverty has put in all she had to live on."

Notice what you think and feel as you read the Gospel.

Jesus watches the poor widow drop two copper coins into the donation box, and he commends her generosity, for she contributed out of her poverty, not her abundance, as others had.

Pray as you are led for yourself and others.

"Lord, give me the trust of the poor widow, the confidence that I will not want if I look to you for my daily bread . . ." (Continue in your own words.)

Listen to Jesus.

God knows what you need, beloved. Seek God first, and you will be rich in spiritual things. Those are the things that endure forever. What else is Jesus saying to you?

Ask God to show you how to live today.

"I pray for those who are poor, Lord—the hungry, the sick. I resolve to share what I have with the needy. Guide my giving. Amen."

Tuesday, November 22, 2016

Know that God is present with you and ready to converse.

"Almighty God, I am here, longing to learn from your holy Word, Jesus Christ."

Read the Gospel: Luke 21:5–11.

When some were speaking about the Temple, how it was adorned with beautiful stones and gifts dedicated to God, Jesus said, "As for these things that you see, the days will come when not one stone will be left upon another; all will be thrown down."

They asked him, "Teacher, when will this be, and what will be the sign that this is about to take place?" And he said, "Beware that you are not led astray; for many will come in my name and say, 'I am he!' and, 'The time is near!' Do not go after them.

"When you hear of wars and insurrections, do not be terrified; for these things must take place first, but the end will not follow immediately." Then he said to them, "Nation will rise against nation, and kingdom against kingdom; there will be great earthquakes, and in various places famines and plagues; and there will be dreadful portents and great signs from heaven."

Notice what you think and feel as you read the Gospel.

Jesus speaks of the end of the age before his coming. There will be wars, destruction, false Christs, earthquakes, famines, pestilence, terrors, and signs in heaven.

Pray as you are led for yourself and others.

"Lord, prepare me to endure all the terrors and violence that may befall. Keep me faithful to you all the days of my life . . ." (Continue in your own words.)

Listen to Jesus.

You have nothing to fear, dear friend, as long as you walk with me. I will never abandon you. What else is Jesus saying to you?

Ask God to show you how to live today.

"I pray for those who are now experiencing war, natural disasters, famine, and disease. How can I help? Amen."

Wednesday, November 23, 2016

Know that God is present with you and ready to converse.

"Lord God of hosts, Father of the Word, thank you for speaking to me now."

Read the Gospel: Luke 21:12–19.

Jesus said, "But before all this occurs, they will arrest you and persecute you; they will hand you over to synagogues and prisons, and you will be brought before kings and governors because of my name. This will give you an opportunity to testify. So make up your minds not to prepare your defense in advance; for I will give you words and a wisdom that none of your opponents will be able to withstand or contradict. You will be betrayed even by parents and brothers, by relatives and friends; and they will put some of you to death. You will be hated by all because of my name. But not a hair of your head will perish. By your endurance you will gain your souls."

Notice what you think and feel as you read the Gospel.

Jesus tells the disciples that the end will not come before they are persecuted, betrayed even by family and friends, and put to death. Do not prepare any answers for your accusers, he says, but rely on God to provide words and wisdom your adversaries cannot contradict. Despite your suffering and even death, not a hair of your head will perish. You will gain your lives.

Pray as you are led for yourself and others.

"Lord, only in you could I withstand persecution and martyrdom. I offer myself to your will, knowing you know what is best for me and will accomplish it . . ." (Continue in your own words.)

Listen to Jesus.

Many have followed me through the gates of persecution and death. I raise them up to glory, these my brothers and sisters. What else is Jesus saying to you?

Ask God to show you how to live today.

"Jesus, send your Spirit upon those who are being persecuted today. Let them glorify you by their endurance, their wisdom, and their love. Amen."

Thursday, November 24, 2016

Know that God is present with you and ready to converse.

"Holy Trinity of love, I long for my redemption for it is still incomplete. I look to your Word."

Read the Gospel: Luke 21:20–28.

Jesus said, "When you see Jerusalem surrounded by armies, then know that its desolation has come near. Then those in Judea must flee to the mountains, and those inside the city must leave it, and those out in the country must not enter it; for these are days of vengeance, as a fulfillment of all that is written. Woe to those who are pregnant and to those who are nursing infants in those days! For there will be great distress on the earth and wrath against this people; they will fall by the edge of the sword and be taken away as captives among all nations; and Jerusalem will be trampled on by the Gentiles, until the times of the Gentiles are fulfilled.

"There will be signs in the sun, the moon, and the stars, and on the earth distress among nations confused by the roaring of the sea and the waves. People will faint from fear and foreboding of what is coming upon the world, for the powers of the heavens will be shaken. Then they will see 'the Son of Man coming in a cloud' with power and great glory. Now when these things begin to take place, stand up and raise your heads, because your redemption is drawing near."

Notice what you think and feel as you read the Gospel.

Jesus speaks of Jerusalem surrounded by armies, fear, refugees, and violence before he comes. People will see terrifying signs in the heavens and on earth, and then they will see the Son of Man coming with power and great glory. He is our redemption drawing near.

Pray as you are led for yourself and others.

"You are the alpha and the omega of human history, Jesus Christ. I embrace your promise of redemption . . ." (Continue in your own words.)

Listen to Jesus.

Beloved servant, do not be afraid. My grace will sustain you to the end. We are lovers. What else is Jesus saying to you?

Ask God to show you how to live today.

"Thank you, Jesus. Let me see others with your eyes of love today. Let me alleviate someone's fears. Amen."

Friday, November 25, 2016

Know that God is present with you and ready to converse.

"Your Word endures forever, almighty God. Your truth is firm and cannot pass away. Let me hear you now."

Read the Gospel: Luke 21:29–33.

Then Jesus told them a parable: "Look at the fig tree and all the trees; as soon as they sprout leaves you can see for yourselves and know that summer is already near. So also, when you see these things taking place, you know that the kingdom of God is near. Truly I tell you, this generation will not pass away until all things have taken place. Heaven and earth will pass away, but my words will not pass away."

Notice what you think and feel as you read the Gospel.

Jesus says that we know how to interpret the fig tree coming into leaf. It is the sign that summer is near. So, too, can we read the signs that the kingdom of God is near. Heaven and earth will pass away, but his words, he assures us, will never pass away.

Pray as you are led for yourself and others.

"I rely on your words, my Savior and my king, for I have nothing but you. You are my hope . . ." (Continue in your own words.)

Listen to Jesus.

I am your rock, servant, and friend. You are absolutely secure in me. What else is Jesus saying to you?

Ask God to show you how to live today.

"How may I praise you in serving others today, my Jesus? Amen."

Saturday, November 26, 2016

Know that God is present with you and ready to converse.

"Lord, almighty God, give me ears to hear your Word today and to take it to heart."

Read the Gospel: Luke 21:34–36.

Jesus taught, "Be on guard so that your hearts are not weighed down with dissipation and drunkenness and the worries of this life, and that day does not catch you unexpectedly, like a trap. For it will come upon all who live on the face of the whole earth. Be alert at all times, praying that you may have the strength to escape all these things that will take place, and to stand before the Son of Man."

Notice what you think and feel as you read the Gospel.

Jesus tells us to take heed, be watchful, and not be weighed down with drunkenness and dissipation while waiting for his return. He tells us to pray for strength when tribulation comes, and to stand before the Son of Man.

Pray as you are led for yourself and others.

"I pray for strength, Lord, as you ask. I pray for strength for all those you have given me . . ." (Continue in your own words.)

Listen to Jesus.

In your weakness turn to me, beloved disciple. In your weakness you are strong, for I am in you. What else is Jesus saying to you?

Ask God to show you how to live today.

"You are a wonderful Savior. My heart and soul reach out to you in love. Let nothing come between us. Let the world know of our love. Amen."

The Apostleship of Prayer is an international Jesuit prayer ministry that reaches more than fifty million members worldwide through its popular website, *ApostleshipofPrayer.org*, and through talks, conferences, publications, and retreats such as Hearts on Fire. Known as "the pope's prayer group," the Apostleship's mission is to encourage Christians to make a daily offering of themselves to the Lord and at whose center is the love of the Sacred Heart of Jesus. Douglas Leonard has served as executive director of the Apostleship of Prayer in the United States since 2006.